STUDIA PATRISTICA

VOL. CI

STUDIA PATRISTICA

Editor:

Markus Vinzent, King's College London and Max Weber Centre,
University of Erfurt

STUDIA PATRISTICA

VOL. CI

Gregory of Nyssa's Mystical Eschatology

Edited by
GIULIO MASPERO, MIGUEL BRUGAROLAS and
ILARIA VIGORELLI

PEETERS
LEUVEN – PARIS – BRISTOL, CT
2021

© Peeters Publishers — Louvain — Belgium 2021

D/2021/0602/28
ISBN: 978-90-429-4138-0
eISBN: 978-90-429-4139-7

A catalogue record for this book is available from the Library of Congress.

Printed in Belgium by Peeters, Leuven

Table of Contents

Abbreviations

AA.SS	see ASS.
AAWG.PH	Abhandlungen der Akademie der Wissenschaften in Göttingen Philologisch-historische Klasse, Göttingen.
AB	Analecta Bollandiana, Brussels.
AC	Antike und Christentum, ed. F.J. Dölger, Münster.
ACL	Antiquité classique, Louvain.
ACO	Acta conciliorum oecumenicorum, ed. E. Schwartz, Berlin.
ACW	Ancient Christian Writers, ed. J. Quasten and J.C. Plumpe, Westminster (Md.)/London.
AHDLMA	Archives d'histoire doctrinale et littéraire du moyen âge, Paris.
AJAH	American Journal of Ancient History, Cambridge, Mass.
AJP	American Journal of Philology, Baltimore.
AKK	Archiv für katholisches Kirchenrecht, Mainz.
AKPAW	Abhandlungen der königlichen Preußischen Akademie der Wissenschaften, Berlin.
ALMA	Archivum Latinitatis Medii Aevi (Bulletin du Cange), Paris/Brussels.
ALW	Archiv für Liturgiewissenschaft, Regensburg.
AnalBoll	Analecta Bollandiana, Brussels.
ANCL	Ante-Nicene Christian Library, Edinburgh.
ANF	Ante-Nicene Fathers, Buffalo/New York.
ANRW	Aufstieg und Niedergang der römischen Welt, ed H. Temporini *et al.*, Berlin.
AnSt	Anatolian Studies, London.
AnThA	Année théologique augustinienne, Paris.
APOT	Apocrypha and Pseudepigrapha of the Old Testament in English, ed. R.E. Charles, Oxford.
AR	Archivum Romanicum, Florence.
ARW	Archiv für Religionswissenschaft, Berlin/Leipzig.
ASS	Acta Sanctorum, ed. the Bollandists, Brussels.
AThANT	Abhandlungen zur Theologie des Alten und Neuen Testaments, Zürich.
Aug	Augustinianum, Rome.
AugSt	Augustinian Studies, Villanova (USA).
AW	Athanasius Werke, ed. H.-G. Opitz *et al.*, Berlin.
AZ	Archäologische Zeitung, Berlin.
BA	Bibliothèque augustinienne, Paris.
BAC	Biblioteca de Autores Cristianos, Madrid.
BASOR	Bulletin of the American Schools of Oriental Research, New Haven, Conn.
BDAG	A Greek-English Lexicon of the New Testament and Other Early Christian Literature, 3rd edn F.W. Danker, Chicago.
BEHE	Bibliothèque de l'École des Hautes Études, Paris.
BETL	Bibliotheca Ephemeridum Theologicarum Lovaniensium, Louvain.
BGL	Benedictinisches Geistesleben, St. Ottilien.
BHG	Bibliotheca Hagiographica Graeca, Brussels.
BHL	Bibliotheca Hagiographica Latina Antiquae et Mediae Aetatis, Brussels.

BHO	Bibliotheca Hagiographica Orientalis, Brussels.
BHTh	Beiträge zur historischen Theologie, Tübingen.
BJ	Bursians Jahresbericht über die Fortschritte der klassischen Altertumswissenschaft, Leipzig.
BJRULM	Bulletin of the John Rylands Library, Manchester.
BKV	Bibliothek der Kirchenväter, ed. F.X. Reithmayr and V. Thalhofer, Kempten.
BKV2	Bibliothek der Kirchenväter, ed. O. Bardenhewer, Th. Schermann, and C. Weyman, Kempten/Munich.
BKV3	Bibliothek der Kirchenväter. Zweite Reihe, ed. O. Bardenhewer, J. Zellinger, and J. Martin, Munich.
BLE	Bulletin de littérature ecclésiastique, Toulouse.
BoJ	Bonner Jahrbücher, Bonn.
BS	Bibliotheca sacra, London.
BSL	Bolletino di studi latini, Naples.
BWAT	Beiträge zur Wissenschaft vom Alten Testament, Leipzig/Stuttgart.
Byz	Byzantion, Leuven.
BZ	Byzantinische Zeitschrift, Leipzig.
BZNW	Beihefte zur Zeitschrift für die neutestamentliche Wissenschaft, Berlin.
CAr	Cahiers Archéologique, Paris.
CBQ	Catholic Biblical Quarterly, Washington.
CChr.CM	Corpus Christianorum, Continuatio Mediaevalis, Turnhout/Paris.
CChr.SA	Corpus Christianorum, Series Apocryphorum, Turnhout/Paris.
CChr.SG	Corpus Christianorum, Series Graeca, Turnhout/Paris.
CChr.SL	Corpus Christianorum, Series Latina, Turnhout/Paris.
CH	Church History, Chicago.
CIL	Corpus Inscriptionum Latinarum, Berlin.
CP(h)	Classical Philology, Chicago.
CPG	Clavis Patrum Graecorum, ed. M. Geerard, vols. I-VI, Turnhout.
CPL	Clavis Patrum Latinorum (SE 3), ed. E. Dekkers and A. Gaar, Turnhout.
CQ	Classical Quarterly, London/Oxford.
CR	The Classical Review, London/Oxford.
CSCO	Corpus Scriptorum Christianorum Orientalium, Louvain.
	Aeth = Scriptores Aethiopici
	Ar = Scriptores Arabici
	Arm = Scriptores Armeniaci
	Copt = Scriptores Coptici
	Iber = Scriptores Iberici
	Syr = Scriptores Syri
	Subs = Subsidia
CSEL	Corpus Scriptorum Ecclesiasticorum Latinorum, Vienna.
CSHB	Corpus Scriptorum Historiae Byzantinae, Bonn.
CTh	Collectanea Theologica, Lvov.
CUF	Collection des Universités de France publiée sous le patronage de l'Association Guillaume Budé, Paris.
CW	Catholic World, New York.
DAC	Dictionary of the Apostolic Church, ed. J. Hastings, Edinburgh.

DACL	see DAL
DAL	Dictionnaire d'archéologie chrétienne et de liturgie, ed. F. Cabrol, H. Leclercq, Paris.
DB	Dictionnaire de la Bible, Paris.
DBS	Dictionnaire de la Bible, Supplément, Paris.
DCB	Dictionary of Christian Biography, Literature, Sects, and Doctrines, ed. W. Smith and H. Wace, 4 vols, London.
DHGE	Dictionnaire d'histoire et de géographie ecclésiastique, ed. A. Baudrillart, Paris.
Did	Didaskalia, Lisbon.
DOP	Dumbarton Oaks Papers, Cambridge, Mass., subsequently Washington, D.C.
DOS	Dumbarton Oaks Studies, Cambridge, Mass., subsequently Washington, D.C.
DR	Downside Review, Stratton on the Fosse, Bath.
DS	H.J. Denzinger and A. Schönmetzer, ed., Enchiridion Symbolorum, Barcelona/Freiburg i.B./Rome.
DSp	Dictionnaire de Spiritualité, ed. M. Viller, S.J., and others, Paris.
DTC	Dictionnaire de théologie catholique, ed. A. Vacant, E. Mangenot, and E. Amann, Paris.
EA	Études augustiniennes, Paris.
ECatt	Enciclopedia Cattolica, Rome.
ECQ	Eastern Churches Quarterly, Ramsgate.
EE	Estudios eclesiasticos, Madrid.
EECh	Encyclopedia of the Early Church, ed. A. Di Berardino, Cambridge.
EKK	Evangelisch-Katholischer Kommentar zum Neuen Testament, Neukirchen.
EH	Enchiridion Fontium Historiae Ecclesiasticae Antiquae, ed. Ueding-Kirch, 6th ed., Barcelona.
EO	Échos d'Orient, Paris.
EtByz	Études Byzantines, Paris.
ETL	Ephemerides Theologicae Lovanienses, Louvain.
EWNT	Exegetisches Wörterbuch zum NT, ed. H.R. Balz et al., Stuttgart.
ExpT	The Expository Times, Edinburgh.
FC	The Fathers of the Church, New York.
FGH	Fragmente der griechischen Historiker, Berlin.
FKDG	Forschungen zur Kirchen- und Dogmengeschichte, Göttingen.
FRL	Forschungen zur Religion und Literatur des Alten und Neuen Testaments, Göttingen.
FS	Festschrift.
FThSt	Freiburger theologische Studien, Freiburg i.B.
FTS	Frankfurter theologische Studien, Frankfurt a.M.
FZThPh	Freiburger Zeitschrift für Theologie und Philosophie, Freiburg/Switzerland.
GCS	Die griechischen christlichen Schriftsteller, Leipzig/Berlin.
GDV	Geschichtsschreiber der deutschen Vorzeit, Stuttgart.
GLNT	Grande Lessico del Nuovo Testamento, Genoa.
GNO	Gregorii Nysseni Opera, Leiden.
GRBS	Greek, Roman and Byzantine Studies, Cambridge, Mass.

GWV	Geschichte in Wissenschaft und Unterricht, Offenburg.
HbNT	Handbuch zum Neuen Testament. Tübingen.
HDR	Harvard Dissertations in Religion, Missoula.
HJG	Historisches Jahrbuch der Görresgesellschaft, successively Munich, Cologne and Munich/Freiburg i.B.
HKG	Handbuch der Kirchengeschichte, Tübingen.
HNT	Handbuch zum Neuen Testament, Tübingen.
HO	Handbuch der Orientalistik, Leiden.
HSCP	Harvard Studies in Classical Philology, Cambridge, Mass.
HTR	Harvard Theological Review, Cambridge, Mass.
HTS	Harvard Theological Studies, Cambridge, Mass.
HZ	Historische Zeitschrift, Munich/Berlin.
ICC	The International Critical Commentary of the Holy Scriptures of the Old and New Testaments, Edinburgh.
ILCV	Inscriptiones Latinae Christianae Veteres, ed. E. Diehl, Berlin.
ILS	Inscriptiones Latinae Selectae, ed. H. Dessau, Berlin.
J(b)AC	Jahrbuch für Antike und Christentum, Münster.
JBL	Journal of Biblical Literature, Philadelphia, Pa., then various places.
JdI	Jahrbuch des Deutschen Archäologischen Instituts, Berlin.
JECS	Journal of Early Christian Studies, Baltimore.
JEH	The Journal of Ecclesiastical History, London.
JJS	Journal of Jewish Studies, London.
JLH	Jahrbuch für Liturgik und Hymnologie, Kassel.
JPTh	Jahrbücher für protestantische Theologie, Leipzig/Freiburg i.B.
JQR	Jewish Quarterly Review, Philadelphia.
JRS	Journal of Roman Studies, London.
JSJ	Journal for the Study of Judaism in the Persian, Hellenistic and Roman Period, Leiden.
JSOR	Journal of the Society of Oriental Research, Chicago.
JTS	Journal of Theological Studies, Oxford.
KAV	Kommentar zu den apostolischen Vätern, Göttingen.
KeTh	Kerk en Theologie, 's Gravenhage.
KJ(b)	Kirchliches Jahrbuch für die evangelische Kirche in Deutschland, Gütersloh.
LCL	The Loeb Classical Library, London/Cambridge, Mass.
LNPF	A Select Library of Nicene and Post-Nicene Fathers of the Christian Church, ed. P. Schaff and H. Wace, Buffalo/New York.
L(O)F	Library of Fathers of the Holy Catholic Church, Oxford.
LSJ	H.G. Liddell and R. Scott, A Greek-English Lexicon, new (9th) edn H.S. Jones, Oxford.
LThK	Lexikon für Theologie und Kirche, Freiburg i.B.
LXX	Septuagint.
MA	Moyen-Âge, Brussels.
MAMA	Monumenta Asiae Minoris Antiqua, London.
Mansi	J.D. Mansi, Sacrorum conciliorum nova et amplissima collectio, Florence, 1759-1798. Reprint and continuation: Paris/Leipzig, 1901-1927.
MBTh	Münsterische Beiträge zur Theologie, Münster.

MCom	Miscelanea Comillas, Comillas/Santander.
MGH	Monumenta germaniae historica. Hanover/Berlin.
ML	Mediaevalia Lovaniensia, Louvain.
MPG	See PG.
MSR	Mélanges de science religieuse, Lille.
MThZ	Münchener theologische Zeitschrift, Munich.
Mus	Le Muséon, Louvain.
NA28	Nestle-Aland, Novum Testamentum Graece, 28th edition, Stuttgart.
NGWG	Nachrichten der Gesellschaft der Wissenschaften zu Göttingen.
NH(M)S	Nag Hammadi (and Manichaean) Studies, Leiden.
NIV	New International Version.
NKJV	New King James Version.
NovTest	Novum Testamentum, Leiden.
NPNF	See LNPF.
NRSV	New Revised Standard Version.
NRTh	Nouvelle Revue Théologique, Tournai/Louvain/Paris.
NTA	Neutestamentliche Abhandlungen, Münster.
NT.S	Novum Testamentum Supplements, Leiden.
NTS	New Testament Studies, Cambridge/Washington.
NTTSD	New Testament Tools, Studies and Documents, Leiden/Boston.
OBO	Orbis biblicus et orientalis, Freiburg, Switz., then Louvain.
OCA	Orientalia Christiana Analecta, Rome.
OCP	Orientalia Christiana Periodica, Rome.
OECS	Oxford Early Christian Studies, Oxford.
OLA	Orientalia Lovaniensia Analecta, Louvain.
OLP	Orientalia Lovaniensia Periodica, Louvain.
Or	Orientalia. Commentarii editi a Pontificio Instituto Biblico, Rome.
OrChr	Oriens Christianus, Leipzig, then Wiesbaden.
OrSyr	L'Orient Syrien, Paris.
PG	Migne, Patrologia, series graeca.
PGL	A Patristic Greek Lexicon, ed. G.L. Lampe, Oxford.
PL	Migne, Patrologia, series latina.
PLRE	The Prosopography of the Later Roman Empire, ed. A.H.M. Jones *et al.*, Cambridge.
PLS	Migne, Patrologia, series latina. Supplementum ed. A. Hamman.
PO	Patrologia Orientalis, Paris.
PRE	Paulys Realenzyklopädie der classischen Alterthumswissenschaft, Stuttgart.
PS	Patrologia Syriaca, Paris.
PTA	Papyrologische Texte und Abhandlungen, Bonn.
PThR	Princeton Theological Review, Princeton.
PTS	Patristische Texte und Studien, Berlin.
PW	Paulys Realencyclopädie der classischen Altertumswissenschaft, ed. G. Wissowa, Stuttgart.
QLP	Questions liturgiques et paroissiales, Louvain.
QuLi	Questions liturgiques, Louvain.
RAC	Rivista di Archeologia Cristiana, Rome.
RACh	Reallexikon für Antike und Christentum, Stuttgart.

RAM	Revue d'ascétique et de mystique, Paris.
RAug	Recherches Augustiniennes, Paris.
RBen	Revue Bénédictine, Maredsous.
RB(ibl)	Revue biblique, Paris.
RE	Realencyklopädie für protestantische Theologie und Kirche, founded by J.J. Herzog, 3e ed. A. Hauck, Leipzig.
REA(ug)	Revue des études Augustiniennes, Paris.
REB	Revue des études byzantines, Paris.
RED	Rerum ecclesiasticarum documenta, Rome.
RÉL	Revue des études latines, Paris.
REG	Revue des études grecques, Paris.
RevSR	Revue des sciences religieuses, Strasbourg.
RevThom	Revue thomiste, Toulouse.
RFIC	Rivista di filologia e d'istruzione classica, Turin.
RGG	Religion in Geschichte und Gegenwart, ed. Gunkel-Zscharnack, Tübingen
RHE	Revue d'histoire ecclésiastique, Louvain.
RhMus	Rheinisches Museum für Philologie, Bonn.
RHR	Revue de l'histoire des religions, Paris.
RHT	Revue d'Histoire des Textes, Paris.
RMAL	Revue du Moyen-Âge Latin, Paris.
ROC	Revue de l'Orient chrétien, Paris.
RPh	Revue de philologie, Paris.
RQ	Römische Quartalschrift, Freiburg i.B.
RQH	Revue des questions historiques, Paris.
RSLR	Rivista di storia e letteratura religiosa, Florence.
RSPT, RSPh	Revue des sciences philosophiques et théologiques, Paris.
RSR	Recherches de science religieuse, Paris.
RTAM	Recherches de théologie ancienne et médiévale, Louvain.
RthL	Revue théologique de Louvain, Louvain.
RTM	Rivista di teologia morale, Bologna.
Sal	Salesianum, Roma.
SBA	Schweizerische Beiträge zur Altertumswissenschaft, Basel.
SBS	Stuttgarter Bibelstudien, Stuttgart.
ScEc	Sciences ecclésiastiques, Bruges.
SCh, SC	Sources chrétiennes, Paris.
SD	Studies and Documents, ed. K. Lake and S. Lake. London/Philadelphia.
SE	Sacris Erudiri, Bruges.
SDHI	Studia et documenta historiae et iuris, Roma.
SH	Subsidia Hagiographica, Brussels.
SHA	Scriptores Historiae Augustae.
SJMS	Speculum. Journal of Mediaeval Studies, Cambridge, Mass.
SM	Studien und Mitteilungen zur Geschichte des Benediktinerordens und seiner Zweige, Munich.
SO	Symbolae Osloenses, Oslo.
SP	Studia Patristica, successively Berlin, Kalamazoo, Leuven.
SPM	Stromata Patristica et Mediaevalia, ed. C. Mohrmann and J. Quasten, Utrecht.

SQ	Sammlung ausgewählter Quellenschriften zur Kirchen- und Dogmenge-schichte, Tübingen.
SQAW	Schriften und Quellen der Alten Welt, Berlin.
SSL	Spicilegium Sacrum Lovaniense, Louvain.
StudMed	Studi Medievali, Turin.
SVigChr	Supplements to Vigiliae Christianae, Leiden.
SVF	Stoicorum Veterum Fragmenta, ed. J. von Arnim, Leipzig.
TDNT	Theological Dictionary of the New Testament, Grand Rapids, Mich.
TE	Teologia espiritual, Valencia.
ThGl	Theologie und Glaube, Paderborn.
ThJ	Theologische Jahrbücher, Leipzig.
ThLZ	Theologische Literaturzeitung, Leipzig.
ThPh	Theologie und Philosophie, Freiburg i.B.
ThQ	Theologische Quartalschrift, Tübingen.
ThR	Theologische Rundschau, Tübingen.
ThWAT	Theologisches Wörterbuch zum Alten Testament, Stuttgart.
ThWNT	Theologisches Wörterbuch zum Neuen Testament, Stuttgart.
ThZ	Theologische Zeitschrift, Basel.
TLG	Thesaurus Linguae Graecae.
TP	Transactions and Proceedings of the American Philological Association, Lancaster, Pa.
TRE	Theologische Realenzyklopädie, Berlin.
TS	Theological Studies, New York and various places; now Washington, DC.
TThZ	Trierer theologische Zeitschrift, Trier.
TU	Texte und Untersuchungen, Leipzig/Berlin.
USQR	Union Seminary Quarterly Review, New York.
VC	Vigiliae Christianae, Amsterdam.
VetChr	Vetera Christianorum, Bari (Italy).
VT	Vetus Testamentum, Leiden.
WBC	Word Biblical Commentary, Waco.
WUNT	Wissenschaftliche Untersuchungen zum Neuen Testament, Tübingen.
WZKM	Wiener Zeitschrift für die Kunde des Morgenlandes, Vienna.
YUP	Yale University Press, New Haven.
ZAC	Zeitschrift für Antikes Christentum, Berlin.
ZAM	Zeitschrift für Aszese und Mystik, Innsbruck, then Würzburg.
ZAW	Zeitschrift für die alttestamentliche Wissenschaft, Giessen, then Berlin.
ZDPV	Zeitschrift des Deutschen Palästina-Vereins, Leipzig.
ZKG	Zeitschrift für Kirchengeschichte, Gotha, then Stuttgart.
ZKTh	Zeitschrift für katholische Theologie, Vienna.
ZNW	Zeitschrift für die neutestamentliche Wissenschaft und die Kunde der älteren Kirche, Giessen, then Berlin.
ZRG	Zeitschrift für Rechtsgeschichte, Weimar.
ZThK	Zeitschrift für Theologie und Kirche, Tübingen.

Introduction

Studies on Gregory of Nyssa are flourishing. The critical edition is now almost complete. The *Colloquia* periodicals, the tools of research like the *Lexicon Gregorianum* and the dictionaries, and the publications which embrace the various disciplines from spirituality to the history of dogma, from philosophy to exegesis, have gradually brought together a *corpus* which is unique compared with the other Fathers of the Church with the exception of Augustine. In this highly valuable collection of works, two areas stand out: mysticism and eschatology. The former has also been at the centre of a lively controversy, which is still partly smouldering under embers that had apparently been extinguished, concerning the possibility that Gregory could be described as the actual initiator of mysticism. For its part, eschatology has received particular attention, especially in three areas: the question of time, the *epektasis* and the *apokatastasis*.

In 2014, the editors of the present volume organised the XIII *Colloquium* on Gregory of Nyssa in Rome, dedicated to the *Commentary on the Canticle of Canticles/Song of Songs*. Despite the expectation that eschatology would be well represented in the conference papers, in line with the overview of scholarly literature outlined above, the quantity and quality of the work presented raised a question leading to the present volume: why does the *Commentary on the Canticle* cause such an overwhelming eschatological interest when there are so many different approaches to this text?

This question led to a study whose results are collected here. The hypothesis is that it is precisely the mystical character of the exegetical writing examined that offers a natural context for the deep understanding of Gregory's eschatology. The result of the research carried out to verify this hypothesis is in the hands of the reader. The question is all the more interesting in that Gregory's eschatology is marked by a hermeneutical tension which is reflected in a dichotomy present in the studies devoted to it. Clearly, Gregory has been inspired by the *apokatastasis* of Origen, but for him, as for the Alexandrian, is it possible to speak of a universal salvation? If the human being is simply a soul which has to be restored to its initial state, what is the value of its history? And what is the value of the body? And of freedom?

Using a metaphor, we could say that the nucleus of the tension consists in the irreducibility of a circular conception, with which Origen's *apokatastasis* is connected according to his writings, to a linear one which is implied by *epektasis*. It seems, therefore, that the two essential elements of Gregory's eschatology point in irreconcilable directions. Thus, in order to reveal the tension, we have deliberately tried to avoid every irenic approach but sought to immerse ourselves in it through the mystical dimension which is dominant in the *Commentary on the Canticle*. From a theological point of view, the way we

Studia Patristica CI, 1-4.
© Peeters Publishers, 2021.

have chosen implies the path through two areas which, in the context of Nyssa studies as a whole, are among the least studied: Christology and ontology. Therefore, these contributions have been chosen *ad hoc* to ensure that the themes treated are covered in such a way as to reveal the profound relationships between the two foci of theological reflection on the mystery of Christ: on the one hand, the Christological focus proper, and on the other, the ontology which emerges from Christological and Trinitarian considerations. Thus, we shall be able to identify the influences and relations, intrinsic and systematic, between the thought about being, the protology and the eschatology, of classical origin, and the thought about Christ in which the divine and the human are united in and through history.

This volume, therefore, is arranged in three main parts. The first, most fundamental, approximates to the question of the point of view of eschatology itself, seeking to indicate the importance of mysticism in its development. The first two contributions, from Giulio Maspero and Miguel Brugarolas, develop, respectively, the ontological and Christological dimensions on which Gregory's mysticism is based. It is a matter of seeing what really is beyond the appearance and to direct one's own life towards it. It is precisely Christ who simultaneously reveals, discloses and incarnates this movement which culminates in the identification of *apokatastasis* and *epektasis*, founded on the identification of the *eschaton* with Christ himself. Next, a contribution by Anna Silvas enables an appreciation of the role of Basil in the origin of this mystical stamp on Gregory's eschatology. This analysis turns out to be particularly valuable because it highlights the mystical origin of Gregory's *epektasis* in Basil and the link with apophatism. This familial origin of Gregory's theology leads naturally to the contribution of John P. Manoussakis who investigates the role of memory and the possibility that it could also be playing a part in the eschatological dimension. This is also interesting because it asks about the possibility of reconciling the tension which, similar to what has been seen, is reproduced in this area too, bringing it back to a tension between the philosophical and theological approaches. Michael Petrin's chapter tackles the relationship between *theôria* and *praxis*, showing how it is precisely the eschatological dimension of divinisation which holds them together. The result is obtained through the analysis of Gregory's exegesis, inspired by Paul, of a passage from the *Canticle*. Thus, little by little, there emerges the role of Gregory's *Commentary* the eschatological significance of which is presented in Françoise Vinel's concluding contribution to the first part of this work. This indicates the paradoxical role of *epektasis* in Gregory's eschatology, linking it to the apophatic, and, therefore, mystical, approach to the very Mystery of God.

The second part of the volume is devoted precisely to Gregory's *Commentary on the Canticle of Canticles*. The first two contributions contextualise it in relation to two other Nyssan works, the *De Infantibus premature abreptis* and the *De Vita Moysis*. The relation with the former is dealt with in the chapter written by Ilaria Vigorelli which points out the ontological novelty of the approach to eternal life developed by Gregory, starting out from the Trinitarian revelation. In particular, she reveals the fundamental role of *apatheia* in the *Commentary on the Canticle* with the connection which it mediates between eschatology and divine filiation. Raphael A. Cadenhead, on the other hand, analyses the *In Canticum* and the *De Vita Moysis* from a diachronic perspective, bearing in mind the difference between the addressees of the two works, indicating the risk of anachronism in reading the *Canticle* from the perspective of *gender* which does not take account of its spiritual and properly mystical dimension. In the following chapter, Jonathan Farrugia focuses on the thematic thread which connects creation, fall and redemption in an original reading which shows how, even in the mystical context of the work in question, the moral themes, generally more common in the homilies, are present. As for *gender*, the question is extremely important on account of the hermeneutical tension which is the starting point of the study because it concerns the historical, in relation to the eschatological, dimension of the human being. In the next chapter, Joona Salminen looks at the paradoxical dimension of the watchful sleep which characterises the commentary on the *Canticle* to illustrate the role, not only mystical but also ascetic, of the doctrine linked with it whose eschatological value depends on the relation with the categories of *anaisthesia* and *apatheia*. In her chapter, Erini Artemi explores the relationship between seeing and knowing, tracing it from the example of Moses. The desire for knowledge and apophatism are thus presented as a further basis for the tension which runs through Gregory's eschatology. The second part of the volume is concluded by Manabu Akiyama who makes clear the role of the *Fourth Gospel* as a source of inspiration for Gregory's eschatology as realised eschatology. Specifically, the Cross itself is presented as the point of attraction through which the glory of the Risen One draws everything to Himself from within time, from a concrete moment in history. Thus, from several points of view, the analysis of the *Commentary of the Canticle* demonstrates the impossibility of releasing the hermeneutical tension found in Gregory's eschatology.

The third part of the volume is devoted to the *apokatastasis*, an essential element of Gregory's eschatology which he inherited from Origen. Thus, the first two contributions of the last section deal with Gregory's relationship with Origen and his tradition, particularly in Evagrius. Vito Limone studies the exegesis of *Ct* 1:5 in Gregory and Origen in such a way as to highlight the points of contact but also the elements of difference between the two interpretations which discuss precisely the relationship between protology and eschatology. Ilaria Ramelli has examined the development of eschatology up to Evagrius, pointing out the closeness between the latter and Gregory, especially with regard to their interpretations of 1*Cor* 15:28. Here, the mystical dimension of eschatology is ascribed to the convergence of *nous* and love. Finally, the two last chapters reveal the interpretative tension in the reading of *apokatastasis*. The contribution of Magdalena Marunová examines Gregory's doctrine through the analysis of the τῶν πάντων, indicating as the reason for the final restoration the rationality of angels and human beings whereas the irrational creation appears to remain outside the eschatological process. Finally, Marta Przyszychowska's contribution identifies the reason for the *apokatastasis* in the unity of human nature and its social dimension. That makes it possible to understand how Gregory can make a powerful assertion of the value of human freedom, the existence of hell and the universal restoration. In fact, the rejection of God is equivalent to the rejection of being human.

The path outlined proposes to be a powerful pointer both to the theological profundity of this hermeneutical tension and to the various interpretative elements which could be working together to create it. We have deliberately not advanced any conclusion, leaving the judgement to the reader. We have sought to present the different, even contrasting positions, providing, simultaneously, some tools which could assist a deeper penetration into the tensions of eschatology through the mystical perspective which is characteristic of the *Commentary on the Canticle of Canticles*. In particular, the Christological and ontological elements linked to *epektasis* seem to promise a greater immersion into Gregory's eschatology and appreciation of its theological significance, not *despite* its tensions but precisely *by means of* them.

G. MASPERO, M. BRUGAROLAS, I. VIGORELLI

Part I
The Eschatological Structure

CHAPTER 1

Eschatological Ontology

Giulio MASPERO

1. Introduction: a hermeneutical tension

The relationship between protology and eschatology is an essential pillar of human thought on both the philosophical and theological levels in that it reveals the conception of the relation of the Divinity with the world and, consequently, with matter and history.

From this perspective, the thought of Gregory of Nyssa is particularly notable: it reveals the rich web of relations which link him to the previous tradition and especially to Origen. The influence of the great Alexandrian on the Cappadocian has been widely studied even if there still remains much to do.[1] Eschatology and the relation between *archê* and *telos* are central from this point of view because the *apokatastasis* is an element clearly transmitted to Gregory from Origen. However, the positions of the two great authors on the relation between *archê* and *telos* merit particular attention because, if the *apokatastasis* were simply the return to the initial state, that would mean that the *telos* differs in no respect from the *archê*, depriving everything between them of real significance in that it is merely provisional. However, that appears to be in clear contrast with the *epektasis*, the true distinctive mark of Gregory's eschatology: the dynamic conception of the definitive union with God as an infinite growth in glory actually seems to clash with the idea of a simple return to the initial condition. Gregory's *epektasis* seems, in fact, to imply that the *telos* is an infinite progress compared with the *archê*. So, at the same time, the beginning and the end should both coincide and be different. There remains, therefore, a hermeneutical tension, evidenced not only in the contemporary academic sphere but right from the time of the Fathers.

This is clear in the comment of Maximus the Confessor. Here, there is certainly also present the echo of the troubled reception of Origen, but, at the same time, Maximus expresses the need to distinguish Gregory's eschatological perspective from that of Origen, pointing out that, for the former, knowledge and

---

[1] *Cf.* I.L.E. Ramelli, *Social Justice and the Legitimacy of Slavery. The Role of Philosophical Asceticism from Ancient Judaism to Late Antiquity*, Oxford Early Christian Studies (Oxford, 2016), 180, n. 24.

participation are not identified. In this way, eternal condemnation can be interpreted precisely as knowledge without participation.[2] Beyond the valuation of this solution, as of those put forward in recent studies, it is clear that the hermeneutical tension refers to the relationship between ontology and eschatology.

In one of her valuable studies, Monique Alexandre has shown[3] that the affirmation of the correspondence of *archê* and *telos* and the possibility of knowing the former in the light of the latter were already present in the work of Origen. In this way, she has also identified the specific features of Gregory's conception, focusing particularly on the anthropological sphere. Leaning on this work, we shall seek to show Gregory's originality from a point of view that is essentially theological and ontological: specifically, the thesis that we shall try to prove is that the particular nature of Gregory's thought in the conception of the inversion of the relationship between protology and eschatology has its foundation in his Trinitarian doctrine and can, therefore, be understood only if one starts out from the body of Gregory's works and teaching. In other words, we shall seek to show that the relationship between *archê* and *telos* refers to the metaphysical relationship between the triune God and the world. It is at this level that the difference in comparison with Origen becomes clear.

The present chapter is divided into a first part, of a more analytical nature, intended to show, through some examples, the presence and the role of inversion in Gregory's writing; a second, more concise part which, through a more systematic treatment, will seek to indicate the structural value of inversion itself, starting from the Trinitarian foundations of Gregory's thought; finally, a third part which will reread the *apokatastasis* in the light of the *epektasis*, seeking to explain how Gregory's ontology can be described as eschatological.

That brings us back to the very foundations of Greek metaphysics. In fact, we can state in outline that it was characterised by a necessary conception of the correspondence of *archê* and *telos*: Plato, in particular, with his doctrine of the relationship between the soul and the world of ideas, seems to place the reason for the necessity of the correspondence in the *archê* whereas Aristotle places it in the *telos* on the basis of his theory of the act and his identification of the unmoved mover with the final cause. In both cases, however, *archê* and *telos* are united by a series of necessary causal connections. Neoplatonic philosophy takes up these traditions, combining them in the conception of history as *exitus-reditus*: everything had its origin from the first principle, through a process of emanation as a corruption, and everything is irresistibly destined to return to unity. In the light of this correspondence, therefore, knowledge of the *archê* is revealed to be sufficient to discover also the *telos*. It is, therefore,

---

[2] *Cf.* Maximus the Confessor, *Quaestiones, interrogationes et responsiones* q. 19 (I,13): J.H. Declerck, *Maximi Confessoris Quaestiones et dubia* (Turnhout, 1982), 17-8.

[3] *Cf.* M. Alexandre, 'Protologie et eschatologie chez Grégoire de Nysse', in U. Bianchi (ed.), *Arché e Telos. L'antropologia di Origene e di Gregorio di Nissa. Analisi storico-religiosa* (Milano, 1981), 122-59.

determined in that the two are necessarily connected, analogously to what happens in the sphere of the natural sciences.[4] We note that, in this metaphysical sphere, the first principle and the world constitute a single, albeit graduated, level in such a way that the relationship between *archê* and *telos* can be deduced starting from that between God and the cosmos. That is clear in the Aristotelian system of movers which enable the ascension to the unmoved mover.

Quite different is the situation in the Jewish-Christian theological sphere where the ontological distinction between the Creator and the creation is absolute. The conception of the relationship between *archê* and *telos* can, then, be linked to the distinction between philosophy and theology since the latter is characterised precisely by an irreducibility of the *telos* to the *archê*, and so by an inversion compared with what happens in a conception marked by necessity and by the eternal return as in pagan Greek thought.[5] Therefore, the present study seeks to show Gregory's originality precisely by starting from the completeness of his Trinitarian formula and from the consequences that follow from it. In other words, the conception of the relationship between *archê* and *telos* can be employed to assess the *chrêsis* of the philosophical elements by the Fathers according to the methodological category introduced by Christian Gnilka.[6] The hermeneutical tension which characterises the relation between Origen's eschatology and that of Gregory can, therefore, be read from the viewpoint of the relation to the use, that is, to the *chrêsis* itself, of Greek metaphysics on the part of these two great Christian thinkers.

2. The inversion between *archê* and *telos*

2.1. *The life of Christ*

Some examples can serve to understand how, for Gregory, there exists a real connection between the *telos* and the *archê*, but a free one, in such a way that the *archê* is comprehensible only in the light of the *telos*, and the space that separates the two extremes acquires an immense value.

In the *Or cat*, Gregory gives an example of his anti-Arian exegesis, showing how essential it is to start from the divine freedom in order to approach the revealed mystery. In fact, men die because they are born whereas, for Christ,

---

[4] Significantly, for classical Greek, the term *historia* indicated both the natural sciences and history. *Cf.* G. Maspero, 'Esegesi e teologia: l'uso del termine historia applicato alla Scrittura nelle Omelie sul Cantico dei Cantici di Gregorio di Nissa', in M. Cassin *et al.* (eds), *Grégoire de Nysse: La Bible dans la construction de son discours*, Études augustiniennes (Paris, 2008), 245-60.

[5] But we should note that inversion is also present at the beginnings of Latin theology, as far back as Tertullian, so that the Trinitarian origin of the phenomenon is confirmed, *cf.* A. Hamman, 'L'homme, image de Dieu chez Tertullien', in J. Granarolo (ed.), *Autour de Tertullien. Hommage à René Braun*, II (Nice, 1990), 106.

[6] *Cf.* Ch. Gnilka, *Chrêsis: Die Methode der Kirchenväter im Umgang mit der antiken Kultur: Der Begriff des 'rechten Gebrauchs'* (Basel, 2012).

who is God, the incarnate Son, it is necessary to say the opposite. He was born for the Cross so that the meaning of his beginning is precisely his end, that is, the salvation of man:

Perhaps one who has meditated on the mystery diligently would say with greater reason that the death did not occur because of the birth but, on the contrary, the birth was assumed with a view to the death: for He who is for ever did not subject himself to bodily birth out of the need to live but to call us back from death to life.[7]

Here is a wonderful combination of the theology of filiation and the theology of the cross: everything is governed by the principle of the end; Christ comes to life in order to die so that we can pass from death to life. In this way, as already in Origen, the end is not determined by the beginning, but, rather, the causal direction is exactly the opposite.[8] For Gregory, therefore, the virginal generation of Christ is united inseparably with the victory of the cross[9] and the whole of his life, his personal story, proclaims his being the consubstantial and only-begotten Son of the Father.

It is precisely the salvation of the human race, in fact, which is the light that, from the end, illuminates the beginning. In the Incarnation, at the moment of the Lord's conception, the Most High was united inseparably with the entire human nature through the work of the Holy Spirit. Thus, our salvation is complete. The same thing happened, says Gregory, at the end of Christ's life. From the end, indeed, one draws knowledge of the beginning:

Therefore, what we understand about the final part, we deduce also about the beginning. In fact, at the end, he ensured that [His] body was separated from his soul in the economy, but His indivisible Divinity, united once for all to its human element, was not separated either from his body or from his soul. But while with [His] soul he enters Paradise (cf. Lk 23:43), opening the path to people in the person of the [Good] Thief, with [His] body he destroys in the heart of the earth (Mt 12:40) the one who has the power of death (Heb 2:14) and, thus, his body is also called Lord on account of the Divinity inherent in it.[10]

---

[7] τάχα δ᾽ ἄν τις δι᾽ ἀκριβείας καταμαθὼν τὸ μυστήριον εὐλογώτερον εἴποι μὴ διὰ τὴν γένεσιν συμβεβηκέναι τὸν θάνατον, ἀλλὰ τὸ ἔμπαλιν τοῦ θανάτου χάριν παραληφθῆναι τὴν γένεσιν· οὐ γὰρ τοῦ ζῆσαι δεόμενος ὁ ἀεὶ ὢν τὴν σῶμα τικὴν ὑποδύεται γένεσιν, ἀλλ᾽ ἡμᾶς ἐπὶ τὴν ζωὴν ἐκ τοῦ θανάτου ἀνακαλούμενος (Or cat, 32, 15-21; J. Srawley, 115-6). Abbreviations for Gregory's works are those in F. Mann, Lexicon Gregorianum (Leiden, 1999-2007).

[8] Origen had replied to the fatalist criticism of Celsus on the basis of which the death of Christ had to happen necessarily because the prophets had foreseen it. He explained that they did not cause the outcome of the Lord's life but had known it in their relationship with God. Thus, it was the Cross that caused their prophecy, not the reverse. Cf. Origen, Contra Celsum, II, 20 (SC 147, 336-44).

[9] Gregory in Virg 2, 1, 1-11 (SC 119, 262-4) also rereads Mary's virginity in a Trinitarian key since the generation in time reveals the eternal generation: cf. M. Gordillo, 'La virginidad transcendente de Maria Madre de Dios en S. Gregorio de Nisa y en la antigua tradición de la Iglesia', Estudios Marianos 21 (1960), 117-55.

[10] ὅπερ οὖν ἐπὶ τοῦ κατὰ τὸ τέλος μέρους καταλαμβάνομεν, τοῦτο καὶ περὶ τῆς ἀρχῆς λογιζόμεθα. ὡς γὰρ ἐκεῖ τὸ μὲν σῶμα τῆς ψυχῆς διαζευχθῆναι κατ᾽ οἰκονομίαν ἐποίησεν, ἡ

We notice the emphasis on the body as place of the manifestation of the divine omnipotence in glory. Although obviously not existing in the *archê*, not only is it present in the *telos*, but remains in it through its union with God. Here, the divinisation of matter reaches its peak. The conjunction of human and divine nature is complete: flesh, time and history are truly saved. This is not a question of symbols alone but of realities *divinised* in Christ and, therefore, *able to be divinised* in every human being. They do not lose their autonomy. The laws of nature and time continue to hold, but they have now become a path for the imitation of God who became Man.

To understand the difference with regard to the correspondence between *archê* and *telos* in Origen,[11] we could look at the following text taken from his commentary of the *Fourth Gospel*:

In fact, there is no need to think that historical realities (τὰ ἱστορικά) are figures of historical realities (ἱστορικῶν) and that corporal realities are figures of corporal realities, but corporal realities are figures of spiritual realities (πνευματικῶν) and historical realities (τὰ ἱστορικά) of intellectual realities (νοητῶν).[12]

The thought behind the exegesis reflects metaphysics in such a way that the space, the *diastêma*, between *archê* and *telos*, has a value but on a different level from the case in Gregory's conception. For Gregory, instead, the body, which arose precisely in the diastematic space, does not refer beyond itself but is the place of the presence of the divine omnipotence. Thus, in Christ, time and movement become realities of salvation. To be perfect no longer means escaping the domination of movement but rather governing movement in order to direct it permanently to the Good.

2.2. *Human nature and history*

From the life of Christ, this dynamic extends to the whole of human history until it becomes an interpretative key in the development of thought. The Platonic theme of the cave is an example of it.[13] In Gregory, it displays an interesting

---

δὲ ἀμέριστος θεότης, ἅπαξ ἀνακραθεῖσα τῷ ὑποκειμένῳ, οὔτε τοῦ σώματος οὔτε τῆς ψυχῆς ἀπεσπάσθη, ἀλλὰ διὰ μὲν τῆς ψυχῆς ἐν τῷ παραδείσῳ γίνεται ὁδοποιοῦσα διὰ τοῦ λῃστοῦ τοῖς ἀνθρώποις τὴν εἴσοδον, διὰ δὲ τοῦ σώματος ἐν τῇ καρδίᾳ τῆς γῆς ἀναιροῦσα τὸν τὸ κράτος ἔχοντα τοῦ θανάτου, καὶ διὰ τοῦτο καὶ τὸ σῶμα κύριος λέγεται, διὰ τὴν ἐγκειμένην θεότητα· (*Ep* 3, 22, 1-10: GNO VIII/2, 25,21-26,1).

[11] Note that for Origen, however, human history is a reflection of angelic history, *cf.* J. Daniélou, *Origène* (Paris, 1948), 193.

[12] Οὐ γὰρ νομιστέον τὰ ἱστορικὰ ἱστορικῶν εἶναι τύπους καὶ τὰ σωματικὰ σωματικῶν, ἀλλὰ τὰ σωματικὰ πνευματικῶν καὶ τὰ ἱστορικὰ νοητῶν (Origen, *Commentarii in evangelium Joannis*, X 18, 110, 4-6; SC 157, 448).

[13] In Gregory, the Aristotelian reformulation of the myth also plays a significant role. *Cf.* W. Blum, 'Eine Verbindung der zwei Höhlengleichnisse der heidnischen Antike bei Gregor von Nyssa', *VigChr* 28 (1974), 43-9.

development.[14] At a first stage, the image is being employed to indicate the present life from which it is necessary to be freed.[15] The difference compared with Neoplatonism is radical because it is no longer matter or the body in themselves that are a prison but the present life, marked by original sin.[16] Evil is no longer ascribed to nature but to freedom.[17] However, the space between *archê* and *telos* is still not significant in itself. After Gregory's journey to Jerusalem, in 382, on the other hand, it is clear that something has changed: in fact, in his subsequent works,[18] probably influenced by his pilgrimage to the grotto in Bethlehem, Gregory points out that God entered the cave. This is a movement exactly symmetrical with the Platonic one.[19] In the *Antirrh* he writes:

We affirm that God who, in essence is immaterial, invisible and incorporeal, through a disposition of love towards men, by the end of the completion of the universe, when evil had already grown to its highest level, at precisely that moment united himself to human nature in order to destroy sin, like a sun which penetrates into a dark cave and with its presence dissipates the darkness by means of the light.[20]

It is extremely interesting to observe how the same philosophical thought is reread in reverse, starting from the incarnation, according to the Johannine perspective of the light which shines in the darkness (*cf. Jn* 1:5). This is possible because the resurrection has illuminated the birth of Christ. In its turn, the latter can illuminate history; and the movement expands further until it acquires cosmic dimensions. It is noticeable that this eschatological perspective is at the base of the exegetical method which not only rereads the Old Testament typologically in the light of Christ but extends the possibility of understanding to the whole history of human thought, recovering the elements of truth found also in the pagan sphere, not in the name of the *Logos*, as the Apologists and the Alexandrian School had done, but in the Body of Christ.

---

[14] Various authors highlight the importance of the diachronic dimension for the study of Gregory's thought: *cf.* A.A. Mosshammer, 'Historical time and the apokatastasis according to Gregory of Nyssa', *SP* 27 (1993), 70-93, and J. Daniélou, 'La chronologie des œuvres de Grégoire de Nysse', *SP* 7 (1966), 159-69.

[15] *Cf. Mort*, GNO IX, 37-8; *Inscr*, GNO V, 151-4 and *Beat*, GNO VII/2, 102-5.

[16] *Cf.* J. Daniélou, *L'Être et le Temps chez Grégoire de Nysse* (Leiden, 1970), 165.

[17] On Gregory's concept of liberty, see G. Dal Toso, *La nozione di* proairesis *in Gregorio di Nissa. Analisi semiotico-linguistica e prospettive antropologiche* (Frankfurt a.M., 1998) and *id.*, article 'Proaresis', in L.F. Mateo-Seco and G. Maspero (eds), *The Brill Dictionary of Gregory of Nyssa* (Leiden, 2010), 647-9.

[18] *Cf. Diem nat*, GNO X/2, 256-8; *Epist* 3, GNO VIII/2, 20 and *Steph I*, GNO X/1, 75.

[19] This would be a similar journey to that of Jerome who abandoned Neoplatonism after he had been to Jerusalem.

[20] ἡμεῖς γάρ φαμεν, ὅτι ἄϋλός τε καὶ ἀειδὴς καὶ ἀσώματος κατ᾽ οὐσίαν θεὸς ὢν οἰκονομίᾳ τινὶ φιλανθρώπῳ πρὸς τῷ τέλει τῆς τοῦ παντὸς συμπληρώσεως ἤδη τῆς κακίας εἰς τὸ ἀκρότατον αὐξηθείσης, τότε ἐπὶ καθαιρέσει τῆς ἁμαρτίας τῇ ἀνθρωπίνῃ κατακιρνᾶται φύσει, οἷόν τις ἥλιος ἐν γνοφώδει σπηλαίῳ εἰσοικιζόμενος καὶ διὰ τοῦ φωτὸς ἐξαφανίζων τῇ παρουσίᾳ τὸ σκότος (*Antirrh*, GNO III/1, 171,11-7).

Thus, in the *Trid spat*, Gregory asks how it was that the Lord, who had the power to choose his own way of dying among so many, actually chose the cross.[21] The question was fundamental for responding to the neo-Arians who considered Christ's obedience and the shame which he underwent a proof of his inferiority to the Father. Gregory claims that the choice of the instrument of the Saviour's death can be understood only in the light of the resurrection and the divinity of Christ: the *telos* illuminates the *archê*. In fact, in harmony with the Johannine approach, the very form of the cross reveals the extending of the divine power to the whole of the cosmos and all history: taking up also the Pauline theology of the cross as power of God (1*Cor* 1:18) and reason for boasting (*Gal* 6:14), Gregory comments on the four dimensions of *Eph* 3:18-9, setting them in relation to the four arms of the cross. He write:

[Paul] sees, in fact, that this figure of the cross, divided into four arms which extend from the central intersection, signifies the all-pervading power and providence of the One who appeared on it. That is why Paul gives each branch a particular name, calling *depth* the one which stands below the centre and *height* the one which stands above, *breadth* and *length* those which extend from the intersection to one side and the other. And it appears to me that with these expressions the discourse clearly shows that there is nothing which is not absolutely under the power of the divine nature: above the heavens, under the earth and to the extreme horizontal limits of what exists.[22]

The whole cosmos is held together by the power of God, that is revealed on the cross, with which the Author of life conquers death. Everything is pervaded with meaning because Christ holds everything together. Commenting on the text of *Ps* 138:7-9, Gregory writes:

Do you see how with his words he portrays the figure of the cross? He says: You are the One who pervades everything, making yourself the bond (*syndesmos*) of everything and including within yourself every extreme limit: You are on high, You are present in the depth, over one extreme stands Your hand and over the other Your right hand governs.[23]

---

[21] Cf. *Trid spat*, GNO IX/1, 298,20-299,3.

[22] εἶδε γὰρ ὅτι τὸ σχῆμα τοῦτο τέσσαρσι προβολαῖς ἀπὸ τῆς ἐν τῷ μέσῳ συμβολῆς μερι-ζόμενον τὴν διὰ πάντων ἤκουσαν τοῦ ἐν αὐτῷ φανέντος δύναμίν τε καὶ πρόνοιαν διασημαίνει καὶ τούτου χάριν ἑκάστην προβολὴν ἰδιαζούσαις κατονομάζει φωναῖς βάθος λέγων τὸ ἐκ τοῦ μέσου κάτω καὶ ὕψος τὸ ὑπερκείμενον, πλάτος δὲ καὶ μῆκος τὸ ἐκ πλαγίου παρατεινόμενον μετὰ τὴν συμβολὴν ἑκατέρωθεν, ὡς τὸ μὲν ἔνθεν τοῦ μέσου πλάτος τὸ δὲ ἑτέρωθεν μῆκος προσαγορεῦσαι, δι᾽ ὧν τοῦτό μοι δοκεῖ σαφῶς διασημαίνειν τῷ λόγῳ, ὅτι οὐδὲν τῶν ὄντων ἐστίν, ὃ μὴ τῇ θείᾳ πάντως διακρατεῖται φύσει, τὸ ὑπερουράνιον, τὸ ὑποχθόνιον, τὸ ἐπὶ τὰ πέρατα τῶν ὄντων πάντοθεν ἐκ πλαγίου παρατεινόμενον· σημαίνει γὰρ διὰ μὲν τοῦ ὕψους τὸ ὑπερκείμενον, διὰ δὲ τοῦ βάθους τὸ ὑποχθόνιον, τῷ μήκει δὲ καὶ τῷ πλάτει τὰ διὰ μέσου πέρατα τὰ ὑπὸ τῆς τὸ πᾶν διακρατούσης δυνάμεως κατεχόμενα (*Ibid.*, GNO IX, 300,8-301,1).

[23] ὁρᾷς πῶς διαζωγραφεῖ τὸ τοῦ σταυροῦ σχῆμα διὰ τῶν λεγομένων; σὺ εἶ, φησίν, ὁ διὰ πάντων ἤκων καὶ σύνδεσμος τῶν πάντων γινόμενος καὶ πάντα ἐν ἑαυτῷ διαλαμβάνων τὰ πέρατα· ἄνω σὺ εἶ, κάτω σὺ πάρει, ἐν τῷ πέρατι τούτῳ ἡ χείρ σού ἐστι καὶ ἐν τῷ ἑτέρῳ ἡ δεξιά σου ὁδηγεῖ (*Ibid.*, 301,17-302,2).

This text is particularly important because it applies to Christ the function of *desmos* of the universe which Philo had attributed to the *Logos*.[24] The cross-over is essential because the function of mediation and union is now performed by Christ in his Humanity which is indissolubly united to the Divinity, and no longer by the *Logos* alone, according to a theology typical of the Alexandrian school and which had been very successful. It had enabled the presentation of the unity of history but it always ran the risk of a subordinationism, at least at the verbal level. Gregory, on the other hand, reasons in terms of nature in such a way as to put at the centre the mystery of the hypostatic union and, therefore, the historicity and bodily nature of Christ.

This also corresponds to the importance of 1*Cor* 15:28 in Gregory's eschatology: he had to refute the Arian interpretation of the final submission of Christ to the Father in a subordinationist, Arian sense. The main elements of his response are two: (a) the conception of evil as a metaphysically finite reality implies its disappearance at the end of time when union with God will be definitive; (b) the affirmation that the Son's submission to the Father will take place in his Body, that is, in bringing back everything into himself.[25] From this point of view, eschatology will be a realisation and a full manifestation of the union of Christ with man. This point is essential for grasping the Trinitarian foundation of Gregory's inversion in his reading of the relationship between *archê* and *telos*.[26]

The theme of the cosmic cross came to Gregory through the mediation of Irenaeus[27] and the majority of authors recognise his direct dependence on this source.[28] However, it is a subject already found in Origen[29] which Gregory redevelops but in an original way starting from the totality of his sources.

This is a properly theological operation through which the sacred history is being reread in the light of its end so that we can understand its meaning, that

---

[24] Cf. Philo, *Quis rerum divinarum heres sit?*, 205.1-206.4; *De plantatione*, 15, 1-16, 1; *De fuga et inventione*, 112, 1-3.

[25] Cf. Gregory of Nyssa, *Tunc et ipse*, GNO III/2, 13-5.

[26] Gregory comments on the same figure in *Or cat*, 32, 40-6.52-61, inserting an almost word for word quotation from Plato's *Symposium* where the role of holding the universe together is attributed to Eros (cf. 202d.8-203a.5). It is particularly significant how Gregory changes the sense of the Platonic text radically though seeking to acknowledge the philosophical and mystical insights contained in it: cf. G. Maspero, 'El Espíritu, la Cruz y la unidad: syndeô, syndemos y syndetikos en Gregorio de Nisa', *Scripta Theologica* 38 (2006) 445-71. See also *Eun* II, GNO I, 121,21-122,5. A cosmic cross (in the form of *chi*) was present also in the *Timaeus* (34ab and 36bc), as a sign of the divinity of the demiurge.

[27] Cf. Irenaeus, *Demonstratio* 34, PO 773. He claims that the cross was chosen by Christ to proclaim the divinity of the Son and his universal power. Hubertus Drobner points out the closeness of this text to Gregory's thought: cf. H.R. Drobner, *Die drei Tage zwischen Tod und Auferstehung unseres Herrn Jesus Christus* (Leiden, 1982), 152.

[28] Cf. D.L. Balás, 'The Meaning of the "Cross"', in A. Spira and C. Klock (eds), *The Easter Sermons of Gregory of Nyssa: Translation and Commentary* (Cambridge, 1981), 305-18, 314-5.

[29] Cf. H. Drobner, *Die drei Tage* (1982), 155. See Origen, *Homelia in Genesim 2,5* (GCS 6, 33,23-36,17) and *Homilia in Jeremiam* 18,2 (GCS 3, 152,31-153,6).

is, the absolute gratuitousness of the gift of God to man. That is why the cross itself is, surprisingly, referred to with the appellative of *theologian*:

Therefore, it seems to me that the divine voice of the Gospel is intending proclaim the existence of One in whom everything has been constituted, who is more eternal than what is included under His power and who, through the figure of the cross, is indicating, as in a mystery and a mirror, the very power which guards all beings. For this reason, it says that it was necessary that the Son of Man should not simply die but be crucified so that, for the most discerning, the cross becomes theologian (*theologos*) in that it proclaims in its form the omnipotent dominion of Him who was exposed on it and who is all in all.[30]

Indeed, the function of theology is precisely that of proclaiming the divinity of the Son, leading in reverse from the *telos* to the *archê* to show that the Trinity is the origin and the end of everything that exists.

3. The theological architecture

3.1. *Analysis*

In her work already cited,[31] Monique Alexandre indicated four specific characteristics of Gregory's concept of the relation between protology and eschatology compared with that of Origen: (1) the end of history is not equivalent to the return to a pre-existing unity of pure spirits; (2) eschatology is understood essentially in terms of the general resurrection; (3) the dimension of progress and successive stages in the closeness to the end is particularly clear, together with the need for a human response; (4) the possibility of other worlds is not contemplated while the final unity is conceived of in terms of infinite movement.

The examples of inversion in Gregory's thought which were adduced in the previous section enable us to set the previous conclusions of Monique Alexandre in the context of Gregory's theology, pointing out its Trinitarian foundation, that is, its link with ontology. In fact, in a movement of gradual expansion from Christ to the cosmos, those texts describe the inversion in such a way as to highlight: (a) the divine freedom in the incarnation of the Son as a sign of His divinity; (b) the entrance of the Light into the cave as the reason for the inversion of the Neoplatonic movement of flight from the material world, to which

---

[30] διό μοι δοκεῖ πρὸς τοῦτο βλέπειν ἡ θεία τοῦ εὐαγγελίου φωνή, ὅτι ἐκεῖνό ἐστιν, ἐν ᾧ τὰ πάντα συνέστηκε, τὸ τῶν ἐν αὐτῷ περικρατουμένων ἀϊδιώτερον, ὃ τὴν ἑαυτοῦ δύναμιν τὴν συντηρητικὴν πάντων τῶν ὄντων οἷον δι᾽ αἰνίγματος καὶ ἐσόπτρου τινὸς διὰ τοῦ κατὰ τὸν σταυρὸν σχήματος ὑποδείκνυσι. διὰ δὴ τοῦτό φησιν, ὅτι δεῖ τὸν υἱὸν τοῦ ἀνθρώπου οὐχ ἁπλῶς ἀποθανεῖν, ἀλλὰ σταυρωθῆναι, ἵνα γένηται τοῖς διορατικωτέροις θεολόγος ὁ σταυρὸς τὴν παντοδύναμον ἐξουσίαν τοῦ ἐπ᾽ αὐτῷ δειχθέντος καὶ πάντα ἐν πᾶσιν ὄντος ἀνακηρύσσων τῷ σχήματι (*Trid spat*, GNO IX, 303,2-12).

[31] *Cf.* M. Alexandre, 'Protologie et eschatologie chez Grégoire de Nysse' (1981), 157-8.

the Greek world ascribed evil, identified with ignorance; (c) the reformulation of that in terms of theology in that it is conceived as the announcement of the divinity of the incarnate Son, through the recognition in the concrete details of the story itself – like the form of the cross – of His power and the unity which He has brought into the cosmos.

Following the three examples proposed, it is possible to show the connection of the inversion between *archê* and *telos* with the Trinitarian thought of Gregory in three successive stages.

(a) The *freedom in the incarnation* is expressed through the passage from the theology of the *Logos*, which had characterised the first three centuries and had served to present Revelation in the context of human thought, to the theology of the natures. It was the necessary response to neo-Arian subordinationism. With Athanasius and the Cappadocians, it became increasingly clear that only the three divine Persons are eternal: if salvation, that is, the fullness and eternity of life, is communicated by Them through baptism, each one must have the fullness of life and so be identified with eternity itself. Every other being, then, including the pure spirits, must have had a beginning in time, in accordance with Monique Alexandre's first conclusion (1). In this way, every possible figure of necessary mediation disappears[32] and the absolute freedom of God in the acts of creation and providence is made explicit: this means the cutting of the fatal and automatic connection which characterised the relationship between *archê* and *telos* and the creation of the possibility of bringing together the two extremes starting from a properly Trinitarian conception of God, characterised, therefore, by freedom.

(b) However, that had some serious gnoseological consequences because the *darkness of the cave*, symbol of human existence could no longer be ascribed to the corruption linked to the descent on the ontological scale which united the world and God, nor to the heaviness of the human body. In fact, driven by the Trinitarian debates with the neo-Arians, Gregory points out the distinction between being and knowing,[33] making a definitive break with the necessary connection which united both according to the Greek way of thinking.[34] The latter identified evil and ignorance, in connection with the historical and material dimension. It is precisely this distinction between being and knowing which creates the space for the awareness of the value of freedom and relation. That could also be related to the exclusion of other possible worlds in M. Alexandre's fourth conclusion (4).

---

[32] Both Neoplatonism and Gnosis explained the relationship between God and the world in terms of intermediate ontological degrees that are gradually degenerating.

[33] He says, for example: 'Bodily health is good for human life, but being happy does not mean just knowing the definition of health but rather living healthily' (*Beat*, GNO VII/2, 142,7-10). See also the distinction between the plane of *being* and that of *being said* in *Eun* II, GNO I, 271,30.

[34] This is precisely the point of the exegesis of Gregory's *apokatastasis* by Maximus the Confessor cited in the introduction.

(c) The *cosmic dimension of the cross* reveals that the incarnate Son is God through the rereading of the Paschal mystery from the starting point of the resurrection, and that explains the properly theological, that is, Trinitarian, depth of Monique Alexandre's second conclusion relating to the importance of the resurrection in Gregory's conception of eschatology (2). In fact, these events reveal that God must be Father from eternity and cannot have a Son solely in view of the creation, as the Arians thought. Therefore, the being of God has to be reread in terms of relation, and the Person has to assume the same ontological value as the substance. But that translates itself into the affirmation of the unknowability of the divine essence: in fact, apophatism follows from the awareness of the infinite distance that separates the being of God from the human capacity of understanding.[35] Instead, the possibility of knowing God has to come through His action (*energeia*) which reveals His being[36] and can be given only in relation (*schesis*),[37] since the action is in harmony with nature, and only God can give Life, create and save and all those actions which are exclusively characteristic of His power.

In this sense, God can be known only *a posteriori*, through his acting in creation and in the history of salvation, and so through His freedom. But that means to say that God can be known in the personal dimension and therefore in that concrete history which is Revelation.[38]

Precisely Gregory's inversion between *archê* and *telos* is linked to this apophatism since only at the end of history will it be possible to know really what God has done and who God is. In fact, where knowledge of Him is concerned, it will be able to be given only in union through the eternal and infinite dynamic of the *epektasis*, that is, a movement of progressive and eternal immersion in the One who is infinite.[39] On the other hand, when it comes to nature, and human nature in particular, precisely on account of its creaturely nature, it can be known only in its temporal and, therefore, social dimension. Here we note the agreement with the final two conclusions of Monique Alexandre: the importance of progress (3) and the impossibility of other cycles which

---

[35] *Cf.* A. Ojell, article 'Apophatic Theology', in L.F. Mateo-Seco and G. Maspero (eds), *The Brill Dictionary of Gregory of Nyssa* (2010), 68-73.

[36] For example, *Abl*, GNO III/1, 44,7-44,16.

[37] *Cf.* G. Maspero, 'Divinization, Relation (schesis) and Ontology in Gregory of Nyssa', in J. Arblaster and R. Faesen (eds), *Theosis / Deification: Christian Doctrines of Divinization East and West*, Bibliotheca Ephemeridum Theologicarum Lovaniensium 294 (Leuven, 2018), 19-34.

[38] For a detailed study on the relation between apophaticism, person and ontology in Gregory, see G. Maspero, *Trinity and Man* (Leiden, 2007), 138-47.

[39] With regard to *epektasis*, *cf.* J. Daniélou, *Platonisme et théologie mystique. Doctrine spirituelle de saint Grégoire de Nysse* (Paris, 1944), 291-307; L.F. Mateo-Seco, 'Progresso o immutabilità nella visione beatifica? Appunti dalla storia della teologia', in M. Hauke and M. Pagano (eds), *Eternità e libertà* (Milano, 1998), 119-40 and G. Maspero, 'Ontology, History and Relation (schesis): Gregory of Nyssa's Epektasis', in A.T.J. Kaethler and S. Mitralexis (eds), *Between Being and Time. From Ontology to Eschatology* (Lanham, 2019), 23-36.

follow the *telos*, precisely because the latter is recognised in its Trinitarian dimension (4).

Trinitarian reflection has driven Gregory to a dynamic conception of the immanence which is reflected in the understanding of the *telos* of history, conceived, in its turn, dynamically. Access to it takes place through freedom in union with history and the Body of the Lord. Automatism of intellectual knowledge is replaced by the necessity of the intervention of the will.

Thus, the imitation (*mimêsis*) of Christ is presented as the other face of apophatism with an authentic dimension that is simultaneously ontological and historical: 'this imitation implies not only having the same feelings as Christ but also participating in the very mysteries of his life'.[40]

3.2. *Apophatism*

The radical nature of Gregory's position is clearly shown by a passage of the *Cant* where he comments on the encounter of the bride with the friends of the bridegroom, here interpreted as symbols of the angelic hosts. The question she addresses to them about the Bridegroom is interpreted in an apophatic key:

Thus the soul went through the entire angelic order and since she did not see that which she sought among the goods that she found, she thought to herself: 'Perhaps for them the one whom I love is comprehensible?' and says to them: 'Have you seen him whom my heart loves?' (*Song* 3:3). However, because they were silent before the question and with their silence they demonstrated that even for them that which she seeks is incomprehensible, as soon as she had gone in mental pursuit throughout the entire spiritual city and did not get to know what she was looking for even among intelligible and incorporeal beings, then renouncing everything she had found, she knew whom she sought, whose existence is known only in the impossibility of comprehending that which He is. In fact, every element that makes it known is an obstacle for those who seek Him to come to find Him.[41]

The angels themselves, then, cannot know God except in submission before His incomprehensibility. The question is, in fact, ontological insofar as it is the consequence of the clear separation between the unique divine nature, infinite

----

[40] L.F. Mateo-Seco, 'Imitación y seguimiento de Cristo en Gregorio de Nisa', *Scripta Theologica* 33 (2001), 601-22, 618.

[41] ἡ μὲν οὖν περιήει διερευνωμένη πᾶσαν ἀγγελικὴν διακόσμησιν καὶ ὡς οὐκ εἶδεν ἐν τοῖς εὑρεθεῖσιν ἀγαθοῖς τὸ ζητούμενον τοῦτο καθ᾽ ἑαυτὴν ἐλογίσατο· ἆρα κἂν ἐκείνοις ληπτόν ἐστι τὸ παρ᾽ ἐμοῦ ἀγαπώμενον; καί φησι πρὸς αὐτούς· μὴ κἂν ὑμεῖς ὃν ἠγάπησεν ἡ ψυχή μου εἴδετε; σιωπησάντων δὲ πρὸς τὴν τοιαύτην ἐρώτησιν καὶ διὰ τῆς σιωπῆς ἐνδειξαμένων τὸ κἀκείνοις ἄληπτον εἶναι τὸ παρ᾽ αὐτῆς ζητούμενον, ὡς διεξῆλθε τῇ πολυπραγμοσύνῃ τῆς διανοίας πᾶσαν ἐκείνην τὴν ὑπερκόσμιον πόλιν καὶ οὐδὲ ἐν τοῖς νοητοῖς τε καὶ ἀσωμάτοις εἶδεν οἷον ἐπόθησεν, τότε καταλιποῦσα πᾶν τὸ εὑρισκόμενον οὕτως ἐγνώρισε τὸ ζητούμενον, τὸ ἐν μόνῳ τῷ μὴ καταλαμβάνεσθαι τί ἐστιν ὅτι ἔστι γινωσκόμενον, οὗ πᾶν γνώρισμα καταληπτικὸν ἐμπόδιον τοῖς ἀναζητοῦσι πρὸς τὴν εὕρεσιν γίνεται (Gregory of Nyssa, *In Canticum canticorum*, GNO VI, 182,10-183,5).

and eternal, which is the Trinity, and finite creatures. Here, however, with great daring, Gregory introduces a surprising element which marks still more powerfully the difference from Origen's conception. In fact, despite their spiritual perfection, even the angels cannot attain knowledge of the divine Bridegroom except through the economy, that is, the history of salvation which unfolds between the *archê* and the *telos*.[42] Rather, in a still more radical way, Gregory claims that the only path on which to come close to the triune God passes through the very Body of Christ which is the Church, and this is true even for the angelic creatures:

And if it is not too bold to say, perhaps [the angelic powers] have marvelled seeing the beauty of the Bridegroom in the Bride, invisible and incomprehensible to all. In fact, He who 'no one has ever seen' (*Jn* 1:18), as John says , and who 'no human being has seen or can see' (*1Tim* 6:16), as Paul testifies, made the Church His Body and built in love through the addition of the saved, 'until we all attain [...] mature manhood, to the extent of the full stature of Christ' (*Eph* 4:13). Therefore, if the Church is the Body of Christ and the Head of the Body is Christ, Who forms the face of the Church with His own image, perhaps the friends of the Bridegroom are heartened watching her because in her they see the invisible more distinctly. Like those who do not manage to see the disk of the sun see it in splendour reflected in the water, so also [the angelic powers] in the pure mirror that is the Church contemplate the Sun of Justice known through that which appears.[43]

The image is extremely powerful because she who searches for the Bridegroom without finding Him discovers that she already has Him in herself, and actually that she herself is the way of access to God even for the angels. The value of the space between *archê* and *telos* cannot be affirmed more powerfully just like the irreducibility of the latter to the former.

Thus, if the *archê* of the life of Christ can be properly considered only if we start at the *telos*, the same has to be said for human life which is saved by being inserted into this movement through grace, and that has an essential sacramental dimension so much so that Gregory conceives Christian initiation as a path which leads gradually to mysticism, passing from baptism through confirmation to be completed in the Eucharist, in parallel with the degrees of spiritual growth. The final stage no longer corresponds to light, as in Origen, but to

---

[42] *Cf. ibid.*, 254,13-20.

[43] εἰ δὲ μὴ τολμηρόν ἐστιν εἰπεῖν, τάχα κἀκεῖνοι διὰ τῆς νύμφης τὸ τοῦ νυμφίου κάλλος ἰδόντες ἐθαύμασαν τὸ πᾶσι τοῖς οὖσιν ἀόρατόν τε καὶ ἀκατάληπτον· ὃν γὰρ Οὐδεὶς ἑώρακε πώποτε, καθώς φησιν Ἰωάννης, Οὐδὲ ἰδεῖν τις δύναται, καθὼς ὁ Παῦλος μαρτύρεται, οὗτος σῶμα ἑαυτοῦ τὴν ἐκκλησίαν ἐποίησε καὶ διὰ τῆς προσθήκης τῶν σωζομένων οἰκοδομεῖ ἑαυτὸν ἐν ἀγάπῃ, Μέχρις ἂν καταντήσωμεν οἱ πάντες εἰς ἄνδρα τέλειον, εἰς μέτρον ἡλικίας τοῦ πληρώματος τοῦ Χριστοῦ. εἰ οὖν σῶμα τοῦ Χριστοῦ ἡ ἐκκλησία, κεφαλὴ δὲ τοῦ σώματος ὁ Χριστὸς τῷ ἰδίῳ χαρακτῆρι μορφῶν τῆς ἐκκλησίας τὸ πρόσωπον, τάχα διὰ τοῦτο πρὸς ταύτην βλέποντες οἱ φίλοι τοῦ νυμφίου ἐκαρδιώθησαν, ὅτι τρανότερον ἐν αὐτῇ τὸν ἀόρατον βλέπουσιν· καθάπερ οἱ αὐτὸν τοῦ ἡλίου τὸν κύκλον ἰδεῖν ἀδυνατοῦντες, διὰ δὲ τῆς τοῦ ὕδατος αὐγῆς εἰς αὐτὸν ὁρῶντες, οὕτω κἀκεῖνοι ὡς ἐν κατόπτρῳ καθαρῷ τῇ ἐκκλησίᾳ τὸν τῆς δικαιοσύνης ἥλιον βλέπουσι τὸν διὰ τοῦ φαινομένου κατανοούμενον (*ibid.*, 256,9-257,5).

Moses' entrance into the darkness of the union with God,[44] where it is necessary to overcome every human conception in infinite union with Him.[45]

Gregory, therefore, recognises the properly Trinitarian dimension of the *telos*, which still coincides with the *archê*, but which is now characterised by an absolute freedom and dynamism. This implies that everything which is included between the two extremes, as the work of the Creator, is characterised once again by freedom and dynamism, understood here in a participatory sense. It can be read as a unity – *oikonomia* – endowed with its own sense thanks to the relationship with the Trinitarian *archê* and *telos*.

Thus, the need for starting with the *telos* to understand the *archê* is not dictated solely by gnoseological reasons but by ontology itself. This passage confers the highest value on history and the body, understood, finally, in a sense that is properly theological and not philosophical thanks to the light issuing from the Trinitarian *telos*.

3.3. *Dynamics*

Thus, the space between the *archê* and the *telos* is no longer characterised by necessity and a function that is merely symbolic but is a source of authentic change. The dynamics become positive to the extent that precisely the capacity for change which characterises human nature gives it the possibility of progressing infinitely towards the better, namely, towards God:

Therefore the reasoning shows that that which seems to be feared – I mean to say that our nature is mutable – is instead a wing for the flight towards the greatest things, since it would be a punishment for us to not be able to undertake a change for that which is better. Therefore let not he who sees in his nature the disposition to change become afflicted, but moving in every thing towards that which is better and transforming himself *from glory to glory*,[46] let him change thus, becoming every day constantly better, in daily growth, and perfecting himself always more, without ever being able to reach the limit of perfection. For in this consists true perfection: never to stop growing towards the best and to place no limits on perfection.[47]

---

[44] *Cf.* G. Maspero, 'Contemplazione ed Eucaristia nelle Omelie sul Cantico dei Cantici di Gregorio di Nissa', in L. Touze (ed.), *La contemplazione cristiana: esperienza e dottrina* (Roma, 2006), 301-18.

[45] Here we note especially the difference to Origen for whom the Eucharist, with its corporal dimension, was for simple people whereas the truly spiritual man had no need of it. On the symbolic value of the Eucharist in Origen, see J. Daniélou, *Origène* (1948), 74-9. Bear in mind that, for Origen, the terms *angel* and *man* indicate substantially the same reality, *cf.* Origen, *Commentarii in evangelium Joannis* II, 23, 144, 6-7 and 146, 6-7; SC 120, 302 and 304.

[46] *2Cor* 3:18. Cfr J. Daniélou and H. Musurillo, *From Glory to Glory* (New York, 1979), 69.

[47] οὐκοῦν τὸ φοβερὸν εἶναι δοκοῦν (λέγω δὲ τὸ τρεπτὴν ἡμῶν εἶναι τὴν φύσιν) οἷόν τι πτερὸν πρὸς τὴν ἐπὶ τὰ μείζω πτῆσιν ὁ λόγος ὑπέδειξεν, ὡς ζημίαν εἶναι ἡμῖν τὸ μὴ δύνασθαι τὴν πρὸς τὸ κρεῖττον ἀλλοίωσιν δέξασθαι. μὴ τοίνυν λυπείσθω ὁ βλέπων ἐν τῇ φύσει τὸ πρὸς τὴν μεταβολὴν ἐπιτήδειον, ἀλλὰ πρὸς τὸ κρεῖττον διὰ παντὸς ἀλλοιούμενος καὶ ἀπὸ δόξης εἰς δόξαν μεταμορφούμενος οὕτω τρεπέσθω, διὰ τῆς καθ᾽ ἡμέραν αὐξήσεως πάντοτε κρείττων γινόμενος καὶ ἀεὶ τελειούμενος καὶ μηδέποτε πρὸς τὸ πέρας φθάνων τῆς τελειότητος. αὕτη

As Spira has rightly emphasised,[48] Gregory's conception of virtue represents a real paradigm shift. Despite the Platonic terminology, it is an infinite movement towards the infinite which demolishes the very foundation of Aristotelian logic. The Greek world identified perfection with the finite as infinitude itself was linked to indetermination.[49] With Revelation, on the other hand, time and history rise to the highest dignity because, in Christ, they have become the way to God; and this has extremely practical consequences such as the consideration, surprising for the period, that the embryo possesses already human rights from the moment of its conception[50] or the clear condemnation of slavery.[51]

All that is possible because the Trinitarian *telos* is made present as eschatological anticipation in Christ, the incarnate Son. Everything passes from and by Him. Daniélou expresses it beautifully when he writes that there is no Christian *eschaton* but an *eschatos*;[52] the *telos* is Christ himself.

The elect will be *images of the Image*,[53] and so each of them will be *alter Christus, ipse Christus*. Thus, commenting on the fact that, on the third day of the creation in *Gen* 1:11-2, the fruit precedes the seed, Gregory claims that this signifies that the resurrection will be nothing else than the return to the original state,[54] explaining that:

Adam, the first man, was in fact the first ear of grain. But after humanity was fragmented into a multitude by the insurgence of malice, as the fruit develops at the interior of the ear, so we single men, stripped of that form of the ear and mixed with the earth, are born anew in the resurrection according to the original beauty, having become, instead of that original ear, infinite myriads of harvests.[55]

γάρ ἐστιν ἡ ὡς ἀληθῶς τελειότης τὸ μηδέποτε στῆναι πρὸς τὸ κρεῖττον αὐξανόμενον μηδέ τινι πέρατι περιορίσαι τὴν τελειότητα (*Perf*, GNO VIII/1, 213,20-214,6).

[48] *Cf.* A. Spira, 'Le temps d'un homme selon Aristote et Grégoire de Nyssa', in J.-M. Leroux (ed.), *Le Temps chrétien de la fin de l'Antiquité au Moyen Âge* (Paris, 1984), 289-90.

[49] *Cf.* E. Muehlenberg, *Die Unendlichkeit Gottes bei Gregor von Nyssa. Gregors Kritik am Gottesbegriff der klassischen Metaphysik* (Göttingen, 1966), 29-58.

[50] *Cf. An et res*, PG 46, 125C-128A; *Mort*, GNO IX, 51,5-52,1. In this, Gregory distances himself from the opinion of Origen and Methodius: I. Ramelli, 'Embrione', in GND, 238-9.

[51] Gregory is the first to formulate this principle explicitly and precisely starting from the infinite value of human freedom as an image of the divine: *cf.* P. Garnsey, *Ideas of Slavery from Aristotle to Augustine* (Cambridge, 1996), 243. On the Trinitarian foundation of the affirmation, see G. Maspero, 'La dimensione trinitaria della dignità dell'uomo. L'Ad Ablabium e l'analogia sociale di Gregorio di Nissa', in A. Rodríguez Luño and E. Colom (eds), *Teologia ed Etica Politica* (Roma, 2005), 149-70. For a more complete study of the question of slavery, see I.L.E. Ramelli, *Social Justice and the Legitimacy of Slavery* (2016).

[52] *Cf.* J. Daniélou, 'Christologie et eschatologie', in A. Grillmeier and H. Bacht (eds), *Das Konzil von Chalkedon* III (Würzburg, 1954), 269-86. For a similar approach to Gregory's theology, see A. Ojell, 'El «telos» escatológico de la vida cristiana. La vida en Cristo según San Gregorio de Nisa', in C. Izquierdo *et al.* (eds), *Escatología y vida cristiana* (Pamplona, 2002), 353-73.

[53] *Perf*, GNO VIII/1, 196,12.

[54] *Cf. An et res*, PG 46, 156D.

[55] Ὁ γὰρ πρῶτος στάχυς ὁ πρῶτος ἄνθρωπος ἦν Ἀδάμ. Ἀλλ᾽ ἐπειδὴ τῇ τῆς κακίας εἰσόδῳ εἰς πλῆθος ἡ φύσις κατεμερίσθη, καθὼς γίνεται ὁ καρπὸς ἐν τῷ στάχυϊ· οὕτως οἱ καθ᾽ ἕκαστον

Sin introduces multiplicity, and multiplicity becomes a positive principle. Jean Daniélou summarises Gregory's novelty thus: 'In Gregory, the idea of change is perfectly positive and represents a valuable contribution to theology. For Plato, every change is a defect, and, if the intelligible world is superior to the sensible world, it is precisely insofar as it is immutable. Origen does not escape this difficulty: for him, change is nothing other than a degeneration from a state of initial perfection. However, with Gregory, the equation good = immutability, evil = change is inverted'.[56] The same conclusion is reached by other authors such as Brooks Otis[57] and, above all, the already-cited Andreas Spira, whose beautiful and learned analysis of how the time of a man of the Greek period was conceived by Gregory highlights the central role and the radical novelty constituted by Nyssa's concept of history – understood as personal life – in the development of thought.[58]

Auguste Luneau, who has studied Gregory's thought from the perspective of the doctrine of the ages of the world also points out the eschatological and ontological connection with Irenaeus, presenting Gregory's theology as the final synthesis of Greek thought in this area. In connection with the relationship between Gregory and Irenaeus, he writes: 'Both believe in human progress without end and give the same reason for it. However, what the Bishop of Lyons simply affirmed, Gregory developed, giving greater space to explanations. Above all, living in the period of Trinitarian disputes, Gregory discovered in the Trinity a new and supreme reason for human 'infinity'. Since, as Revelation has taught, the God-Being is simultaneously the God-Love. Consequently, the insatiable human desire, transformed into the tension of love by the grace of the Word, becomes the best image of the divine life, of that 'super-movement' in the bosom of the Trinitarian life.'[59]

Jean Daniélou saw precisely in Irenaeus the first outlines of an authentic theology of history.[60] Gregory's attention to the temporal development and the historical conception of human nature represents, again according to Daniélou, an Asiatic tradition precisely together with Irenaeus.[61] That can also be seen in the comparison with Origen: the latter, in fact, follows the *archê – telos* scheme,

---

γυμνωθέντες τοῦ κατὰ τὸν στάχυν ἐκεῖνον εἴδους, καὶ τῇ γῇ καταμιχθέντες, πάλιν ἐν τῇ ἀναστάσει κατὰ τὸ ἀρχέγονον κάλλος ἀναφυόμεθα, ἀντὶ ἑνὸς τοῦ πρώτου στάχυος ἀνάπειροι μυριάδες τῶν ληΐων γενόμενοι (*ibid.*, 157B).

[56] J. Daniélou, in the introduction to M. Canévet, *La colombe et la ténèbre: textes extraits des «Homélies sur le Cantique des Cantiques» de Grégoire de Nysse* (Paris, 1967), 13-4.

[57] *Cf.* B. Otis, 'Gregory of Nyssa and the Cappadocian Conception of Time', *SP* 14 (1976), 327-57.

[58] *Cf.* A. Spira, 'Le temps d'un homme selon Aristote et Grégoire de Nysse' (1984), 283-94.

[59] A. Luneau, *L'histoire du salut chez les Pères de l'Église. La doctrine des âges du monde* (Paris, 1964), 180.

[60] J. Daniélou, 'Saint Irénée et les origines de la théologie de l'histoire', *RSR* 34 (1947), 227-31.

[61] *Cf. id.*, *L'Être et le Temps chez Grégoire de Nysse* (1970), vii.

but the body is excluded from this movement. Precisely the reinclusion of bodiliness in the dynamic of the *exitus* and the *reditus* was to be the specific work of Gregory, founded on the perfection of the Trinitarian formula.

4. *Apokatastasis* and *epektasis*

4.1. *Angels*

This means that the identification of eschatology with the perpetual movement of the *epektasis* can be considered as the distinctive mark of Gregory's approach to the relation between *archê* and *telos*. From this perspective, the study of the perfection of angels expressed through the category of impassibility can help us to reread the *apokatastasis* in such a way as to highlight the differences with respect to Origen.

The latter had to contrast two opposite tendencies simultaneously: (a) the gnostic gradual conception of ontology, which made any real progress impossible on account of its static understanding of differences; (b) the Plotinian mystic dissolution in the One, which denied difference itself. Along these lines, he stressed the dynamic possibility of progress that can elevate the human being to the level of angelic creatures.[62] So the perfect man becomes similar to the angels (*isanghelos*)[63] as they are the necessary path to divinisation.[64] This seems to be exactly specular compared with Gregory's presentation of the meeting between the bride and the angels in *Cant*, quoted in section 3.2, where even the pure spiritual creatures need to go through the body of Christ to know the triune God. In this case the difference of natures is clearly affirmed.

By contrast, Origen's theology seems to be dependent on the thought of Philo, who identified human beings and angels as mere names of souls:

In favour of the thesis one can further add the fact that the names assigned to the superior powers are not names of living natures, but of orders, where this or that rational nature is assigned by God. In fact, *throne, principality, dominion,* and *power* are not a living species, but names of the reality into which those that are denominated have so been classified. Their subject is none other than a *man* and to the subject is added as accident being *throne* or *dominion* or *principality* or *power*.[65]

---

[62] Cf. Origen, *De principiis*, I 8, 1, 15 and 23, ed. Samuel Fernández (Madrid, 2015), 306.

[63] Cf. id., *Contra Celsum*, IV 29, 16-18, SC 136, 252 and *De principiis*, IV 4, 2, ed. S. Fernández (Madrid, 2015), 934.

[64] Cf. id., *Contra Celsum*, VIII 29, 21-28, SC 150, 252.

[65] Καὶ ἔτι μᾶλλον παραμυθήσεται, ὅτι ἐπὶ τῶν κρειττόνων δυνάμεων τὰ ὀνόματα οὐχὶ φύσεων ζῴων ἐστὶν ὀνόματα ἀλλὰ τάξεων, ὧν ἤδε τις καὶ ἤδε λογικὴ φύσις τέτευχεν ἀπὸ θεοῦ. Θρόνος γὰρ οὐκ εἶδος ζῴου οὐδὲ ἀρχὴ οὐδὲ κυριότης οὐδὲ ἐξουσία, ἀλλὰ ὀνόματα πραγμάτων, ἐφ᾽ ὧν ἐτάχθησαν οἱ οὕτως προσαγορευόμενοι, ὧν τὸ ὑποκείμενον οὐκ ἄλλο τί ἐστιν ἢ ἄνθρωπος, καὶ τῷ ὑποκειμένῳ συμβέβηκε τὸ θρόνῳ εἶναι ἢ κυριότητι ἢ ἀρχῇ ἢ ἐξουσίᾳ (id., *Commentarii in evangelium Joannis*, II 23, 146, 1-9, SC 120, 304).

In Origen's reading, Scripture itself would not know the difference between angels and human beings, so that the Saviour can become man for men and angel for angels.[66]

From the dogmatic perspective, the point is that Origen lacks a terminological and ontological instrument to express the difference of nature between angels and human beings.[67] He has recourse to pure spirituality as the very distinctive characteristic of the divine nature with respect to creatures. This means that even angels have a thin but corporeal body whereas only the Father, the Son and the Holy Spirit are purely incorporeal. This implies that the material dimension has to decrease along with the ascent to perfection.[68] Human perfection consists in being transfigured so to have bodies similar to the angelic ones which are eternal and resplendent.[69] In fact, the tendency toward evil is attributed to the body that in itself is dead and joined to the soul only by accident.[70]

It should be noted that this point is closely related to the negative role of movement, so that the ontological equation behind Origen's thought is still good = immutability:

It was necessary that the intelligible nature makes use of bodies, because, by the very fact of being created it is subject to mutation and change. In fact, a reality that was not but came to be, for this same reason it is said to be of a mutable nature and therefore has virtue or vice not substantially but as an accident.[71]

Perfection is thus understood as the return to a static and original condition of pure intelligibility.[72] For human beings, this can be defined as *isanghelia*. In turn, this is defined as an adoring disposition (*diathesis*) that consists in being always turned toward the Father.[73]

Gregory's approach is similar, but the ontological framework is quite different, yielding a real novelty in the final picture. *Isanghelia* is still a defining

---

[66] Cf. *ibid.*, II 23, 144, SC 120, 302 and I, 31, 217, SC 120, 166.
[67] Cf. Cécile Blanc, in SC 120 (Paris, 1966), 30 and Peter Nemeshegyi, *La Paternité de Dieu chez Origène* (Paris, 1960), 81.
[68] Cf. Origen, *Homeliae in Exodum*, VI 5, 21-25, SC 321, 184.
[69] Cf. *id.*, *Commentarium in evangelium Matthaei*, 17, 30, 48-59, ed. Erich Klostermann, GCS 40, 671.
[70] Cf. *id.*, *De principiis*, III 4, 1, ed. S. Fernández (Madrid, 2015), 722. On the role of the body in Origen's theology, see Mark J. Edwards, 'Origen No Gnostic; or On The Corporality of Man', *JThS* 43 (1992), 23-37.
[71] *Ut quoniam necesse erat uti corporibus intellectualem naturam, quae et commutabilis et convertibilis depraehenditur ea ipsa conditione, qua facta est (quod enim non fuit et esse coepit, ex hoc ipso naturae mutabilis designatur et ideo nec substantialem habet vel virtutem vel malitiam, sed accidentem)* (Origen, *De principiis*, IV 4, 8: 360,10, ed. S. Fernández [Madrid, 2015], 956-8).
[72] Cf. *ibid.*, II 8, 3, ed. S. Fernández (Madrid, 2015), 462.
[73] Cf. *id.*, *Commentarii in evangelium Joannis*, XIII 16, 99, 1-9, SC 222, 82 and *Selecta in Psalmos*, PG 12, 1281B.

characteristic of eschatological perfection and a binding moral indication for human life.[74] Moreover, *apokatastasis* does coincide with the achievement of the angelic condition:

If, therefore, the life of those who are returned (ἀποκαθισταμένων) to the primitive state is similar to that of the angels (πρὸς τὴν τῶν ἀγγέλων οἰκείως ἔχει), it is clear that the life preceding the fall was in a certain way angelic; for this reason, even the return of our life to the ancient state makes us like the angels (τοῖς ἀγγέλοις ὡμοίωται).[75]

Telos and *archê* seem to overlap perfectly with *isanghelia* even more intensely than in Origen because Gregory does not distinguish image and likeness in *Gen* 1:26-7, as Origen does.[76] Beyond any diachronic argument, it seems that the hermeneutic tension is even stronger.

However, the confrontation with Apollinaris introduces an element fundamental in grasping the full meaning of Gregory's position. In this context, he had to contest his rival's reading of 1*Thess* 2:7 in a divisive sense where spirit, body and soul were considered as separate elements, division that was applied even to Christ. The Cappadocian's response is based on 1*Cor* 3:1 and 15:44, according to a unitary reading of the carnal man, the spiritual man and the animal (or natural) man as a single human being in which freedom assigns the prominence to the carnal, spiritual or material element.[77] This means that perfection does not require the overcoming of the historical and corporeal dimensions, but can be achieved even through material activities when they are accomplished with one's gaze turned towards God.[78] In this way, salvation is extended to all of the human being and certainly also to the body.[79] The latter is no more *per se* negative; *isanghelia* is identified with liberation from corporeal constraints (*sômatikoi desmoi*) and bad passions, not from matter as such.[80]

4.2. *Impassibility*

This shows that Gregory's and Origen's eschatologies are very close, but at the same time they differ substantially. The reason seems to depend on the ontological framework. The description of Macrina's death in *Macr* confirms both the role of *isanghelia* and the identification between perfection and a

---

[74] *Cf.* Gregory of Nyssa, *De virginitate*, 14.4.13-20, GNO VIII/1, 8-15.

[75] Εἰ τοίνυν ἡ τῶν ἀποκαθισταμένων ζωὴ πρὸς τὴν τῶν ἀγγέλων οἰκείως ἔχει, δηλονότι ὁ πρὸ τῆς παραβάσεως βίος ἀγγελικός τις ἦν· διὸ καὶ ἡ πρὸς τὸ ἀρχαῖον τῆς ζωῆς ἡμῶν ἐπάνοδος τοῖς ἀγγέλοις ὡμοίωται (*id.*, *De opificio hominis*, PG 44, 188D).

[76] *Cf.* Origen, *De principiis*, III 6, 1: ed. S. Fernández (Madrid, 2015), 764-8.

[77] *Cf.* Gregory of Nyssa, *Antirrheticus adversus Apollinarium*, GNO III/1, 208,28-210,6.

[78] *Cf. ibid.*, 210,23-4.

[79] *Cf. ibid.*, 211,14-5.

[80] *Cf. ibid.*, 212,4-10 and *Vita sanctae Macrinae* 11,33-45, GNO VIII/1, 382,19-383,5.

disposition toward God as common elements between the two authors, but at the same time the text highlights the anthropological and ontological novelty:

And it seemed to me that she [Macrina] no longer behaved like human beings, but as if an angel had providentially taken on a human form, an angel who did not have any relationship and affinity with life in the flesh and whose thought in no way was unlikely to remain in impassibility (ἐν ἀπαθείᾳ), insofar as the flesh does not pull it down toward the passions that characterise it. Thus, it seems to me that she showed to everyone that divine and pure love for the invisible Bridegroom, whom she harboured hidden in the depths of her soul, and that she made known to all the disposition (διάθεσιν) that she carried in her heart to cast herself towards the One she desired (ποθούμενον) in order to be with Him free from the constraints of the body as soon as possible. In fact, her haste (δρόμος) was indeed directed as at a lover (ἐραστήν), without any other pleasures of life being able to divert her gaze.[81]

Here perfection is described as impassibility and freedom from fleshly constraints, that is, the eschatological condition shared by the angels. The literary form is extraordinary at both the poetic and the theological level as the purity of Macrina is expressed with recourse to erotic language. Through passionate words, Gregory says that his sister was free from passions. This has an ontological reason: her perfection is identified with a disposition (*diathesis*), as already in Origen, but this is now understood in dynamic terms. Perfection is, then, a passion, that is, a tendency towards the real and eternal Lover. This is the 'impassible passion' (*apathes to pathos*)[82] which is the core of *epektasis*.[83]

---

[81] οὐκέτι μοι ἐδόκει τῶν ἀνθρωπίνων εἶναι, ἀλλ᾿ οἷον ἀγγέλου τινὸς οἰκονομικῶς ἀνθρωπίνην ὑπελθόντος μορφήν, ᾧ μηδεμιᾶς οὔσης πρὸς τὸν ἐν σαρκὶ βίον συγγενείας ἢ οἰκειώσεως οὐδὲν ἀπεικὸς ἐν ἀπαθείᾳ τὴν διάνοιαν μένειν, μὴ καθελκούσης τῆς σαρκὸς πρὸς τὰ ἴδια πάθη. διὰ τοῦτό μοι ἐδόκει τὸν θεῖον ἐκεῖνον καὶ καθαρὸν ἔρωτα τοῦ ἀοράτου νυμφίου, ὃν ἐγκεκρυμμένον εἶχεν ἐν τοῖς τῆς ψυχῆς ἀπορρήτοις τρεφόμενον, ἔκδηλον ποιεῖν τότε τοῖς παροῦσι καὶ δημοσιεύειν τὴν ἐν καρδίᾳ διάθεσιν τῷ ἐπείγεσθαι πρὸς τὸν ποθούμενον, ὡς ἂν διὰ τάχους σὺν αὐτῷ γένοιτο τῶν δεσμῶν ἐκλυθεῖσα τοῦ σώματος. τῷ ὄντι γὰρ ὡς πρὸς ἐραστὴν ὁ δρόμος ἐγίνετο, οὐδενὸς ἄλλου τῶν κατὰ τὸν βίον ἡδέων πρὸς ἑαυτὸ τὸν ὀφθαλμὸν ἐπιστρέφοντος (*id.*, *Vita sanctae Macrinae* 22, 26-39, GNO VIII/1, 396,1-14).

[82] Cf. *id.*, *In Canticum canticorum*, GNO VI, 23,10. On this topic, see Jean Daniélou, *Platonisme et théologie mystique. Doctrine spirituelle de saint Grégoire de Nysse* (Paris, 1944), 92-103 and 201-7.

[83] On this fundamental topic of Gregory's thought, see Theodorus Alexopoulos, 'Das unendliche Sichausstrecken (Epektasis) zum Guten bei Gregor von Nyssa und Plotin. Eine vergleichende Untersuchung', *ZAC* 10 (2007), 302-12; Paul M. Blowers, 'Maximus the Confessor, Gregory of Nyssa, and the concept of "perpetual progress"', *VigChr* 46 (1992), 151-71; J. Daniélou, *Platonisme et théologie mystique* (Paris, 1953), 291-307; Everett Ferguson, 'Progress in perfection: Gregory of Nyssa's Vita Moysis', *SP* 14 (1976), 307-14; Marguerite Harl, 'Recherches sur l'origénisme d'Origène: la satiété (κόρος) de la contemplation comme motif de la chute des âmes', *SP* 8 (1966), 373-405; Ronald E. Heine, *Perfection in the Virtuous Life. A Study in the Relationship between Edification and Polemical Theology in Gregory of Nyssa's De vita Moysis* (Cambridge MA, 1975); Lucas F. Mateo-Seco, '¿Progreso o inmutabilidad en la visión beatífica?

For the discussion of Gregory's eschatology, it is fundamental to stress how he identifies his sister with an angel, not at the level of nature, because her *physis* is different, but at that of the relation with respect to God. Like the angels, she is definitely turned towards the Bridegroom.

This eschatological end suggests the importance of impassibility for the question at hand as it is presented by Gregory in his *Commentary on the Song of the Songs*. These homilies were preached in Lent, probably between 391 and 394, as a preparation for Easter. The resurrection of the body is consequently the main focus:

Indeed, the person who before such words, whose immediate meaning speaks of carnal pleasures, does not slip into impure thoughts, but by these words is conducted as by hand to the philosophy of the divine realities, that is, to pure thoughts, shows himself to be no longer human and no longer to have a nature composed together of flesh and blood, but shows himself to have that life of the saints that we hope to receive in the resurrection, in that such a person has become like the angels on account of impassibility (ἰσάγγελος διὰ τῆς ἀπαθείας). In fact, after the resurrection, the body, becoming changed in its elements to enter into incorruptibility, is united (συμπλέκεται) to the soul of the man while the passions that now plague us through the flesh will not rise along with those bodies, but our life will receive as a gift a condition (κατάστασις) of peace.[84]

Again, as in *Macr*, impassibility and *isanghelia* are pulled together. In a similar way, freedom from the constraints of passions is expressed with erotic language, as the verb *sumpleketai* points to the act of spousal union. This means that the resurrected body will be passionless so as to be in a peaceful condition (*katastasis*). But such a condition will be deeply dynamic:

In fact, since it was announced that the life after the resurrection will be similar (ὅμοιον) to the condition (καταστάσει) of the angels – and the One who announces it does not lie –, it would be proper that even life in the world would be a preparation for the life we hope for after it, in such a way that those who live in the flesh and in the field of the world do not lead a life according to the flesh nor configure themselves to this world, but practice, in anticipation, the life they long for during their life in this world. Thus the bride inspires in the souls of those who follow her a confirmation, by means

Apuntes de la historia de la Teología', *Scripta Theologica* 29 (1997), 13-39; Ovidiu Sferlea, 'On the Interpretation of the Theory of Perpetual Progress (epektasis). Taking into Account the Testimony of Eastern Monastic Tradition', *RHE* 109 (2014), 564-87; A. Spira, 'Le temps d'un homme selon Aristote et Grégoire de Nyssa' (1984), 283-94.

[84] ἀληθῶς γὰρ ὁ διὰ τῶν τοιούτων ῥημάτων, ὧν ἡ πρόχειρος ἔμφασις τὰς σαρκώδεις ἡδυπαθείας ἐνδείκνυται, μὴ κατολισθαίνων εἰς τὴν ῥυπῶσαν διάνοιαν ἀλλὰ πρὸς τὴν τῶν θείων φιλοσοφίαν, ἐπὶ τὰς καθαρὰς ἐννοίας διὰ τῶν ῥημάτων τούτων χειραγωγούμενος δείκνυσι τὸ μηκέτι ἄνθρωπος εἶναι μηδὲ σαρκὶ καὶ αἵματι συμμεμιγμένην τὴν φύσιν ἔχειν, ἀλλὰ τὴν ἐλπιζομένην ἐν τῇ ἀναστάσει τῶν ἁγίων ζωὴν ἐπιδείκνυται ἰσάγγελος διὰ τῆς ἀπαθείας γενόμενος. ὡς γὰρ μετὰ τὴν ἀνάστασιν τὸ μὲν σῶμα μεταστοιχειωθὲν πρὸς τὸ ἄφθαρτον τῇ ψυχῇ τοῦ ἀνθρώπου συμπλέκεται, τὰ δὲ νῦν διὰ σαρκὸς ἡμῖν ἐνοχλοῦντα πάθη τοῖς σώμασιν ἐκείνοις οὐ συνανίσταται ἀλλά τις εἰρηνικὴ κατάστασις τὴν ζωὴν ἡμῶν διαδέξεται (Gregory of Nyssa, *In Canticum canticorum*, GNO VI, ed. Hermann Langerbeck [Leiden, 1986], 29,20-30,12).

of a vow, that their life in this field will be directed at contemplating the Powers, imitating the angelic purity through impassibility (ἀπαθείας). In fact, just as love (ἀγάπης) becomes more and more kindled, that is, is lifted up and, with addition, grows always toward the better, it is said that the good will of God is carried out in heaven as in earth because the impassibility of the angels is realised in us as well.[85]

So impassibility is the most dynamic condition ever since it coincides with *epektasis*. This is achieved, not without one's body, but within it, as an unerring movement towards the Trinity, shared by angels and human beings. In Gregory's understanding, perfection is a condition, a *diathesis* or *katastasis*, that consists in a definitive tendency, which is both dynamical and static, as the perfected person cannot be diverted any more from God. Thus, movement becomes, absolutely positive, as the example of the soul-bride shows:

Rendered more divine and transformed by the beautiful change into a higher glory with respect to the glory she had, in such a way as to inspire awe in the choir of angels surrounding the Bridegroom who together address to her the astonished greeting 'You have ravished my heart, our sister and bride' (*Song* 4:9). In fact, having obtained impassibility, this very condition of impassibility, which shines both in her and in the angels, introduces her into kinship and fraternity with the incorporeal beings.[86]

Epektasis is this condition of progress from glory to glory, something that is an eternal and beautiful change as the increasing participation of the finite creature in God's infinity. Gregory's ontology does not negate classical metaphysics because he does not say that any movement is good, erasing the difference between substantial and accidental dimensions. However, he works with a different ontological background since the Trinity and the world are separated in an absolute way by an infinite gap so that the only infinite and eternal nature is the divine one.

---

[85] *Ibid*. 134,9-135,6: ἐπειδὴ γὰρ τὸν μετὰ τὴν ἀνάστασιν βίον ὅμοιον ἐπήγγελται τῇ ἀγγελικῇ καταστάσει [τῶν ἀνθρώπων] γενήσεσθαι (ἀψευδὴς δὲ ὁ ἐπαγγειλάμενος), ἀκόλουθον ἂν εἴη καὶ τὴν ἐν τῷ κόσμῳ ζωὴν πρὸς τὴν ἐλπιζομένην μετὰ ταῦτα παρασκευάζεσθαι, ὥστε ἐν σαρκὶ ζῶντας καὶ ἐν τῷ ἀγρῷ τοῦ κόσμου διάγοντας μὴ κατὰ σάρκα ζῆν μηδὲ συσχηματίζεσθαι τῷ κόσμῳ τούτῳ, ἀλλὰ προμελετᾶν τὸν ἐλπιζόμενον βίον διὰ τῆς ἐν τῷ κόσμῳ ζωῆς. διὰ τοῦτο τὴν διὰ τοῦ ὅρκου βεβαίωσιν ἐμποιεῖται ταῖς ψυχαῖς τῶν μαθητευομένων ἡ νύμφη, ὥστε τὴν ζωὴν αὐτῶν τὴν ἐν τῷ ἀγρῷ τούτῳ κατορθουμένην πρὸς τὰς δυνάμεις βλέπειν, μιμουμένην διὰ τῆς ἀπαθείας τὴν ἀγγελικὴν καθαρότητα· οὕτω γὰρ ἐγειρομένης τῆς ἀγάπης καὶ ἐξεγειρομένης (ὅπερ ἐστὶν ὑψουμένης τε καὶ ἀεὶ διὰ προσθήκης πρὸς τὸ μεῖζον ἐπαυξομένης) τὸ ἀγαθὸν εἶπε θέλημα τοῦ θεοῦ τελειοῦσθαι ὡς ἐν οὐρανῷ καὶ ἐπὶ γῆς τῆς ἀγγελικῆς καὶ ἐν ἡμῖν ἀπαθείας κατορθουμένης.

[86] Gregory of Nyssa, *In Canticum canticorum*, GNO VI, ed. Hermann Langerbeck (Leiden, 1986), 253,15-254,4: μεταποιηθεῖσα πρὸς τὸ θειότερον καὶ ἀπὸ τῆς δόξης ἐν ᾗ ἦν πρὸς τὴν ἀνωτέραν δόξαν μεταμορφωθεῖσα διὰ τῆς ἀγαθῆς ἀλλοιώσεως, ὡς θαῦμα γενέσθαι τῷ περὶ τὸν νυμφίον τῶν ἀγγέλων χορῷ καὶ πάντας εὐφήμως πρὸς αὐτὴν τὴν θαυμαστικὴν ταύτην προέσθαι φωνὴν ὅτι Ἐκαρδίωσας ἡμᾶς, ἀδελφὴ ἡμῶν νύμφη· ὁ γὰρ τῆς ἀπαθείας χαρακτὴρ ὁμοίως ἐπιλάμπων αὐτῇ τε καὶ τοῖς ἀγγέλοις εἰς τὴν τῶν ἀσωμάτων αὐτὴν ἄγει συγγένειάν τε καὶ ἀδελφότητα τὴν ἐν σαρκὶ τὸ ἀπαθὲς κατορθώσασαν.

5. Conclusion: an eschatological ontology

The sequence of steps proposed in the present exploration of Gregory's eschatology brings us to the conclusion that the return to the *archê* is real, but at the same time the *telos* does not simply coincide with it as a mere repetition that overcomes the historical and corporeal dimensions. The final status will be dynamic and not static, corresponding to God's will from the beginning. This means that the inversion between *archê* and *telos* is structural because only in the definitive eschatological movement will the beginning be revealed. This is not a matter of knowledge alone, but also of ontology. Man was created for the infinite progress of the eternal and ever-growing union with the triune God, so that eschatological perfection is not a mere return to a condition, but, more deeply, a definitive relation that makes possible a constantly increasing participation in the life of the Trinity.

This can be restated by saying that Gregory's ontology is an eschatological one because it cannot be grasped by analysing the cosmos and the human being at a fixed moment of time, as a still image, that reveals the metaphysical constants of reality. This level of inquiry is valid, but, to catch the deeper content of the world, one should look at relations. *Epektasis* is, in fact, the true being of the human person: it is constituted by the relation with God and can be perfect only through and in that relation.

This picture of Gregory's eschatology implies that the ontological dimension is essential to understanding his differences compared with Origen: the inversion between *archê* and *telos* depends, in fact, on a different metaphysics in which the triune God and creation are distinguished in an absolute way by an infinite gap. For this reason, there is no way of climbing the ontological ladder, as in Aristotle, getting to know the essence of God though intellect alone. On the contrary, apophatism obliges us to take into account history, the body and personal relations. The dimension between *archê* and *telos* is not overcome, but is perfected in the dynamic progress of participation in the life of the Trinity.

If this is so, Gregory's eschatology cannot be understood only from the perspective of Origen's: the ontological categories oblige us also to take into account Irenaeus' and Athanasius' contributions since the Trinitarian rereading of the *exitus* and the *reditus* was made possible by the introduction of the absolute gap between the divine nature and creation. In this way the hermeneutic tension seems to be solved by the identification of *epektasis*, *apokatastasis* and eschatology which appear simply as different faces of the one reality. This is the dynamic union with God where progress is not caused by imperfection but, on the contrary, is the effect of the reality of the relation between the finite human being and the infinity of the Trinity.

CHAPTER 2

Christological Eschatology

Miguel BRUGAROLAS

1. Introduction[1]

From the perspective of the theology of history, the main idea in the New Testament is that the coming of Christ brings with it the fullness of time. The incarnation of the Son of God happens when 'the fullness of time' arrives (*Gal* 4:4), in these 'last days' (*cf. Heb* 1:2; 1*Pet* 1:20), 'at the end of the age' (*cf. Heb* 9:26). However, this fullness of time is not understood as something extraneous to the incarnation: it is God himself who takes history to its plenitude by sending his Son to implement the plan of salvation. 'For he has made known to us, in all wisdom and insight, the mystery of his will, according to his purpose which he set forth in Christ as a plan for the fullness of time, to unite all things in him, things in heaven and things on earth' (*Eph* 1:9-10).

Indeed, this 'fullness of time' would make no sense if it were understood merely as a temporal concept, as the mere chronological ending (πέρας) of a series of events. On the one hand, history has not come to an end, and the end of time has not arrived. On the other, if we were to understand time as a mere chronological succession of events, it would amount to no more than the passing of time. Following this, if the end took place, it would be an ending devoid of any meaning.

The idea of fullness or consummation implies the existence of an expectation, of a hope, which implies that there is something more than a simple conclusion: there is an end (τέλος) that must be achieved, a goal to attain, which gives meaning to everything. The end gives time consistency, it transforms it into history and its consummation does not only consist in its ending, but in its perfection. This is a theological perspective that places time in relation to God as its origin and end. For Gregory of Nyssa, 'the one who had power both to lay down his life of his own accord and to take it up again had power when he wished as creator of the temporal orders not to be bound by time for his actions, but to

---

[1] This article was prepared as part of the research project under M.J. Soto-Bruna's direction: 'Unity and Plurality of the Logos in the World: *Explicatio* and *Ratio Naturae* (4th-14th Centuries): Medieval Hermeneutics' (ref.: FFI2015-63947/PIUNA 2015-24).

create time to fit his actions'.[2] The main point about time is not the mere succession of events, but divine action, that is, the history of salvation that God, through
the Logos,[3] puts into place in the economy of time. Divine action encompasses
everything, so there is no past or future in God's power.[4] In this sense, nothing
separates the beginning and the end.[5] So, because of this, the fullness of time can
only be understood in the light of the beginning, in the light of the divine will,
and as a call to its fulfilment, to perfection: it consists in the consummation of
the meaning of history as a history of salvation. Consummation takes place
because the divine plan of salvation is revealed and definitively realized.

However, since the life of man is completely embedded in time, between what
was and what will be, 'the fullness of time' as a consummation of history is made
intelligible to our eyes precisely because this plenitude is realized through the
real and historical fulfilment of a promise: the promise and hope of salvation that
imbues the Old Testament. Thanks to the fact that Christ has declared Himself
as He who fulfils the Old Covenant we can understand the 'end of the age',
which is made present in Him (*cf. Heb* 1:2; 9:26), as the start of a *new* time.[6]

In effect, properly speaking the *evangelium* consists not in the announcement
of the future realities of salvation that are yet to come, but in the affirmation
that in Christ, salvation has been made definitively present. That is why there
is a stress on the *hodie*, the *ecce*. The messianic expectations of the Old Testament are not promises of the past or realities entrusted to the future: they have
been made present in Christ himself, who is the fulfilment and plenitude of the
divine plan of salvation. The resurrection of Christ plays a central role here.[7]
Human beings can understand their life as a *historia* and a journey returning to
the Good precisely because in the resurrection of Christ they understand that
their own destiny is not an endpoint in time, but a plenitude of life (ζωή) which
consummates their own temporal existence (βίος). For Gregory, the Incarnate
Logos transforms all of human life (ζωή) by the assumption of a perfect human
existence (βίος), that is the entirety of human life and history.[8]

[2] Gregory of Nyssa, *Trid spat* (GNO IX, 279; tr. Hall 40-1).

[3] The whole creative work of God, the Creator's *fiat*, is brought to its conclusion in the incarnation, since the same *Logos* of creation has been made flesh in historical form. In his historical form
He Himself leads creation to its appointed goal. *Cf.* J. Daniélou, *The Lord of History: Reflections
on the Inner Meaning of History* (original title in French: *Essai sur le Mystère de l'Histoire*) (London, 1958), 191.

[4] *Cf.* Gregory of Nyssa, *Op hom* (PG 44, 185CD).

[5] *Cf.* M. Alexandre, 'Protologie et eschatologie chez Grégoire de Nysse', in U. Bianchi (ed.)
*Arché e Telos. L'antropologia di Origene e di Gregorio di Nissa. Analisi storico-religiosa. Atti del
Colloquio, Milano, 17-19 Maggio 1979* (Milano, 1981), 122-59, 136.

[6] *Cf.* J. Daniélou, 'Christologie et eschatologie', in A. Grillmeier and H. Bacht (eds), *Das
Konzil von Chalkedon: Geschichte und Gegenwart, III: Chalkedon heute* (Würzburg, 1954), 270-7;
id., *The Lord of History* (1958), 183-202.

[7] *Cf.* R. Winling, *La Résurrection et l'Exaltation du Christ* (Paris, 2000), 372.

[8] *Cf.* T. Špidlík, 'L'eternità e il tempo, la *zoé* e il *bíos*, problema dei Padri Cappadoci', *Augustinianum* 16 (1976), 107-16.

To clarify this issue we turn to a fragment of *Homily XI* from *In Canticum canticorum* in which, starting from the text *Cant* 5:4 ('My brotherkin extended his hand from the opening, and my abdomen was stirred for him'), Gregory proceeds to make a short Christological *excursus*. The hand of the Bridegroom that touches the door of the Bride's house is an image of the descent of the Word to the life of men:

I think – writes Gregory – that the bride's house represents the whole of human life (ζωή), and thus the hand that creates all beings, has contracted itself to reside in our small, worthless human existence (βίος), by participating in our human nature *in everything like us except sin* (*Heb* 4:15).[9]

The distinct way in which Gregory refers to the life of the human being (the house of the Bride is the image of the human ζωή, and the Word descends to his/her βίος) stresses that the Incarnation not only implies the assumption of a perfect humanity, but also means taking on the life and the history of humankind.[10]

Starting from the framework we have just outlined I will now show some aspects of the relationship between Christ and the final consummation of history according to Gregory of Nyssa. The background used as reference is the profound theology of time and history that Gregory developed and which has been the subject of many studies.[11] However, rather than discussing this, we will focus on some of the issues which highlight the eminently Christological character of Gregory of Nyssa's eschatology. We will first examine the medicinal character of the incarnation of the Word. Through this we can adequately perceive the salvific perspective within which Gregory's teachings are placed, and where the *dynamic* dimension of his Christology takes on great importance. We will then cover two essential aspects of Gregory's Christology: an understanding of Christ as the firstborn of the new humanity, and the centrality of

[9] Gregory of Nyssa, *Cant* XI (GNO VI 338, 2ff.).

[10] This has important consequences for the spiritual life of the Christian, which consists in imitating (μίμησις) the life of Christ. *Cf.* L.F. Mateo-Seco, 'Imitación y seguimiento de Cristo en Gregorio de Nisa', *Scripta Theologica* 33 (2001), 601-21.

[11] Amongst other publications: *cf.* J. Daniélou, *Platonisme et théologie mystique: Doctrine spirituelle de Saint Grégoire de Nysse* (Paris, 1944), 291-307; *id.*, *L'être et le temps chez Grégoire de Nysse* (Leiden, 1970); P. Zemp, *Die Grundlagen heilsgeschichtlichen Denkens bei Gregor von Nyssa* (München, 1970); D.L. Balás, 'Eternity and Time in Gregory of Nyssa's *Contra Eunomium*', in H. Dörrie, M. Altenburger and U. Schramm (eds), *Gregor von Nyssa und die Philosophie: Zweites Internationales Kolloquium über Gregor von Nyssa* (Leiden, 1976), 128-55; B. Otis, 'Gregory of Nyssa and the Cappadocian Conception of Time', *SP* 14 (1976), 327-57; M. Mees, 'Mensch und Geschichte bei Gregor von Nyssa', *Augustinianum* 16 (1976), 317-35; A.A. Mosshammer, 'Historical Time and the Apokatastasis according to Gregory of Nyssa', *SP* 27 (1993), 70-93; P. Plass, 'Trascendent Time and Eternity in Gregory of Nyssa', *Vigiliae Christianae* 34 (1980), 180-92; G. Maspero, Θεολογια, οικονομια e ιστορια: *La teología della storia di Gregorio di Nissa*, Diss. Universidad de Navarra (Pamplona, 2003); I. Ramelli, 'Αἰώνιος and Αἰών in Origen and in Gregory of Nyssa', *SP* 47 (2010), 57-62; H. Boersma, 'Overcoming Time and Space: Gregory of Nyssa's Anagogical Theology', *JECS* 20 (2012), 575-612.

resurrection. Both issues, as well has having an undoubtable Christological interest, are very important for Gregory's understanding of anthropology and eschatology. Finally, we will analyse how Gregory comprehends the end of time from the point of view of the Son's 'submission' to the Father. This 'submission' of the Son to the Father has been described by Gregory in regard of the return to unity, a unity which is consummated in the filial surrender of the Son to the Father.

2. The medicinal aspect of the Incarnation

The reason for the Incarnation of the Word is, according to Gregory, mainly a soteriological one. That is, it finds its origin in the divine *economy* of love for humankind and its purpose is medicinal. Divine *philanthropy* is the principle that informs Christology to the point that Christ Himself receives this name: 'your name has become love for humankind'.[12] The descent of the Word is a descent of love, an authentic divine 'condescension'. Indeed, the Incarnation – as Daniélou has emphasised – is the union of the Word not merely with human nature as such, but with fallen nature, the *sarx*, which is characterised by death.[13] The Word, by the Incarnation, has assumed humanity unto its ultimate consequences. *Philanthropy* is not only the reason for the Incarnation but the reason for the death and resurrection. Gregory expresses this idea in a multitude of ways throughout his writings. The best known ones in this sense are his readings on the meaning behind the parables of the Good Samaritan[14] and the Good Shepherd,[15] or statements such as the following, which we find in *Oratio catechetica magna*:

Christ did not suffer death because he had been born; rather, it was because of death that he chose to be born. Eternal Life had no need of life, but he entered our bodily existence in order to restore us from death to life [...] Indeed he came so close to death as to touch mortality itself, that he might make of our own nature, in his body, a principle of resurrection.[16]

---

[12] Gregory of Nyssa, *Cant* IV (GNO VI 107,4-5).

[13] J. Daniélou, *From Glory to Glory. Texts from Gregory of Nyssa's Mystical Writings* (London, 1962), 16-7.

[14] *Cf.* Gregory of Nyssa, *Cant* XV (GNO VI, 436,2-16).

[15] *Cf.* Gregory of Nyssa, *Cant* II (GNO VI, 61,1-62,13). Gregory's exegesis on the parable of the lost sheep is also eloquent: the Word descends by means of the Incarnation in search of the lost sheep, and takes all of human nature on His shoulders, restoring the hundred sheep to the joy of the choir of angels. *Cf.* Gregory of Nyssa, *Eccl* II (GNO V, 304-5); *Cant* II (GNO VI, 61); *Antirrh* (GNO III/1, 151-2); L.F. Mateo-Seco, 'Eschatology', in L.F. Mateo-Seco and G. Maspero (eds), *The Brill Dictionary of Gregory of Nyssa* (Leiden, 2010), 284; R. Hübner, *Die Einheit des Leibes Christi bei Gregor von Nyssa. Untersuchungen zum Ursprung der 'physischen' Erlösungslehre* (Leiden, 1974), 125-9.

[16] Gregory of Nyssa, *Or cat* XXXII (GNO III/4, 84).

Christ's act of 'touching mortality' to make His body the 'principle of resurrection' for us shows the salvific objective of the Incarnation. Gregory stresses this point in the short treatise *Ad Theophilum adversus Apollinaristas*, in which he refers to Christ as the true Physician who healed the sickness of fallen human nature.[17] The context of the treatise is anti-Apollinarist, but it is mainly a defence of those who (like Gregory) are falsely accused of stating the existence of two subjects – two sons – in Christ. This requires on the one hand, a clear description of the Incarnation as a true and inseparable union (ἕνωσις)[18] of the divine and human in Christ, the exact unity of the flesh and the Divinity that assumed it;[19] and, on the other hand, showing the salvific and divinizing meaning of this union. Indeed, when the Word assumes humanity he 'touches' it and transforms it from corruptible to incorruptible. This dynamism of divine transformation requires that the humanity Christ assumed is complete and that from this union the result is not two sons but the divinisation of the human being. Christ, Gregory states, 'healed the sick as the disease demanded, cared for the weak by becoming weak in a sense with the weakness of our nature, and became flesh'.[20] This means that taking on human nature corresponds to divinisation. The key to understand the union of human and divine in Christ is therefore profoundly dynamic; the Word, when incarnated, makes humanity his own, and, when making it his own, he makes it divine.[21] Drecoll has summarized Gregory's teaching on this point:[22] the assumption of what is human, which is by nature weak, mortal and corruptible, signified its transformation through immorality, strength, and incorruptibility. Christ's divine nature remains always identical in the incarnate – 'The Word', says Gregory, 'both before assuming the flesh and after His corporeal dispensation, both was and is the Word. And God, both before assuming the form of a slave and afterward, is God. And the true Light, both before He shone upon the dark and afterward, is the true Light'[23]– and redeems the human nature assumed by transforming it. Thus, one cannot speak of a duality of sons, because the divine nature remains immutable, while the properties of human nature are transformed.

Gregory became familiar with Apollinarism during his visit to Jerusalem. On his return he wrote *Letter* 3, which also deals with Christological issues.[24]

---

[17] Gregory of Nyssa, *Theoph* (GNO III/1, 124,14-5); *Eun* III 4,30 (GNO II, 145).

[18] *Cf.* Gregory of Nyssa, *Theoph* (GNO III/1, 128,3-4).

[19] *Cf.* Gregory of Nyssa, *Theoph* (GNO III/1, 127,15-6).

[20] *Cf.* Gregory of Nyssa, *Theoph* (GNO III/1, 124,15-8).

[21] *Cf.* Gregory of Nyssa, *Antirrh* (GNO III/1, 169-71).

[22] *Cf.* V.H. Drecoll, 'Ad Theophilum', in L.F. Mateo-Seco and G. Maspero (eds), *The Brill Dictionary of Gregory of Nyssa* (2010), 734-5.

[23] Gregory of Nyssa, *Theoph* (GNO III/1, 125,11-5).

[24] *Cf.* P. Maraval, 'La lettre 3 de Grégoire de Nysse dans le débat Christologique', *RSR* 61 (1987), 74-89.

In this text we see him following the path of that long Christological-medical tradition, so close to Origen's heart,[25] and depicting the economy of salvation in terms of a therapeutic economy for the healing of human sin. He writes:

And inasmuch as the deity is incorruptible, though it had come to be in a corruptible body, so it was not altered by any change even as it healed what was changeable in our soul, just as in the art of medicine, he who is treating bodily ills, in touching the patient, does not himself become infected, but thoroughly heals that which is diseased.[26]

Gregory explains in this letter that healing – the transformation or divinisation – of the humanity of Christ does not only affect the body, but also the soul: 'He who shone in our darkened nature dispersed the ray of His divinity through our whole compound, through soul I say and body too, and so accommodated our entire humanity to his own light'.[27] In the anti-Apollinarist context this is particularly appropriate: in Christ the Word does not take on the role of the higher human soul as Apollinaris defended, but rather he assumes an integral humanity. 'The Lord', says Gregory, 'truly came to be in our composition'.[28]

We can also find the medical metaphor in the same sense in *Antirrheticus adversus Apolinarium*, alongside the theme of light and darkness. The One who is immaterial, formless and incorporeal in substance, in a kind of philanthropic economy towards the end of the world, combined himself with human nature to purify it of sin, like a sun that comes to dwell in a gloomy cave and annihilates the darkness through the presence of its light.[29] Gregory goes on: '"The light", John says, "shone in the darkness, but the darkness did not overcome it" (*John* 1:5). It is also like a medical treatment: when the remedy is applied to the disease, the illness passes into oblivion; it isn't transferred into the medical art'.[30]

This medical character is also essential, as many scholars have pointed out,[31] in order to understand a well-known image that Gregory uses to describe the relationship between the divine and the human in Christ: the *drop of vinegar mingled with the ocean*.[32] In the Hippocratic medical tradition, with which

[25] *Cf.* S. Fernández, *Cristo médico según Orígenes. La actividad médica como metáfora de la acción divina*, Studia Ephemeridis Augustinianum 64 (Roma, 1999).

[26] Gregory of Nyssa, *Epistula* 3,15 (GNO VIII/1, 23-4; tr. A. Silvas, 128).

[27] Gregory of Nyssa, *Epistula* 3,15 (GNO VIII/1, 23-4; tr. A. Silvas, 128).

[28] Gregory of Nyssa, *Epistula* 3,16 (GNO VIII/1, 23-4; tr. A. Silvas, 128).

[29] *Cf.* Gregory of Nyssa, *Antirrh* (GNO III/1, 171,9ff.).

[30] Gregory of Nyssa, *Antirrh* (GNO III/1, 171,20ff.).

[31] *Cf.* J.-R. Bouchet, 'À propos d'une image christologique de Grégoire de Nysse', *RThom* 67 (1967), 586-8; M. Ludlow, *Gregory of Nyssa, Ancient and (Post)modern* (Oxford, 2007), 99; A. Radde-Gallwitz, 'Contra Eunomium III 3', in J. Leemans and M. Cassin (eds), *Gregory of Nyssa: Contra Eunomium III. An English Translation with Commentary and Supporting Studies* (Leiden, 2014), 308. On the use of this image in relation to the christological language of Gregory of Nyssa see M. Brugarolas, 'Theological Remarks on Gregory of Nyssa's Christological Language of "Mixture"', *SP* 84 (2017), 39-58.

[32] *Cf.* Gregory of Nyssa, *Eun III* 3,68 (GNO II, 133), *Antirrh* (GNO III/1, 201,10-17), and *Theoph* (GNO III/1, 126,17-21).

Gregory was familiar,[33] vinegar blended with seawater was considered to be a therapeutic remedy.[34] In using this metaphor Gregory is modifying an existing image of mixture among different philosophical theories (a drop of wine dissolved into a vast mass of water) and is changing its meaning for theological reasons. He is not just describing the relation between the two elements (the human and the divine nature of Christ), but pointing out the healing effect of the Incarnation. That is, he takes this example of a physical union of elements in order to explain the profound salvific – medicinal – sense which the Word's assumption of humanity contains. Thus, the drop of vinegar blended with the boundless sea is not only an image of the relation between the human and the divine in Christ, but an explanation of the therapeutic character of the Incarnation for our human nature.

Along with the medical-soteriological significance of this metaphor, another aspect that is also very much in line with Gregory's thought appears: the dynamic transformation of human nature into the divine, or better, the divinisation of human nature through its assumption by the Logos and its final perfection accomplished in the Resurrection. With the Resurrection, the mortal nature of Christ was transformed into the divine inasmuch as it is no longer mortal or perishable, but immortal and glorious. What matters here is that this Christological dynamic is essentially soteriological. That is, the sense of this transformation is not the absorption of humanity into divinity and the mix of natures in a Monophysite sense, but rather the divinization of the humanity of Christ and, in Christ, of the whole of humanity. This divinization is an authentic transformation of humanity, but it is not a dissolution. Divine and human are not confused.

This means that Gregory's Christology cannot be explained separately from its soteriological meaning. When Gregory speaks about the divine and the human in Christ, he is always alluding to divine nature, which is immutable, perfect, full of love, and human nature, which is sinful, weak, separated from life. In Gregory, one cannot separate Incarnation and divinisation, just as one cannot understand the 'first fruits' apart from the 'whole dough',[35] nor the 'Good Shepherd' without the 'whole sheep' that are restored upon his shoulders.[36] But

[33] On the medical knowledge of Gregory of Nyssa see M. E. Keenan, 'Saint Gregory of Nyssa and the Medical Profession', *Bulletin of the History of Medicine* 15 (1944), 150-61; J. Janini Cuesta, *La antropología y la medicina pastoral de san Gregorio de Nisa* (Madrid, 1946); M. Dörnemann, *Krankheit und Heilung in der Theologie der frühen Kirchenväter* (Tübingen, 2003), 247-73; A. Lallemand, 'Références médicales et exégèse spirituelle chez Grégoire de Nysse', in V. Boudon-Millot and B. Pouderon (eds), *Les Pères de l'Église face à la science médicale de leur temps* (Paris, 2005), 401-26.

[34] *Cf.* J.-R. Bouchet, 'À propos d'une image christologique de Grégoire de Nysse' (1967), 587.

[35] *Cf.* J. Zachhuber, 'Phyrama', in L.F. Mateo-Seco and G. Maspero (eds), *The Brill Dictionary of Gregory of Nyssa* (2010), 612-4.

[36] Daniélou, commenting on these images, states as follows: 'Some scholars have wrongly thought that Gregory is here teaching that the Word has hypostatically united with all humanity; but it is clear from a good number of texts that he is merely emphasizing, in a very real sense,

this leads us to the next step. How can those who are saved participate in the divine transformation realized in Christ's humanity, or, in other words, how can the Incarnate Logos 'heal' all those who share the same human ancestry and nature?

3. Christ's Resurrection: the first fruit of divinized humanity

In Gregory, the salvific dimension of Christology and its dynamic character lead towards eschatology. Gregory's eschatology is completely based on the resurrection of Christ, because it relates not only to Jesus' personal destiny, but to the destiny of humanity as a whole. The resurrection of Jesus is the anticipation of the eschatological end, because the resurrection of the dead will occur in the image of the resurrected and glorified Christ.[37] This means that the person of Christ is indissolubly linked to the salvation of humanity, and that therefore, as we said at the beginning, the 'last times' have begun in Christ.

Some of Gregory's best known texts on the resurrection are those found in *Oratio catechetica*,[38] both in chapter XVI on the resurrection of Christ, and in XXXII, on the role of the death and resurrection of Christ in the salvation of human beings. Gregory states that, through Christ's Resurrection, God reunited the separated elements by His divine power. Body and soul, which were separated at death, are fitted together into a union which cannot be broken. The resurrection is then the return to oneness of body and soul, which are knitted together in an indissoluble union. Gregory states that the resurrection is the restoration of human nature to its original grace.[39] In fact, Christ's resurrection from the dead 'becomes to this race of mortals the beginning of the return to the immortal life'.[40] And this is so because, according to Gregory:

Just as the principle of death, becoming operative in the case of one man, passed therewith throughout the whole of human nature, in like manner the principle of resurrection extends through one to all humanity (*cf. Rm* 5:15; 1*Cor* 15:21).[41]

The implicit parallel between Adam and Christ in this text leads Gregory to highlight the fact that the resurrection of Christ is the source of the resurrection of humanity.[42] Christ took the soul he had assumed and joined it to his own

the solidarity of all mankind' (J. Daniélou, *From Glory to Glory* [1962], 17-8). *Cf.* L.F. Mateo-Seco, *Estudios sobre la Cristología de Gregorio de Nisa* (1978), 53.

[37] *Cf.* R. Winling, *La Résurrection et l'Exaltation du Christ* (2000), 143.

[38] *Cf.* R. Winling, 'La résurrection comme principe explicatif et comme élément structurant dans le *Discours catéchetique* de Grégoire de Nysse', *SP* 22 (1989), 74-80.

[39] *Cf. e.g.* Gregory of Nyssa, *Or cat* XVI (GNO III/4, 48-9); *Eccl* 1 (GNO V, 296).

[40] Gregory of Nyssa, *Or cat* XXV (GNO III/4, 64 ; tr. J. H. Srawley, 80).

[41] Gregory of Nyssa, *Or cat* XVI (GNO III/4, 48-9; tr. J. H. Srawley, 63-4).

[42] Christ is the new Adam, and Gregory of Nyssa understands this with all its theological and eschatological consequences (*cf.* Gregory of Nyssa, *Or cat* XVI [GNO III/4, 45-9]; *Antirrh* [GNO

body by means of his own power, constituting in this way the principle of resurrection that extends to all of human nature: the re-junction of the separated elements is extended from the individual case of Christ to the whole of humanity.[43] Gregory insists on the solidarity of all humankind in such a way that the Logos could not be united with a specific human nature without having an effect upon the whole of humanity.[44] This solidarity of humanity in the resurrection corresponds with the unity of the human nature created by God in his image.[45] Gregory refers to the humanity created 'in the image of God' as 'a unique body', the *pleroma* of humanity, which carries within itself the divine image and which will be born as a new humanity in the consummation.[46]

The text does not, however, emphasize humanity's participation in the resurrection of Christ as a necessary process, or one regulated by the physical principle of the solidarity of universal human nature,[47] but rather stresses that Christ is the author of the resurrection – He resurrects through his own power (τῇ δυνάμει) – and the cause, beginning (ἀρχή) and hope of all resurrection: the resurrection of Christ reveals that death, caused by sin, falls within the divine providence of God for the salvation of humankind:

And this is the mystery of God's economy with regard to death and the resurrection from the dead; that while God has not prevented the soul from being separated from the body by death in the inevitable course of nature, yet he has brought them together again by the resurrection, in order that he himself might become the meeting-point of both, that is of death and life, in his own person arresting the process of dissolution effected in our nature by death, and himself becoming a principle of reunion for the separated elements.[48]

Indeed, if when talking about creation Gregory uses the distinction between the first creation – that of the *pleroma* of humanity – and the second creation, to distinguish the creation *in principio*, which refers to the eternal and indivisible moment wherein God embraces the whole universe in its totality, and the creation in *six days*, which is the ordered development of God's plan in time;[49]

III/1, 160-1]; *Tunc et ipse* [GNO III/2, 16-8]); his resurrection is the starting point and cause of the resurrection of man. *Cf.* R. Winling, *La Résurrection et l'Exaltation du Christ* (2000), 372.

[43] *Cf.* J. H. Srawley, 64.

[44] *Cf.* J. Daniélou, *From Glory to Glory* (1962), 18.

[45] *Cf.* R.M. Hübner, *Die Einheit des Leibes Christi bei Gregor von Nyssa* (1974), 107-11; J. Zachhuber, *Human Nature in Gregory of Nyssa: Philosophical Background and Theological Significance* (Leiden, 2000), 231.

[46] *Cf.* Gregory of Nyssa, *Op hom* XVI (PG 44, 185).

[47] For a commentary on this text and the notion of universal nature in dialogue with stoicism and neo-Platonism see: J. Zachhuber, *Human Nature in Gregory of Nyssa* (2000), 228-37.

[48] Gregory of Nyssa, *Or cat* XVI (GNO III/4, 48-9; tr. J. H. Srawley, 64).

[49] *Cf.* M. Brugarolas, 'Divine Simplicity and Creation of Man: Gregory of Nyssa on the Distinction between the Uncreated and the Created', *American Catholic Philosophical Quarterly* 91 (2017), 29-51, especially 44-5; M. Alexandre, 'L'Exégèse de *Gen.* 1-1,2ª dans l'*In Hexaemeron* de Grégoire de Nysse', in H. Dörrie, M. Altenburger and U. Schramm (eds), *Gregor von Nyssa und*

then when speaking of resurrection – which is the new creation of humanity –
the resurrection of Christ has an effect on the *pleroma* of humanity analogous
to that of the act of creation in the image of God. In a similar way to God's
creative act, viewed from the perspective of God's *theologia*, it is global and
simultaneous, but creation from within itself (that is, from the perspective of
God's *oikonomia*) will not be complete without its temporal development.
The resurrection of humankind has its unique *theological* principle in Christ's
resurrection that embraces the whole human nature,[50] but it will not reach the
final consummation without the *economy* of the Church, that is, without the
mystical growing of the entire body of Christ, the restored humankind.

Gregory states that Christ himself came into contact with mortality, 'raising
up along with Him the whole man'.[51] This 'whole man' refers to the participation of humanity as a whole in the resurrection of Christ. For Gregory, the
whole of humanity has an organic unity analogous to that of the human body
in relation to the resurrection of Christ.[52] In the case of the human body the
action of one of the organs of sense communicates a common sensation to
the whole organism. Analogously, the whole of our human nature is like a
single living being, so the resurrection of the part extends to the whole,
and in virtue of the unity of nature communicates itself from the part to the
whole.[53]

This organic unity of human nature that Gregory uses to express the solidarity of the resurrected Christ with all humanity can be better understood if
we consider a soteriological image that Gregory appreciates greatly: the first
fruits and the whole lump of nature in *Rom* 11:16. We can see below an example taken from the relevant Christological *excursus* that Gregory develops in
Homily XIII of *In Canticum*.

What I am chiefly referring to here is the great mystery of piety, by which God was
revealed to us in the flesh (*cf. 1Tim* 3:16), he who was 'in the form of God' (*Phil* 2:6)
lived with men through the flesh in 'the form of a slave'. And since he, once for all, by
the sacrifice of first fruits, had reunited to himself the mortal substance of the flesh (τὴν
ἐπίκηρον τῆς σαρκὸς φύσιν) – which he had received from an immaculate Virgin –, he
continually sanctifies the whole lump of nature together with the first fruits, nourishing

---

die Philosophie: Zweites Internationales Kolloquium über Gregor von Nyssa (Leiden, 1976), 159-
86; D.L. Balás, 'Eternity and Time', in L.F. Mateo-Seco and G. Maspero (eds), *The Brill Dictionary of Gregory of Nyssa* (2010), 289; M. Canévet, *Grégoire de Nysse et l'Herméneutique
Biblique: Étude des Rapports entre le Langage et la Connaissance de Dieu* (Paris, 1983), 90.

[50] The word *theological* is employed here to be consistent with the analogy of God's creative
act. It designates the *Logos*' act of returning to unity in Christ's human body and soul, restoring
in Him the whole of human nature. In this sense, Christ's resurrection, being the core of the
economy of salvation, could be considered also from the standpoint of God's *theology*.

[51] Gregory of Nyssa, *Or cat* XXXII (GNO III/4, 78).

[52] L.F. Mateo-Seco, 'Resurrection', in L.F. Mateo-Seco and G. Maspero (eds), *The Brill Dictionary of Gregory of Nyssa* (2010), 668.

[53] *Cf.* Gregory of Nyssa, *Or cat* XXXII (GNO III/4, 78).

his body, the church, through those who are united to him by communion in the mystery (διὰ τῶν ἑνουμένων αὐτῷ κατὰ τὴν κοινωνίαν τοῦ μυστηρίου).[54]

In this text, one can notice the complexity of Gregory of Nyssa's soteriology. The realism with which he describes the Incarnation, far from generating an unconditioned conception of salvation – be it of a spiritualistic or physical nature – shows that God has effectuated salvation while adapting his action to the being of man in his totality, in his corporality and freedom. Thanks to the communion and kinship (κοινωνία, συγγενεία) of natures between Christ and human beings, salvation is a ἀναγέννησις by means of which man's life is incorporated into that of Christ through μίμησις and sacramental life.[55]

Those who unite themselves with Christ through the communion in his mystery are grafted into him by faith and are integrated as members into the common body. The first fruits are for Gregory the divinized humanity of Christ. Through it, God sanctifies all humanity ('the whole lump of nature'). The action is divine, but takes place in and through the humanity of Christ.[56] And this is truly important. Because the sanctification of humanity is for Gregory precisely this: that the divine is made present in the human: the authentic interiority of the divine in the human happens in Christ. From this we can understand that salvation, which consists in the incorporation of human beings in the mystery of Christ, will not take place because of a mere ethical decision to follow Christ, because the divinisation would then just be the mere effect of virtue. Nor will it happen for the simple reason that we possess the same nature as Christ.[57] If this were so, salvation would be reduced to the physical relationship of solidarity between the human nature of Christ and of the rest of humanity. Being incorporated into Christ is a complex reality in which both the action of God and human freedom play a part, and which follows the Christological dynamic of 'assumption' and 'communication': when God makes Christ's humanity His, He communicates with the human being; and the human being, when joining Christ, is assumed by God in his filiation, which in turn is communicated to the soul, making it participate in the gifts of his paternity. We can

---

[54] Gregory of Nyssa, *Cant* XIII (GNO VI, 381,16-382,2).

[55] *Cf.* Gregory of Nyssa, *Or cat* XXXV (GNO III/4, 91). Salvation's ontological reality corresponds to the Incarnation's ontological reality: in the same way that the Incarnation is not an extrinsic or Docetic reality, salvation cannot be Docetically or extrinsically conceived. About soteriology in Gregory of Nyssa, see L.F. Mateo-Seco, *Estudios sobre la Cristología de Gregorio de Nisa* (1978), 229-60.

[56] *Cf.* L.F. Mateo-Seco, 'Notas sobre el lenguaje cristológico de Gregorio de Nisa', *Scripta Theologica* 35 (2003), 89-112, 101.

[57] On the disjunction of understanding salvation in an ethical or physical sense see J. Zachhuber, 'From First Fruits to the Whole Lump: the Redemption of Human Nature in Gregory's *Commentary on the Song of Songs*', in G. Maspero, M. Brugarolas and I. Vigorelli (eds), *Gregory of Nyssa: In Canticum Canticorum. Analytical and Supporting Studies. Proceedings of the 13th International Colloquium on Gregory of Nyssa* (Leiden, 2018), 234-55.

say that salvation is not a mere physical relationship – at the level of our nature, because of solidarity –, nor is it merely ethical; but rather it is mystical, that is, personal. It is a union with God so strong that the divine gift dilates nature, and the virtue reaches a level at which it transcends its own possibilities: the union that makes man son of God.[58] Christ, writes Gregory in *De perfectione*,

assuming the first fruit of our common nature, made it holy through His soul and body, unmixed and unreceptive of all evil, preserving it in Himself. He did this in order that, having taken it up to the Father of incorruptibility through His own incorruptibility, the entire group might be drawn along with it because of its related nature, and in order that the Father might admit the disinherited to 'adoption' as sons (*Eph* 1:5), and the enemies of God to a share in His own Godhead.[59]

The movement of God towards the creature and the creature towards the creator is crucial in the work of sanctification of the first fruits and the whole lump. God unites with humanity and transforms it when attracting it towards Him, and by divinizing it He returns to it divine filiation. That is why we can say that the union that occurs in Christ of the divine and human constitutes the τέλος of humanity, in terms of τελείωσις, that is, in terms of constituting its perfection and not only its end. In Christ, the end towards which human nature has been directed since creation is perfectly realized.[60] Indeed, in the last times, Christ, because of love of humanity, took into Himself all our nature so that through His union with the divine our nature would be sanctified with Him; all of the mass ('lump') is thus sanctified by the 'first fruits'.[61]

Gregory sees in the resurrection of Christ not only the possibility of the resurrection, but also the source of the resurrection of the body and the manner in which it will occur.[62] He conceives eschatology as an eternal Easter, in which

---

[58] The incorporation of human beings into Christ requires freedom and is achieved through faith, virtue and the sacraments, *cf.* E. Ferguson, 'The Doctrine of Baptism in Gregory of Nyssa's Oratio catechetica', in S.E. Porter and A.R. Cross (eds), *Dimensions of Baptism: Biblical and Theological Studies* (London, 2002), 224-34. A beautiful passage in *De perfectione* refers to this through the Lord's crown of thorns: men whom sin had transformed into thorns are, through the passion of Christ, transformed into a crown of glory and honour. That is why Gregory states 'we must take care to avoid every thorny deed and word and thought throughout our entire life, so that having become an honor and glory through a pure and innocent regimen, we ourselves shall crown the Head of all, having become, as it were, a treasure and a possession for the Master' (Gregory of Nyssa, *Perf* [GNO VIII/1, 207; tr. V. Woods Callahan, 118]).

[59] Gregorio de Nisa, *Perf* (GNO VIII/1, 206; tr. V. Woods Callahan, 117).

[60] *Cf.* J. Daniélou, 'Christologie et eschatologie', in A. Grillmeier and H. Bacht (eds), *Das Konzil von Chalkedon III* (1954), 277.

[61] *Cf.* Gregory of Nyssa, *Antirrh* 15 (GNO III/1, 151). Interesting affirmations about union with the divinity and the effects of Resurrection can be found also in Gregory of Nyssa, *Ref Eun* 177 (GNO II, 386) and *Trid spat* (GNO IX, 294).

[62] Gregory of Nyssa, *Salut Pasch* (GNO IX, 245-53); *Or cat* XXXVII (GNO III/4, 93-5); *cf.* L.F. Mateo-Seco, 'Resurrection', in L.F. Mateo-Seco and G. Maspero (eds), *The Brill Dictionary of Gregory of Nyssa* (2010), 668.

all will be united to Christ in the praise of the Lord.[63] Indeed, as B. Daley states, 'the mystery of Christ's resurrection reveals to us the mysterious, unimaginable character of the promised end of history – the mystery of Christ's own form, as well as of our own fulfilment'.[64]

4. The final 'submission' of Christ to the Father and eschatological unity

What we have stated so far on the resurrection of Christ and his salvific power leads us to the reality of the mediation of Christ and towards the eschatological exercise of this mediation. The incarnate Logos is the mediator between the inaccessible nature of God and humankind;[65] He leads the Spouse towards what is good, and receives her in the participation of His incorruptible eternity.[66] The exercise of this mediation encompasses the end of history in which all intelligent beings will be 'submitted' by Christ to the Father, in which man will return to Paradise and recover the splendour of his likeness to God.[67]

Gregory gives an eschatological sense to a text that is complicated to explain within the context of the Arian crisis, 1Cor 15:28: 'When all things are subjected to him, then the Son himself will also be subjected to him who put all things under him, that God may be everything to every one'. Gregory devoted considerable attention to this text. Eunomius, and the Arians in general, used it to argue for the subordination of the Son to the Father. They understood that this submission implied a substantial submission within the Trinity: the Son was subordinated to the Father and the Holy Spirit to the Son. As might be expected, there was a profound theological discussion on the interpretation of this verse, seeking to clarify the real meaning of this submission (ὑποταγή) of the Son to the Father. Gregory covers this issue in *Contra Eunomium*,[68] but dedicates his brief treatise *In illud: Tunc et ipse filius*[69] to this issue in particular.

Gregory's explanation consists of reading 1Cor 15:28 from an eschatological viewpoint: at the end of history Christ will offer the Father all things, and especially human beings, who will form a close unity in Him.[70] Christ is the

[63] Gregory of Nyssa, *Sanct Pasch* (GNO IX, 254-7).

[64] B. Daley, '"Heavenly Man" and "Eternal Christ": Apollinarius and Gregory of Nyssa on the Personal Identity of the Savior', *Journal of Early Christian Studies* 10 (2002), 469-88, 486.

[65] *Cf.* M. Brugarolas, 'La mediación de Cristo en Gregorio de Nisa', *Scripta Theologica* 49 (2017), 301-26.

[66] *Cf.* Gregory of Nyssa, *Cant* IV (GNO VI, 129,5-7).

[67] *Cf.* Gregory of Nyssa, *Op hom* (PG 44, 256C).

[68] *Cf.* Gregory of Nyssa, *Eun* I, 187-204 (GNO I, 81-6).

[69] *Cf.* Gregory of Nyssa, *Tunc et ipse* (GNO III/2, 28).

[70] *Cf.* H. Drobner, 'Die biblische Argumentation Gregors von Nyssa im ersten Buch *Contra Eunomium*', in M. Brugarolas (ed.), *Gregory of Nyssa:* Contra Eunomium I. *An English Translation with Supporting Studies* (Leiden, 2018), 333-5.

one who leads the entire spiritual creation to unity.[71] Gregory's exegesis is
sustained by the exercise of the mediation of Christ: the Son has made himself
a 'participant in our humanity' and *through Himself and in Himself* he offers
the Father the obedience of all humanity.[72] He who descended from and ascended
to Heaven is 'the Mediator between the Father and the disinherited, the One who
reconciled the enemies of God to the true and only Godhead'.[73] That is, Christ is
the mediator (μεσίτης) of our obedience through his own obedience.[74]

Christ unifies all things in Himself – especially humanity – and, united in
Him, he leads them to the Father. It is *in Himself*, in His being God and man,
where Christ gives unity to all creation and submits it to the Father. This we
can see in Gregory's commentary, in which he links *1Cor* 15:28 to *Jn* 17:21-
3's verse on the prayer for unity, and he speaks of the eschatological presence
of God *in* and *through* Christ. For Gregory, Christ is called by Peter 'mediator
between God and man' (*1Tim* 2:5) because He is the one who is in the Father
and lived among men. He accomplishes his mediation by returning humankind
to the unity of the Father, uniting all in Him, and through Himself, unifying
them in the Father. According to Gregory, Christ shows in the Gospel that 'by
unifying us in Him, He who is in the Father, through Himself causes our union
with the Father: "That they may all be one; even as thou, Father, art in me,
and I in thee, that they also may be one in us" (*Jn* 17:21)'.[75]

The union with God and eschatological plenitude – the submission of all to
the Father – are Christological in essence. Christ is in fact the *eschatos*; because
it is in Him that history is fulfilled and that humanity reaches its final end in
union with God. That is why Gregory believes it is important to highlight the
equality of Christ with the Father, because this is necessary for his work of
mediation, precisely because of the radical way in which it is conceived: it is in
Himself that Christ performs this unity.[76] Gregory does not understand this mediation as something transient, and the encounter with Christ is not conceived as a
milestone that man reaches and then leaves behind in his eternal ascension to
God. It is *in* the Son Himself that the human being reaches God. In this sense, it
is revealing that Gregory uses the *epektasis* as proof of the divinity of Christ
against Eunomius:[77] to complete his work of mediation, the Son has to possess

[71] *Cf.* Gregory of Nyssa, *Cant* VIII (GNO VI, 254).
[72] *Cf.* L.F. Mateo-Seco, 'Christology and Soteriology in the *Contra Eunomium* I', in M. Brugarolas (ed.), *Gregory of Nyssa:* Contra Eunomium I (2018), 581ff., 396-400.
[73] Gregory of Nyssa, *Perf* (GNO VIII/1, 205; tr. V. Woods Callahan, 116).
[74] *Cf.* Gregory of Nyssa, *Eun* I, 193 (GNO I, 83,6-14).
[75] Gregory of Nyssa, *Tunc et ipse* (GNO III/2, 21).
[76] *Cf.* L.F. Mateo-Seco, 'Christology and Soteriology in the *Contra Eunomium* I' (2018), 583-4.
[77] *Cf.* Gregory of Nyssa, *Eun* I, 288-9 (GNO I, 111-2); J. Daniélou, *Platonisme et théologie
mystique. Essai sur la doctrine spirituelle de saint Grégoire de Nysse* (Paris, 1944), 291-307;
E. Ferguson, 'God's Infinity and Man's Mutability: Perpetual Progress according to Gregory of
Nyssa', *Greek Orthodox Theological Review* 18 (1973), 59-78.

the fullness of God in Himself in a way in which He is not subject to the laws of change and indefinite progress because of not possessing the plenitude of all good. The stepping stone for rising up toward God in the eternal and infinite movement of *epektasis* is Christ Himself: He, who is the stone, is perfect virtue.[78]

The 'submission' saint Paul talks about refers therefore to the eschatological future and is applied to the Lord in his role as Firstborn and Mediator. Submission means unity and subjection: unity, because when uniting with Christ, all things are unified among themselves and with God; and submission, because it is not the divinity of the Word, but the body of the Lord, which is all humanity,[79] and because this submission is none other than the rejection of evil.[80] This is why Gregory, when explaining the title of Firstborn to Eunomius, links the soteriological and eschatological dimensions. The title of 'Firstborn' is found in scripture with various meanings.[81] We read about 'the Firstborn of all creation' (*Col* 1:15), but also of the 'Firstborn among many brothers' (*Rom* 8:29) and of the 'Firstborn from the dead' (*Col* 1:18) and the Firstborn is also mentioned in: 'And when again he brings the Firstborn into the world, he says, *Let all his angels worship him*' (*Heb* 1:6). According to Gregory, the text says 'again' because it refers to the manifestation of the Judge at the end of time, not in the form of the servant (*Phil* 2:7), but majestically sitting on the throne of his kingdom, surrounded by all His adoring angels. He who came to the world, making himself Firstborn among the dead, His brothers and all creation, will come again to justly judge all things, without rejecting the description 'Firstborn' 'which he once received for our sake'. The Lord, says Gregory, 'rejoices in the reclamation of mankind, which by becoming our Firstborn he has again reclaimed to its original grace'.[82]

Gregory highlights the importance of not separating both titles of the Son: Firstborn and Only-begotten, because it is only possible to understand that He accomplishes humankind's salvation through the unity of both names: He is saviour because He is God and man, the Son of God and Son of man: His transcendent nature means He is God; while the economy of love towards man made Him take on the condition of a servant. So 'being Only-begotten God, he becomes the Firstborn of all creation: Only-begotten as he who is at the paternal breast (*cf. Jn* 1:17), but, in those who are being saved through the new creation, Firstborn of creation both in deed and in name'.[83]

---

[78] Gregory of Nyssa, *Vit Moys* II, 244 (GNO VII/1, 118); *cf.* G. Maspero, 'Deification, Relation (*schesis*) and Ontology in Gregory of Nyssa', in J. Arblaster and R. Faesen (eds), *Theosis/Deification. Christian Doctrines of divinisation East and West* (Leuven, 2018), 32.

[79] *Cf.* L.F. Mateo-Seco, 'La unidad y la gloria. Jn 17,21-23 en el pensamiento de Gregorio de Nisa', in J. Chapa (ed.), *Signum et testimonium* (Pamplona, 2003), 195.

[80] *Cf.* Gregory of Nyssa, *Eun* I, 193 (GNO I, 83).

[81] *Cf.* Gregory of Nyssa, *Eun* III/2, 43-57 (GNO II 66-71).

[82] Gregory of Nyssa, *Eun* III/2, 48 (GNO II 68; trans. S.G. Hall, 82).

[83] Gregory of Nyssa, *Eun* III/2, 55 (GNO II 70f.; trans. S.G. Hall, 82).

5. Conclusion

Throughout this chapter we have considered the nucleus of the Christological question – the union of the divine and human in Christ – first, from the perspective of its intrinsic salvific meaning, and then in its dynamic character. It is the union that is realized in Christ that transforms humanity: the Logos acting in the humanity of Christ (the first fruits), through the resurrection, gives back to the whole of humanity their incorruptible life and the dignity of children of God. Both aspects of this Christology – the soteriological and the dynamic – are closely linked to the theology of time that is so characteristic of Gregory. Gregory understands the resurrection as the return to the original grace, and that is why we can establish a convergent reading of his doctrine of creation and resurrection. The analogy between the first creation and the new glorified creation of humanity opens up the way to a better understanding of the solidarity of all humanity, a solidarity which exists in virtue of the creating act of the Logos and the power of the Logos incarnate to resurrect and regenerate humanity. From here, it is clear that Jesus Christ is, for Gregory, not only the beginning and cause of the resurrection of man, but the very end and ultimate perfection of humanity. His eschatology is, therefore an eternal Easter. Finally, setting out from Gregory's commentary on 1*Cor* 15:28, we have seen the depth with which Gregory understands the role of humanity in the divine economy of salvation: the 'submission' of Christ to the Father as a surrender made by the Logos to the Father of all humanity, united to Him in Himself. All this great 'coherence' or Christological *akolouthia* is sealed by the inseparability of the Christological titles *Unigenitus* and *Primogenitus*. Both titles make evident something that Špidlík expressed beautifully: 'Time and eternity are not radically opposed, but they are rather like a life pulsation of varying intensity. The eternal pulsation gives sense and rhythm to the pulsation of life within time'.[84]

Lastly, we cannot end without referring to some words by Daniélou which summarize the issue in question: the union of both natures in the person of Christ is the true fulfilment of eschatology. This does not consist of knowledge about the ἔσχατον – the last days – but of ἔσχατος, that is, Christ, who constitutes the fullness of time.[85] The ἔσχατος is not a relative term, the fulfilment of a certain *history*, but rather, it is the absolute end, beyond which nothing is possible, because it constitutes the ultimate realization of the divine plan. This brings us to the paradox, so characteristic of Christian thought, that, though the passing of time continues and we expect a chronological ἔσχατον, the final reality is already present in the person of the incarnate Word.[86]

---

[84] T. Špidlík, 'L'eternità e il tempo, la *zoé* el il *bíos*, problema dei Padri Cappadoci', *Augustiniaum* 16 (1976), 116; *cf.* T. Boman, *Das hebräische Denken in Vergleich mit dem Griechischen* (Göttingen, 1968, 5th ed.), 114ff.

[85] *Cf.* J. Daniélou, 'Christologie et eschatologie', in A. Grillmeier and H. Bacht (eds), *Das Konzil von Chalkedon III* (1954), 273-4.

[86] *Cf. ibid.*, 275; O. Cullmann, *Cristo y el tiempo* (Madrid, 2008), 105-18.

CHAPTER 3

A *Paradosis* of Mystical Theology between Basil the Great and Gregory of Nyssa

Anna M. Silvas

1. Introduction

Recently, through the season of Lent we were treated to the book of *Exodus* in the Liturgy of the Hours and in the Mass. I do not know what is happening to this soul clamoring for *Lectio Divina*, out of an inept and failing life, but I was shaken to see what seemed to be three stages or modalities of theophany experienced by Moses.

First there is the theophany of light, as in the flame of fire: *And the angel of the Lord appeared to him in a flame of fire out of the midst of a bush* (*Ex* 3:2) and later, a *pillar of fire to give light* (*Ex* 13:21).

Second there is the theophany of cloud, a theme which occurs throughout the Scriptures, even to the Annunciation to Mary and the Mount of Transfiguration: *And the Lord said to Moses, 'I am coming to you in a thick cloud, that the people may hear when I speak with you, and may also believe you for ever'* (*Ex* 19:9).

Third we have the most paradoxical of theophanies, the theophany of deep darkness, *And the people stood afar off, while Moses drew near to the thick darkness where God was* (*Ex* 20:21). This is like to that hour of darkness (cf. *Lk* 22:53), the hour in the Garden and on the Cross (*Jn* 12:23, 13:31) when the Son of Man was glorified, such a darkness, both moral and cosmic when God never seemed so absent, and was never so intensely present.

I checked the Hebrew and the Septuagint, and found the discrete terms, so resonant with meanings, firstly בְּלַבַּת־אֵשׁ / ἐν φλογὶ πυρός (in a flame of fire) and לְהָאִיר (to give light), secondly, בְּעַב הֶעָנָן / ἐν στύλῳ νεφέλης (in a column of cloud), and thirdly, אֶל־הָעֲרָפֶל אֲשֶׁר־שָׁם / εἰς τὸν γνόφον, οὗ ἦν ὁ θεός (into the darkness where God was). This darkness, unlike the generic σκότος, has the connotations of a dense, *thick* darkness.

All of this could not but forcefully remind me of St Gregory of Nyssa, with whom I have had a few dealings over the years. Let us hear his exposition of the theophanic darkness in *Ex* 20:21:

Why did Moses wish to enter the darkness and thus to see God therein? For this present account seems in some way to contradict that of the first theophany. For then it was in *light*, but now the Divine is seen in *darkness* (ἐν γνόφῳ το θεῖον ὁρᾶται).

Yet we must not imagine this to be at variance with our normal experience of divine contemplations (τῶν ... θεωρηθέντων). By these things the Word teaches us that the knowledge proper to piety comes first to us as light, so that all that is understood to be opposed to piety is darkness, and the dispelling of darkness comes from participation in the light.

But as the intellect advances (προϊὸν δὲ ὁ νοῦς), and by ever increasing and more perfect attention attains a comprehension of realities, and the more it approaches contemplation, the more clearly it sees that the divine nature is invisible. Having left behind all appearances, not only those perceived by the senses but also those which the mind (ἡ διάνοια) seems to see, it plunges ever more deeply within itself, until by much diligence of the mind it penetrates to the invisible and the incomprehensible (διαδυῇ ... πρὸς τὸ ἀθέατόν τε καὶ ἀκατάληπτον), and there it sees God.

For in this is the true knowledge of what is sought, and this is to see, in not seeing, because that which is sought transcends all knowledge, being separated on all sides by incomprehensibility as by a kind of darkness.

This is why the lofty John, who had penetrated this luminous darkness (τῷ λαμπρῷ γνόφῳ), said that *no one has ever seen God* (*Jn* 1:18), defining by this *negation* (τῇ ἀποφάσει ταύτῃ διοριζόμενος) that the knowledge of the divine substance (τῆς θείας οὐσίας τὴν γνῶσιν) is beyond the reach not only of human beings but of every intellectual nature (τῇ νοητῇ φύσει)[1] as well.

And so, when Moses had advanced in knowledge, it was then that he professed that he saw God in darkness (ὁμολογεῖ ἐν γνόφῳ τὸν θεὸν ἰδεῖν), or in other words, that he recognized that the Divine is that which by nature transcends all knowledge and comprehension. For *Moses entered*, it says, *the deep darkness where God was* (*Ex* 20:21). What God? The one *who made the darkness his covering*, as David said (*Ps* 17:12) who was initiated into the same ineffable inner shrine (ὁ ἐν τῷ αὐτῷ ἀδύτῳ μυηθεὶς ἀπόρρητα).[2]

So, we fly into the heart of Christian mysticism. The meaning and history of the words 'mysticism', 'mystical' etc. of course, might detain us for some time.[3] For now let me briefly say that Christian mysticism very much concerns *mystery,* and supremely that *mystery hidden for ages and generations but now made manifest to his saints ... this mystery which is Christ among you, your hope of glory* (*Col* 1:26-7). Which delivers us to *the* Mysteries, to the sublime

---

[1] Meaning the bodiless angels, who are purely 'noetic' creatures.

[2] Translated from Gregory of Nyssa, *The Life of Moses*, Bk 2, 162 in *de Vita Moysis*, PG 45, 1365-1382; *Gregorii Nysseni De Vita Moysis*, ed. Herbert Musurillo, GNO VII,I (Leiden, 1964), 86,11-87,20.

[3] 'Now it seems to me obvious that the word 'mysticism' has a past, has a history: it is not all innocent, and its use cannot be separated from a whole host of religious concerns *that have a history,* and a history that demands to be understood', Andrew Louth, in the 'Afterword' of *The Origins of the Christian Mystical Tradition*, 2nd ed. (Oxford, 2007), 201. The later Louth points to several studies, notably an essay originally published by Louis Bouyer in *La Vie Spirituelle, Supplément* in 1952, and republished in English as '"Mysticism" and "Mysterion": an essay on the history of a word', in A. Plé *et al.* (eds), *Mystery and Mysticism: a Symposium* (London, 1956), 119-37; Michel de Certeau, 'Mystique au XVIIᵉ siècle; le problème du langue "mystique"', in *L'Homme devant Dieu: Mélanges offerts au père Henri de Lubac* II, Théologie 57 (Paris, 1964), 267-91.

secret of the Father disclosed and communicated in the Incarnation, and now in the Divine Liturgy while the world lasts.

2. Gregory of Nyssa, Father of Christian Mysticism

One can now see why St Gregory of Nyssa had been called 'the founder of Mystical Theology' in the Church.[4] So Jean Daniélou, in his 1944 doctoral thesis. Pope Benedict XVI fairly endorsed this judgment in his catecheses on St Gregory, when he named him 'a great Father of Christian Mysticism'.[5]

On this account Gregory's elder brother, Basil the Great, with whom I have also had a bit to do over the years, was essentially the practical ascetic and a moralist, while Gregory was the one who had the chance to explore the theology of the further reaches of the life in Christ and to write about it. But this tidy categorization of the two brothers may be questioned. I was part of a workshop of Gregory of Nyssa scholars at the Oxford Patristics Conference in 2011, when it was suggested that since the great *Gregorii Nysseni Opera* series was nearly at an end, we ought to be thinking of doing the same for his brother. The relation between the two brothers, and the idea of looking at the Cappadocian Fathers *together* rather than as individual luminaries was advocated. For myself, I was already sensitive to the significant *paradosis* (tradition, handing on) from the elder brother to the younger.

In this chapter then, I will address two specific questions: Did Basil himself personally attain to the mature flowering of a sound Christian asceticism, the ever deepening, ever more contemplative intuition of God in prayer? Was Basil, in short, a mystic, and secondly, was he a mystical theologian, one who articulated some written account of the *teleiosis* or perfection of the life in Christ? The answers to these two questions will then affect our estimation of Gregory's own attainments in this field.

3. Was Basil a mystic? Gregory's Testimony

For an answer to the first question, let us first hear what Gregory of Nyssa says of his brother, of one whom he always called his 'Father', for he was indeed his spiritual father, who effectively dragged him out of a virtuous 'secular' life

---

[4] J. Daniélou, *Platonisme et théologie mystique: Essai sur la doctrine spirituelle de saint Grégoire de Nysse* (Paris, 1944), 6. He was called ὁ τῶν Πατέρων Πατήρ ('the Father of the Fathers') by Epiphanius the Deacon at the 7th ecumenical council, Nicaea II (787), 6th session (Mansi XIII 203-364 at 293E / Labbé and Cossart, *Concilia* vol. VII, 477), and ὁ τῶν Νυσσαέων φωστήρ ('the shining light of Nyssa'), Nicephorus Callistus *H.E.* 11.19.

[5] Pope Benedict XVI, *The Fathers* (Huntingdon, IN, 2008), Chapter 14, 'St Gregory of Nyssa' (comprising two addresses given on August 29 and September 9, 2007), 91-100, 93.

for service to Christ and his Church as bishop. He wrote his *Eulogy for his Brother* in the winter of 381/2. This is an important work, because its purpose is to advocate giving Basil a memorial day, just like the martyrs. Thanks to Gregory, Basil may have been the very first non-martyr saint to receive the honours of the altar. Gregory says:

He forsook the tumults of the city and the clamour of material attractions and philosophized with God in his retreat (καὶ ἦν ἐπὶ τῆς ἐσχατιᾶς προσφιλοσοφῶν τῷ Θεῷ). [Moses] was irradiated by the light from the bush (*cf. Ex* 3:2-5); with this vision we may draw a comparison: at night an irradiation of light came upon [Basil] while at prayer in his house (νυκτὸς οὔσης γίνεται αὐτῷ φωτὸς ἔλλαμψις κατὰ τὸν οἶκον προσευχομένῳ); an immaterial light filled his hut by divine power, kindled from no material source (ἄϋλον δέ τι τὸ φῶς ἦν ἐκεῖνο θείᾳ δυνάμει καταφωτίζον τὸ οἴκημα, ὑπ᾽ οὐδενὸς πράγματος ὑλικοῦ ἐξαπτόμενον) ... We know that *he often entered 'the darkness where God was'* (*cf. Ex* 20:21) (πολλάκις ἔγνωμεν αὐτὸν καὶ ἐντὸς τοῦ γνόφου, οὗ ἦν ὁ Θεός). The mystagogy of the Spirit rendered intelligible to him what was unfathomable to others (τὸ γὰρ τοῖς ἄλλοις ἀθεώρητον, ἐκείνῳ ληπτὸν ἐποίει ἡ μυσταγωγία τοῦ πνεύματος), since it seemed to transpire in the embrace of the darkness, in which the discourse concerning God was concealed (ὡς δοκεῖν ἐντὸς εἶναι τῆς περιοχῆς τοῦ γνόφου, ᾧ ὁ περὶ τοῦ Θεοῦ λόγος ἐναποκρύπτεται).[6]

Here Gregory proclaims the great distance Basil travelled inwardly with God in prayer, and that this perfecting of prayer in outward and inward darkness was the source of his infused wisdom, his theology. Anyone familiar with Gregory's accents, will recognize amid the rhetorical set pieces, that his 'we know' is an assertion of personal witness. The occasion for such personal observation of his brother leading to these later interpretations, came during visits by the young Gregory to the hidden retreat by the Iris River between the late 350s and early 360s, a sacred spot I have had the exceptional privilege of visiting. During the years 358-362, Gregory was visiting, and one sleepless night, perceived a strange luminosity around his brother's hut. In that region of the Church, children were brought up in the catechumenate. Basil had only come to Holy Baptism, Chrismation and Communion in the Mysteries in his late twenties. But for him this moment was simultaneously his commitment to vocational virginity, and to seeking a life of renunciation and ascetic endeavor. The Holy Spirit found in Basil a very apt pupil, and just as well, for there was not going to be much time. Basil departed this earth only twenty years later, in 378.

Gregory shows a Basil who was perfected – and when I use this word I always have the Greek *teleiosis* (attaining the *telos*, the 'end') in mind – *perfected* in intimacy with God, through his docility to the mystagogy of the Spirit who leads the lover of Christ into divine secrets which before had been inaccessible, a mystagogy consummated in the embrace of the darkness where God is.

---

[6] Otto Lendle (ed.), *In Basilium Fratrem* (*Eulogy for Basil the Great*), GNO X/1 (Leiden, 1990), 127,4-10, 129,5-9.

4. Was Basil a mystic? His own testimony

Let us seek what evidence we may have from Basil's own writings. We need go no further than the Second of his Question/Answers in the *Small Asketikon*, redacted in 365/366, as it is testified in Rufinus' Latin translation.[7] This section deals with Christian anthropology: what Basil understands man is constituted to *be*, and what his *end* is, as the basis of all engagement in the ascetical life.

10 Having received a commandment to love God, we possess the capacity to love implanted at the moment we were first constituted by God.[8] 11 And the proof is not from without, for anyone may discover the traces of what we have said from himself and within himself. 12 For we all are by nature enamoured of the beautiful,[9] even if what exactly is the beautiful appears differently from one to another,[10] 13 and, untaught, we show affection toward our friends and blood kin, and spontaneously display every goodwill towards our benefactors.
14 Now what is more wonderful than the divine beauty (indeed, *what other good is there but God alone?* (see *Lk* 18:19), 15 what thought more alluring than the splendour of God? 16 What yearning of the soul is so keen and intolerable as that which comes from God upon the soul cleansed of all vice, which, from a true affection declares: '*I am wounded with love*' (*Song* 2:5)?
18 Wholly ineffable and indescribable, as I at any rate experience it, are the lightning flashes of the divine beauty; speech cannot express it, hearing cannot take it in. 19 Invoke if you will the rays of the morning star, the brightness of the moon, or the light of the sun itself; none of them are worthy of being likened to that glory – indeed, the comparison falls far shorter of the true light than deep night and the moonless dark compared with (the flawlessly clear light of) the high noon sun.
20 Yet such beauty is not visible to fleshly eyes; it is comprehended only by the soul and the mind. 21 Whenever it illumined any of the saints it left embedded in them *an intolerable sting of yearning*,[11] 22 till at length, as if languishing in the fires of such

---

[7] Basil later re-edited and expanded this answer as *Longer Rules* 2-6 in the surviving Greek *Great Asketikon*.

[8] Basil seems to be tributary to Origen here. The natural, implanted love of God that needs to be trained and released so it can soar upward to its home in the absolute beauty of God is the theme of Origen's *Homilies on the Song of Songs* – to which book of scripture Basil shortly refers. Origen's doctrine in turn has antecedents in Plato's writings. The trapped finite soul impelled by the dynamism of *eros* to regain its ultimate home, once it has been kindled by moral *ascesis*, is told vividly in the analogy of the cave in *Republic* Bk 7, and in the argument of the *Symposium*.

[9] τῶν καλῶν, the 'beautiful', also comprising the 'good', hence the Latin translation, *bonum*.

[10] Basil touches on the differing opinions of the philosophers in *Hom. on Ps 48.1* (PG 29, 432-60, 432A-B) (Way, 311-31, 311): 'Some, even among the pagans (τῶν ἔξω) have imagined for themselves what the end of man might be, and have arrived at different conceptions about that end. There are those who declared that the end was knowledge [Platonists], others practical activity [Aristotelians], others an alternative use of life and body [Stoics], whereas the bestial declared that the end is pleasure [Epicureans]. But for us [Christians], the end for the sake of which we do everything and to which we press forward, is the blessed life in the world to come, which will be fulfilled when we have God reigning over us. Till now, no better conception than this has been found in rational nature'.

[11] εἴπου τινα περιέλαμψε τῶν ἁγίων, καὶ ἀφόρητον τοῦ πόθου τὸ κέντρον αὐτοῖς ἐγκατέλιπεν, *RBas* 2.21-2: if it should happen that this loveliness has bruised the mind and heart of the saints

love and chafing at this present life, they said: *Alas for me, that my sojourning is prolonged!* (*Ps.* 119:5), *when shall I come and appear before the face of God?* (*Ps.* 41:3) and this: *To depart and to be with Christ would be far better* (*Phil.* 1:23).

Rufinus preserves for us in Latin what has disappeared in the Syriac and in the later Greek re-editing, a rare expression of personal testimony: '*as I at any rate experience it*'. Here then is a man smitten with the divine beauty, in whom all the powers of *eros* are trained on their consummate end. He is a Christian imbued with the culture of Hellenic *paideia*, who uses a more or less Platonic discourse in an attempt to convey his intuitions of the highest end in Christ. His use of the famous phrase *wounded with love* indicates that he knew the exposition of *Song of Songs* by Origen of Alexandria, who transposes the mysticism of the Bride and the Bridegroom from the Church to the individual believer.[12] Another passage from Basil confirms this impression. It comes from his first recorded homily, *on the Beginning of Proverbs*, preached in the early 360s, still in his monastic years. He says:

I. The *Song of Songs* sketches the way in which souls are perfected. For it comprises the symphony of the Bride and the Bridegroom (περιέχει γὰρ συμφωνίαν νύμφης καὶ νυμφίου), that is, of the soul's intimacy with God the Word (τούτεστι, ψυχῆς οἰκείω-σιν πρὸς τὸν Θεὸν Λόγον). (PG 31, 388B)

Clearly then, to infer from the overwhelmingly moral thrust of Basil's many exhortations to the faithful, that he was somehow a mere moralist or rigorist, or 'only' an ascetic, is to make a serious mistake. Without doubt a depth of theocentric intensity, a vibrant and dynamic spiritual *tonos* is the wellspring of all Basil's teaching on the life in Christ. Thus from Basil's own testimony, we have Gregory's reading of him abundantly confirmed.

5. *Tonos*

We now ask whether Basil has anything in him of the mystical theologian, a theologian of the holy life. Can we find in his writings an ordered account of the further reaches of the life in Christ?

To begin with, we trace a burning Godward desire running through all of Basil's discourse. In *LR* 8.2 he speaks of a certain *tonos*, 'the tension yolked with desire (τὸν συνεζευγμένον τόνον τῇ ἐπιθυμίᾳ) of those who follow the Lord'; in *SR* 34/*RBas* 60, he says that we overcome the passion for cultivating human

---

and left embedded in them a most fiery sting of yearning after it (*qui decor, si cuius forte sanctorum mentem animumque perstrinxit, flagrantissimum in eis amoris sui stimulum defixit*) 22 till at length, as if languishing in the fires of such love and shuddering in horror at this present life, such as these go on to say: '*When shall I come and appear before the face of God?*' (*Ps* 41:3).

[12] See *Commentary on the Song of Songs* III.8, GCS, 1899ff., 194, and A. Louth, *The Origins of the Christian Mystical Tradition* (2006), 61-2.

favour 'by an undistracted concern (*cf.* 1*Cor* 7:35) for being well-pleasing to God and *by a* burning *desire* (διαπύρῳ ἐπιθυμίᾳ) *for the blessings promised by the Lord*; *SR* 197/*RBas* 58 speaks of an '*undistracted and intense desire* (ἀμετεωρίστῳ καὶ τεταμένη ἐπιθυμία τῆς πρὸς Θεὸν εὐαρεστήσεως) to be well pleasing to God, that strives wholeheartedly not to fall from the right path...'

In Basil's teaching, this *tonos*, deriving from the verb τείνω, 'to stretch', 'to pull tight', is the dynamic underpinning of a genuine striving to please the Lord, a tension stretching between present realities with the goal not yet fully realized. This same verb famously appears in a compound form in *Phil* 3:13-4: *but one thing I do, forgetting what lies behind and straining forward* (τοῖς δε ἔμπροσθεν ἐπεκτεινόμενος) *to what lies ahead, I press on toward the goal* (κατὰ σκόπον διώκω) *of the upward call of God in Christ Jesus*. Basil cites or alludes to this very passage, and the form of this word as used by Paul, throughout his works, many of them quite early.[13] For example, he uses ἐπεκτείνω[14] in *SR* 211, which is brief enough to quote in full:

SR 211 (*RBas* 151)
Q: What is the measure of love for God?
R: 1 *To be ever stretching the soul* (τὸ ... ἀεὶ τὴν ψύχην ἐπεκτείνεσθαι) *beyond its strength* (ὑπὲρ δύναμιν) towards the will of God, having his glory[15] as its goal and desire.

Thus already in Basil we find a doctrine of *epektasis* as an unceasing 'dynamic', or forward 'thrust' in the life in Christ. For the most part, however, Basil considers that perfection will only be reached in the life to come. Let us not forget that 'to be perfected', τελειωθῆναι is a key concept in Basil's teaching. It means that process of growth by which the end, the τέλος, is finally attained, the goal is reached, all potential is realized. We can easily defuse the negative connotations of 'perfectionism' in English, by thinking in terms of maturity, of completion, of fruition, which accords with one of Basil's favorite expressions, of bearing fitting and worthy fruit. All this we find in Basil's sense of *tonos*, this 'stretching out' the soul to its true end in Christ.

6. Anamnesis and Thanksgiving

Before we explore any further, it is vital to note that Basil's discourse is the very antithesis of every gnostic, hyper-spiritualizing or elitist tendency. There is nothing in him of a discarnate intellectualism, but a very practical, social,

---

[13] *Contra Eunomium* I 7 and I 16, *SR* 121/*RBas* 82.6, *SR* 32/*RBas* 55, *SR* 211/*RBas* 151, *Homily on Ps. 32.2* (*Homilia in Psalmum 32*, PG 29, 324-49, Way 230), *Homily on Ps 44* (*Homilia in Psalmum 44*, PG 29, 388-413, Way 276), and *On Renunciation of the World* (*On Renunciation of the World and Spiritual Perfection*, 4, PG 31, 625C-648B, 636B).

[14] As he does also in *SR* 32/*RBas* 55, to judge from the *extendimus* of Rufinus' translation.

[15] *RBas* 151.1: keeping in view and desiring whatever leads to the glory of God.

ecclesial and obediential piety. In Basil's account, the burning Godward desire spoken of above, takes motive power from the remembrance of God's over-flowing *philanthropia* towards us, both in creating us and providing for us on the one hand, and in the *kenosis* of his Only-Begotten Son in order to save us, on the other. Gratitude to such a Benefactor must inspire us to make some return for God's love towards us, inspire us to cleave to him through grateful obedience to his commandments. Indeed, he says in a striking phrase from his *Homily that there are Not Three Gods*, ch. I: 'love is the root of the command-ments'. Basil is completely penetrated by the Johannine teaching that love for God is in the obediential moral act (*Jn* 14:15): 'This is knowledge (γνῶσις) of God', says Basil, 'the keeping of God's commandments'.[16]

He constantly returns to this dynamic of remembrance and gratitude. You could well say that this is the heart of Basil's heart, a theme I designate *anamnesis and thanksgiving*, or *eucharistia*, for indeed it has every liturgical connotation. In fact, I detected phrases from Basil's *Anaphora* sprinkled throughout his extended expression of it in *RBas* 2 of his *Small Asketikon*. A sample of the many instances of this feature in in his writings, is this passage from his *Homily on Psalm 115*, ch. IV:

After he [the psalmist] became aware of God's innumerable gifts – that he was brought into being from nothing, that he was formed from the earth and honored with reason, by virtue of which he can also bear the heavenly *image*; then, turning his attention to the economy for the human race, that the Lord gave himself as a ransom for us all – he is at a loss and searches among all his possessions for a gift worthy of the Lord. So then, *what shall I return to the Lord* (*Ps* 115:13), 'Neither sacrifices, nor the service based on the ritual duties of the Law, but the entirety of my life.'[17]

This theme might be thought to belong more properly under the heading of Basil's ascetical doctrine, *i.e.* his study of the practical ways and means of making progress in the life in Christ. Yet, as Basil constantly teaches us, the goal we keep in view is already operative in us *now*, even in the O so humbling toil of our return to God. The God-breathed power of grace, of *tonos* and *epek-tasis,* of love in return for love, these energies of the Spirit which shall never end, already waft our flagging sails and steady our uncertain rudder as, trembling, we sail the back of the vast sea towards the sublime horizon.

7. Basil and the Infinity of God's Nature

Yet that horizon seems ever to elude us even as we draw nearer and nearer, because it has no limit. In the *Contra Eunomium* Basil uses the verb ἐπεκτείνω

---

[16] *Homily on the Martyr Mamas*, PG 31, 597A.
[17] *Homily on Psalm 115*, in Mark DelCogliano (tr., annot and introd.), *On Christian Doctrine and Practice St Basil the Great* (Yonkers NY, 2012), 218-26, 222.

in passages where he speaks of God's *infinity*, his boundlessness, his having no end. Consider the following example:

Whenever we consider the ages past, we find that the life of God transcends every beginning and say that he is 'unbegotten'. Whenever *we stretch our mind forward* into the ages to come (ὅταν δὲ τοῖς ἐπερχομένοις αἰῶσι τὸν νοῦν ἐπεκτείνωμεν), we designate the one who is *without boundary, infinite,* and comprehended by no terminal point, as 'incorruptible' (τὸν ἀόριστον καὶ ἄπειρον καὶ οὐδενὶ τέλει καταληπτὸν προσαγορεύομεν ἄφθαρτον).[18]

The *CE* comes from relatively early in Basil's career, about 364. He returns to the infinitude of God's nature again and again in later writings. All of which corrects me of a misapprehension under which I had labored long: that it was Gregory who added the note of 'infinity' to the Cappadocian teaching on the 'incomprehensibility' of the Divine nature. But it is not so. There is no doubt that contemplation of the divine 'infinity' was already on the theological agenda handed down by Basil to his brother.

8. The dogmatic touchstone of mystical theology

A small batch of Basil's *Letters to Amphilochius*, 232-235, especially 233-235 (Deferrari III, 364-385) is of culminating interest to our investigation. They were written late in his life, in 376, so they represent the maturity of his thought. He works out his argument against the extravagant claim of the Eunomians, or as he puns it, the Anomians, that they have definite knowledge of the *ousia* or substance/essence of God. In *Letter* 234 (Deferrari III, 370-377) especially, we light upon the dogmatic touchstone of all later mystical theology:

If you say that you know His substance, then Him you do not know (εἰ τὴν οὐσίαν λέγεις εἰδέναι, αὐτὸν οὐκ ἐπίστασαι) ... I do know that he *is*, but what His substance is I deem beyond understanding (ὅτι μὲν ἔστιν οἶδα, τί δὲ ἡ οὐσία ὑπὲρ διάνοιαν τίθεμαι). How then am I saved? *Through faith*, and it is faith enough to know that God *is*, not *what* He is, and that He will be the recompense of those who seek Him. *Knowledge, then, of His divine substance, is the perception of His incomprehensibility* (εἴδεσις ἄρα τῆς θείας οὐσίας, ἡ αἴσθεσις αὐτοῦ τῆς ἀκαταληψίας).

9. Basil and *Apophasis*

At a particularly crucial point of his argument, Basil says, in Deferrari's translation of his letters:

If they [the Eunomians] find us confessing that we know, demand of us knowledge of the substance (ἀπαιτοῦσιν ἡμῖν τῆς οὐσίας τὴν εἴδησιν), and if they see that we are

---

[18] PG 29, 525C, *cf.* alternative translation in Mark DelCoglio and Andrew Radde-Gallwitz (trans. and annot.), *St Basil of Caesarea, Against Eunomius* (Washington DC, 2011), 100.

cautious about making our answer (ἐὰν δὲ ἴδωσιν ἡμᾶς εὐλαβουμένους πρὸς τὴν ἀπόφασιν), turn upon us the reproach of impiety.[19]

This passage turns on the word *apophasis*, from which of course comes 'apophatic'. I think that the proper significance of the word eluded Deferrari. That *apophasis* here in fact concerns 'denial' or 'negation', is corroborated in the opening lines of *Letter* 234, as cited above: 'If we confess *that we do not know* the substance' (ἐὰν δὲ ἀγνοεῖν ὁμολογήσαμεν τὴν οὐσίαν). *Apophasis* in this context, therefore, is the theological correlate of *agnosis*: not knowing. We might attempt to retranslate the above passage in its fuller context as follows:

For since the word 'knowledge' has many meanings (ἐπειδὴ πολύσημον τὸ τῆς γνώσεως ὄνομα), and a thing can be known in respect to number, and size, and power, and manner of subsistence, and time of generation, and substance, they, taking it in a general sense in their questioning, if they find us confessing that we know, demand of us knowledge of the substance (ἀπαιτοῦσιν ἡμῖν τῆς οὐσίας τὴν εἴδησιν); and if they see us maintaining reverence with a denial (ἐὰν δὲ ἴδωσιν ἡμᾶς εὐλαβουμένους πρὸς τὴν ἀπόφασιν), turn upon us the reproach of impiety. But we for our part confess that we do know what is knowable about God, while on the other hand, to 'know' anything that escapes our comprehension is impossible … But 'knowledge' is manifold (πολλαχῶς ἡ γνῶσις), as we have said. For it is the apprehension of Him who created us, and the understanding of his wonders, and the keeping of His commandments, and intimacy with Him (καὶ ἡ οἰκείωσις ἡ πρὸς αὐτόν).

10. Knowing *in part*

It is a principle with Basil that our knowledge of God is in proportion to our limited human capacity. Elsewhere he expresses this in the phrase of Paul in 1*Cor* 13:9,12, 'we know *in part*'. In his *On the Faith*, later used as a preface for the *Moralia*, he explains how progress in the knowledge of God is gradual and tentative. Such knowledge grows by steps towards a relative plenitude in the life that is to come, to which we are always striving. He begins with the principle of the incomprehensibility of God's nature:

The nature of the majesty and glory of God is incomprehensible in word and uncontainable by mind (λόγῳ ἀπερίληπτον οὖσαν καὶ νῷ ἀκατάληπτον), and cannot be demonstrated or understood by one phrase or thought, but requires a number of those in current use. The God-breathed Scripture with difficulty hints darkly to the pure in heart, *as in a mirror*. For to see *face to face* (1*Cor* 13:12) and to know perfectly is promised in the age to come to those who are worthy of receiving it. But now, even though it be a Peter or Paul, one sees truly what one sees, and is neither deceived nor the victim of a phantasm, yet one sees *in a mirror* and *darkly* (cf. 1*Cor* 13:12), and receiving now with gratitude what is only *in part* (1*Cor* 13:9,10,13), one waits with joy for that perfection that is to come (τὸ τέλειον εἰς τὸ μέλλον περιχαρῶς ἀπεκδέχεται)…

---

[19] *Letter* 235, Deferrari III, 376-85, 380-1.

Similarly, that which now seems perfect in knowledge, if compared with the knowledge that shall be revealed to the worthy in the age to come, is so slight and obscure that it falls shorter of the clarity of the age to come than *seeing through a glass* and that *darkly*, falls short of *face to face*...

The God-breathed Scripture is as greatly conscious of the unlimited character of knowledge (τῆς ἐπιγνώσεως τὸ ἀπέραντον), as it is of the unattainability of the divine mysteries at the present time by human nature (τῆς ἀνθρωπίνης φύσεως τὸ τῶν θειῶν μυστηρίων ἐν τῷ παρόντι ἀνέφικτον), since to each, according to his progress, *more is* always *being added* (*cf. Mk* 4:24, *Mt* 25:29) (ἀεὶ μὲν κατὰ προκόπην ἑκάστῳ προστιθεμένου τοῦ πλείονος), and yet he ever falls short of worthy achievement (ἀεὶ δὲ τοῦ πρὸς ἀξίαν ἀπολιμπάνου ἁπάντων), until that which is perfect comes, when *that which is in part shall be done away with* (1*Cor* 13:10).[20]

11. Maturing in the Knowledge of God

In *Letter* 233 Basil acknowledges that the knowledge of God in the affective, experiential sense, does grow and mature, but that it is always, as we have seen, 'in part'. The letter begins abruptly, possibly indicating that its original introduction is missing:

I too have heard of this and know it, and I understand the constitution of human beings (γνωρίζω τὴν ἀνθρώπων τὴν κατασκεύην). What then shall we say concerning this? That the intellect is something noble (ὅτι καλὸν μὲν ὁ νοῦς), and in it we have what is according to the image of the Creator, and the activity of the intellect is something noble (καὶ καλὸν τοῦ νοῦ ἡ ἐνέργεια) ... But if it [ὁ νοῦς] inclines to its more divine part [ἐὰν δὲ πρὸς τὴν θειοτέραν ἀπονεύσῃ μερίδα], and accepts the graces of the Spirit, then it becomes sensitive to the more divine things (τότε γίνεται τῶν θειοτέρων καταληπτικός), insofar as is commensurate with its nature (ὅσον αὐτοῦ τῇ φυσει σύμμετρον) ... But the intellect that is tempered / blended / suffused / admixed / *melded with the divinity of the Spirit* (ὁ μέντοι τῇ θεότητι τοῦ Πνεύματος ἀνακραθείς) is already initiated into/brought into view of the great things contemplated (οὗτος ἤδη τῶν μεγάλων ἐστι θεωρημάτων ἐποπτικός), and observes the divine beauties (καὶ καθορᾷ τὰ θεῖα κάλλη), but only to the extent that grace allows and its constitution admits. Let them therefore dismiss those dialectical questions and enquire into the truth, not mischievously, but reverently. The discriminating power of the intellect (τὸ τοῦ νοῦ κριτήριον) has been given us in order to apprehend the truth (εἰς τὴν τῆς ἀληθείας σύνεσιν). But our God *is* Truth itself. Therefore it is the first concern of the intellect to recognize our God (τὸν Θεὸν ἡμῶν ἐπιγινώσκειν), but to recognize Him *in such a way as the infinitely great can be known by the very small* (γνωρίζεσθαι τὸν ἀπειρομεγέθη ὑπὸ τοῦ μικρότατου).[21]

Here we see further aspects of mystical theology adumbrated: the Spirit as the protagonist of our progress, gradually curing the coarseness and opacity of

---

[20] *On the Faith*, PG 31, 681A, 684A; quoted from Clarke, 93-4, with retranslations from the Greek. A very similar passage is found in his *Homily on the Martyr Mamas* quoted earlier.
[21] *Letter* 233, Deferrari III, 364-7, 368-9.

our spiritual senses to divine realities in the measure that the *noos* is receptive
to his influences. Note Basil's use of 'mingling' language, when he speaks of
the intellect as *anakratheis* with the divinity of the Spirit – *i.e.*, 'melded' or 'shot
through' with the Spirit, not in any monist or gnostic sense, but penetrated,
pervaded by. Basil describes this maturing of prayer as an initiation into contemplation of divine realities, of the divine beauty, and as a strange and wonderful
dialogue between the divine *infinitely great* and the human *exceedingly small*.

12. Conclusion

In conclusion: was Basil a mystic, *i.e.* a man of advanced holiness who had
matured in an ever deepening experiential knowledge of God? The evidence
of his own testimony confirms Gregory of Nyssa's interpretation that Basil was
by any reckoning a Christian mystic of a high order. But was he also a mystical *theologian*, in the sense of one who attempts to articulate an account of the
more mature reaches of the life in Christ? When beginning this essay I had
been expecting to find that perhaps he was not. Instead I was surprised to find
his discourse planted thickly with the seeds of a mystical theology, even with
the elements of an *apophatic* mystical theology. It seems that in the last years
before his all too premature death, Basil was tentatively probing the implications for the experience of the Christian spiritual life of the theology of the
divine infinitude and incomprehensibility.

Privileged to be at his brother's death bed, Gregory of Nyssa conceived a
strong sense of mission to continue Basil's theological task. It was a true *paradosis*. Whether the dying Basil personally spoke to Gregory in this vein we
do not know, but the aftermath strongly suggests he did. When he delivered his
teaching on *tonos* to Gregory, Basil's theology of the life in Christ was already
disposed to the greatly expanded use that Gregory would make of it later. These
seeds germinated slowly in Gregory's active years after his brother's death,
occupied as he was with many responsibilities, until they bore rich fruit in his
own later years, when he had fallen somewhat out of political favour. In artic-
ulating his own profound intuitions of Christian mystical theology, it is clear
that Gregory was taking up Basil's already existing preparatory work and car-
rying it forward. A deeper synthesis of the mystical *telos* to which all Basil's
Trinitarian theology and his ascetic doctrine tends, and the threads of ideas that
link this with Gregory's magisterial credentials in this field await further careful
investigation.

CHAPTER 4

Time, Memory, Identity

John Panteleimon Manoussakis

1. Introduction

It is only when Charles Ryder realizes that he has been in Brideshead *before*[1] that his Augustinian conversion of heart is set in motion, recognizing who he is by revisiting his past. Similarly, Oedipus in Sophocles' drama could not possibly know his true identity until he comes to recognize the terrible double crime he investigates as his own – that is, until he realizes that, like Charles Ryder in Evelyn Waugh's *Brideshead Revisited*, he has been in Thebes *before*.[2]

Remembering that 'we have been here before' – even if that *before* and that *here* refer to a time and a place as immemorial as Gregory of Nyssa's 'first creation'[3] – is absolutely essential in recognizing ourselves, our true identity, as seen from the perspective of eternity. To know oneself is to know oneself as he or she is known by God.[4] Yet such knowledge is possible only by knowing God (as much as *such* knowledge is possible and in the ways that it becomes possible, precisely, as impossible), which, for Gregory in particular, can only mean a kind of knowledge arrived at by the eschatological perspective of the end.[5]

---

[1] Evelyn Waugh, *Brideshead Revisited* (New York, 1972), 17.

[2] On such a reading of Oedipus see my article: 'Thebes Revisited: Theodicy and the Temporality of Ethics', *Research in Phenomenology* 39 (2009), 292-306.

[3] This idea, to my knowledge unique to Gregory, finds a variety of expressions. Thus we read about πρώτη δημιουργία (*Insc* XVI, GNO V, 188), πρώτη κτίση (*Cant* XV, GNO VI, 458 and in *Or dom* V, PG 44, 1181), πρώτη κατασκευή, πρώτη ζωή and πρώτη κοσμογένεια (in *An et res*, GNO III, 115, 112 and 119 respectively), πρώτη κατασκευή and διπλὴ κατασκευή (*Op hom* XVI, Μπρούσαλης, 150 and 142 respectively). See also, Morwenna Ludlow, *Universal Salvation: Eschatology in the Thought of Gregory of Nyssa and Karl Rahner* (Oxford, 2000), 46-50.

[4] See the opening line from Augustine's X book of his *Confessions*: 'Let me know you, O you who know me; then shall I know even as I am known'. Translation Maria Boulding (New York, 1997), 237.

[5] On the impossibility of knowledge of God as the only possibility of 'knowing' God, see Gregory's reading of *Song* 3:1-4 in *Cant* VI (GNO VI, 181-3). On an exploration of this theme, central to Gregory's theology, see my *God After Metaphysics* (Bloomington, 2007), 93-108.

Studia Patristica CI, 59-66.
© Peeters Publishers, 2021.

I think the bishop of Nyssa would have been in agreement with the conviction that at this end,

(…) the end of all our exploring
Will be to arrive where we started
And know the place for the first time (*Little Gidding*, V 240-3)[6]

2. Gregory of Nyssa's Eschatology

Time, memory, identity: it is this cluster of interlocking notions that I try to briefly sketch in this opening in order to pose the following question: is the unfolding of time and the nostalgia of a future that is at the same time our past that sets us upon this eschatological return (Gregory is using the stronger term 'recapitulation' [ἀποκατάστασις][7])? And if so, once we are there, are time and memory to be discarded like a ladder that one is not using anymore? Does time abide at the eschaton? And if not – as Gregory, in following a long tradition, invites us to imagine a timeless eternity, that is an eternity without duration[8] – does this also mean that in the resurrection and hereafter humanity is bereft of memory?[9] And what good is the resurrection itself, and indeed salvation, if those saved do not remember who they were, or from what evils they have been saved, or, worse of all, by what means and who their savior is? For at a timeless time one could hardly entertain the possibility of remembering – as much as to remember is to re-present what is not present any more, to intend a *before*. Yet, without the recollecting and synthetic capacity of memory, it seems to me that the person's very identity would remain fragmentary.

One might indeed expect in a work entitled Περὶ ψυχῆς καὶ ἀναστάσεως – especially when styled after a Platonic dialogue[10] – to find Platonism's influence a little more pronounced than it is usually the case with the Greek Fathers

---

[6] T.S. Eliot, *Four Quartets* (San Diego, 1971), 59.

[7] For example, in *An et res* (GNO III, 112 and 119). Daniélou advises caution in taking this term too literally and, as a consequence, reaching some unfavorable conclusions for Gregory's eschatological vision, see J. Daniélou, 'L'apocatastase chez Saint Grégoire de Nysse', *Recherches de Science Religieuse* 30 (1942), 342, as cited by M. Ludlow, *Universal Salvation* (2000), 49.

[8] τὴν δὲ [ἔξω τοῦ σώματος ζωὴν] παρατείνας εἰς τὸ ἀΐδιον (...) κατὰ τοὺς ἀτελευτήτους αἰῶνας, ὧν πέρας ἡ ἀπειρία ἐστίν, *An et res* (GNO III, 60).

[9] The eschatological eradication of memory has been more recently supported by Metropolitan John Zizioulas in his essay 'Ἐσχατολογία καὶ Ὕπαρξη', *Σύναξη* 121 (January-March) (2012), 43-72; I have attempted to respond to Zizioulas' argument in my article 'The Dialectic of Communion and Otherness in St Maximus' Understanding of the Will', in Maxim Vasiljević (ed.), *Knowing the Purpose of Creation through the Resurrection* (Los Angeles, 2013), 159-81.

[10] I do not enter here into the debate whether Macrina is merely a character in Gregory's text, styled perhaps so as to voice a more Platonic version of Christianity than what Gregory himself espouses in other works of his. However, I believe that such a possibility should be taken seriously into consideration in further readings of the dialogue.

of the fourth century. Nevertheless, to the extent that this is also a work περὶ ἀναστάσεως and not only περὶ ψυχῆς, it could have provided an excellent opportunity for a Christian to defend Christianity's kerygma over against the metaphysics of the Academy. Unfortunately, this opportunity was rather missed here.

One could begin justifying this assessment by noting that Christ's name is mentioned only a couple of times and even those are in passing. This silence is indicative, in my view, of a defective Christology, or rather the lack of any detectable Christological context. Christ's resurrection is indeed mentioned[11] but no more than as the last example in a series of scriptural examples of resurrections.[12] It does not constitute any particular event in this discourse on the resurrection. I attribute to this work's absence of a robust Christology some, if not most, of the problems identified below.

Furthermore, the metaphysical structure within which Gregory's thought operates is, as expected, one divided between the sensible (τὸ αἰσθητόν) and the suprasensible or intelligible (τὸ νοητό). To these two orders Gregory gives his own particular coloring by further denominating the former as διαστημικό and the latter as ἀδιάστατον. Yet, the mediation between these two orders is not the incarnate Word of God – never is the incarnation mentioned in this work – but the soul itself which participates in both orders by being on the one hand ἀδιάστατος and on the other κτιστή (i.e., created – in our text γενητή, p. 15). To make the soul a third term, a *tertium quid*, that is both created and yet without diastemic properties renders the Christological mediation between created and uncreated orders, as it will be defined later on by Chalcedon, superfluous.

This last point regarding the dual character of the soul requires a considerable explanation for in a number of other works, Gregory specifically restricts the character of τὸ ἀδιάστατον to the divine nature alone, that is, he makes it a characteristic of the uncreated (read, divine) nature.[13] If the soul, however, is created (on pains of lapsing into Origen's error) then how is it also ἀδιάστατος?[14] A soul that is unlimited by space and time (as well as by any other diastemic characteristic) cannot but be only *one* soul. How are we to account for the soul's plurality and individuality in the absence of *diastema*? Perhaps the answer here is the body and the soul's connection to it – a connection which

---

[11] *An et res* (GNO III, 105).

[12] Absent here is the distinction between resuscitation and resurrection as found, for example, in Epiphanios of Salamis.

[13] *Eun* III, GNO II, 210: Ἡ δὲ θεία φύσις [...] ἀδιάστατος καὶ ἄποσος καὶ ἀπερίγραπτος; 217: οὐδὲ τινος διαστηματικῆς ἐννοίας περὶ τὴν θείαν φύσιν τὴν ἄποσον τε καὶ ἀδιάστατον θεωρουμένης.

[14] See, for example: τὴν νοερὰν ταύτην καὶ ἀδιάστατον φύσιν, ἣν καλοῦμεν ψυχήν (*An et res*, GNO III, 29); ἡ δὲ νοερά τε καὶ ἀδιάστατος φύσις ... οὐκοῦν ἐστιν ἐν αὐτοῖς ἡ ψυχή (*An et res*, GNO III, 31).

Gregory is willing to allow enduring even after death.[15] Yet, the question of identity and individuality, even though raised in most unambiguous terms by Gregory himself,[16] was never sufficiently answered in the course of this work.

In a sense my objection is the reverse of that which Gregory voices to Macrina. If the risen body is not identical to and with itself then 'one person will become a crowd of human beings'.[17] Nevertheless, it seems more dangerous to me that, with every physical difference removed, a proposition that the resurrection as the return to the first creation[18] not only implies but also necessitates, then this crowd of humans, indeed the entire humanity, might collapse into one human being – or less than one.

Yes, Marcina indeed provides for one last difference: the ethical difference not of bodies but of lives. Such a difference would distinguish between the various degrees of virtue and it would subsequently determine the manner of our participation in God's blessedness (μετασχεῖν τῆς μακαριότητος, 116). Yet, there is a further problem here: this difference in degrees of participation translates into a time difference (παράτασις), *for not all souls will participate to the eschatological perfection at the same time.* Hence the paradox that confronts Gregory. For, on the one hand, he asserts that there is *no time* at the eschata, yet, on the other hand, the conformity of the wicked to the good will take *longer* as opposed to the almost *instantaneous* enjoyment of the eschatological bliss reserved for the virtuous. How do these temporal indications apply on a timeless eternity? This language of eschatological duration is more than a figure of speech employed in a slip of Gregory's pen. It is an argument of a central importance in his eschatological vision, as the following passage makes clear:

...when the complete whole of our race [παντός τοῦ τῆς φύσεως ἡμῶν πληρώματος] shall have been perfected through each man – some having at once in this life been cleansed from evil, others having afterwards in the necessary periods been healed by fire, others having in their life here been unconscious equally of good and of evil – to offer to every one of us participation in the blessings which are in Him, which, the Scripture tells us, 'eye has not seen, nor ear heard, nor thought ever reached'. But this is nothing else, as I at least understand it, but to be in God Himself; for the good which

---

[15] See, *An et res* (GNO III, 54): τῇ γνωστικῇ δυνάμει τοῦ οἰκείου [ἡ ψυχὴ] ἐφαπτομένη καὶ παραμένουσα; 55: τούτοις καὶ μετὰ τὴν διάλυσιν [ἡ ψυχὴ] παραμένει οἰονεὶ φύλακα τῶν οἰκείων καθισταμένην. It is interesting that on the basis of this affinity between soul and body Gregory is able to sketch a theory on relics (and perhaps in defence of their veneration), see *An et res* (GNO III, 57). The term λείψανον allows him to use the metaphor of the broken pottery and, at the same time, allude to the saint's relics.

[16] This is Gregory's (as one of the *personae dramatis*) longest contribution to the dialogue; it runs from *An et res*, GNO III, 105 to 111.

[17] δῆμος τις ἀνθρώπων πάντως ὁ εἷς γενήσεται, *An et res* (GNO III, 109).

[18] ἡ εἰς τὸ ἀρχαῖον τῆς φύσεως ἡμῶν ἀποκατάστασις, *An et res* (GNO III, 112). And again: ὅταν δὲ πρὸς τὴν πρώτην τοῦ ἀνθρώπου καταστευὴν δι'ἀναστάσεως ὁ θεὸς ἐπανάγῃ τὴν φύσιν, *An et res* (GNO III, 115).

is above hearing and eye and heart must be that good which transcends everything. But the difference [διαφορά] between the virtuous and the vicious life will be illustrated in the future condition in this way; namely in the quicker [θᾶττον] or more tardy [σχολαιότερον] participation of each in that promised blessedness. For the duration [παράτασις] of one's cure will be analogous to the measure of the ingrained wickedness in each person. This cure consists in the cleansing of one's soul, and that cannot be achieved without an excruciating condition, as has been expounded in our previous discussion.[19]

The same objection can be raised against Gregory's celebrated notion of *epektasis*. Twice in the present work Gregory has Macrina assertaining that the participation of the human nature to the good (*i.e.*, to God) will expand 'without ever ceasing to increase'[20] and it will be 'without any limit'.[21] The dynamism suggested by these expressions cannot be reconciled with the static *nunc stans* of a timeless eternity. These inconsistencies might have been resolved, had Gregory distinguished between two notions or kinds of the eternal: one reserved for God properly called *aeternitas* and denoting a lack of succession (ἀϊδιότης), while the other describing an endless time is more properly called *sempiternitas*. The same difference has been expressed by St. Maximus the Confessor as an eternity without neither beginning nor ending (ἀνάρχως) which belong to God and an eternity with a beginning but without end (ἀτελευτήτως) to which creation might aspire.[22]

3. Temporality and the Body

Underneath this rather technical discussion hides the philosophical problem of *kinesis* (motion, movement) in St. Gregory's thought. The problem is connected with the metaphysical question of the relation between the one and the many, namely, with the effort to account for multiplicity without denying the ontological and chronological priority of the one. A clear expression of this question is found in Macrina's following words: 'The question presents, on the face of it, many insuperable difficulties. How, for instance, could movement come from a nature that is at rest? How from the simple and undimensional [nature] that which shows dimension and compositeness?'[23] I am afraid that

---

[19] *An et res* (GNO III, 115-6, Moore and Wilson (trs.) in NPNF 5 (Buffalo, NY, 1893); translation modified.

[20] καὶ μὴ λήγει ποτὲ τῆς αὐξήσεως, *An et res* (GNO III, 78).

[21] ἐφ'ὧν ὅρος οὐδεὶς ἐπικόπτει τὴν αὔξησιν, *An et res* (GNO III, 79). Gregory's emphasis here is also directed against Origen's doctrine of satiation (κόρος) which he has addressed earlier (see, *An et res*, GNO III, 71). For Origen's position, see *De principiis*, II 8 (Koetschau, 123-5).

[22] Maximus, *Cap. caritate*, 3, 25 (PG 90, 1024C). See also the distinction in Zizioulas's 'Ἐσχατολογία καὶ Ὕπαρξη' (2012), 62-4. This distinction between the two kinds of eternity is also found in Heidegger's *Hölderlins Hymnen Germanien und Der Rhein*, ed. S. Ziegler, Martin Heidegger Gesamtausgabe 39 (Frankfurt am Main, 1999), 55.

[23] *An et res* (GNO III, 92).

Gregory was not either willing or bold enough to vindicate *kinesis* by making it an intrinsic and inseparable characteristic of God's creation as such. The Eleatic suspicion against movement surfaces in such passages where Gregory speaks of multiplicity as the result of evil. The expression 'by the entrance of evil [to creation] nature was divided into a multiplicity'[24] seems to justify the fears concerning Gregory's eschatology as the return (ἐπαναγωγή) to the undifferentiated *pleroma* of the first creation.[25] Such a return – if nothing more than a return to the beginning – would render Gregory's eschatology into archaeology. For when he says that 'the resurrection is nothing else than the *apokatastasis* of our nature to *the ancient condition* of our nature (εἰς τὸ ἀρχαῖον)'[26] he, in fact, establishes a circle where the final consummation is the Ulyssean return to the *archē*. And what was this *archē* to which we ought to hope to return?[27] Gregory explains, 'at the *archē* the life of the human beings was μονοειδής'.[28] Μονοειδής is rather an interesting term: it suggests a singularity of kind, it excludes multiplicity and differentiation (things which as we have seen Gregory attributes to evil) and it raises our suspicion that the eschatological return to the beginning might be taken to amount to a catastrophic – if it was not, in fact, *epistrophic* – undoing of creation's plurality, difference, and otherness. The *archē* is not only μονοειδής, it is also monotonous. In such circular schema there is little room for the dynamic movement of history, for a vision that vindicates movement and affirms time and the temporality of desire.[29] To this extent, therefore, and in spite of whatever modification he is willing to undertake, Gregory's view of history shows its weakness in resisting the allure of the origin – or, better yet, the allure of Origen.[30]

---

[24] τῇ τῆς κακίας εἰσόδῳ εἰς πλῆθος ἡ φύσις κερματίσθη, *An et res* (GNO III, 120).

[25] Ludlow writes with respect to Gregory's notion of the first creation: 'It is almost as if Gregory thinks that ideal humanity or human nature (ἡ ἀνθρώπινη φύσις) is akin *to a Platonic form in the mind of God*. It thus already in a sense exists...' (49, my emphasis). We would like to add that not only it exists 'in a sense', but preeminently so, for to be 'in God's mind' is to exist most truly and properly. We will avoid entering here into a discussion of Patristic exemplarism.

[26] *An et res* (GNO III, 119).

[27] What sense is one to make out of such a hope which is nothing more than the return to the first condition (τὸ ἐλπιζόμενον οὐδὲν ἕτερον ἐστιν ἢ ὅπερ ἐν πρώτοις ἦν, *An et res*, GNO III, 120) other than nostalgia for an imaginary beginning?

[28] *An et res* (GNO III, 59).

[29] Desires (conceived precisely as the movements of the soul – τὰ τῆς ψυχῆς κινήματα, *An et res*, GNO III, 65) were altogether and indiscriminately ruled out from the eschatological condition (see, *An et res*, GNO III, 66-8).

[30] Cardinal Ratzinger (Pope Benedict XVI) raises a very pertinent point with regards to the relation between the dead and history: 'When we die, we step beyond history. In a preliminary fashion history is concluded – for me. But this does not mean that we lose our relation to history: the network of human relationality belongs to human nature itself. History would be deprived of its seriousness if resurrection occurred at the moment of death', *Eschatology: Death and the Eternal Life*, Michael Waldstein (tr.) (Washington, D.C., 1988), 184. To corroborate this idea, Ratzinger calls upon a beautiful passage from – surprisingly – Origen's commentary on *Leviticus*

On the other hand, in Gregory's exegetical works the relation of the beginning to the end is regulated by the notion of *prolepsis* (which is rather missing here). For example, in a passage from the commentary on the *Song of Songs*, Gregory understands creation's *archē* as a proleptic foreshadowing of the eschatological end – which is to say that the beginning was only a preview of the end:

When at the beginning [κατ'ἀρχάς] the nature of creation was established by the divine power, for each of the beings' beginning was conjoined [τῇ ἀρχῇ συναπηρτίσθη] without any dimension [ἀδιαστάτως] to the end [τὸ πέρας] of all things that came from the non-being to being, having together with their beginning [τῇ ἀρχῇ συνανασχούσης] their perfection.[31]

The two terms employed in this passage – συναπηρτίσθη, 'being cojoined', and συνανασχούσης, 'having together' – spell out the connection between the beginning of creation and its end, making creation a *prospect* of the future perfection of beings so much so that their eschatological *apokatastasis* is not any more merely a return to the beginning as it is rather the completion of the unfolding of the end that began at that beginning.

These questions cannot be fully considered apart from the eschatological destiny of the human body. Embodiment and temporality are two inseparable aspects of one and the same phenomenon: of personhood. In a passage cited above, Gregory seems to suggest that a consequence of the fall was the division of the human life into two periods: a short time living in the body and an infinite period living *without the body*. Let us hear his own words:

God divided the life of man into two parts, namely, this present life, and that *out of the body* [ἔξω τοῦ σώματος] hereafter; and He placed on the first a limit of the briefest possible time, while He prolonged the other into eternity [εἰς τὸ ἀΐδιον].[32]

Giving St. Gregory the benefit of the doubt (what did he mean by 'body' here? How is it possible that he assumes the eternal life to be 'out of the body' in light of everything else he says in defence of the body's resurrection), let us briefly take into examination the body's status in his eschatology. When, in the course of the dialogue,[33] Gregory raises the objection of the purpose that different parts of the body will serve once their function has ceased on account of the resurrection, Marcina's response is simply to reiterate that the resurrection will signal the reconstitution (*apokatastasis*) of our ancient nature,[34] which she

---

(*In Leviticum Homiliae* VII 1-2) where Christ, the holy apostles, and all the saints are said to be waiting for us (*Eschatology*, 185-6).

[31] *Cant* XV, GNO VI, 457-8. See also M. Ludlow, *Universal Salvation* (2000), 49.

[32] *An et res* (GNO III, 60, translation from *NPNF*).

[33] *An et res* (GNO III, 110).

[34] As we have already seen above (*An et res*, GNO III, 112 and 115). On the other hand: '… not only will the body not be such [eschatologically] as it is now, even when it is in the best of health; *it will not even be such as it was in the first human beings prior to sin*' (Augustine, *De civ. Dei*, XIII 20, William Babcock [tr.], volume II [New York, 2013], 87 my emphasis).

avoids to describe in any detail, except for saying that 'all of these [meaning such conditions as infancy and old age, and illnesses and 'anything else of the bodily affliction'] were brought about by the entry of evil'.[35] One wonders, then, how humans might have looked like in that first creation: without the need for food there would have been no digestive system, no mouth nor teeth; without the need for sexual procreation, there would have been no reproductive system; and so on (there is no need to be exhaustive here). What is left from the human body? What kind of body does he envision in the resurrection? And why, at this crucial moment, he fails to look at the body of the risen Lord as the exemplar and promise of our resurrection? Indeed, Christ at his resurrection did not assume a perfect body that was blank of any traces of (his) history, but He appeared in that very same body, even down to the marks and wounds of his passion (*Jn* 20:27). It is in such moments that one feels more strongly this work's Christological deficiency.[36]

The reason for this deficiency is this work's pronounced Platonic atmosphere as witnessed by the many references to the dialogues of the great master of the Academy. Above all, however, what determines the problematic character of this work is the Platonic metaphysics of participation that frames Gregory's exposition from beginning to end. More specifically, the human soul is here an image (εἰκών) of the divine nature, both in its genesis as well as in its eschatological destiny. At the very beginning of Gregory's dialogue with Macrina the soul is conceived precisely in terms of bearing a *similitude* (ὁμοιότης, 26) to the archetype of divinity.[37] The same sentiment is reiterated in the dialogue's last words, only now the term εἰκών is extended to the whole human nature and not only the soul. The language of likeness (εἰκών) is of course corroborated by the foundational text of the creation of humankind in God's image (κατ' εἰκόνα ἡμετέραν, *Gen* 1:26). It is not our task at the present moment to trace Gregory's extensive interpretation of this verse. Rather, what we are interested in is Gregory's adoption of Plato's so-called affinity argument (*Phaedo*, 78b4-84b8) on the expense of a more scriptural and Pauline understanding of the term εἰκών, reserved primarily for Christ as the 'image of the invisible God' (εἰκὼν τοῦ Θεοῦ τοῦ ἀοράτου, *Col* 1:15). One indeed wonders how much different a work the dialogue *On the Soul and the Resurrection* could have been, had Gregory chosen to stir a course closer to Paul than to Plato.

---

[35] Ταῦτα δὲ πάντα τῇ εἰσόδῳ τῆς κακίας ἡμῖν συνεισέβαλεν, *An et res* (GNO III, 113).

[36] Contrast St. Gregory's silence over Christ's risen body to this: 'Even after his [*i.e.*, Christ's] resurrection, in his already spiritual but still real flesh, he took food and drink with his disciples. For it is not the ability but rather the need to eat and drink that will be removed from such bodies. These bodies will be spiritual, therefore, not because they will cease to be bodies but because they will be sustained by a life-giving spirit' (Augustine, *De civ. Dei*, XIII 22, 89).

[37] On this similitude between the divine nature and the human soul see, Salvatore R.C. Lila, *Neuplatonisches Gedankengut in den 'Homilien über die Seligpreisungen' Gregors von Nyssa*, ed. H. Drobner (Leiden, 2004), 61-7.

CHAPTER 5

Theôria and Praxis

Michael J. PETRIN

1. Introduction

The relationship between *theôria* and *praxis* ('contemplation' and 'action,' or 'theory' and 'practice') has been a standard topic in Christian theology since Late Antiquity. The first traces of Christian interest in the topic are found in the works of Clement of Alexandria, but it was his younger contemporary Origen who set the basic agenda for subsequent Christian reflection.[1] Especially important was Origen's treatment of the story of Mary and Martha (*Lk* 10:38-42), in which he interpreted the two sisters as symbols of *theôria* and *praxis* (among other things).[2] Origen explicitly claimed that both *theôria* and *praxis* are necessary, but he also elevated the former as 'the good portion' (*Lk* 10:42) and emphasized the preparatory role of the latter. Although later Christian reflection on *theôria* and *praxis* tended to follow the basic lines of Origen's approach, I will argue that there are two distinctive and under-appreciated ways in which Gregory of Nyssa contributed to the Christian conversation about this topic.[3]

2. The Best Way of Life

Early Christian discussions of the relationship between *theôria* and *praxis* were, of course, extensions of a pre-existing conversation in Greek and Roman philosophy – a conversation originally focused on identifying the best *bios*, or way of life.[4]

---

[1] See B. McGinn, 'Asceticism and Mysticism in Late Antiquity and the Early Middle Ages', in V.L. Wimbush and R. Valantasis (eds), *Asceticism* (Oxford, 1998), 61-4.

[2] Origen, *Frag Luc* 171.

[3] A thorough comparison of Gregory's position with those of other early Christian theologians is unfortunately beyond the scope of the present chapter. Especially worthwhile would be a comparison with the position of Gregory of Nazianzus, on which see S. Elm, *Sons of Hellenism, Fathers of the Church: Emperor Julian, Gregory of Nazianzus, and the Vision of Rome* (Berkeley, 2012); F. Gautier, *La retraite et le sacerdoce chez Grégoire de Nazianze* (Turnhout, 2002).

[4] There is a vast amount of scholarship on the ancient philosophical conversation about the best way of life. Useful starting points include T. Bénatouïl and M. Bonazzi (eds), *Theoria, Praxis,*

Studia Patristica CI, 67-77.
© Peeters Publishers, 2021.

68 M.J. PETRIN

Plato laid the groundwork for this conversation by advocating a philosophical life centered on contemplation, but Aristotle must be credited with establishing the standard terminology.[5] In the *Nicomachean Ethics*, for example, Aristotle distinguishes three kinds of life, each of which testifies to a different conception of happiness, or the good.[6] The first kind of life is the *apolaustikos bios*, or 'life of enjoyment', which is embraced by those who foolishly identify the good as pleasure.[7] The second kind of life is the *politikos bios*, or 'political life' (called elsewhere the *politikos kai praktikos bios*), which is the life embraced by those who identify the good as honor – or as ethical virtue.[8] Such a life is regarded by Aristotle as genuinely happy, but only 'in a secondary degree' (*deuterôs*).[9] The happiest kind of life is the third: the *theôrêtikos bios*, or 'contemplative life', which is embraced by those who pursue the 'perfect happiness' of contemplative virtue, that is, the virtue of the intellect (*nous*).[10] It is useful to compare Aristotle's terminology for these different kinds of life to his terminology for the different kinds of science and philosophy: the 'active' (*praktikê*), the 'productive' (*poiêtikê*), and the 'contemplative' (*theôrêtikê*).[11]

As the philosophical conversation about the best way of life progressed, a number of different ways of understanding the proper relationship between *theôria* and *praxis* emerged. Because of the ambiguity of Aristotle's own views – especially his inconsistency in affirming the superiority of the contemplative life[12] – the Peripatetic tradition itself gave rise to a variety of positions: some philosophers recommended the *theôrêtikos bios*, some the

---

and the Contemplative Life after Plato and Aristotle (Leiden, 2012); A. Grilli, *Vita contemplativa: Il problema della vita contemplativa nel mondo greco-romano*, 2nd ed. (Brescia, 2002); W. Vogl, *Aktion und Kontemplation in der Antike: Die geschichtliche Entwicklung der praktischen und theoretischen Lebensauffassung bis Origenes* (Frankfurt, 2002); N. Lobkowicz, *Theory and Practice: History of a Concept from Aristotle to Marx* (Notre Dame, 1967); R. Joly, *La thème philosophique des genres de vie dans l'Antiquité classique* (Brussels, 1956).

[5] *E.g.*, Plato, *Resp* IX 580d-583a. On the contemplative life and Pre-Socratic philosophers, see W. Jaeger, 'Ueber Ursprung und Kreislauf des philosophischen Lebensideals', in *Scripta minora*, vol. I (Rome, 1960), 347-93.

[6] *Cf.* Aristotle, *Eth Eud* I 1215a-1216a; Diogenes Laertius V 31.

[7] Aristotle, *Eth Nic* I 1095b.

[8] *Ibid.*, I 1095b-1096a; *id.*, *Pol* VII 1324a. Care must be taken when interpreting Aristotle's use of the term *praktikos*. See *ibid.*, VII 1325b, where Aristotle claims that autotelic *theôriai* are especially worthy of being considered *praktikai*.

[9] *Id.*, *Eth Nic* X 1178a (tr. H. Rackham, *The Nicomachean Ethics*, 2nd ed., LCL 73 [Cambridge, MA, 1934], 619).

[10] *Id.*, *Eth Nic* X 1177a (tr. Rackham 613). On the relationship between the *theôrêtikos bios* and the *praktikos bios* in this work, see G.R. Lear, *Happy Lives and the Highest Good: An Essay on Aristotle's 'Nicomachean Ethics'* (Princeton, 2004).

[11] See Aristotle, *Metaph* VI 1025b-1026a.

[12] Compare Aristotle's approach to the different ways of life in *Eth Nic* with his remarks in *Pol* and *Eth Eud*.

praktikos bios, and some the *synthetos bios* (*i.e.*, the 'composite life').[13] The Stoics, for their part, tended to support involvement in existing political society; however, they too affirmed, in their own way, the importance of both *theôria* and *praxis*. Thus, according to Diogenes Laertius, the Stoics recommended the *logikos bios*, or 'rational life', within which both *theôria* and *praxis* were subordinated to the end of living in agreement with nature: for 'a rational being is expressly produced by nature for contemplation and for action (*pros theôrian kai praxin*)'.[14] It should be noted, however, that the word *theôria* meant something different for the Stoics, as they were not interested in the contemplation of transcendent realities.[15] Instead, they tended to focus on the coherence of *logos* and *ergon* ('word' and 'deed') – and it was not uncommon for them to prioritize the importance of actions and deeds within the philosophical life.[16] Within Middle and Neo-Platonism, on the other hand, there was a general return to the position of recommending the *theôrêtikos bios* as the best way of life.[17] Yet this was not done by completely neglecting *praxis*, but by subordinating it to *theôria* as secondary and/or preparatory – a necessary and/or purificatory good inferior to contemplation of the intelligible realm. As the second-century Platonist Alcinous puts it, 'the theoretical life (*ho theôrêtikos bios*) is of primary value; the practical (*praktikos*) of secondary, and involved with necessity'.[18] More specifically, he says that *praxis* and the *praktikos bios*, 'being pursued through the body, are subject to external hindrance, and would be engaged in when circumstances

---

[13] On the *controversia* mentioned in Cicero, *Att* II 16, see P.M. Huby, 'The *Controversia* between Dicaearchus and Theophrastus about the Best Life', in W.W. Fortenbaugh and E. Schütrumpf (eds), *Dicaearchus of Messana: Text, Translation, and Discussion* (New Brunswick, 2001), 311-28. On the *synthetos bios*, see G. Tsouni, 'Antiochus on Contemplation and the Happy Life', in D. Sedley (ed.), *The Philosophy of Antiochus* (Cambridge, 2012), 146-9.

[14] Diogenes Laertius VII 130 (tr. R.D. Hicks, *Lives of Eminent Philosophers*, vol. II, LCL 185 [Cambridge, MA, 1925], 235). On the difference between the *logikos bios* and the 'mixed life', see T. Bénatouïl, 'Le débat entre platonisme et stoïcisme sur la vie scolastique: Chrysippe, la Nouvelle Académie et Antiochus', in M. Bonazzi and C. Helmig (eds), *Platonic Stoicism – Stoic Platonism: The Dialogue between Platonism and Stoicism in Antiquity* (Leuven, 2007), 10-3.

[15] *Cf.* T. Bénatouïl, 'Θεωρία et vie contemplative du stoïcisme au platonisme: Chrysippe, Panétius, Antiochus et Alcinoos', in M. Bonazzi and J. Opsomer (eds), *The Origins of the Platonic System: Platonisms of the Early Empire and Their Philosophical Contexts* (Leuven, 2009), 3-11.

[16] *Cf.* J. Sellars, *The Art of Living: The Stoics on the Nature and Function of Philosophy*, 2nd ed. (London, 2009), 20-1 and 75-8; P. Hadot, *Philosophy as a Way of Life: Spiritual Exercises from Socrates to Foucault*, tr. M. Chase (Malden, 1995), 266-8.

[17] For a useful distillation of the debate between the Platonists and the Stoics on the best way of life, see G. Reydams-Schils, '"Unsociable Sociability": Philo on the Active and the Contemplative Life', in F. Calabi *et al.* (eds), *Pouvoir et puissances chez Philon d'Alexandrie* (Turnhout, 2015), 305. On the distinctive position of Plutarch, see M. Bonazzi, '*Theoria* and *Praxis*: On Plutarch's Platonism', in T. Bénatouïl and M. Bonazzi (eds), *Theoria, Praxis, and the Contemplative Life after Plato and Aristotle* (2012), 139-61.

[18] Alcinous, *Didasc* 2 (tr. J. Dillon, *The Handbook of Platonism* [Oxford, 1993], 3-4).

demand, by practising the transferral to human affairs of the visions of the contemplative life'.[19]

It is against the background of this philosophical conversation that we will now examine Gregory of Nyssa's treatment of the relationship between *theôria* and *praxis*. As we will see, Gregory, like Origen before him, holds a rather Platonic understanding of the intellectual activity of *theôria*; however, in his *Life of Moses*, Gregory, unlike Origen, presents *theôria* and *praxis* as equally important parts of the life of virtue, that is, the life of becoming like God. Gregory's position thus resembles, in important ways, that of the Stoics. In addition, in the thirteenth and fourteenth of his *Homilies on the Song of Songs*, Gregory integrates his balanced approach to *theôria* and *praxis* into a Pauline understanding of the Church as the body of Christ, thereby opening a space for different ways of life (with different emphases) within the life of one and the same body.

3. The Heart and the Arms

Gregory's understanding of *theôria* has already been studied by many.[20] The scholarship on his treatment of the relationship between *theôria* and *praxis*, however, has tended to focus on his appropriation and transformation of Origen's tripartite spiritual itinerary of *êthikê*, *physikê*, and *epoptikê* (stages that came to be known in Evagrian theology as *praktikê*, *physikê*, and *theologikê*).[21] This approach to Gregory's writings, while valuable in itself, has unfortunately led to a less than complete appreciation of at least two distinctive ways in which Gregory addresses the relationship between *theôria* and *praxis*.[22]

---

[19] *Ibid.*, 2 (tr. Dillon 4). *Cf.* D. Sedley, 'The *Theoretikos Bios* in Alcinous', in T. Bénatouïl and M. Bonazzi (eds), *Theoria, Praxis, and the Contemplative Life after Plato and Aristotle* (2012), 163-81.

[20] *E.g.*, G. Maspero, '*Theôria* / θεωρία', in L.F. Mateo-Seco and G. Maspero (eds), *The Brill Dictionary of Gregory of Nyssa* (Leiden, 2010), 736-8; T. Böhm, *Theoria – Unendlichkeit – Aufstieg: Philosophische Implikationen zu 'De vita Moysis' von Gregor von Nyssa* (Leiden, 1996), 69-106; A. Louth, *The Origins of the Christian Mystical Tradition: From Plato to Denys* (Oxford, 1981), 80-97; J. Daniélou, *L'être et le temps chez Grégoire de Nysse* (Leiden, 1970), 1-17; *id.*, *Platonisme et théologie mystique: Doctrine spirituelle de saint Grégoire de Nysse*, 2nd ed. (Paris, 1953), 117-72.

[21] Origen, *Comm Cant* prol. 3. *Cf.* Gregory of Nyssa, *Cant* I (GNO VI, 17-27); XI (GNO VI, 322-3). On Origen's third branch, see J. Kirchmeyer, 'Origène, Commentaire sur le Cantique, prol. (GCS Origenes 8, Baehrens, p. 75, ligne 8)', *SP* 10 (1970), 230-5.

[22] See, however, R.E. Heine, *Perfection in the Virtuous Life: A Study in the Relationship between Edification and Polemical Theology in Gregory of Nyssa's 'De vita Moysis'* (Cambridge, MA, 1975), 115-91; A.-M. Malingrey, '*Philosophia*': Étude d'un groupe de mots dans la littérature grecque, des Présocratiques au IVᵉ siècle après J.-C. (Paris, 1961), 253-5. See also the discussion of Gregory's 'praktische Metaphysik' in T. Kobusch, 'Metaphysik als Lebensform bei Gregor von Nyssa', in H.R. Drobner and A. Viciano (eds), *Gregory of Nyssa: Homilies on the Beatitudes:*

The first of these may be found in the *Life of Moses*. Let us begin with Gregory's treatment of the straps that hold up the pectoral adornments of Aaron, the high priest (*cf. Ex* 28,6-30; 36,9-28):

The straps by which these frontal adornments are tied to the arms seem to me to provide a teaching for the sublime life: namely, that active philosophy (*tên praktikên philosophian*) must be joined to that which is enacted contemplatively (*têi kata theôrian energoumenêi*). So the heart becomes a symbol of contemplation (*tês theôrias*) and the arms symbols of deeds (*tôn ergôn*).[23]

Gregory offers here a balanced affirmation of both contemplative and active philosophy, both *theôria* and *praxis*.[24] He advocates the union of contemplation and deeds as a necessary characteristic of the sublime life, and he finds a symbolic representation of this union in the body parts of Aaron.[25]

Elsewhere in the *Life of Moses* Gregory seems to use different terms for more or less the same conceptual distinction.[26] For example, when discussing the value of 'foreign education', he twice uses the phrase *êthikê te kai physikê* ('ethical and physical' philosophy).[27] More important, however, are those passages that seem to be closely related to our topic but employ fewer philosophical terms, such as when Gregory says the following in a discussion of the Decalogue:

Virtue in accordance with piety is divided into two parts: into that which pertains to the Divine and that which pertains to the rectification of conduct (*eis te to theion kai eis tên tou êthous katorthôsin*) – for purity of life is also a part of piety. Moses learns

An English Version with Commentary and Supporting Studies: Proceedings of the Eighth International Colloquium on Gregory of Nyssa (Paderborn, 14–18 September 1998) (Leiden, 2000), 467-85.

[23] Gregory of Nyssa, *Vit Moys* II 200 (GNO VII/1, 102-103; tr. A.J. Malherbe and E. Ferguson, *The Life of Moses* [Mahwah, 1978], 106 alt.).

[24] On the Cappadocian use of the word *philosophia*, see A.-M. Malingrey, '*Philosophia*' (1961), 207-61.

[25] Gregory does not speak of Aaron's *stêthos* (*cf. Ex* 28:29.30) and *ômoi* (*cf. Ex* 28:12.29), but of his *kardia* and *brachiones* (terms not found in *Ex*). I suggest that the word *sphragis* (*cf. Ex* 28:11.21) has reminded Gregory of *Song* 8:6: 'Set me as a seal (*sphragida*) upon your heart (*tên kardian sou*), as a seal (*sphragida*) upon your arm (*ton brachiona sou*)...' Indeed, there may even have been a precedent – perhaps dating back to Origen himself – for interpreting *Song* 8:6 as a teaching on *theôria* and *praxis*. Cf. Origen, *Schol Cant* (PG 17, 285B-C); Ambrose, *Myst* 7,41; id., *Virg* I 8,48; and Theodoret, *Cant* (PG 81, 204D-205A).

[26] *Cf.* Gregory of Nyssa, *Eccl* VI (GNO V, 373); *Epist* 24,2 (GNO VIII/2, 75).

[27] *Id.*, *Vit Moys* II 37 (GNO VII/1, 43); 115 (GNO VII/1, 68). The phrase *êthikê te kai physikê* could be taken as a reference to the first two branches of Origen's tripartite itinerary of *êthikê*, *physikê*, and *epoptikê* (*Comm Cant* prol. 3); however, I suggest that – at least in the case of *Vit Moys* II 37 – Gregory is referring to the entirety of pagan philosophy. On the distinction between *êthikê/praktikê* and *physikê/theôrêtikê* in ancient commentary on Aristotle, see R. Bodéüs, *Le philosophe et la cité: Recherches sur les rapports entre morale et politique dans la pensée d'Aristote* (Paris, 1982), 34-9. Cf. the distinction between *êthikê philosophia* and *theôrêtikê [te kai epoptikê] philosophia* in Gregory of Nyssa, *Inscr* II 3 (GNO V, 75-6).

at first the things which must be known about God (but to know him is to perceive about him none of the things known by human comprehension). Then, he is taught the other form of virtue, learning by what pursuits the virtuous life is rectified.[28]

Gregory does not explicitly address the topic of *theôria* and *praxis* in this passage, but his distinction between two different kinds of virtue – and his affirmation of the necessity of both – is very similar to his exegesis of Aaron's heart and arms.

Two other passages should also be mentioned here, both of which use the vocabulary of 1*Tim* 1:19 ('faith and a good conscience') instead of the terms *theôria* and *praxis*. In the first passage, Gregory interprets the alternating bells and pomegranates on the hem of Aaron's undergarment (*cf. Ex* 28:33; 36:31-3) as 'the two pursuits through which virtue is acquired, namely, faith toward the divine and conscience toward life (*hê te peri to theion pistis kai hê peri ton bion suneidêsis*)'.[29] Gregory thus exhorts his reader: 'Let faith sound forth pure and loud in the preaching of the holy Trinity, and let life imitate the nature of the pomegranate's fruit' (*i.e.*, let life be hard and sour on the outside, but beautiful and sweet on the inside).[30] In the second of the aforementioned passages, Gregory interprets the two small shields on Aaron's shoulders (*cf. Ex* 28:13-4; 28:29; 36:23-5) as 'the two-handed character of our weaponry against the Adversary' (*cf.* 2*Cor* 6:7), thereby reaffirming that virtue is accomplished 'in a two-fold way', that is, 'by faith and a good conscience concerning this life' (*dia te pisteôs kai tês kata ton bion touton agathês suneidêseôs*).[31]

If these passages are all variations on the same basic theme, then we can begin to flesh out Gregory's understanding of the two parts of the life of virtue. For example, *theôria* not only includes a form of knowledge so elevated that it exceeds the limits of human comprehension, but also a more common form of knowledge: a faith that can be proclaimed 'in the preaching of the holy Trinity'.[32] As for Gregory's comments on *praxis*, they emphasize the marks of asceticism, such as 'purity of life' and 'philosophical and austere behavior'.[33]

Gregory's emphasis on purification and his affirmation of a form of knowledge that transcends normal comprehension are both reminiscent of the Platonist

---

[28] *Id., Vit Moys* II 166 (GNO VII/1, 88; tr. Malherbe and Ferguson 96 alt.).

[29] *Ibid.*, II 192 (GNO VII/1, 99; tr. Malherbe and Ferguson 104).

[30] *Ibid.*

[31] *Ibid.*, II 198 (GNO VII/1, 102; tr. Malherbe and Ferguson 106 alt.).

[32] *Ibid.*, II 166 (GNO VII/1, 88); 192 (GNO VII/1, 99; tr. Malherbe and Ferguson 104). See also *ibid.*, II 162 (GNO VII/1, 86-7; tr. Malherbe and Ferguson 95), in which the intellect, despite pursuing *theôria*, paradoxically transcends it: 'As it approaches more nearly to contemplation (*têi theôriai*), it sees more clearly what of the divine nature is uncontemplated (*to tês theias physeôs atheôrêton*)'.

[33] *Ibid.*, II 166 (GNO VII/1, 88; tr. Malherbe and Ferguson 96); 193 (GNO VII/1, 99; tr. Malherbe and Ferguson 104 alt.).

approach to *theôria* and *praxis*. However, the balanced way in which he advocates the constitutive importance of both forms of virtue is closer to what we find in the *logikos bios* of the Stoics.[34] Indeed, Gregory subordinates both *theôria* and *praxis* to the primary concern of perpetual progress in virtue, that is, to the end of becoming like God, who is himself 'absolute virtue' (*hê pantelês aretê*).[35] As Gregory sees it, the significance of every event in Moses' life comes from its being a step forward in virtue, regardless of whether that step is contemplative or active.[36] Moreover, the two sides of virtue are mutually complementary, for each advancement in virtue builds on the last.[37] The *Life of Moses* thus offers a balanced treatment of the constitutive importance of both *theôria* and *praxis* (albeit one largely expressed in other terms), while at the same time presenting the possibility of a form of theological knowledge that equals – if not exceeds – the heights of Platonic contemplation.[38]

4. The Eye and the Hand

There is, of course, another way in which Gregory's position on *theôria* and *praxis* is similar to the position of the Platonists, and that is in his high regard for the monastic life, a 'philosophical' life that stands apart from the existing political order and is dedicated primarily to *theôria*.[39] One significant difference, however, is that Gregory affirms the enduring importance of *praxis* even for monks – and not just the importance of purgative behaviors that lay the foundation for higher levels of contemplation, but also of interpersonal actions like caring for the elderly and feeding the hungry during a time of famine.[40] In addition, Gregory does not reduce Christianity to a single way of life (monastic

[34] An important precedent for Gregory's approach to *theôria* and *praxis* may be found in the approach of Philo of Alexandria. See G. Reydams-Schils, '"Unsociable Sociability": Philo on the Active and the Contemplative Life' (2015), 305-18; F. Calabi, 'Vita pratica e vita teoretica in Filone di Alessandria', in C. Trottmann (ed.), *Vie active et vie contemplative au Moyen Âge et au seuil de la Renaissance* (Rome, 2009), 19-42.

[35] Gregory of Nyssa, *Vit Moys* prol. 7 (GNO VII/1, 4; Malherbe and Ferguson 31). On the place of *homoiôsis theôi* (*cf.* Plato, *Theaet* 176b) in the writings of Gregory, see H. Merki, Ὁμοίωσις Θεῷ: *Von der platonischen Angleichung an Gott zur Gottähnlichkeit bei Gregor von Nyssa* (Freiburg in der Schweiz, 1952). *Cf.* L.F. Mateo-Seco, 'Imitation / Μίμησις', in L.F. Mateo-Seco and G. Maspero (eds), *The Brill Dictionary of Gregory of Nyssa* (2010), 502-5.

[36] *Cf.* R.E. Heine, *Perfection in the Virtuous Life* (1965), 63-114.

[37] *Cf.* J.W. Smith, *Passion and Paradise: Human and Divine Emotion in the Thought of Gregory of Nyssa* (New York, 2004), 148-82.

[38] The balance of Gregory's approach is likely indebted, at least in part, to Basil (see, *e.g.*, *Epist* 295). There are, however, some cases in which Gregory grants a measure of superiority to *theôria*: *e.g.*, *Epist* 24,2-3 (GNO VIII/2, 75); *Vit Moys* I 47 (GNO VII/1, 22-3).

[39] *Cf.* G. Reydams-Schils, '"Unsociable Sociability": Philo on the Active and the Contemplative Life' (2015), 305.

[40] *E.g.*, Gregory of Nyssa, *Macr* (GNO VIII/1, 379; 384).

or other[41]), a point that is made quite clearly in his thirteenth and fourteenth *Homilies on the Song of Songs*, where he employs the Pauline image of the Church as the body of Christ, a body composed of many different members.

Gregory's use of this ecclesiological image in the aforementioned homilies is prompted by the description of the Bridegroom's body in *Song* 5:10-6; and his hermeneutic approach to this passage is summed up well by the following statement: 'Anyone, therefore, who focuses attention on the Church is in fact looking at Christ – Christ building himself up and augmenting himself by the addition of those who are being saved (*cf. Acts* 2:47)'.[42] Using this principle, Gregory interprets the various members of the Bridegroom's body (*i.e.*, Christ's body) in light of the various members of the Church. This interpretation, which spans two homilies, includes many points; however, we will focus our attention here on how Gregory deals with the Bridegroom's 'eyes' and 'hands' (*Song* 5:12.14).

The reference to the Bridegroom's 'eyes' reminds Gregory of 1*Cor* 12:21, and it is in view of this connection that he discusses the relationship between *theôria* and *praxis*:

The divine apostle observes somewhere in his letters that the eye cannot say to the hand, 'I have no need of you' (1*Cor* 12:21). In these words, he formulates a basic teaching, that it is fitting for the body of the Church to act well by means of both, combining discernment of the truth (*tou dioratikou tês alêtheias*) with activity (*to drastêrion*), for contemplation (*tês theôrias*) does not of itself bring the soul to perfection unless it makes room for works that rectify the ethical life (*ta erga … ta ton êthikon katorthounta bion*), nor does active philosophy (*tês praktikês philosophias*) offer any profit in its own right unless true piety (*tês alêthinês eusebeias*) guides what comes to pass.[43]

In this passage, Gregory reaffirms the constitutive importance of both *theôria* and *praxis* for the Christian life.[44] He associates the Bridegroom's eyes with 'discernment of the truth', 'contemplation', and 'true piety', and he associates the hands with 'activity', 'works that rectify the moral life', and 'active philosophy'. He then goes on, in the rest of homily XIII and later in homily XIV, to identify the members of the Church that are symbolized by the Bridegroom's eyes and hands.

---

[41] Note, *e.g.*, the continuity that Gregory recognizes between monastic *philosophia* and priestly *philosophia* in *ibid.* (GNO VIII/1, 385).

[42] *Id., Cant* XIII (GNO VI, 383; tr. R.A. Norris, *Homilies on the Song of Songs* [Atlanta, 2012], 403 alt.).

[43] *Ibid.*, XIII (GNO VI, 393-4; tr. Norris 415 alt.). *Cf.* XIV (GNO VI, 406; tr. Norris 431): 'From the great Paul we have learned that in the body which is the church the gift of the eye falls short of its purpose when it is not associated with the service of the hands, for he states, "The eye cannot say to the hand, 'I have no need of you'" (1*Cor* 12:21). The function of the eyes is shown to their greatest advantage when deeds bear witness to the acuteness of their vision, deeds that, by the zeal they exhibit for what is excellent give evidence of being soundly guided'.

[44] *Cf. ibid.*, prol. (GNO VI, 5); XII (GNO VI, 353); and XIII (GNO VI, 376-7).

He begins his identification of the eyes by citing three epithets found in Scripture: the 'looker' (*blepôn*), used of Samuel (1*Kgs* 9:9); the 'seer' (*horôn*), used of Amos (*Am* 7:12); and the 'watchman' (*skopos*), used of Ezekiel (*Ez* 3:17; 33:7).[45] These titles lead Gregory to claim that 'it is those who are ordained to oversee (*ephoran*), to look upon (*epiblepein*), and to watch over (*episkopein*) who are called eyes'.[46] Although he never says so explicitly, the vocabulary that Gregory uses – especially the verb *episkopein* – makes it apparent that he understands the eyes to represent bishops (*episkopoi*).[47]

As for the hands, Gregory first notes that they are praised as 'golden', and this reminds him of *Song* 5:11, where the Bridegroom's head is described as '*kephaz* gold'.[48] Gregory has already argued that the head symbolizes Christ in homily XIII, where he also explains that the word *kephaz* signifies 'that which is completely pure, as well as unmixed with and unreceptive to any base material'.[49] Gregory imports this meaning and identifies as a 'hand' (*cheir*) 'the one who administers (*diacheirizousan*) the common goods of the Church in the service of the command-ments – whose praise it is to be likened to the nature of the head in respect of purity and sinlessness'.[50] Gregory also cites 1*Cor* 1:9 and 4:2, connecting the trustworthi-ness of God to the trustworthiness required of stewards (*oikonomoi*). According to Gregory, 'the trustworthy and prudent steward (*oikonomos*), who in the Church plays the role of the hand, shows the body's hand to be golden after the likeness of its head (*kath' homoiotêta tês kephalês*) by imitating his wise master through his life'.[51] Gregory cites Judas here as a cautionary tale: a hand who was 'entrusted with the stewardship (*oikonomian*) of the poor', but who failed to imitate the head of the body.[52] It is uncertain if, in his treatment of the Bridegroom's hands, Greg-ory is speaking of stewardship (*oikonomia*) in a technical sense – that is, if he understands the hands to symbolize only the official *oikonomoi* of the episcopal treasury, or if he also includes others (especially deacons) in the same category.[53] Regardless, Gregory makes it clear that *praxis* involves not just ascetic practice and purification, but also concrete philanthropic action on behalf of the poor.

---

[45] *Ibid.*, XIII (GNO VI, 394; tr. Norris 417).

[46] *Ibid.*, XIII (GNO VI, 394; tr. Norris 417 alt.).

[47] *Cf. ibid.*, XIII (GNO VI, 398; tr. Norris 419): 'The Word wants the seers and watchers (*tous horôntas te kai episkopountas*) to be people who set the surety of the divine teachings before them like the brow of an encompassing wall but conceal by a humility like an enclosing eyelid the purity and radiance of their way of life, lest the beam of self-conceit, falling upon the pure pupil of the eye, become an obstacle to sight'.

[48] The standard text of the LXX does not read *chrysion kephaz*, but rather *chrysion kai phaz*.

[49] Gregory of Nyssa, *Cant* XIII (GNO VI, 390; tr. Norris 413 alt.). The Hebrew word *paz* does, in fact, mean 'pure/refined gold'.

[50] *Ibid.*, XIV (GNO VI, 407; tr. Norris 433 alt.).

[51] *Ibid.*, XIV (GNO VI, 408; tr. Norris 433 alt.).

[52] *Ibid.*, XIV (GNO VI, 408-9; tr. Norris 433 alt.).

[53] On those who assisted with episcopal almsgiving, see R. Finn, *Almsgiving in the Later Roman Empire: Christian Promotion and Practice (313–450)* (Oxford, 2006), 77-8.

The most interesting aspect of all of this for our purposes is Gregory's distribution of the responsibility for *theôria* and *praxis* to two different groups within the Church. Gregory thus engages with the question of different ways of life (not just with the question of different aspects of the same life).[54] Especially noteworthy here is his dependence on 1*Cor* 12:21, which ensures that he grants constitutive importance to both of the two ecclesial groups (both the 'eyes' and the 'hands'), subordinating both of their ways of life to the greater good of the building up of Christ's body.[55] Gregory thus stands apart from the standard Platonist view of the active life as merely secondary or preparatory. This is perhaps unsurprising, given that Paul's ecclesiological image of the body of Christ is a reapplication of a traditional political *topos* that was commonly adopted by Stoic philosophers.[56] There is, to be sure, a degree of tension between Gregory's distribution of the responsibility for *theôria* and *praxis* to different groups within the Church and his balanced account elsewhere of the place of both *theôria* and *praxis* within one and the same life of virtue. But these two approaches are not entirely opposed, as it is possible even within Gregory's respective discussions of the eyes and the hands to detect hints of both forms of virtue.[57] The greatest point of continuity, however, is to be found in Gregory's subordination of the different ways of life to the primary concern of the building up of Christ's body; for we once again see Gregory treating *theôria* and *praxis* not as ultimate goods, but as complementary ways of striving toward something greater: 'for the equipment of the saints, for the work of ministry, for the building up of the body of Christ, until we all attain to the unity of the faith and of the knowledge of the Son of God, to perfect manhood, to the measure of the stature of the fullness of Christ' (*Eph* 4:12-3).[58]

[54] Although Gregory identifies specific groups (*episkopoi* and *oikonomoi*) as the Bridegroom's eyes and hands, his position has implications for other members of the Church as well. After all, there are many different ways to build up Christ's body through *praxis*, and bishops are certainly not the only ones who are especially dedicated to *theôria* (consider, *e.g.*, the life of monks).

[55] *Cf.* Bénatouïl's remarks on the *logikos bios* in T. Bénatouïl, 'Le débat entre platonisme et stoïcisme sur la vie scolastique: Chrysippe, la Nouvelle Académie et Antiochus' (2007), 11-2: 'La question des genres de vie se trouve donc profondément transformée voire subvertie dans l'éthique stoïcienne: le seul 'choix' de vie important devient en effet celui d'Héraclès dans le fameux apologue de Prodicos, à savoir le choix de la vertu et d'elle seule contre toutes les autres valeurs et motivations, en particulier le plaisir. Mais la vertu n'impose aucune manière déterminée de vivre, puisqu'elle est suffisante pour atteindre le bonheur dans toutes les circonstances. Le problème du choix d'un mode de vie spécifique se trouve donc ravalé à un rang secondaire, celui de la 'sélection' entre divers indifférents en fonction des circonstances'.

[56] On the general political background of Paul's image, see M.M. Mitchell, *Paul and the Rhetoric of Reconciliation: An Exegetical Investigation of the Language and Composition of 1 Corinthians* (Louisville, 1991), 157-64. On the specifically Stoic background, see M.V. Lee, *Paul, the Stoics, and the Body of Christ* (Cambridge, 2006).

[57] *Cf.* Gregory of Nyssa, *Cant* XIII (GNO VI, 395-8); XIV (GNO VI, 410-1).

[58] *Ibid.*, XIII (GNO VI, 382; tr. Norris 403 alt.).

5. Conclusion

We have thus examined two distinctive ways in which Gregory of Nyssa contributed to the early Christian conversation about the relationship between *theôria* and *praxis*. First, in his *Life of Moses*, Gregory subordinates both *theôria* and *praxis* to the greater concern of perpetual progress in virtue. His understanding of *theôria* is, in many ways, Platonic; however, he offers a more balanced account of the constitutive importance of both contemplative and active virtue, an account that is similar in certain respects to the Stoic understanding of the virtuous life. Second, in the thirteenth and fourteenth of his *Homilies on the Song of Songs*, Gregory offers an ecclesiological interpretation of the body of the Bridegroom (*i.e.*, Christ), identifying the 'eyes' as those members of the Church who bear the primary responsibility for *theôria* and the 'hands' as those who bear the primary responsibility for *praxis*. He thus engages with the question of different ways of life, but he does not advocate one over and against the other. Instead, he affirms the constitutive importance of each member of the Church, and he subordinates their distinctive characteristics to the common goal of building up Christ's body. Although there is a degree of tension between these two contributions to the Christian conversation about *theôria* and *praxis*, Gregory's general position is consistent. He strives to balance the importance of *theôria* with that of *praxis*, and he subordinates both contemplative and active virtue to greater goals: that of becoming like God through perpetual progress in virtue, and that of building up Christ's body by 'grow[ing] up in every way into him who is the head' (*Eph* 4:15).[59]

---

[59] *Cf. id.*, *Vit Moys* II 318 (GNO VII/1, 143); *Cant* XIII (GNO VI, 382).

CHAPTER 6

The Key Eschatological Role of the *Song of Songs*[1]

Françoise VINEL

1. Introduction

As is well known, the fifteen *Homilies on the Song of Songs* are undoubtedly the final work of Gregory of Nyssa – written around 390 – and it is thus legitimate to ask if the eschatological question has a specific place in them that would renew or, rather, recapitulate the reflections of Gregory concerning the *eschaton*.[2] A passage from the fifteenth homily will serve as a sketch for an initial approach:

Being are not re-created in the same sequence and order in which they were created. For when at the beginning the created order came into existence by God's power, it was the case for each of these that its start and its full actualization were achieved together without any interval, since for all that were brought from nonexistence to existence their perfection coincided with their beginning. Now the human race is one of the things that were created.[3]

Then, after recalling *Gen* 1:26-7 (the human being is created in the image and likeness of God), Gregory notes what change comes about because of the intrusion of evil:

In the case of the first creation, then, the final state appeared simultaneously with the beginning, and the race took the starting point of its existence in its perfection; but from the moment it acquired a kinship with death by its inclination toward evil and so ceased to abide in the good, it does not achieve its perfect state again all at once, as at its first creation. Rather does it advance toward the better along a road of sorts, in an orderly

---

[1] My thanks go too to Xavier Morales for his careful reading. English translation by Kira Howes, revised by Matthieu Smyth.
[2] For quotations from *Homilies on the Song of Songs*, we refer to the Greek text edited by H. Langerbeck in GNO VI (Leiden, 1960), and to the English translation published by R.A. Norris Jr, SBL (Atlanta, 2012) [henceforth: GNO VI and Norris] – we shall note any changes made to the translation. There is a french translation by Dom A. Rousseau (Brussels, 2008). Reference may be made to the extracts translated by M. Canévet, *La colombe et la ténèbre* (Paris, 1967). About Gregory of Nyssa's eschatology, see L. Mateo-Seco, 'Eschatology', in L.F. Mateo-Seco and G. Maspero (eds), *The Brill Dictionary of Gregory of Nyssa*, SVC 99 (Leiden and Boston, 2010); G. Maspero, M. Brugarolas and I. Vigorelli (eds), *Gregory of Nyssa: In Cantico Canticorum: Analytical and Supporting Studies. Proceedings of the 13th International Colloquium on Gregory of Nyssa (Rome, 17-20 September 2014)* (Leiden, 2018); H. Boersma *Embodiment and Virtue in Gregory of Nyssa: An Anagogical Approach* (Oxford, 2013).
[3] Hom. XV, GNO VI, 457,19-458,4 – Norris, 487.

Studia Patristica CI, 79-100.
© Peeters Publishers, 2021.

fashion, one step after another, and rids itself bit by bit of its susceptibility to that which opposes its fulfillment. For when it was first created, since evil did not exist, there was nothing to prevent the race's perfection from going hand in hand with its birth, but in the process of restoration, lapses of time necessarily attend those who are retracing their way toward the original good.[4]

Moving from creation to the re-creation (Gregory rarely uses the verb ἀνα-κτίζεσθαι), to find at the end the perfection of the origin, the *archè-telos* scheme for Gregory of Nyssa was analyzed by Monique Alexandre,[5] and the definition of perfection as a return to the beginning – is clearly expressed, to take but an example, in the first *Homily on Ecclesiastes*: 'it is certain that the resurrection is nothing else but the restoration of the primitive state.'[6] Nonetheless, we note that the term ἀποκατάστασις is absent from the homilies on the *Song of Songs*. However, in the passage we are examining, Gregory opposes πρώτη κατασκευή, without a temporal mark, to δευτέρα ἀναστοιχείωσις.[7] Even if the latter term seems to signify the same thing as ἀποκατάστασις, Gregory, by choosing a compound of στοιχεῖα, the 'elements,' may want to insist upon a sort of reconfiguration of created realities that will draw us, with the insight provided by the reflections of H. Boersma,[8] to the question of the becoming of sensible and material creation after the resurrection. And, with matter beckoning the categories of space and time, what follows the passage cited above invokes the interval of time (διαστηματικὴ παράτασις) that 'necessarily attend[s] those who are retracing their way toward the original good' – an unclear expression that we must nonetheless associate with the problem of the relation between space and time.

More important for the purpose of this article is the accent placed, along these lines, on the connection between temporality and attachment to evil, by opposition to the immediacy of the first creation. The adverb ἀδιαστάτως is repeated in order to characterize the principle and the lost perfection, which, at a price, are to find a path to explore – ὁδῷ τινι –, with temporal extension (διάστημα) characterizing this path. H. Boersma wonders, along with other researchers, about the limits of διάστημα within the framework of the doctrine of *epektasis* fully illustrated in the *Life of Moses* and taken back up in the *Homilies on the Song of Songs*: if even in God the movement toward attaining

---

[4] Hom. XV, GNO VI, 458,10-459,1; Norris, 487.

[5] M. Alexandre, 'Protologie et eschatologie chez Grégoire de Nysse', in U. Bianchi (ed.), *Archè e telos. L'antropologia di Origene e di Gregorio di Nissa. Analisi storico-religiosa. Atti del Colloquio di Milano* (Milan, 1981), 122-59.

[6] *Homélies sur l'Ecclésiaste*, I 13, SC 416, 145. English translation by St. Hall, 45.

[7] Hom. XV, GNO VI, 458,18-2; trans. p. 324. In *De an. et res.*, ἀναστοιχείωσις is connected with ἀνάστασις (GNO III/3, 54,23-4).

[8] H. Boersma, 'Overcoming time and space: Gregory of Nyssa's Anagogical Theology', *Journal of Early Christian Studies* 20 (2012), 575-612; included in *id.*, *Embodiment and Virtue in Gregory of Nyssa* (2013), Chap. 1, Measured Body, 19-52.

the inaccessible is endless, is it not the case that Gregory imagines or conceives a sort of infinite space-time, even beyond death? The verses of the *Canticle*, organized as a dialogue between the bride and the groom, express precisely in the most concrete way the path without end of human life and the way in which the coming of Christ makes the 'recreation' of the original perfection possible. It is the whole mystery of salvation that Gregory's commentary highlights in the biblical book[9] and, paradoxically, it is the carnal, erotic aspect of the *Canticle* that becomes the place of a confession of faith whose key word may be *sarx*, the flesh of a humanity that is sinful and aspiring toward salvation, and the flesh of the bridegroom Word who 'became flesh'. Thus we must without doubt underline that this final work serenely recapitulates his previous theological battles, especially those against Eunomius and Apollinaris; to this effect, as soon as he judges it useful for the attention of his listeners and even for his own intention as part of his interpretation of the *Song*, he abandons the concrete, pictoral expression of the biblical text and translates it into a conceptual language that in the course of the reading appears as a synthesis of his theology. The place given to the eschatological dimension can be approached in three stages : 1) human life, an endless race; 2) the mystery of the flesh and the salvific movement of the incarnation; 3) the figures of beatitude – the optimism of the eschatological conceptions of Gregory of Nyssa.

2. An Endless 'Race' toward God: The Bride, Moses, and Paul

In her endless, hesitant, and sometimes erratic movement, the Bride appears to double for two other personages, Moses and Paul.[10] It is because they have several traits in common: they are seekers of God, one might say in contemporary language, always in motion and ready to take the risk of death.

2.1. *Three Personages for the Same Movement toward God*

The identification of the Bride with Moses is indeed suggested several times, and certain passages of the *Life of Moses* are clearly echoed.[11] From the first

---

[9] In this sense, see H. Boersma, 'Saving bodies: anagogical transposition in St Gregory of Nyssa's, Commentaries on the Song of Songs', *Ex Auditu* 20 (2010), 168-200, 170: 'The paradox is more than an interesting peculiarity: it points to what Gregory is convinced is the Song's ultimate concern, salvation itself' (Review accessible online on ATLA).

[10] This is an identification that pushes the distinction between masculine and feminine into the background – See V. Harrison, 'A Gender Reversal in Gregory of Nyssa's *First Homily on the Song of Songs*', *SP* 27 (1993), 34-8.

[11] Researchers were hesitant about the respective dates of the two works, but H. Dünzl gave convincing arguments about *Life of Moses'* anteriority (*cf.* H. Dünzl, 'Gregor von Nyssa's *Homilien zum Canticum* auf dem Hintergrund seiner *Vita Moysis*', *VC* 44 [1990], 371-81). Actually there

homily, we read: 'The bride Moses kissed the Bridegroom in the same way as the virgin in the Song who says *Let him kiss me with the kisses of his mouth* – φιλησάτω με ἀπὸ φιλημάτων στόματος αὐτοῦ' (*Song* 1:2), and through the face-to-face converse accorded him by God (as the Scripture testifies [see *Num* 12:8: στόμα κατὰ στόμα λαλήσω αὐτῷ], he became more intensely desirous of such kisses after these theophanies...'[12] In homily XI, which comments on *Song* 5:2-4, Gregory resumes the three stages of the life of Moses: 'The revelation of God to the great Moses began with light as its medium (see *Ex* 3:2), but afterwards God spoke to him through the medium of a cloud (*Ex* 19:9), and when he had become more lifted up and more perfect, he saw God in darkness – ἐν γνόφῳ τὸν θεὸν βλέπει'.[13] And then *Ex* 20:21 is explicitly cited, after which its equivalence with the bride's history is suggested: 'Now that we have thus interpreted these statements, we are bound to ask whether the words before us are compatible with what I have been saying'.[14] The whole beginning of the *Canticle* (with citations of *Song* 1:6; 1:2; 1:9 and 10) is repeated through the lens of the stages of the life of Moses and the situation of the Bride in *Song* 5:2 (who forms the object of the beginning of homily XI) defined in these terms: 'Now, however, she is already surrounded by the divine night, in which the Bridegroom draws near but is not manifest – ὑπὸ τῆς θείας νύκτος περιέχεται καθ' ἣν ὁ νυμφίος παραγίνεται μὲν οὐ φαίνεται δέ'[15] – the same experience of mystery: to see God without seeing Him. The term μυσταγωγία appears again in the discourse of Gregory – the same term that defines the σκοπός (goal) of the *Song* at the beginning of the first homily: 'What is the initiatory process (μυσταγωγία), then, that this night causes the soul to undergo? The Word touches her door'.[16] However, the resemblance between Moses and the Bride also relates to the purification that they must go through in order to approach the divine: the deed indicated in *Song* 5:3 ('*I have washed my feet. How shall I soil them?*') is in some way justified by the fact that 'furthermore, it is related that Moses, after, at God's command, he had liberated his feet from their dead clothing of skins upon entering the holy and luminous ground (see *Ex* 3:5), did not put those shoes back on'.[17] Even the silence or what is not said in the Scripture take on a meaning, which is a sign in our opinion that Gregory read into the texts two modes of narrating the same experience.

---

are several passages of the *Life of Moses* that are clearly evoked in the *HomCt*, whereas there is no allusion to the *Song* in the *Life of Moses*, in order to go in the direction of this anteriority of the *Life of Moses* with respect to *HomCt*.

[12] Hom. I, GNO VI, 31; Norris, 33.
[13] Hom. XI, GNO VI, 322,9-12; Norris, 339.
[14] Hom. XI, GNO VI, 323,10-12; Norris, 341.
[15] Hom. XI, GNO VI, 324,7-8; Norris, 343.
[16] Hom. XI, GNO VI, 324,12-3; Norris, 343.
[17] Hom. XI, GNO VI, 329,17-330,2; Norris, 349.

Paul is also compared to the Bride: commenting on *Song* 1:12 ('My spike-nard gave off his scent') in homily III, Gregory wrote: 'So it was with the Bride Paul (οὕτω καὶ Παῦλος, ἡ νύμφη). He imitated the Bridegroom by his virtues (1*Cor* 11:1), and inscribed within himself the unapproachable Beauty by means of their sweetness, and out of the fruits of the Spirit ... he said that he was "the aroma of Christ" (2*Cor* 2:15)'.[18] The omnipresence of Paul is not only linked to the repeated reference to the body of his letters. It is also Paul as a personality, a witness of his own experience of God, that suggests the comparison with the Bride: indeed they have in common the incessant movement that carries them toward God. The greatest mode of expression for this, for Gregory, is the verse of *Phil* 3:13, often repeated, sometimes by mere allusion.[19] However, at the same time the perhaps 'unidirectional' movement of Paul described in *Phil* 3:13, unfolds in more variated movements; thus in *Song* 3:2: 'I will arise, then, and go around the city', she 'circles', Gregory interprets, through the whole Angelic hierarchy.[20] Others, the guards who strike the Bride, 'the watchmen who go their rounds in the city – *Song* 5:7 – οἱ φύλακες οἱ κυκλοῦντες ἐν τῇ πόλει)'. However, the movements of the Bride appear equally as a succession of entrance and exit – the paradoxical equivalent of an ascension:

For this reason she always 'strains forward toward what lies ahead' (*Phil* 3:13). She does not stop departing from where she is, or working her way inwards where she has not yet been, or judging that what at every point appears great and marvelous to her is nonetheless inferior to what comes after it; for that which is ever in process of being discovered is at every point more lovely than what has already been apprehended. Just so Paul also died every day.[21]

The two verses *Song* 5:7 and *Phil* 3:13 that are so intimately intertwined, superimpose in this race, with the final allusion to 1*Cor* 15:31, the passage through death that is inseparable from the coming into the flesh.

Thus, three life stories (The Bride/Moses/Paul) are superimposed or intersecting with one another, and this corresponds to a scheme of three stages: life-death-obscure presence. None of them reaches the luminous presence: although the ascension of Paul to the third heaven, mentioned at the beginning of the eighth homily,[22] seems to be for Gregory a sign of a more accomplished mystical

---

[18] Hom. III, GNO VI, 91; Norris, 101.
[19] On the importance of *Phil* 3:13, see M. Canévet, *Grégoire de Nysse et l'herméneutique biblique* (Paris, 1983), 207-13; the verse is quoted nine times in the *Homilies on the Song of Songs*, suggesting a connection between the movements of the characters of the song and the race of Paul: *e.g.* in Hom. XII where we read about the bride: πάντοτε τοῖς ἔμπροσθεν ἐπεκτεινομένη – 'always stretched out toward what is ahead' (Hom. XII, GNO VI, 366,14-5; trans. p. 224).
[20] See Hom. VI, GNO VI, 182; Norris, 195.
[21] Hom. XII, GNO VI, 366,14-20; Norris, 385-7.
[22] Hom. VIII, GNO VI, 245,15-6; Norris, 257.

life that remains unfinished. Indeed, after having cited *Phil* 13:3, Gregory adds: '[Paul] shows that after that "third heaven" that he alone knew (for Moses told nothing about it in his cosmogony) and after the ineffable audition of the mysteries of paradise, he is still hastening toward something higher and never leaves off his ascent by setting the good he has already grasped as a limit to his desires'.[23] The accent is instead placed on the difference between Moses and Paul, within the perspective of a typological exegesis where the Pauline preaching and his very life manifest the accomplishment of what Moses prefigures.

2.2. *A Race that is an Exchange of Movement*

The Bride, Moses, and Paul are running toward God – but in the *Song* and the *Homilies on the Song*, the Bride has a 'vis-à-vis', so to speak, the Bridegroom who is himself in movement. Here we find the *drama*, the theatrical action and the game of *prosopological* exegesis – to cite the explanation of M.J. Rondeau:[24] 'When he considers the text as a drama, the exegete examines the relations of the different characters to each other... The characters are defined by their mutual relations'. Through this exchange of words/dialogue, the course of the Bride is sustained by the movement of the Word himself, the very movement of the incarnation. It is thus fitting to take a closer look at the subject of the words of movement: an ascending and descending movement. And unlike the Bride compared to Moses and Paul, the Bridegroom does not have a 'double', he is the Word, who has experienced the trial of the flesh. He is 'descended', according to the word given to the Bridegroom in *Song* 5:1 ('I have come down into my garden') and confirmed by the word of the Spouse in *Song* 6:3, on which Gregory comments at the beginning of homily XV: 'Hence when we hear *My kinsman has descended into his garden*, we learn the mystery of the gospel, since each of these terms illuminates the mystical meaning of the passage. ... it is right and appropriate that God-manifest-in-flesh be assigned the title "kinsman"'.[25] Another effect of dialogue and encounter is the Bridegroom who had triggered the initial movement of the Bride: 'Arise ... come' (*Song* 2:10b, commented on in Homily V).

It has been said above how, in the dialogue between the Bridegroom and the Bride, as interpreted by Gregory of Nyssa, two other personages do not cease to get involved, Moses and even more so Paul: the experience of Moses, commented on in the *Life of Moses*, alternates between light and shadow up until

---

[23] Hom. VIII, GNO VI, 245,17-22; Norris, 259. The last part of the phrase emphasizes how the doctrine of *epektasis* is more appropriate to Paul than to Moses – οὐ λήγει τῆς ἀναβάσεως οὐδέποτε τὸ καταλαμβανόμενον ἀγαθὸν ὅρον τῆς ἐπιθυμίας ποιούμενος.

[24] In retracing the history of the patristic exegesis of the Psalter, Marie-Josèphe Rondeau highlights the importance of this method: *Les commentaires patristiques du Psautier*, 2 vol. (Rome, 1982), vol. I 43-8, 43.

[25] Hom. XV, GNO VI, 436,4-6; Norris, 463.

the luminous darkness of Sinai and that of Paul leads to entry into a mystery of life and death. The words exchanged in the *Song of Songs* become for Gregory of Nyssa words of the history of salvation – a movement inscribed in time, and the decisive moment is the coming of the Bridegroom, the Word, in the flesh – the descending of the Bridegroom into the garden, preceded by the calls he makes to the Bride.

Concerning this endless movement, we should clarify that it is inscribed in places, like the mountain that is to be climbed by Moses; in the *Song* it is the city, the garden, and the fields... Each place is interpreted symbolically, but to return to the analyses of A. Conway-Jones,[26] the finish-line of the race is the entrance into the 'holy of holies', the image of the tabernacle thus superimposes itself over that of creation. And we read in homily V, with a new reference to *Phil* 3:13: 'If then the soul ... is shown not truly to have seized her goal, what is likely to become of us, or in what category may those be reckoned who have not yet drawn near even to the entrances into the sanctuaries of contemplation?'[27] From the first homily onward, Gregory resorts to this image of the ἄδυτον: 'Let each depart from himself and get beyond the material cosmos and ascend somehow, by way of impassibility, into paradise, and having by purity been made like to God, let him in this fashion journey to the inner shrine of the mysteries manifested to us in this book'.[28] With the image of the holy of holies we connect the association between the Bride and Moses, but the image of the sanctuary is evidently more present in the *Life of Moses*.[29]

Is this place finally reached?[30] The entrance into the inaccessible does not mean immediate and full knowledge, to which gives witness Gregory's explanation of the dew (*Song* 5:2: 'My head is covered with dew'): '[for one who has entered the place of things beyond our grasp and vision] ... it is enough if Truth drizzles down knowledge of them by way of thoughts that are subtle and only just discernible, pouring out reason's drop through persons who are holy and inspired'.[31] If the race is endless, even beyond death, if access to the knowledge of God remains progressive, is it not the case that even the great beyond is inscribed within duration, a διάστημα? The response of Gregory to this

---

[26] See below n. 29.

[27] Hom. V, GNO VI, 138,17-8; Norris, 151.

[28] Hom. I, GNO VI, 25,8-10; Norris, 27.

[29] See the commentaries of A. Conway-Jones of the *Life of Moses* II 188, p. 188-202.

[30] In homily XI, one finds the term ἄδυτον to comment on the journey of the soul compared to that of Moses (GNO VI, 323,3-4: ἐντὸς τῶν ἀδύτων τῆς θεογνωσίας, the phrase ending with the quote from *Ex* 20:21).

[31] Hom. XI, GNO VI, 326,2-5; Norris, 345 (ἀγαπητὸν εἰ λεπταῖς τισι καὶ ἀμυδραῖς διανοίαις ἐπιψεκάζοι τὴν γνῶσιν αὐτῶν ἡ ἀλήθεια διὰ τῶν ἁγίων τε καὶ θεοφορουμένων τῆς λογικῆς σταγόνος ἀπορρεούσης. We note, along these lines, the use of the rare verb ἐπιψεκάζειν, used willingly by Philo – for example, concerning the cloud of *Ex* 14:14 (*Quis heres*, 204) or the manna (*De fuga*, 138). Is it enough to see in the choice of this verb by Gregory an influence of Philo? It is difficult to prove!

question remains paradoxical, so it seems to us, and we shall attempt to analyze it in the last part.

However, besides the two principal protagonists, the Bridegroom and the Bride, there intervene on several occasions the 'maiden daughters' of Jerusalem and the 'friends of the Bridegroom';[32] their role, within the interpretation of Gregory, is also inserted into the eschatological aim of the *Song*. The maidens, like the friends, address the Bride and not the Bridegroom. The maidens (*Song* 1:4; 2:7; 5:7; 6:1; 6:9) are carried by a desire to imitate the Bride and to receive from her testimony and teaching – and it is the growth of the Church that is thus symbolized: 'We will run after you…' (*Song* 1:4). The following expression unveils in the Word the dispensation of the Church. Those who were first made disciples by grace and became 'eyewitnesses … of the Word' (*Lk* 1:2) did not keep the Good to themselves. Rather did they work the same grace, by transmission, in those who were their companions'.[33] If the Bride encourages them,[34] she is also attentive to their question (*Song* 5:9: 'What is your kinsman … ?') and, by her response, she 'initiates the young women into the truth'.[35] The relation between the Bride and the maidens is that of a witness and apostle and a believer, as it is expressed in the opening of homily XV concerning *Song* 6:1, where Gregory establishes a parallel between the Apostles and the Bride. He notes: 'This, then, is the outward and literal guidance with which the text provides the maidens; from it they learn both where he is and where he is looking'.[36] Thus, it is the transmission of faith and the knowledge of God that the exchange of words between the Bride and the maidens translates – the mystery of the Church.

As for the friends of the Bridegroom, they face the Bride to advise her (*Song* 1:8, but they also honor her – *Song* 3:6-8 – in words that do not seem to be an address of a precise interlocutor. Gregory seeks to explain the 'stupor' of the friends of the Bridegroom and for this purpose he brings together the words that they pronounce (*Song* 1:8; 1:11; 3:6)[37] in honor of the Bride, not for her beauty alone but because they perceive her as a model of ascension

---

[32] The recognition that there are changes of interlocutor poses textual problems on several occasions, already underlined by Origen: *Philocalie. Sur les Écritures*, 7 ('the confusion of the personages who speak in the Scriptures [*Song of Songs* and *Acts*]', [our translation] SC 302, éd M. Harl [Paris, 1983]). See also Origène, *Commentaire sur le Cantique des Cantiques*. The manuscript tradition of the *Canticle* also gives way to this difficulty – see *Le Cantique des Cantiques*, *Bible d'Alexandrie*, by J.-M. Auwers (Paris, 2019). Other personages are mentioned: the concubines and queens (Homily XV, *Song* 6), or the 'powerful ones surrounding the litter of Solomon' (Hom. VI, *Song* 3:7) and there are other personages, but they do not express themselves directly and do not have a 'role' in the 'drama'.

[33] Hom. I, GNO VI, 40,13-7; Norris, 43.

[34] *Song* 2:7 – Hom. IV, GNO VI, 129,21-130,1; Norris, 143: 'And what she utters is an exhortation, brought forward with an oath, always to increase and multiply love'.

[35] ἡ νύμφη μυσταγῶγει τὰς νεάνιδας (Hom. XIII, GNO VI, 387,2; Norris, 407).

[36] Hom. XV, GNO VI, 435; Norris, 463.

[37] Hom. VI, GNO VI, 185-6; Norris, 197-9.

toward God. It is notable that when discussing them Gregory makes reference to theater characters,[38] to the mobility of certain roles: in *Song* 3:7-8, commenting on what is said of the 'litter of Solomon', Gregory is well aware to add to this what is said in the historical books (1*Kgs* 7 and 10), and the friends of the Bridegroom are thus intermediary figures between the King and the Bride: '... [they] point out to her the beauty of the royal bed, so as to induce the Bride to desire a divine and unspotted cohabitation with the Bridegroom[39] – εἰς ἐπιθυμίαν ... τῆς θείας τε καὶ ἀχράντου μετ' αὐτοῦ συμβιώσεως; she is also their model, even more so a witness, as Gregory concludes concerning *Song* 4:9: 'In her (= the Bride) they saw the Invisible more clearly – τρανότερον ἐν αὐτῇ τὸν ἀόρατον βλέπουσιν'.[40]

The presence of these two groups enriches the scenario of the *Song* and contributes to make way for the ecclesial interpretation that will especially have its place in the final two homilies. To the Church are linked simultaneously both the concept of *plerôma*, so present in Gregory's theology and which speaks of the plenitude and perfection of the Body of Christ, and also that of growth, suggested in the verse of *Eph* 4:13, cited in homily VIII – it is this question of the growth of the Church, in our opinion, that closely links ecclesiology and eschatology. What is the necessary time for this growth? Again there is the question of space-time, on access to the place of salvation, and on the final number of the saved.

After the developments concerning the ascension of Moses leading up to the encounter with God in the luminous cloud, the movement in the *Homilies on the Song* no longer appear linear and especially God Himself, in the abasement of the incarnation – which is also movement – colors the doctrine of the *epektasis*: only the necessary realism of the incarnation, by means of the words and action of the Bridegroom-Word, helps to bring to realization this movement of the desire of the Bride. And many of the concrete evocations and images of the *Song* come, in the commentary of Gregory, to illustrate or make palpable the salvific coming of the Word in flesh.

3. A Deployment of Images to Express the Expectation of Salvation

Four sets of images will further grab our attention, those which entail life and death and in this sense are more specifically adapted to the mystery of the incarnation: the evocation of the seasons; the house of wine (red color); myrrh

---

[38] Hom. VI, GNO VI, 185-6. 'For consider an example: in theatrical performances, even though it is the same actors who take the parts assigned them in the drama, nevertheless different persons seem to appear in different instances as the actors alter their look by changing their masks' (Norris, 199).

[39] Hom. VI, GNO VI, 190,2-3; Norris, 203.

[40] Hom. VIII, GNO VI, 256,21-257,1; Norris, 269.

and seasons. With even greater coherence, the descriptions of the body of the Bride and that of the Bridegroom, put in relation with the Pauline metaphor of the head and of the body (1*Cor* 12:12-31) gives Gregory an opportunity to display the ecclesial dimension of the *Song*. In fact, different parts of the body are understood as symbols of this or that function within the Church, for example, 'the golden hands' of the Bridegroom that 'administer the common goods of the church'.[41] But the growth toward which the Church is called once again directs Gregory's interpretation toward eschatology.

3.1. *From Winter to Spring, Life and Its Promises: The Wine of the Kingdom*

While temporality was the negative mark of the creature distant from God, and is in some sense connected with evil, the coming of Christ restores to it a positive value, even to the point, it seems to us, of making fragile the distinction between created and uncreated. The passage of time is signified by the succession of seasons, by the passage of winter to spring: the latter results in the first fruits of the fig tree (*Song* 2:13a) and it is followed by the flowering of the vines: 'For behold, the winter is past ... the flowers are seen on the earth' (*Song* 2:11-2). Gregory comments on these verses in two stages. Winter is at first a symbolic expression of the different forms of evil: 'Winter, rain, and drops are the same; each of the names labels some particular trial ... [During winter] all things mimic the misery of death: the blossom is killed; the grass of the field dies'. But, 'by taking them in a transferred, figural sense – τὰ τοιαῦτα πάντα μεταλαμβάνων εἰς τροπικὴν σημασίαν', one finds the origin of these *sadnesses* of winter in the ceaselessly repeated evil chosen by human beings: 'The winter of disobedience having dried up the root. The blossom was shaken off and fell to the earth'.[42] The return to life is not possible until the coming of 'the One who works in us the springtime of souls'[43]: The good is restored and the men turn to him again by choosing the virtuous life.[44] With the seasons and his symbolic explanation of the springtime that is the coming of Christ, Gregory is not satisfied with the metaphor: 'This season, he says, is a halfway house between two others-between wintry desolation and the summer's sharing in the harvest – ὁ δὲ καιρὸς οὗτος μεθόριός ἐστιν τῶν δύο καιρῶν'.

---

[41] Hom. XIV, GNO VI, 407; Norris, 433. See the same in Homily VII, the teeth and lips of the bride refer to those who have a teaching function in the Church and in the rest of Homily XIV, the 'legs' of the Bridegroom symbolize the 'columns of the Church'.

[42] Hom. V, GNO VI, 151,8-9, 153,3-4; Norris, 165.

[43] Hom. V, GNO VI, 153,9-10; Norris, 165 – ἐλθόντος τοῦ τὸ ἔαρ ἡμῖν τῶν ψυχῶν ἐμποιήσαντος.

[44] This symbolism of the succession of seasons and the paschal significance of the seasons is particularly developed in the *Paschal Homilies* of Ephrem, not unconnected with the Lenten question (SC 502, French translation of F. Cassingena-Trévédy, who marks as a parallel in his introduction the praise of springtime made by Gregory in his twelfth letter).

The qualification of spring as μεθόριος[45] recalls the mediating function of Christ, making the promised summer the fulfillment: 'And what "summer" means, Gregory adds, you know well enough from the words of the Lord, which say: "The harvest is the consummation of the age" (*Mt* 13:39)'.[46] The evocation of summer is made through the image of the 'vines in flower', promise of wine, promise 'of a good and sober drunkenness.[47] What I am referring to is the drunkenness that occasions that self-transcendence by which people move out of the material sphere toward what is more divine'.[48] We shall return at the end of this article to this utilization of ἔκστασις ('self-transcendence', here) to say that the climb to God passes through the 'moving out of the material sphere', as Gregory says it here.

The commentary of *Song* 2:13 ('Arise...') completes the commentary on the seasons by reintroducing – thanks to the repetition of the call of the Bridegroom 'Arise', already put forth in *Song* 2:10 – the dynamic of a ceaseless movement: 'For to one who has risen up in this manner there will never be wanting an up-rising without end; nor for one who runs to the Lord will opportunity for the divine race be used up[49] for the one who runs to the Lord'. We should note again the mention of a space (εὐρυχωρία - Norris' translation by 'opportunity' is too much abstract) that seems unlimited.

3.2. *The Virtues of the Myrrh*

Interpreted through the lens of *Jn* 1:14 ('the Word became flesh') and of 1*Tim* 3:16[50] ('[He] who was manifested in the flesh'), several verses of *Song* 5, commented on in homilies X to XIII, refocus the discourse of Gregory on the

---

[45] Hom. V, GNO VI, 155,15-6; Norris, 167. On the importance of the term, see J. Daniélou, 'La notion de confins (*methorios*) chez Grégoire de Nysse', *RSR* 49 (1961), 161-87; the article '*methorios*' of G. Maspero in the *Brill Dictionary of Gregory of Nyssa*, s. v.

[46] Hom. V, GNO VI, 155; Norris, 169.

[47] Concerning this 'sober drunkenness' we refer along with Langerbeck to the study of H. Lewy, *Sobria ebrietas. Untersuchungen zur Geschichte der antiken Mystik* (Giessen, 1929).

[48] Hom. V, GNO VI, 156,19-20; Norris, 169. In Homily III, already, the expression 'my kinsman is for me a cluster of grape blossoms – βότρυς τῆς κύπρου ἀδελφιδός μου ἐμοί' (*Song* 1:14a) is read as the announcement of the blood of the Passion and a promise of a fruit that will not come to full maturity until 'the fullness of the times' (Hom. III, GNO VI, 97,1; Norris' translation – cf. *Gal* 4:4). The eschatological significance of this 'sober drunkenness' is affirmed in the following homilies: Hom. X, GNO VI, 308,17-8; Hom. XII, GNO VI, 362,12.

[49] Hom. VI, GNO VI, 159,13-5; Norris, 171.

[50] The 'manifestation' in the flesh is a particular match to the manner in which the verses of the *Song* speak concerning the visibility (palpable and impalpable at once) of the Bridegroom. It is important then to recall that 1*Tim* 3:16, recurring in the *Homilies on the Song of Songs*, plays a decisive role in the Pauline argumentation against Apollinarius, see F. Vinel, 'Grégoire de Nysse et la référence aux épîtres pauliniennes dans le *Contre Apollinaire*', in O. Munnich, M. Cassin and H. Grelier (eds), *Grégoire de Nysse: la Bible dans la construction de son discours* (Paris, 2013), 101-13, 103-7 on the role of 1*Tim* 3:16 as a structuring reference of the treatise. To a lesser extent,

incarnation of the Word, his descent in the flesh (*Song* 5:1: 'I have come into my garden') and his manifestation.[51] However, the evocation of myrrh with spices, of bread and honey, of wine and milk, as well as the call to 'be drunken'[52] closely associates incarnation with the promise of salvation that is already partially present.

In the New Testament, myrrh evokes, as we know, the passion and burial of Christ.[53] In our homily, Gregory associates the death of Christ with the necessary purification, by 'mortification' (see *Col* 3:5), of those who aspire to participate in the death and resurrection of Christ, to become 'the aroma of Christ'[54] according to the Pauline expression recalled by Gregory. In an article published in 2002, Annick Lallemand was interested in saffron and cinnamon,[55] both perfumes and plants, having healing properties. Moreover, with the symbolism of myrrh, the charm of perfumes is heavily weighed down by an eschatological telos. 'But no one becomes a participant in the divine glory without first being conformed to the likeness of death', an affirmation that precedes the explanation given in Homily IX[56] of the 'myrrh and aloe' (*Song* 4:14) by which 'is meant a sharing in burial (even as the sublime Gospel records that the One who tasted death on our behalf [*Heb* 2:9] was prepared for his burial by these very spices [*Jn* 19:39])'. It is noteworthy that Gregory stops at each mention of myrrh to recall this symbolism.[57]

As a sign of death and burial, however, myrrh is also a sign of life and healing[58] for those who receive the testimony of truth and are baptized into Christ: 'His lips are lilies, dropping abundant myrrh' (*Song* 5:13) is indeed in

the remark could be extended to the *Against Eunomius*. This is one of the features of the recapitulative scope of the *Homilies on the Song of Songs* within Gregory's theology.

[51] See the double interpretation of the symbol of the hand in *Song* 5:4: The 'hand' of the Beloved (*Song* 5:4: 'My beloved put his hand through the opening') is at once the sign of the creative work ('all things were made by him') and the symbol of the coming of the Word in humanity (Hom. XI, GNO VI, 338). And in the paragraph that ends shortly after this Homily XI, we perceive that Gregory is conscious of the importance of this double interpretation of the hand: 'One of them lays it down that the divine nature is altogether incomprehensible and incomparable and so is known solely by its activity. The second asserts that in these words the grace of gospel was announced ahead of time by the Bride' (*ibid.*, 339,5-9; Norris, 357).

[52] See *Song* 5:1b-d: ἐτρύγησα σμύρναν μου μετὰ ἀρωμάτων μου, ἔφαγον ἄρτον μου μετὰ μέλιτός μου. Φάγετε, οἱ πλησίον μου, καὶ πίετε καὶ μεθύσθητε, ἀδελφοί μου.

[53] *Lk* 23:56.

[54] *2Cor* 2:15, cited several times in the Homilies.

[55] A. Lallemand, 'Le safran et le cinnamome dans les *Homélies sur le Cantique* de Grégoire de Nysse', *L'antiquité classique* 71 (2002), 121-30.

[56] Hom. IX, GNO VI, 290,6-7; Norris, 305 – Οὐδεὶς δὲ κοινωνὸς τῆς τοῦ θεοῦ γίνεται δόξης μὴ σύμμορφος πρῶτον τῷ ὁμοιώματι τοῦ θανάτου γενόμενος. For the rest of the citation, *ibid.*, 290,10-15 Norris, 305-7.

[57] See Hom. VI (GNO VI, 189; Norris, 201), Hom. VII (GNO VI, 243; Norris, 253), Hom. XII (GNO VI, 343-4; Norris, 363), Hom. XIV (GNO VI, 404; Norris, 427-8).

[58] On this theme, see the rich set of texts analyzed by B. Caseau, 'Parfum et guérison dans le christianisme ancien et byzantin: des huiles parfumées des médecins au myron des saints byzantins',

Homily XIV the place of a development on the dissemination of the faith –
Gregory takes the conversion of Thecla[59] through the word of Paul as an
example, and then adds that of Peter's role with the conversion of Cornelius
(*Acts* 10) – and the consequent growth of the Church. Like the vine, myrrh
produces fruit, and Gregory underlines the evidence for his interpretation: 'But
there is no need to spin out our discourse about these matters. The meaning has
become plain through what has already been said: how the church's mouth
becomes a lily, and myrrh drips from the lily, and the soul of its recipients is
filled with these drops'[60] – the economy of salvation has its fulfillment in the
growth of the Church, and myrrh gives life. The descriptions of the bodies of
the Bride and the Bridegroom and the mention of different parts of the bodies
in the poetry of the *Song*, like a 'blason', a poetic form used during French
Renaissance, are read, thanks to the likeness to 1*Cor* 12, as an announcement
of the mystery of the Church like nowhere else in Gregory's work, and its
eschatological scope will be analyzed. But first, a few reminders about the
prophetic beauty of these bodies.

3.3. *Body of the Bride, Body of the Bridegroom – The Pleromatic Growth of the Church, The Body of Christ*

In the fifteen homilies, the five passages of the *Song*[61] that mention parts of
the body of the Bridegroom or Bride give rise to a commentary, and Gregory
of Nyssa demonstrates his allegorical skill, carefully giving meaning to every
detail. However, as he points out in the Prologue to the *Homilies*, it is not so
much the exegetical method as defining the theological scope of the biblical
book that matters to him[62] and, in this sense, the reconciliation between the
allusion to the parts of the body along with 1*Cor* 12 is immediately brought
to light, and it determines the ecclesiological meaning given to these verses.
The important thing to note for our eschatological perspective is the dynamic
of growth that gives the deep meaning of the corporeal metaphors, both of
the *Song* and the Pauline epistle – just as the Bride and Paul are, as we have seen,
in an endless movement, always 'straining forward', the body never ceases to

---

in V. Boudon-Millot and B. Pouderon (eds), *Les Pères de l'Église face à la science médicale de leur temps* (Paris, 2005), 141-91.

[59] See the story of *Actes de Paul* (F. Bovon and P. Geoltrain [eds], *Écrits apocryphes chrétiens*, vol. I [Paris, 1997] – the history of Thecla is found in Chapters III and IV). As Langerbeck notes (GNO VI, 405), Gregory also mentions the personage of Thecla in the *Life of Macrina* (2, 25-7, SC 178). On the development of the cult of Thecla in Asia Minor, see the study of S.J. Davis, *The Cult of Saint Thecla: A Tradition of Women's Piety in Late Antiquity* (Oxford, 2001) – the first part is about the cult of Thecla in Asia Minor (p. 1-80).

[60] Hom. XIV, GNO VI, 406,2-6; Norris, 431.

[61] *Song* 4:1-7; 4:10-2; 5:10-2 and 13-6; 5:6-9.

[62] See Prologue, GNO VI, 5-6; Norris, 5-6.

grow thanks to Christ who 'ever sanctifies the common dough of that nature through its first fruits, nourishing his body, the church, in the persons of those who are united to him in the fellowship of the mystery'.[63] The metaphor that refers to the legs of the Bridegroom as 'marble pillars' (*Song* 5:15) ensures the link with the role of those who are 'the pillars of the Church'[64] in Homily XIV. The nourishing image (τρέφων in the passage we have just cited) recalls the charism of the Apostle, 'the wet nurse of newborn in the Church'[65] (allusion to 1*Thess* 2:7). Finally, in Homily XV there is the distinction between the 'young maidens' 'still young in spiritual stature',[66] the 'queens', and the 'concubines' who symbolize different stages of growth in the virtuous and spiritual life. Does the birth of faith and incorporation into the Church go hand in hand, for Gregory, with the idea of unlimited growth?

There is a convergence, or, to borrow one of Gregory of Nyssa's favorite terms, an *akolouthia* of all these images, as if a strong link associated poetry and theology. It is now necessary to see how Gregory himself cares to synthetically and dogmatically translate the meaning that is so difficult for the human intellect to grasp: a teaching on the ultimate ends.

4. A Happy Eschatology: Figures of the Beatitude

Two central questions about Gregory's eschatological conceptions have arisen and have remained suspended in the previous analyses: that of the *diastèma*, of the temporality which, with the image of the endless race (see Part I), seems to go past the created and characterizes the beyond; the second relates to the way in which Gregory solves the apparent antinomy between his recurring assertion of the growth of the body of the Church, in other words, of the number of those saved, and that of the pleromatic character – full plenitude – of life in the end times. We shall return to these questions, but, in the end, we may ask whether Gregory gives a clear response? His responses to the objections of Eunomius or Apollinaris were argued, but with the reminder that 'we only know in part' (1*Cor* 13:9-12). Similarly, the last section of the *Catechetical Discourse* focuses precisely on considering the promised eternal goods, 'what no eye has seen, no ear has heard, no human heart has conceived'.[67] This verse of 1*Cor* 2:9 is dear to Gregory of Nyssa, in that it serves to describe the

---

[63] Hom. XIII, GNO VI, 381,21-382,2; Norris, 403.
[64] Hom. XIV, GNO VI, 415,20; Norris, 441. A similar interpretation starting from the description of the tabernacle is found in the *Life of Moses* II 184.
[65] Hom. XIV, GNO VI, 399,16-7; Norris, 423: τροφὸς τῶν ἀρτιγενῶν ἐν τῇ ἐκκλησίᾳ.
[66] Hom. XV, GNO VI, 460,20-1; Norris, 489.
[67] Gregory of Nyssa, *Catechetical Discourse* XL, l. 67-92, French Translation by R. Winling, SC 453 (Paris, 2000).

contemplation of God in the *Life of Moses* (II 157), or the mystery of life in God in *Homily XI on the Song of Songs*:

Perhaps, in the age to come, when everything that is seen passes away in accordance with the Lord's word to the effect that 'the heaven and the earth shall pass away' (*Mt* 24:35), and we are transported into that life that transcends sight and hearing and thinking, then no longer shall we know the Good's nature 'in part' (*cf. 1Cor* 13:9) as we do now, nor shall the transcendent be conceived by way of the workings of things that appear. On the contrary, the form of the ineffable Blessedness shall be apprehended in another fashion, and the mode of its fruition will be different, a mode that cannot now 'enter into the human heart' (*cf. 1Cor* 2:9).[68]

'Perhaps', ἴσως, two allusions to the verse of Paul in these lines and these apophatic reminders are not lacking in the *Homilies*.

4.1. *From Desire to Desire, 'from Beginning to Beginning' – Is there an End to Temporality?*

The desire to know, the desire to see, the desire to love: the amorous connotations of the *Song of Songs* are obviously ideal gateways to attempt to speak of this endless capacity for desire inscribed in the human being; and it is not surprising that the verse of *1Cor* 2:9 is also used to address this subject in the preamble of Homily VII:

Neither, moreover, does the one who is mounting up ever cease to promote one starting point into another, nor does the starting point of ever-greater things find fulfillment simply in itself. For the desire of the soul that is ascending never rests content with what has been known. In turn mounting upwards by way of one greater desire toward another that surpasses it, that soul is always journeying toward the infinite by way of higher things.[69]

It is not without importance to note that Gregory's long sentence ends with the expression πρὸς τὸ ἀόριστον. Throughout the opening, Gregory gives the theological meaning of *Song* 4:8 in advance. The rise is at once a sign of the growing desire and of the progressive purification of desire – a purification affected by the 'mortifications' that we have already mentioned (see above, in connection with myrrh) – and also a sign, since it knows no end, that the object of desire remains inaccessible. Martin Laird, who revisited the question of desire in the *Homilies on the Song of Songs*, observes that there is a point of divergence between Origen and Gregory; according to him, 'the pedagogy of the *Song of Songs* focuses, unlike Origen, on exposing desire to the apophatic'.[70]

---

[68] Hom. XI, GNO VI, 336,1-6 and 7-9; Norris, 355 – we used 'perhaps' to translate ἴσως (the same in the French translation, 'peut-être'), instead of Norris' 'in the same way'.

[69] Hom. VIII, GNO VI, 247,12-8; Norris, 261.

[70] M. Laird, 'Under Solomon's Tutelage: The Education of Desire in the *Homilies on the Song of Songs*', in S. Coakley (ed.), *Re-Thinking Gregory of Nyssa* (Oxford, 2003), 77-95.

His article shows how this understanding of infinite desire is inscribed in the logic of the rest of Gregory's work.[71] The purification of desire with regard to the created realities is already mostly accomplished, since it had been proposed with the *Proverbs* and *Ecclesiastes*; concerning the prologue of the *Homilies on the Song of Songs*, Laird notes that the union with God is defined as 'incorporeal, spiritual, and undefiled marriage – ἡ ἀσώματός τε καὶ πνευματικὴ καὶ ἀμόλυντος τοῦ θεοῦ συζυγία'.[72] Henceforth, therefore, through the nuptial dialogue of the *Song*, this purification rests in the fact that desire infinitely experiences the elusive character of the One who is desired – the desire becoming more and more ἀπαθὲς πάθος.[73] The apprehension of eschatological realities can henceforth only be ineffable – which agrees with Gregory's statements in the *Catechetical Discourse* (see above). The darkness of the *Life of Moses* meets the mystagogy of the *Song*.

But does such an infinite desire not presuppose that the duration is rooted in eternity itself? On this point, let us summarize the article of H. Boersma that was already cited:[74] Beginning with the state of the research, he defines two opposed positions that differ according to whether or not the *eschaton* retains a spatial-temporal dimension.[75] Through the question of the *diastèma*, two central aspects of Gregory's doctrine are at issue: Does the affirmation that a *diastemic* expansion continues after death undermine the distinction between created and uncreated, which is so fundamental for Gregory? And inversely, if all expansion disappears into the hereafter, does it not mean that the resurrected are confused with the divine, in a sort of fusion? Maintaining a spatial-temporal expansion, which is consistent with the conception of the *epektasis*, would then be the possibility of retaining the distinction of nature between created and uncreated, and of making room for the idea of union as a participation in the divine. The response of Boersma moves through the examination of several texts, in particular the last *Homilies on Ecclesiastes* and the place given to *kairos* and *eukairia*, concepts of times without duration – if we can imagine this! –, but it is in the *De Tridui Spatio* that the overcoming of the human categories of space-time is in play, thanks to which Boersma names 'a Christological

---

[71] Building on the recent research of M. Hart, J. Behr, and R. Williams, which sets in a series, if you will, the *De virginitate*, the *De hominis opificio*, the *De anima et resurrectione*, and it refers to the broader study of M. Ludlow, *Universal Salvation: Eschatology in the Thought of Gregory of Nyssa and K. Rahner* (Oxford, 2000), on the purification of desire.

[72] Hom. I, GNO VI, 15,14-5; Norris, 15.

[73] See the definition of Gregory's *apatheia* proposed by M. Ludlow: 'Ἀπαθεία is thus not the absence of desire but freedom from any materialistic impulse or passion', cited by M. Laird, 'Under Solomon's Tutelage' (2003), 79. This may sound reminiscent of the *Phaedrus*, but the role assigned to the Bridegroom in the *Song* emphasizes that this cannot be done without the condescension of the Word made flesh (see II above).

[74] See H. Boersma, 'Overcoming time and space: Gregory of Nyssa's Anagogical Theology' (2012).

[75] *Ibid.* 576-80.

realignment of time'.[76] It is this intuition, or conviction, that is expressed in the *De Tridui Spatio*: 'You see what world this day is ushering in, this "day the Lord has made" and that the Prophet says it is neither a day like the other days nor a night like the other nights'.[77] In the paschal mystery, which the liturgy celebrates, the *eschaton* intrudes into created time, and the explanations of Gregory of Nyssa on 'the eighth day', in his commentary on *Psalm* 6, suppose – Boersma says – a bracketing of the *diastemic* character of the eighth day.[78] In our opinion, this is to recognize that Gregory is in a paradoxical position, which does not truly stop, and he keeps in his discourse the mythical and analogous categories of 'heaven' and 'paradise'.[79] The way in which Gregory uses the concept of *epektasis* in the *Homilies on the Song of Songs* can accurately symbolize what from this passage is incomprehensible and indescribable from time to 'non-time', from one form of a *diastèma* to another. What, in fact, is this 'departure from self' evoked in Homily I?[80] It is directed toward the divine realities. In Homily X, there is clearly participation in the Eucharist that makes it possible.[81]

4.2. *What Place is Left for the Final Judgment?*

What place does this leave for the theme of the Final Judgment? The reflection on sin as the source of death has a place in the *Song*; however, we would suggest that it is only a minor place.

In commenting on the eschatological aspects of the *Homilies on the Beatitudes*, Monique Alexandre[82] highlighted the way in which, 'the reason for the

---

[76] *Ibid.* 591-7.

[77] Our translation. French Translation by M. Canévet, in *Grégoire de Nysse, Le mystère pascal* (Paris, 1994), 51.

[78] *Ibid.* 603. The mystery of the eighth day is that it is both in time and outside of time, a paradox that assumes in a way the paschal liturgy ('For the eighth day' is the title of *Psalm* 6 – commentary of Gregory of Nyssa in GNO V, 176-93).

[79] It is interesting that, concerning these, Boersma endeavours to propose Gregory's definition of the matter: 'Gregory chooses to define matter in such a way that it is, potentially at least, capable of the adiastemic life of the eschaton (and, by implication, of the original paradisal state)', so H. Boersma, 'Overcoming time and space: Gregory of Nyssa's Anagogical Theology' (2012), 605. A careful re-reading of *In Hexaemeron* would be necessary in order to advance on this issue, largely addressed in the thesis of F. Dubois: *Le corps comme un syndrome. Une théorie de la matière chez Grégoire de Nysse*, Collection Patrimoines (Paris, 2018).

[80] See the quoted text on p. 85.

[81] See GNO VI, Hom. X, p. 310-1; Norris, p. 327 : the vision of Peter in *Acts* 10:10-6 has just been recalled and Gregory concludes on the theme of sober drunkenness: '... it is the drunkenness of this sort that is occasioned by the wine that the Lord sets before his companions – a drunkenness that causes the soul to depart (*ekstasis*) from itself in the direction of things more divine' (we translate 'to depart from itself' instead of Norris' 'to move out of itself').

[82] Monique Alexandre, 'Perspectives eschatologiques dans les *Homélies sur les Béatitudes* de Grégoire de Nysse', in H.R. Drobner and A. Viciano (eds), *Gregory of Nyssa: Homilies on the*

judgment several times comes to be superimposed, so to speak, over the text of the Beatitudes, which is absent'; also present is the theme of the 'healthy fear': to live as a call to move away from evil and sin. The pericope of *Mt* 25, the paradigm of the discourse on Judgment so to speak, is not absent from the homilies on the *Song*. In *Song* 1:8 the image of the Bride [leading] the goats to graze' is, for Gregory, an easy link with that of the Shepherd separating the sheep and goats, and Homily II ends with the address to the Bride as to the listeners of Jesus's invitation in *Mt* 25:34 ('Come, you who are blessed by my Father ...').

The violent separation of the sheep and goats is, however, not the last word of the Shepherd Bridegroom. Indeed, the 'grazing among the lilies' and the effect of the inclusion of the trifold repetition (*Song* 1:7; 1:8; 6:3) of the verb ποιμαίνω merits some attention. In *Song* 6:3 ('I am for my kinsman, and my kinsman is for me; he grazes his flock among the lilies'),[83] it is now the Bride-groom who acts, as in response to the questioning of the Bride: 'Speak to me, you whom my soul loves, where you pasture your flock?' (*Song* 1:7). The sym-bolism of the lily speaks both of the recovered purity of the Bride, 'the splendors of the saints' (allusion to *Ps* 109:3) and 'the brightness of the Lord our God' (citation of *Ps* 89:17). In other words, the Beauty of God overcomes those who are now compared to 'a hollow vessel made of glass. Everything that is placed in it shows through for whatever it is, whether the contents be soot or some-thing purer and more shining. Well then, when Christ has filled souls with the splendor of lilies, by their means he renders the souls shining in splendor'.[84] The nuptial dialogue orchestrated in the *Song* is consonant, so to speak, with the Cappadocian's optimistic view of human existence. The concepts may still seem to be marked by Platonism, but we find its mark in all the works of Gregory (Beauty, archetype); nevertheless, the place taken by the motif of the incarnation, the descent of the Word into the flesh, profoundly transforms them. The comparison with the *Life of Moses* may well lead to the conclusion that the *Homilies on the Song of Songs* mark a greater achievement in the economy of Gregory's theology, precisely because the incarnation, associated with the personage of the Bridegroom in dialogue with the bride, becomes inscribed in the theme of the *epektasis*.

Beatitudes. An English Version with Commentary and Supporting Studies (Paderborn, 14-18 Sep-tember 1998) (Leiden, 2000), 257-91. She analyzes in particular 'the long rewriting of Matt 25:31-46' at the end of Homily V (*ibid.*, 262-3) and she gives some parallel passages in the work of Gregory (*Contra usurasios, sext ps*).

[83] This is one of the last verses commented on by Gregory in Homily XV, and the inclusion effect that we emphasize may not be without interest for reviving the question of the completeness or incompleteness of Gregory's commentary on the *Song of Songs*.

[84] Hom. XV, GNO VI, 441; Norris, 469.

4.3. *Praise of Beauty*

The Archetype/image relationship, the original beauty of the Archetype, is enriched in these Homilies with emotional and sensible manifestations, which mark the gradual and mutual recognition between the Bridegroom and the Bride. Thus Beauty itself becomes flesh, it is the object of a desire sharpened by the experience of the senses: perfume ('She touches the one she seeks through her sense of smell'[85]), or the visual sensation shared by the Bridegroom himself of an increasing proximity in Homily IV when Gregory interprets his repeated affirmation: "... contemplating her in the increase and increment of her beauty, he repeats the same expression: Behold, you are beautiful"'.[86] These experiences belong to the spiritual senses, that is to say, they pass to the bride through a purification and conversion to which the Bridegroom himself leads her. In this way, the coming of the Word into the flesh opens the way for the bride, for every human being, to the fullness of time, and one could again read a passage from Homily IV:[87] he who has invited souls to 'turn to divine things' and has guided them to the heavenly life – πρὸς τὴν οὐράνιον πολιτείαν – makes possible within them a conversion of emotions and attitudes. The reminder of the Pauline counsel – 'Let this mind be in you that was also in Christ Jesus' (*Phil* 2:5) – is followed by the list of goods promised: sweetness, equanimity, benevolence[88] – virtues at once promised, to wait for, and to acquire in this life. The way from virtue to beatitude, according to the definition of it given by Gregory in his treatise *On the Inscriptions of the Psalms*: 'The goal of the virtuous life is beatitude'.[89] But the fact that in Homily IV Gregory associates this necessity of the virtuous life with the 'mind that was in Christ', actually makes it more of an imitation of Christ than a moral effort.[90] It is already a participation in divine life, a bliss already begun.

4.4. *'God will be All in All' – A Pleromatic Eschatology*

Some paragraphs of our second part stopped at the images of the body and its members. Thus the Church is built and it manifests, makes visible, the beauty of the Bride; and this is truly a 'new creation', as attest the concatenation

---

[85] Hom. III, GNO VI, 88,13; Norris, 99.

[86] Hom. IV, GNO VI, 104,16-105,2; Norris, 117.

[87] Hom. IV, GNO VI, 126-7; Norris, 139: Gregory comments on the strange demand of the Bride in *Song* 2:5: 'Refresh me with apples' – playing on the white and red colors of the apples, he makes them symbols of Christ.

[88] Hom. IV, GNO VI, 127,1-6; Norris, 139.

[89] *On the Inscriptions of the Psalms* I I, 2, SC 466, p. 163.

[90] The word of Christ is recalled in the same passage: 'Learn from me, for I am meek and humble of heart' (*Mt* 11:29).

of biblical allusions, the repetition of the word 'new' and, at the end, the view
of God 'all in all' (1*Cor* 15:28) in Homily XIII:

For the creation of the cosmos signifies the foundation of the church – κόσμου γὰρ
κτίσις ἐστὶν ἡ τῆς ἐκκλησίας κατασκευή –. For the creation of the cosmos signifies
the foundation of the church, in which, according to the word of the prophet, both a
new heaven is created (which is 'the firmament of faith in Christ' [*cf. Col* 2:5], as Paul
says) and a new earth is established (*cf. Isa* 65:17), which drinks 'the rain that ... falls
upon it' (*cf. Heb* 6:7), and another humanity, renewed by the birth from above 'after
the image of its Creator' (*cf. Col* 3:10) is fashioned, and a different race of heavenly
lights comes to be, about which it says, 'You are the light of the cosmos' (*Mt* 5:14) ...
so too the person who attends to this new cosmos that appears in the creation of the
church sees in it the One who is and is becoming 'all in all – ὁρᾷ ἐν αὐτῷ τὸν πάντα
ἐν πᾶσιν ὄντα τε καὶ γινόμενον (*cf.* 1*Cor* 15:28)'.[91]

The use of the present tense dominates in these lines, not that eschatology is
yet fully realized, but the never-ending growth of this new world situates the
Church in what already exists of the new world. Moreover, the assimilation of
the 'foundation of the Church' to the 'creation of a world', reintroduces us to
the passage of Homily XV, which we cited at the beginning: the salvific economy ends in re-creation – which is none other than the plentitude of 'God all
in all' – the expression finding an eminent place in the last sentence of the
commentary. However, we need to ask ourselves about the redoubling, 'the one
who at the same time *is* and *becoming* all in all', especially as an allusion to
Eph 4:15-6, introduced the related idea of Christ's growth a little earlier in the
same homily: 'We are to grow up in every way into him who is the head, into
Christ, from whom the whole body, joined and knit together by every joint with
which it is supplied, when each part is working properly, makes bodily growth
and upbuilds itself in love' (*Eph* 4:15-6). Anyone, therefore, who focuses attention on the church is in fact looking at Christ – Christ building himself up and
augmenting himself by the addition of people who are being saved'.[92] Do note
the addition of the verb γίγνεσθαι to the quotation from 1*Cor* 12:28 and the
passage in the lines just quoted, 'we are to grow' (an appeal to the Christians
of Corinth) to Christ who 'augments himself' take us back to the question of
duration? And what then of the *plerôma*,[93] of the finished and definitive character of the 'all'?

On this point, the hesitance is ever present at the end of Homily XV: how
is the concept of *plerôma* compatible with the possibility of unending growth?

---

[91] Hom. XIII, GNO VI, 384,21-385,7 and 386,4-7; Norris, 405-7.
[92] Hom. XIII, GNO VI, 382-3; Norris, 403.
[93] It's quite surprising that neither E. Corsini, 'Plérôme humain et plérôme cosmique chez
Grégoire de Nysse', in *Epektasis. Mélanges offerts au Cardinal Daniélou* (Paris, 1972), 111-25
nor J. Zachhuber, 'Plérôma', in *Brill Dictionary of Gregory of Nyssa*, s. v. take Gregory' *Homilies
on the Song of Songs* in consideration when they try to define what *plerôma* means in his thought.

Once again, Gregory of Nyssa remains in a paradoxical position when, after his developments on the *epektasis*, in the *Life of Moses* as in the *Homilies on the Song of Songs*, he agrees with the traditional explanations of the value of the numbers mentioned in *Song* 6:8 ('There are sixty queens, eighty concubines, and young maidens without number'[94]). We need to look more closely at these last paragraphs of Homily XV where Gregory begins by referring to *Jn* 14:2 ('In my Father's house there are many places to stay'), on which he comments: '[It is] corresponding to the degree of each individual's inclination to the good and withdrawal from the worse, since there is a reward prepared for all of them'.[95] The important word here is *all*, and it is very present in these pages. From this point on, the proposed explanation for the three groups, young girls, queens and concubines, presupposes that salvation is for all but that access to the 'reward', the full vision of God, continues to take place in stages (to which the different residences correspond, it seems), as without end, because God adapts to the capacities of each one. 'God receives each in his own rank', quoting a somewhat truncated version of 1*Cor* 15:23. Indeed, the young girls signify the 'spiritual stature' of those who are still on the road to perfect conversion and the fact that they are innumerable seems to indicate that the number of the saved is not closed, that the movement toward salvation is ongoing. On the contrary, the explanations for 60 and 80[96] affirm completion, the plentitude: 'queens' and 'concubines' also represent two stages, that of the desire of God through love and that of desire linked to fear. Yet, without giving way to a form of imagination that is too psychologizing, Gregory himself hardly seems satisfied with such calculations: 'If this interpretation of the number in our text seems a bit forced, remember that at the start we confessed that it is not possible to attain the truth that lies in these words. We have touched on them only to the extent that we have not left the enigmas entirely without treatment'.[97] What is important, rather, is the conviction that, paradoxically, the *plerôma* is still growing!

Homily XV, however, ends with the promise of a perfect unity, with the explanation that is given of *Song* 6:9: 'One is my dove'. For this verse, Gregory attaches less importance to the image of the dove, symbol of the Spirit, than to the adjective μία: the great quantity and variety of the goods that can be desired are substituted with the unique promised good – 'that they may all be one, even as you, Father, are in me and I in you, that they also may be one in us', as Gregory comments on *Jn* 17:21. Coming after the subtle considerations – but hardly convincing for a contemporary reader! – concerning the numbers, the

---

[94] See also Hom. VI as regards the 'sixty valiant men of Solomon' (*Song* 3:7).

[95] Hom. XV, GNO VI, 459,4-6; Norris, 487.

[96] The two numbers, broken down as multiples of ten and twelve, are reminiscent of the Philonian explanations.

[97] Hom. XV, GNO VI, 465-6; Norris, 495.

skillful gathering of one and the multiple signals that the infinite tension towards union with God remains: 'If the concubines and queens praise the dove, this is a token that they too are eager for that which is worthy of praise – *until* that time when, since all have become one in desiring the same goal and there is no vice left in any, God may become all in all persons, in those who by their oneness are blended together with one another in the fellowship of the Good in our Lord Jesus Christ'.[98] The enigmatic word remains this *until* – ἕως: does the growth continue, like a race, in the eschaton itself? While remaining within the paradox, Gregory acknowledges that we cannot know the answer.

5. Some Concluding Remarks

With respect to the *Life of Moses* and the *Homilies on the Song of Songs* there is no longer room for controversy; the former is undoubtedly addressed to a monk, and with the latter, Gregory responds to the pressing demand of Olympias, whose perfection he celebrates. The debates with Eunomius and Apollinaris recede and with the doctrine of *epektasis* developed in those two works, Gregory moves the issues onto the grounds of eschatology. We have tried to show how, by highlighting the eschatological orientation of the dynamics of the *Song*, he is still facing a dual enigma – undoubtedly the very mystery of salvation – and he assumes the paradox of the two contradictory possibilities: Is the anticipated union with God ever total or only by participation, which endlessly maintains a gap, a distance between the creature and its Creator, and, on the other hand, is the growth of the body of Christ without end or is it necessary to conceive a definite, perfect number of those who are saved? For the coherence of Gregory's ontology, the introduction of a *diastèma* into the eschaton guarantees, in a way, as we have seen above, the distinction that is so fundamental between created and uncreated. However, it seems to us that it is also Gregory's optimism that leads him to imagine the possibility of an infinite growth in God of the number of the saved, which is consistent with the logic of the *epektasis*. There is no doubt that it is to the detriment of the theme of the Final Judgment, which has no more than a restricted place – with so much poetry and with the amorous language of the *Song* – coming after the stages of conversion and purification associated with *Proverbs* and *Ecclesiastes*: showing that the way of salvation is open to all.

---

[98] Hom. XV, GNO VI, 469,1-9; Norris, 497.

PART II
THE *SONG OF SONGS*

CHAPTER 7

De Infantibus and In Canticum

Ilaria VIGORELLI

1. Introduction

Gregory's treatise *De infantibus premature abreptis* is characterized by its stunning prose and the intensity of its dogmatic content.[1] Although the date of its composition is debated,[2] we can nevertheless, with a certain degree of certainty, consider it to have been written at the same time as or after the composition of *Contra Eunomium* (380-383) and before the composition of the fifteen homilies *In Canticum Canticorum*.[3]

Here I want to draw attention to the sequence of these two works with the intention of developing the notion of human *physis* as it relates to human participation in the divine life and as a reflection of the relationship between *theologia* (or the inner divine life) and *oikonomia* (or divine action *ad extra*) in Gregory of Nyssa's theology.

His argument, which was written to ease the grief over an infant's death, leans on the assumption taken from the Apostles' teaching that the human being is created because of an overabundance of love[4] and that this love is particularly manifested in being created 'in the likeness' of the divine image (κατ'εἰκόνα θεοῦ), as is read in *Gen* 1:26-7.[5]

---

[1] Addressed to the prefect Hierius of Cappadocia, and most likely the anonymous *egemon* of *Epist* 8 (G. Pasquali, GNO VIII/2, 36 no. 14), it finds its place amidst the cultural panorama as a work of great literary value in addition to being a clear advancement in doctrine. It will henceforth be referred to as the *De infantibus*.

[2] Jean Daniélou dates the *De infantibus* as prior to 386. *Cf.* J. Daniélou, 'La chronologie des œuvres de Grégoire de Nysse', *SP* 7 (1966), 159-69. G. Maturi moves the date back to 381: *cf.* G. Maturi, 'Infant', in L.F. Mateo-Seco and G. Maspero (eds), *The Brill Dictionary of Gregory of Nyssa*, VCS 99 (Boston, Leiden, 2010), 421-2.

[3] See G. Maspero, '*Cant*', in L.F. Mateo-Seco and G. Maspero (eds), *The Brill Dictionary of Gregory of Nyssa* (2010), 121-5.

[4] ἀλλ'ἀγάπης περιουσία: *Or cat*, GNO III/4, 17,2; *cf.* also *Beat*, GNO VII/2, 141,13; *Op hom*, PG 44, 202B.

[5] Leys claims that the treatise *De infantibus* contains the whole of Gregory's anthropology. See R. Leys, *L'image de Dieu chez saint Grégoire de Nysse* (Brussels, 1951), 60. Expressions that are very similar to those of the *De infantibus* are found in the *Oratio catechetica magna*, which – unlike Daniélou (1955), Barbel (1971) and May (1971) – Winling dates as prior to the *Contra*

Studia Patristica CI, 103-115.
© Peeters Publishers, 2021.

On account of the Christian notion of creation, Gregory affirms that *divine life* is the very *kata physin* good of man.[6]

Throughout this article I would like to observe the correspondence between the human *physis* – that is, created *kat'eikona theou* (*Gen* 1:26), whose *energeia* appears to be related to divine life – and the theological concept of *epektasis* that appears in Homily VI of *In Canticum*. Through the comparison between the treatise and the homily, a very intriguing parallelism comes to light: in both writings human nature is compared to childhood, and the child appears to be the one who has the same disposition as the divine Son; as we will see, the disposition of the Son is perfectly narrated in the Trinitarian formula which was developed in *Contra Eunomium* I. The communion of nature between the Father and the Son is expressed there as a reciprocal relation/disposition (*schesis*) that indicates not only communion of nature but also of will (*Eun* I, 498,1-499,4 and *Eun* I, 502,4-6).

Here, one can see how the maturation of the Trinitarian doctrine encourages the maturation of an anthropology that is equipped to overcome the necessity of Greek finalism.

A new ontology opens the notion of human nature to the freedom of reciprocal relation between the Creator and His creature and thereby also reconfigures the notion of participation in divine life, and the divinization of man. This is the aspect of Gregory's Eschatology that we are about to analyze.

2. κατὰ φύσιν and κατ'εἰκόνα in Gregory of Nyssa's *De infantibus*

Let us therefore begin with the way in which the expressions *kata physin* and *kat'eikona* are used in the treatise *De infantibus*, wherein Gregory of Nyssa offers an important development regarding the theological notion of the end of the soul.

Gregory was compelled to challenge a fierce Origenist variety of the doctrine of the soul's pre-existence, as well as the Platonic metempsicosis that was still circulating in Middle and Neo-Platonist thought. He thus found himself with the task of giving a reason for the goodness of God and His Providence, even in the context of such grave circumstances as the premature death of a child, and likewise having to explain that it is always worth living and struggling against the passions for all one's life rather than dying immediately after birth.[7]

As regards the argument, the issue is treated on the basis of the reasonableness of divine wisdom (σοφία), God's will (βουλήσις) and God's sense (λόγος).

Eunomium I and contemporaneous with the *De anima et resurrectione* and *De hominis opificio*, that is, between 379 and 380 (SC 453; Paris, 2000).

[6] GNO III/2, 79,21-80,1.

[7] GNO III/2, 72,17ff.

But it is also based on the goodness of human beings and the giving of life, on divine judgment and remuneration (ἀντίδοσις), and on the opposition between good and evil that does not allow a third intermediate (ἄμεσος).[8]

This treatise is particularly interesting when read within a study of the relationship between philosophy and theology, for Gregory compares the Apostles' preaching with the requirements of reason. The problem is about remuneration principles.

The matter of children who die soon after birth is in fact taken above all as a question that is relevant to the very coherence of the Gospel. If Paul claims the Kingdom to be a kind of recompense (*Rm* 14:10 and *2Cor* 5:10), what recompense is there for those who were unable to take action (πρᾶξις) and make a choice (προαίρεσις)?[9] In this case, what would justice in the heavenly court be based upon?

Without going so far as to analyze Gregory's argument point by point, I shall only highlight the theological matter and the ontological innovation introduced in this convergence of creation *kat'eikona* and the vision of God as *energeia kata physin*. The theologian seems, in fact, to turn *energeia* from a matter of fulfillment to a matter of personal relationship.

The argument hinges on the two Biblical premises:

a) God is the creator of all things and all things have life from Him (τὸ εἶναι ἔχειν),[10] He rules all things and governs with order.
b) Human nature is created in the image of God (κατ'εἰκόνα θεοῦ: *Gen* 1:27).

The Cappadocian father remains consistent above all with philosophical theology, and yet at any given moment also with the sphere of faith. In citing the Bible, he remarks that there is only one uncreated nature[11] and professes the absolute transcendence of God and God's freedom to create. But he also notes philosophical monotheism, taking it as something commonly known and in no need of demonstration.[12]

The same can be said of the manner in which the anthropological argument is approached.

Although the divine transcendence is considered from a perspective of the Middle or Neo-Platonic tradition – which is called to mind and reproduced here[13] – as in some way united to man *by way of the mixing of elements both*

---

[8] GNO III/2, 72,17-22 and 74,9-10.

[9] GNO III/2, 74,21ff.

[10] GNO III/2, 74,6.

[11] It is only here that Gregory uses the term *physis* to mean the nature of God. *Cf.* J. Zachhuber, 'Physis', in L.F. Mateo-Seco and G. Maspero (eds), *The Brill Dictionary of Gregory of Nyssa* (2010), 614-20.

[12] GNO III/2, 77,4ff.

[13] For more on the philosophical sources running through the *De infantibus*, see the vast work done by G. Maturi, *Gregorio di Nissa, Paradiso precoce* (Rome, 2004), 31-94.

material and immaterial used in the creation of human nature,[14] Gregory does
not offer a different argument regarding the composition of man but only
embraces the philosophical assumption and traces it back to the Biblical language of *Gen* 1:27 where man is said to have been created 'in the image of
God' (κατ'εἰκόνα θεοῦ ἐποίησεν αὐτόν)[15].

He engages the anthropological argument beginning with what was inherited
from philosophy and the *mixing* with divine characteristics (those that are
immaterial and intellectual) to then connect it with the theological notion of the
icon. He thereby introduces a new element; that is, he claims that what Scripture adds – that human nature is fashioned κατ'εἰκόνα θεοῦ – indicates a way
of understanding what the nourishing good consists of, that is to say, the good
that gives life to man.

> If, then, this is the life-nourishment of an intellectual nature, namely, to have a part in
> God (τὸ τοῦ θεοῦ μετέχειν), this part (μετουσία) will not be gained by that which is
> of an opposite quality; the would-be partaker must in some degree be akin to that which
> is to be partaken of.[16]

This argument stays close to the heart of the Platonic and Aristotelian traditions as Gregory's statement is imprinted with that same desire for the fullness
of life, a tradition that maintains contemplating God as the human being's
proper act (ἡ δὲ τοῦ βλέπειν πρὸς τὸν θεὸν ἐνέργεια),[17] *i.e.*, the life that corresponds to its nature. Gregory likewise holds this to be possible by virtue of
the fact that human nature is 'mixed': one part is, in fact, intellectual (τῇ νοερᾷ
φύσει)[18] and suitable to the intelligible nature of God.

The theological innovation emphasized here is seen in the observation that
in order for nourishment to give life it must be suitable (συγγενές)[19] for the
one who is nourished, for only in such a way can life pass from one subject to
another. For Gregory, likeness to God is precisely what ensures that the vision
of Him – as stated in philosophical discourse – will actually *nourish*, or facilitate the passing of His life to man[20] in a proper sense. It is therefore important
to understand what he means by such affinity. He states that this likeness is

---

[14] GNO III/2, 77,13-21. On this point see M. Brugarolas, 'Theological Remarks on Gregory
of Nyssa's Christological Language of "Mixture"', *SP* 84 (2017), 39-57.

[15] GNO III/2, 77,22-3.

[16] εἰ οὖν αὕτη ἐστὶν ἡ οἰκεία τε καὶ κατάλληλος τῇ νοερᾷ φύσει ζωή, τὸ τοῦ θεοῦ μετέχειν,
οὐκ ἂν διὰ τῶν ἐναντίων γένοιτο ἡ μετουσία, εἰ μὴ τρόπον τινὰ συγγενὲς εἴη τῷ ὀρεγομένῳ
τὸ μετεχόμενον (GNO III/2, 79,13-6). See also the parallel passage in the *Or Cat* (GNO III/4,
17,7-16): here Gregory still stays committed to his interest in the question of remuneration.

[17] GNO III/2, 79,2.

[18] GNO III/2, 79,2-3.

[19] GNO III/2, 79,15.

[20] 'The act of seeing God is simply the most fitting life according to the nature of the intellect'
(ἡ δὲ τοῦ βλέπειν πρὸς τὸν θεὸν ἐνέργεια οὐδὲν ἄλλο ἐστὶν ἢ ζωὴ τῇ νοερᾷ φύσει ἐοικυῖα
τε καὶ κατάλληλος, GNO III/2, 79,2-3). *Cf.* also GNO III/2, 79,9ff.

found in the *disposition by nature* (τῷ κατὰ φύσιν διακειμένῳ), whose *energeia* is the vision of God and that this is the innovation that emerges from an accurate analysis of Gregory's writing *actual relation with God*. The argument comes through a classical metaphor of sight:[21]

With the eye in a natural state, sight follows necessarily (τῷ κατὰ φύσιν διακειμένῳ); with it vitiated by disease, failure of sight necessarily follows. In the same way, the life of blessedness is as a familiar second nature (ἡ μακαρία ζωὴ συμφυής ἐστι καὶ οἰκεία) to those who have kept clear the senses of the soul; but when the blinding stream of ignorance prevents our partaking in the real light, then it necessarily follows that we miss that, the enjoyment of which we declare to be the life of the partaker (οὗ τὴν μετουσίαν ζωὴν εἶναί φαμεν τοῦ μετέχοντος).[22]

At first, these words do not seem to be too far from the metaphysical discussions of his own day that called for participation. However, there are differences. Here the vision of God is an act of the intellectual nature, but it is also the relation that gives life to man. Gregory argues that as vision is to the eye a natural relation with light,[23] or as knowledge and ignorance are in relation (τὸ πρός τί πως ἔχειν),[24] so too for the soul of man the vision of God is a natural relation.[25]

The *energeia* of *physis* is hereby placed within the category of relation (πρός τι), and *physis* in itself has life that is proper to it by way of relation with God.[26] One can see, then, that for Gregory the *physis* of man is an *original disposition toward God*,[27] yet something which originates in the love that has created man in His image (κατ'εἰκόνα θεοῦ). The love of God is the ontological novelty about relation, because it is free and doesn't work as necessity but as will.

---

[21] On this, see, E. Cain, 'Through a mirror darkly: Mystical metaphors of sight from Paul to Gregory of Nyssa and Augustine of Hippo' (2016). ETD Collection for Fordham University.

[22] ἀλλ' ὡς ἀναγκαίως ἕπεται τῷ κατὰ φύσιν διακειμένῳ τὸ βλέπειν τῷ τε ἀπὸ πάθους παρενεχθέντι τῆς φύσεως τὸ μὴ ἐνεργὸν ἔχειν τὴν ὅρασιν, τὸν αὐτὸν τρόπον καὶ ἡ μακαρία ζωὴ συμφυής ἐστι καὶ οἰκεία τοῖς κεκαθαρμένοις τὰ τῆς ψυχῆς αἰσθητήρια, ἐφ' ὧν δὲ καθάπερ τις λήμη τὸ κατὰ τὴν ἄγνοιαν πάθος ἐμπόδιον πρὸς τὴν μετουσίαν τοῦ ἀληθινοῦ φωτὸς γίνεται, ἀναγκαίως ἕπεται τὸ μὴ μετέχειν ἐκείνου, οὗ τὴν μετουσίαν ζωὴν εἶναί φαμεν τοῦ μετέχοντος, GNO III/2, 81,15-22.

[23] GNO III/2, 81,10ff.

[24] 'Thus knowledge and wisdom indicate the soul's mode of being in relation' (ὅτι ἡ γνῶσις καὶ ἡ ἄγνοια τὸ πρός τί πως ἔχειν τὴν ψυχὴν ἐνδείκνυται), GNO III/2, 80,13-4.

[25] GNO III/2, 81,6-7.

[26] 'Seeing God is the life of the soul' (τὸ δὲ βλέπειν τὸν θεόν ἐστιν ἡ ζωὴ τῆς ψυχῆς), GNO III/2, 80,1.

[27] On the disposition toward God, see the studies on *schesis* in Gregory of Nyssa done by G. Maspero and myself. The term *schesis* does not appear in *De infant*, but the matrix of terms that normally appear with it can be found, as is the word διατίθημι, which is used synonymously with *schesis*, διάθεσις (here in a contrary position to physis: 'Turned away from nature one is thus deprived of that which is according to nature and one excludes himself from relation and from its corresponding life' [παρὰ φύσιν διατεθεὶς ἠλλοτρίωται τοῦ κατὰ φύσιν καὶ ἀμέτοχος γίνεται τῆς οἰκείας ἡμῖν καὶ καταλλήλου ζωῆς], GNO III/2, 82,26-8.

The discussion on the remuneration principles regarding infants leads Gregory to employ the difference between nature and relation, and this includes linking them together.

If *physis* is relational openness to God – for relation with God is relation *par excellence*, the one that is most natural (κατὰ φύσιν)[28] – the individual who has not had the means to corrupt his nature with the passions and who dies with pure senses reaches blessedness as a kind of *natural conclusion* of his likeness to God, because of God's love.[29] God gives this individual His own life by virtue of the very same nature in which the individual was created.

Hence, the essential difference between the single, uncreated, and eternal nature (μίαν μὲν φύσιν εἶναι ἄκτιστον καὶ ἀΐδιον)[30] and nature created in likeness (κατ'εἰκόνα) is certainly upheld in the difference of hypostases (the child remains as he is and never becomes God), yet the true life of created nature, and as endowed with intellectual essence (νοερᾶς οὐσίας)[31] akin to that of God, *comes to be the very same life of God*. In death the beatific vision is attained because it is the fulfillment of the child's very nature.

The topic of remuneration is thereby articulated by way of his commentary on the *purity* of human nature, highlighting that *God is already positioned toward human nature* so as to be its fullness inasmuch as He is its Creator. One realizes from these passages that Gregory's ontology alters the doctrine of participation of a Platonic variety and likewise the doctrine regarding contemplation as read in Aristotle. Contemplative relation actually gives man the divine life itself *as it is so willed by God*, i.e., as affinity with God's own intellectual and loving nature that is the most fitting to human *physis*.[32]

Divinization of the human being is not assimilation of one reality to another by way of necessity, but rather it is one, single life (the divine and eternal life only) that God grants the child through an act most fitting to the child's own nature: that of seeing God according to the creating will of God Himself.

Divine life is given to the child by way of the actual disposition/relation of his *physis*, which naturally *corresponds* to the creating disposition/relation of the Creator (i.e., to the *physis* of the Creator).

Doctrine in *Gen* 1:26-7 rushes into the philosophical ontology with Gregory of Nyssa and enables a noticeable transformation of the doctrine of likeness to the divine and the perfection of human life.[33]

---

[28] GNO III/2, 81,15.

[29] GNO III/2, 81,15ff.

[30] GNO III/2, 77,6.

[31] GNO III/2, 77,17.

[32] The term συγγενές occurs three times in *De infantibus*: cf. GNO III/2, 78,23, GNO III/2, 79,15, and GNO III/2, 79,22. Here we can see a foreshadowing of the argument of *epektasis*: what in Homily 6 *In Cant* leads Gregory to interpret human nature as infinite even though it is created.

[33] Cf. D.L. Balás, *Metousia theou: Man's participation in God's perfections according to Saint Gregory of Nyssa* (Rome, 1966), 18.

Being an *icon* of God means actually being *turned toward* a relation of love, a conclusion according to nature because nature itself is a *mirror of relation*, a reflection of the communion one has with God. But man receives eternal life from God because creation provides the basis for reciprocity according to nature (ἐν τῇ ζωῇ τῇ κατὰ φύσιν):[34] 'The life of blessedness is as familiar second nature to those who have kept clear the senses of the soul'.[35] This clarity is the same as *apatheia*.

So, for Gregory, what does it mean that human nature possesses in itself this intimate familiarity with God? Affinity through *physis* is interpreted by Gregory as the *original disposition toward God*[36] that allows for the inclusion of a prematurely deceased child to be fulfilled in his *physis*. And it is not because the child carried out deeds worthy of recompense or as an individual agent (according to *praxis*). And it is not because the vision of God is due to him according to his essence (οὐσία).[37] The vision of God, and therefore the divinization that is communion with divine life or everlasting life – occurs by way of *energeia* of the human *physis*. But this *energeia* is now intended as relational: it is vision *of God* because the creating God wants to position Himself as the most relevant relationship to the *human physis*.

An understanding of this leads one to see the similarity between this treatise and what will be expressed in a spiritual way through the Homily VI of *In Canticum Canticorum*.

3. *Epektasis* and *Apatheia* in Homily VI of *In Canticum Canticorum*

Homily VI of the comment on the *Song* opens with a metaphysical analysis that is very similar to the one presented in the treatise *De infantibus*.

It seems that Gregory wants to revive a Porphyrian tree based on the material-immaterial and created-uncreated distinctions, at the end of which, however, the human being is presented as a being that is created from composed and changeable nature: participated. Here, however, unlike the discourse on human nature that was developed in *De infantibus*, rather than bringing attention to the creation of the human being in the image and likeness of God (*Gen* 1:26-7), Gregory emphasizes the fact that we cannot identify its limits, because it is always reaching towards a greater good (*Phil* 3:13).[38]

The doctrine of *epektasis* thus appears to initiate the spiritual reading of the third book of the *Song*. The central element is the thalamus of *Song* 1:16, which

---

[34] GNO III/2, 82,23. *Cf.* also *De anima et resurrectione*, PG 46, 120C-121A.
[35] GNO III/2, 81,18.
[36] GNO III/2, 83,11.
[37] GNO III/2, 80,17.
[38] *Cant* 6: GNO VI, 174,15.

is resumed here by connecting it to the exegesis of the nuptial bed of Solomon being surrounded by sixty warriors (*Song* 3:7) and to the image of the bed in which the children are already sleeping in *Lk* 11:7.[39]

In Gregory's *Commentary*, the thalamus is the Christological image *par excellence*: God's being veiled in the flesh has made it possible for human beings to know Him; this knowledge is given in the darkness of personal intimacy, in the union between the Bridegroom and the Bride, which takes place precisely in the thalamus.[40] The fact that this occurs in the presence of the warriors, who have overcome the impulses of the flesh with the sword of virtue, offers Gregory the opportunity to compare the warriors to children.

The image of the children and of the thalamus is revived by *Lk* 11:7 where the protagonist of Jesus' parable replies to the friend that the door is already closed and the children (παιδία) are in bed.

The text appropriately uses the term *children* (παιδία) to describe those who, through the arms of justice, have brought the impassive state (τὸ ἀπαθές) to fulfillment in themselves, thus leading us to the teaching that the good that comes from such care is not different from that which had been placed in nature from the beginning (τὸ ἐξ ἀρχῆς ἐναποτεθὲν τῇ φύσει). In fact, whoever has bound his sword to his flank by means of the diligence of the life according to virtue is free from passions and is now a child (νήπιον) in their age insofar as they are insensitive to such passions. In childhood (νηπιότης), indeed, there is no room for passions.[41]

The *apatheia* of the flesh – understood, according to the language of Gregory, as the freedom from sensuality that goes along with the tunic of the skin – and the insatiable passion for the good, are therefore characteristics of human nature 'from the beginning' (ἐξ ἀρχῆς). Therefore, as we have already pointed out in *De infantibus*, it is in itself a disposition toward the good that can be deviated but which craves relation with God from the beginning, because God has voluntarily placed Himself as the end of the relation to which human nature tends.

At the end of Homily VI, however, Gregory highlights the stable disposition assumed by the Bride toward the Bridegroom: a disposition aquired for the love of the Bridegroom:

Then in the discourse [the Bride] describes the house of virtue, of which the material of the roof is cedar and cypress that does not admit corruption or putrefaction, which

---

[39] Cf. *Cant* 6: GNO VI, 189,16-199,7.

[40] Cf. *Cant* 4: GNO VI, 107,9-108,4.

[41] καλῶς δὲ τοὺς διὰ τῶν ὅπλων τῆς δικαιοσύνης τὸ ἀπαθὲς ἑαυτοῖς κατορθώσαντας παιδία κατονομάζει ὁ λόγος δόγμα διὰ τούτων ἡμῖν ὑφηγούμενος, ὅτι τὸ ἐξ ἐπιμελείας προσγινόμενον ἡμῖν ἀγαθὸν οὐκ ἄλλο τί ἐστι παρὰ τὸ ἐξ ἀρχῆς ἐναποτεθὲν τῇ φύσει· ὅ τε γὰρ τῷ μηρῷ τὴν ῥομφαίαν διαζωσάμενος διὰ προσοχῆς τοῦ κατ᾽ ἀρετὴν βίου τὸ πάθος ἀπεσκευάσατο τό τε νήπιον τῇ ἡλικίᾳ ἀναισθήτως ἔχει τοῦ τοιούτου πάθους· οὐ γὰρ χωρεῖ τὸ πάθος ἡ νηπιότης (*Cant*. 6: GNO VI, 198,6-13).

in the discourse means the stability and immutability of the disposition toward the good (τῆς πρὸς τὸ ἀγαθὸν σχέσεως).[42]

The σχέσις of the Bride, turned firmly toward the good, is here to signify the state of human nature that has aquired virtue, that is, a mode of being in relation that has assumed the characteristics of stability and immutability in the capacity to choose the good.

It is important to remember that the context describes the condition of the soul loved by Christ: by His love it is in fact made beautiful and able to learn of the beauty of the Logos. Suprised by seeing Him adumbrated by the material nature of the human body (τῇ ὑλικῇ τοῦ ἀνθρωπίνου σώματος φύσει συσκιαζόμενος),[43] it is led by His voice to perfection through an even higher asceticism.

The σχέσις that is πρὸς τὸ ἀγαθόν points to the κατάστασις,[44] that is, to the definitive position to which the soul reaches through asceticism in faith (πίστις),[45] asceticism made possible by the vision (θεωρία) offered by Scripture.[46]

Here too, therefore, the final condition is posed as the fulfillment of the disposition toward the good that dwells in human nature since its origins,[47] whose desire is made known – in the union achieved with the Bridegroom[48] – as the capacity to host the divinity itself,[49] to be indwelt by it.

The correlation between the σχέσις which is πρὸς τὸ ἀγαθόν and the κατάστασις of the divine indwelling, is highlighted by the reference to the τὸ ἀπαθές of children.[50]

The definitive conditon of the human being will thus not be subject to the passions in the corporeal sense, just as it is not the condition of children.

Gregory thus interprets the state of the virtuous man, freed from the fluctuations of the will driven by passions, in light of that precise insensitivity (ἀναισθήτως)[51] that children have for the bodily passions and that is therefore linked to their innocence from the start. Gregory explicitly states: 'The text teaches us that the good to which we adhere with our care is nothing other than that originally reserved to [our] nature'.[52]

---

[42] πρὸς τούτοις τὸν τῆς ἀρετῆς οἶκον διαγράφει τῷ λόγῳ, οὗ γίνεται ἡ ἐρέψιμος ὕλη κέδρος τε καὶ κυπάρισσος σηπεδόνος τε καὶ διαφθορᾶς ἀνεπίδεκτος, δι' ὧν τὸ μόνιμόν τε καὶ ἀμετάβλητον τῆς πρὸς τὸ ἀγαθὸν σχέσεως διερμηνεύει τῷ λόγῳ. *Cant* 6: GNO VI, 176,15-177,3 (our translation).

[43] *Cant* 6: GNO VI, 176,14.

[44] *Cant* 6: GNO VI, 183,12.

[45] *Cant* 6: GNO VI, 183,8.

[46] *Cant* 6: GNO VI, 180,11.

[47] Cf. *Cant* 2: GNO VI, 56,5-11.

[48] Cf. *Cant* 6: GNO VI, 179,7.

[49] ἣ τότε γίνεται δεκτικὴ τῆς θείας αὐτοῦ ἐνοικήσεως (*Cant* 6: GNO VI, 183,11-2).

[50] Cf. *Cant* 6: GNO VI, 198,6ff.

[51] *Cant* 6: GNO VI, 198,12.

[52] ὁ λόγος δόγμα διὰ τούτων ἡμῖν ὑφηγούμενος, ὅτι τὸ ἐξ ἐπιμελείας προσγινόμενον ἡμῖν ἀγαθὸν οὐκ ἄλλο τί ἐστι παρὰ τὸ ἐξ ἀρχῆς ἐναποτεθὲν τῇ φύσει. *Cant* 6: GNO VI, 198,8-10 (our translation).

Thus, in the argumentative strategy of Homily VI, the identification of the state of the child with perfection constitutes a new beginning, a leap to *epektasis*, in the new ontological perspective that makes impassibility the very core of the divinization by virtue of the relation desired by God.

That is why it ends in a convergent exegesis where the figures of the child, the soldier, and the true Israelite can no longer be distinguished:

Therefore, it is the same to learn that there are soldiers around the bed and children (νήπια) resting in it. In fact, in both there is only one impassibility (ἀπάθεια); the latter because they are not disposed to passions, and the former because they have driven them out. Thus, the children do not know them yet, while the soldiers in their struggle have risen to this disposition and become children (παιδία) thanks to impassibility (ἀπαθείᾳ). Thus the bliss of the child (παιδίον), the soldier, and the true Israelite is found in them, since the true Israelite contemplates God in his pure heart, the soldier protects the bed of the King, that is, his own heart, in the impassibility and purity, and the child (παιδίον) rests in the blessed bed in Jesus Christ our Lord, to whom be glory forever and ever. Amen.[53]

The connection between childhood and impassibility makes it possible to link childhood with *epektasis*. In fact, from the Nyssen perspective, impassibility is not statically conceived, but it is that condition of stability and indefectibility in the movement toward God, which characterizes the ontological fullness that is already enjoyed by the angels.[54]

Gregory's proposal is therefore ontologically vertiginous and founded on Christ. He juxtaposes the divine word incarnate who saves with the creating word that gives life, in such a way that the divinization of man is assured by the very power of the Creator Logos by the love that descends from the creator over human nature when He assumes its flesh and blood.

We can note here in action a fundamental element of Gregory's thought, for which the mutability of the creature becomes positive, as the possibility of turning forever toward the Creator in a growing participation: the man who remains faithful to God will reach the state of the angels whose will is definitively turned toward the Trinity in the perpetual progress of *epektasis*.

Perfection is therefore given by the docility of the will and the abandonment of that force of attraction that always draws higher and higher toward the infinitude of the will of good that is God Himself.

---

[53] οὐκοῦν ταὐτόν ἐστιν ὁπλίτας τε περὶ τὴν κλίνην εἶναι μαθεῖν καὶ νήπια ἐπὶ τῆς κοίτης ἀναπαυόμενα· μία γὰρ ἐπ' ἀμφοτέρων ἡ ἀπάθεια τῶν τε μὴ παραδεξαμένων καὶ τῶν ἀπωσαμένων τὸ πάθος· οἱ μὲν γὰρ οὔπω ἔγνωσαν, οἱ δὲ πρὸς τὴν τοιαύτην κατάστασιν ἑαυτοὺς ἐπανήγαγον στραφέντες καὶ παιδία τῇ ἀπαθείᾳ γενόμενοι, ὡς μακάριον τὸ ἐν τούτοις εὑρεθῆναι ἢ παιδίον ἢ ὁπλίτην ἢ ἀληθινὸν Ἰσραηλίτην γενόμενον, ὡς μὲν Ἰσραηλίτην ἐν καθαρᾷ καρδίᾳ τὸν θεὸν ὁρῶντα, ὡς δὲ ὁπλίτην ἐν ἀπαθείᾳ καὶ καθαρότητι τὴν τοῦ βασιλέως κλίνην, τουτέστιν τὴν ἑαυτοῦ καρδίαν φυλάσσοντα, ὡς δὲ παιδίον ἐπὶ τῆς μακαρίας κοίτης ἀναπαυόμενον ἐν Χριστῷ Ἰησοῦ τῷ κυρίῳ ἡμῶν, ᾧ ἡ δόξα εἰς τοὺς αἰῶνας τῶν αἰώνων. Ἀμήν. *Cant.* 6: GNO VI, 198,14-199,7 (our translation).

[54] *Cf. Cant* 4: GNO VI, 134,9-135,6.

We can thus note that the creation in the image of God in *Gen* 1:26-7 does not mean, according to Gregory's perspective, one state, but rather a movement of infinite growth.

4. Trinitarian *oikeia* and Trinitarian Indwelling: *eis ton theon metoikizetai* (*Cant 6:* GNO VI, 179,7)

The full relevance of the depth of the anthropological inquiry undertaken by Gregory, as well as the dynamic of desire described in light of creation and image, shines through when they are read in reference to the Trinitarian theology of *Contra Eunomium*. The treatise was composed either prior to or simultaneously with *De infantibus* and certainly before the homilies *In Canticum*.[55]

Gregory of Nyssa's Trinitarian doctrine is characterized by his development of an ontology of reciprocal relation/disposition (*schesis*) of the Father and the Son, indicated by the connaturality of the terms in relation.[56]

When they hear the title of 'Father' and that of 'Son', they immediately recognize from the names themselves the reciprocal relationship of affinity of nature (τὴν οἰκείαν αὐτῶν καὶ φυσικὴν πρὸς ἄλληλα σχέσιν). In fact, these names mean *per se* a link of nature (τὸ γὰρ τῆς φύσεως συγγενές).[57]

It is interesting to note that the communion of nature between the Father and the Son can be witnessed not only through the logic of *natural* reciprocity offered by the revealed names – which would have led Eunomius to rank generated being below ungenerated being – but also through reference to the communion of the will along with the communion of nature.

In this way the very same nature that is present in the reciprocal relationship of the Father and the Son does not multiply the terms in relation into different substances. Rather, it makes it so that the two live the same one life. An example of this can be produced here, one among many, in *Contra Eunomium*, Book I:

We have heard from Truth the names 'Father' and 'Son', and we have understood the unity of nature (τὴν ἑνότητα τῆς φύσεως) in two subjects (ἐν δύο τοῖς ὑποκειμένοις), as this unity is naturally (φυσικῶς) indicated by names and by way of reciprocal relation (τῆς πρὸς ἄλληλα σχέσεως), and this we have heard from the Lord's own voice. For He has said: 'The Father and I are one'. What can this mean if not that He Himself cannot be without beginning (μὴ ἄναρχον ἑαυτοῦ), through His disposition to profess

---

[55] See P. Maraval, 'Chronology', in L.F. Mateo-Seco and G. Maspero (eds), *The Brill Dictionary of Gregory of Nyssa* (2010), 153-69, 153.

[56] For more on this point, see the insightful work by G. Maspero, *Essere e Relazione* (Rome, 2013).

[57] ὅτι πάντες ἄνθρωποι πατρὸς καὶ υἱοῦ προσηγορίαν ἀκούσαντες εὐθὺς τὴν οἰκείαν αὐτῶν καὶ φυσικὴν πρὸς ἄλληλα σχέσιν ὑπ᾽ αὐτῶν τῶν ὀνομάτων ἐπιγινώσκουσι. τὸ γὰρ τῆς φύσεως συγγενὲς ἐκ τῶν προσηγοριῶν τούτων αὐτομάτως διερμηνεύεται. *Eun* I 159, 3-7: GNO I, 75,3-7 (our translation).

the Father, and the fact that nature (τῆς φύσεως), between them is common (τὸ κοινόν), through unity with the Father (διὰ τῆς πρὸς τὸν πατέρα ἑνότητος)?[58]

Later it appears to be in explicit reference to the will:

So too are the Father and Son one, as they are concurrent in one nature and one will (τῆς κατὰ τὴν φύσιν καὶ τὴν προαίρεσιν κοινωνίας).[59]

Observing that in order to maintain faith in the evangelic tradition the difference of Trinitarian hypostases, and so also union, is described by way of nature and the will, one sees how Gregory places *relational disposition* not only on the plane of anthropology and voluntary decision-making, but also within the divine *physis* itself.

In Homily VI of *In Canticum*, Gregory stays that when the soul is ready to see God, a new οἰκεία between God and human nature is given:

The two actors (the soul and God, the bride and Bridegroom) move into one another. God comes into the soul, and correspondingly the soul is brought into God (εἰς τὸν θεὸν ἡ ψυχὴ μετοικίζεται). For she says, 'My beloved is mine, and I am his. He does his pasturing among the lilies' and transfers human life from the realm of shadowy images to the truth of that which is.[60]

This passage uses the verb *metoikizetai*, and this leads us to compare it with the Trinitarian *oikeia*. Human life is so surprisingly destined to participate in this same intimate familiarity of being and of love that exists between the Father and the Son and which constitutes the intimate life of God.

5. Conclusions

From this brief but close examination of the manner in which the interpretation of *Gen* 1:26-7 appears to be linked in two of Gregory of Nyssa's most powerful works, it is possible to find a description of human *physis* as the open disposition of reciprocal relation with the divine. This facilitated the passage of divine life from the Creator to created being, not as due remuneration according to some *praxis*, but as a new kind of *energia* which is proper to being

---

[58] Πατέρα καὶ υἱὸν παρὰ τῆς ἀληθείας ἀκούσαντες ἐν δύο τοῖς ὑποκειμένοις τὴν ἑνότητα τῆς φύσεως ἐδιδάχθημεν, ὑπό τε τῶν ὀνομάτων φυσικῶς [διὰ] τῆς πρὸς ἄλληλα σχέσεως σημαινομένης καὶ ὑπ' αὐτῆς πάλιν τῆς τοῦ κυρίου φωνῆς. ὁ γὰρ εἰπὼν Ἐγὼ καὶ ὁ πατὴρ ἕν ἐσμεν, τί ἄλλο ἢ τό τε μὴ ἄναρχον ἑαυτοῦ διὰ τῆς τοῦ πατρὸς ὁμολογίας παρίστησιν καὶ τὸ κοινὸν σημαίνει τῆς φύσεως διὰ τῆς πρὸς τὸν πατέρα ἑνότητος. *Eun* I 498,1-499,4: GNO I, 170,13-20 (our translation).

[59] καὶ ὁ πατὴρ καὶ ὁ υἱὸς ἕν εἰσι, τῆς κατὰ τὴν φύσιν καὶ τὴν προαίρεσιν κοινωνίας εἰς τὸ ἓν συνδραμούσης (*Eun* I 502,4-6: GNO I, 171,18-20).

[60] *Cant* 6: GNO VI, 179,5-10. *Cf.* Gregory of Nyssa, *Homilies on the Song of Songs*, trans. R.A. Norris Jr. (Atlanta, 2012), 191.

relational and relationally connatural to God.[61] Here it is possible to see how deeply Gregory changes the meaning of mystical knowledge through the practice of the sacraments, and how strongly ontology and eschatology are intertwined within his theology.

Gregory of Nyssa's eschatological anthropology can then be said to contain the two following characteristics:

1. Man exists inasmuch as he is *the second term of God's creational relation.* God is always looking upon His creation to give all life. This disposition of the human *physis* is marked by the Biblical terminology of the icon as read in *Gen* 1:26-7, as is that of the mirror in the Platonic thought which Gregory revisits. Man's being an icon means he has in himself the disposition of love for God, who puts His own being in the origins of His image.

2. Man exists in *a position of active reciprocal relation* with respect to the divine presence from which he is given life, for he possesses the perceptive faculties of the soul.[62] If his disposition were simply turned toward God in that he is still not subject to his passions or without any capacity to exercise deliberation (as is the case with infants), the life of God could be fully poured into human nature as *relational energeia* that is accomplished by the second term in the relation – namely, God Himself. However, where man instead finds himself yet again in the exercise of his own free will in turning, Gregory affirms, to the good, it is here that human *physis* reaches fulfillment. For here, by way of the will, it orders its *natural* being-through-and-in-relation toward God.

We hereby see that human and divine natures are brought together in Gregory's description via two new characteristics: (1) the fact that *physis bears disposition* and (2) *the actuality of existence in reciprocal relation*, by nature and also voluntarily, which in God is eternal among the three divine Persons, and in the human being appears to be finite and subject to history, but is by creation destined to be infinite in the love of God.

---

[61] This theme emerges strongly in the homilies commenting on the *Song of Songs* as well. I can cite my previous work, I. Vigorelli, 'Desiderio e beatitudine' (2014).

[62] *Cf.* GNO III/2, 81,10ff.

CHAPTER 8

In Canticum Canticorum and *De Vita Moysis*

Raphael CADENHEAD

1. Introduction

Even since Jean Daniélou (1905-1974) foregrounded the theme of desire in his seminal study on Gregory's *Théologie mystique*, so-called,[1] there has been a flurry of interest in the associative themes of spiritual ascent, eros and epektasis in the thought of the youngest and last of the Cappadocian Fathers. Following suit, particularly in more recent decades, Anglo-American scholarship has been almost mesmerised by Gregory's theorisation of desire for its perceived contributions to modern-day discussions on 'gender', 'sexuality' and 'feminism', as charted in a recent survey of the literature by Morwenna Ludlow.[2] However, I believe something in all this has been missed – namely, a full appreciation of the way in which the soul's shifting 'gendered' identifications are, for Gregory, coordinated with key moments in spiritual maturation.

To anticipate the outcome of my analysis: the maturational trajectory that Gregory adumbrates begins with the moral faults of worldly 'femininity', afterwards superseded by virtuous 'masculinity' and then ultimately displaced by a supreme, spiritually passionate 'femininity'.[3] In Gregory's earlier works, he argues that a sexually excessive form of youthful 'masculinity' must also be renounced in spiritual ascent.[4] For the purposes of this chapter, however, I want to focus on the late commentary texts of the *Vit Moys* and the *Cant* – which have received greatest attention by far in discussions on 'gender' – to offer a detailed account of the spiritual maturational process described by Gregory. These two texts – one addressed to the spiritually immature who still 'wander outside virtue' (*Vit Moys* I 11; tr. Malherbe and Ferguson 32), the other, to

---

[1] J. Daniélou, *Platonisme et Théologie Mystique: doctrine spirituelle de Saint Grégoire de Nysse* (Paris, 1944) (1st Edition); (Paris, 1953) (2nd Edition).

[2] M. Ludlow, *Gregory of Nyssa ancient and (post)modern* (Oxford, 2007).

[3] Throughout, I shall frame 'masculinity' and 'femininity' in inverted commas to highlight the potential anachronism in using theory-laden contemporary categories such as these in late antique studies. It is my intention to use Greek terms wherever relevant to provide a clearer picture of Gregory's own linguistic repertoire.

[4] R.A. Cadenhead, *The Body and Desire: Gregory of Nyssa's Ascetical Theology* (Berkeley CA, 2018), 93-5.

Studia Patristica CI, 117-124.
© Peeters Publishers, 2021.

those of mature spiritual standing who 'with [Christ] have been transformed for impassibility and the life divine' and who read the *Song of Songs* with the aim of being 'led as a bride toward an incorporeal and spiritual and undefiled marriage with God' (GNO VI 14,19-15:2; 15,13-5; tr. Norris 15) – provide insights into two moments of spiritual progress, revealing how spiritual maturity inflects the 'gendered' identity of the soul.

The bulk of this chapter will be devoted to a renewed and detailed analysis of the maturational shift between these two commentary texts. I shall also include, by way of framing and comparison, appreciative and critical analyses of two commentators, differently motivated in their retrievals of Gregory's theology, whose interpretations of the *Vit Moys* and the *Cant* have been particularly illuminating. One commentator – Verna Harrison – writing in the 1980s, reflected something of the quasi-Jungian complementarian view of 'masculinity' and 'femininity' that was popular at the time. The other – Sarah Coakley – writing in the 1990s, reflected prevailing notions of gender 'fluidity' popularised by post-structuralist gender theorist Judith Butler.[5]

Some really important insights arose from their respective analyses. Harrison identified in Gregory's theology a crucial shift in the soul's identity from 'male' to 'female' at the very heights of ascent. Coakley underscored the 'gender switches and reversals'[6] that accompany the soul's advances in spiritual growth and emphasised, *contra* Judith Butler, the importance of lifelong asceticism in Gregory's theorisation of desire as well as its eschatological focus. At the same time, however, both Harrison and Coakley imposed categories of interpretation onto the texts that, I shall argue here, distract us from what is truly at stake. It is the burden of this chapter to look afresh at Gregory's theorisation of desire through a close examination of the *Vit Moys* and the *Cant*. In doing so, I shall make clear the implications of the maturational process of ascent for the soul's 'gendered' identification.

So let us begin with the *Vit Moys* to examine how immature desire is 'gendered' by Gregory.

2. The *Vit Moys*: Disavowing 'Womanish' Passion

In the *Vit Moys*, there is an apparent contradiction between the first and second halves of the treatise. How this contradiction is resolved hermeneutically can open up different interpretations of Gregory's construal of stereotypically 'female' vice, as we shall now see, which contribute contrasting insights into spiritual ascent as a process of progressive 'gendered' transformation.

---

[5] J. Butler, *Gender Trouble: Feminism and the Subversion of Identity* (New York, 1990).
[6] S. Coakley, *Powers and Submissions: Spirituality, Philosophy and Gender* (Oxford, 2002), 165.

In the first half of the treatise, Gregory invokes the physiological division in 'human nature' (ἡ ἀνθρωπίνη ... φύσις) between 'male' (ἄρρην) and 'female' (θῆλυς) (*Vit Moys* I 12; tr. Malherbe and Ferguson 32), and argues that Abraham and Sarah (*cf. 1Pt* 3:6) are 'male' and 'female' exemplars of virtue. Through them, he says, men and women have a 'corresponding example of virtue' to emulate (*Vit Moys* I 12; tr. Malherbe and Ferguson 32). In the second part of the treatise, however, Gregory claims that both men and women need to appropriate 'manly' virtue. He claims that 'free will' (προαίρεσις) is responsible for the person whom one chooses to become, 'whether male or female' (*Vit Moys* II 3; tr. Malherbe and Ferguson 56). The 'manly[7] birth' (ὁ ἀνδρώδης τόκος), Gregory writes, represents 'austerity and intensity of virtue ... which is hostile to the tyrant and suspected of insurrection against his rule'. By contrast, 'the female form of life' (τὸ θῆλυ τῆς ζωῆς) denotes 'the material and passionate disposition' (*Vit Moys* II 2; tr. Malherbe and Ferguson 55). These comments reveal what is, for Gregory, the 'real intention' (*Vit Moys* II 2; tr. Malherbe and Ferguson 55) behind the narrative of *Ex* 1, in which Pharaoh tries to curb the growth of the Israelite population (*Ex* 1:16) by ordering Israelite midwives to murder all newborn males. The fact that *male* offspring were singled out for destruction in the biblical narrative is hugely significant for Gregory. It suggests, at the level of allegory, that 'the tyrant' (*Vit Moys* II 2, 5, 49; tr. Malherbe and Ferguson 32, 55, 56, 65), the Devil, whom Pharaoh represents, wants to destroy the practice of virtue among human beings. The Devil, says Gregory, incessantly 'bears hostility' (*Vit Moys* II 49; tr. Malherbe and Ferguson, 65) against male offspring, that is, virtue, and must therefore be defeated through prayer and ascetical practice. For this reason, using the Exodus narrative as an opportunity to expound 'moral teaching' (*Vit Moys* II 49; tr. Malherbe and Ferguson 65), Gregory summons his readers to pursue the 'manly' life of virtue against the Devil.

So which is it? Do women emulate Sarah? Or do they emulate 'manly' virtue? One solution to this apparent contradiction is offered by Verna Harrison.

Keen to eschew 'the monolithic character of ... androcentrism',[8] Verna Harrison claims that Gregory is integrating 'masculine and feminine symbols' in the *Vit Moys* rather than privileging the former above the latter. This is of a piece with her remarks on pagan and Christian thought in the late antique period in which female imagery, she says, is reclaimed at the heights of spiritual ascent alongside 'masculine' qualities.[9] It would appear that Jungian presumptions about

---

[7] Malherbe and Ferguson have 'male' instead of 'manly'. For the purposes of clarification, I have chosen the latter because I want to differentiate ἄρρην (which refers to a physical differentiation, 'male') from ἀνδρώδης (which carried specific moral and spiritual evocations).

[8] V.E.F. Harrison, 'A Gender Reversal in Gregory of Nyssa's First Homily on the Song of Songs', *SP* 27 (1993), 38.

[9] V.E.F. Harrison, 'The Feminine Man in Late Antique Ascetic Piety', *Union Seminary Quarterly Review* 48 (1994), 49-71, particularly 53.

'gender' are at work here. For Jung, the *anima* in men denotes a contrasexual archetype of the collective unconscious,[10] which needs to be integrated into the conscious mind in order to give rise to 'wholeness' and 'individuation'.[11] In Harrison's commentary we find similar ideas at play: the 'virtuous human person', she says of Gregory, is 'at once the mother giving birth and the male child being born' and '[t]he qualities represented by these masculine and feminine symbols are together affirmed as positive'. The 'mature human person', she remarks, 'must possess both'.[12]

At least two presumptions here call for critique and renewed consideration. In the first instance, Harrison presupposes that 'masculine and feminine qualities' (as she herself puts it) are settled, concretised characteristics. In fact, for Gregory, they are differently signified depending on the soul's stage of maturity in ascent – an insight soon to become apparent in our discussion of the *Cant*. In the second instance, she posits a relationship of complementarity between 'masculinity' and 'femininity' – a view that contradicts the *Cant*, in which, as we shall shortly see, the Virgin Bride of Christ supersedes the 'male birth' of the *Vit Moys*.

Gregory's description of spiritual ascent does not, therefore, attempt to integrate two complementary parts of the soul; instead, it schematises the soul's transition in identity from 'male' to 'female' within a framework of diachronic spiritual growth. Harrison pre-empts the reclamation of what she calls 'feminine qualities' at an immature stage of ascent at which 'womanish' passion is in fact renounced *tout court*.

If not in the way Harrison suggests, how will it be possible to reconcile the first and second halves of the *Vit Moys*? To answer this question, it is important to point out that Gregory does not think that women are inexorably or exclusively implicated in 'the female form of life'. It is clear, for instance, that both Miriam and Aaron were 'wounded by the passion of [envy's] influence ...'

---

[10] Its counterpart is the *animus* in women (although Jung wrote relatively little on this).

[11] C.G. Jung, *The Archetypes and the Collective Unconscious*, trans. R.F.C. Hull (London, 1959); *id.*, *Alchemical Studies*, trans. R.F.C. Hull (London, 1968); *id.*, *Psychology of the Unconscious: A study of the transformations and symbolisms of the libido: a contribution to the history of the evolution of thought*, trans. Beatrice M. Hinkle (New York, 1946); *id.*, *Man and his Symbols*, ed. *id.* and after his death, M.-L. von Franz (London, 1964).

[12] V.E.F. Harrison, 'Gender, Generation and Virginity in Cappadocian Theology', *Journal of Theological Studies* 47 (1996), 38-68, 64. It is also revealing that in an article entitled, 'The Feminine Man in Late Antique Ascetic Piety', which does not mention Gregory's *Vit Moys* as such, Harrison characterises late antique theology and philosophy as 'a serious ascetic quest for human wholeness' that seeks the integration of 'both masculine and feminine qualities'. Harrison, 'The Feminine Man' (1994), 49. Note that Harrison invites us to compare this late antique 'ascetic quest' with the thought of Carl Jung, a suggestion she makes *en passant* in a footnote. Harrison, 'The Feminine Man' (1994), 69 n. 2. This gives further credence to the view that her reading of Gregory and her presumptions about 'gender' are underlyingly, if not at times explicitly, Jungian.

(*Vit Moys* II 260; tr. Malherbe and Ferguson 121), even though envy is described as 'most female-like' (γυναικωδέστερα) (*Vit Moys* I 62; tr. Malherbe and Ferguson 47).

It follows, therefore, that when Gregory summons women to emulate Sarah in the first half of the treatise (*Vit Moys* I 12; tr. Malherbe and Ferguson 32), he is rehearsing what has been described as one of his many 'reversals' of 'stereotypical' expectations about 'gender'.[13] Or – to put it more precisely – Abraham's wife exemplifies the kind of 'manly birth' that Gregory later advocates in the second half of the treatise. This is how the two halves of the *Vit Moys* form a coherent unity, despite their apparent contradiction. Although the first half presents Abraham and Sarah as separate exemplars for men and women to emulate respectively, it is evident by the second half that the virtuous life amounts to the same thing for both men and women – it is a 'manly' endeavour, and Sarah's virtue is as 'manly' as Abraham's.

So we have seen that Gregory consistently associates 'female' characteristics with vice in the *Vit Moys* – a text addressed to spiritually immature Christians. But what, we may wonder, is expected of those of greater spiritual stature? It is to these mature individuals, further along the diachronic maturational continuum, that our attentions now turn.

3. The *Cant*: Transforming 'Female' Vice into Passionate Desire for Christ

As stated in the introduction, the *Cant* is addressed to spiritually advanced Christians. This is evidenced by Gregory's own words (as previously cited) and confirmed by the stark absence of the adjectives 'womanish' (γυναικεῖος) and 'soft' (μαλακός),[14] which are evocative of stereotypically 'female' vice, in the text. If I am right therefore to think that the *Vit Moys* and the *Cant* form a progressive continuum in what Martin Laird calls the 'education of desire',[15] then 'womanish' recalcitrance has already – from the perspective of the *Cant* – been repudiated. The soul is now ready to identify with the Virgin Bride in the Song of Songs.

A crucial 'gendered' transition is operative here. Gregory describes the immature soul as a man courting female Wisdom (σοφία) – that is, Jesus Christ, who is described in paradoxical terms as 'the manly woman' (τῆς ἀνδρείας γυναικός) (GNO VI, 22,6-7; my translation). However, Gregory avers that at

[13] S. Coakley, *Powers and Submissions* (2002), 164.

[14] The adjective μαλακός does appear on one occasion, but not without any moral significance. It is used in connection to Elijah, who dressed in 'goatskin' rather than '*soft* raiment' (*Cant* GNO VI, 222,17; tr. Norris 235; emphasis mine).

[15] M. Laird, 'Under Solomon's Tutelage: The Education of Desire in the *Homilies on the Song of Songs*', in Sarah Coakley (ed.), *Rethinking Gregory of Nyssa* (London, 2003), 77-95.

a mature stage of spiritual development – the level at which the *Song of Songs* operates – the soul must relinquish its desire to possess σοφία, so that it may be transformed into the Bride of Christ (GNO VI, 23,1-4; tr. Norris 25). Male courtship of σοφία is therefore ultimately provisional giving way to a further change in identity as the soul matures.

There is a particularly vivid description of the supersession of 'manly' virtue by the Virgin Bride in the Sixth Homily of the *Cant*. Here, Gregory is exegeting *Song* 3:7, which refers to Solomon's marriage surrounded by sixty armed soldiers. Initially, these soldiers are described by Gregory as 'intermediaries with the pure Bride', who 'point out to her the beauty of the royal bed, so as to induce the Bride to desire a divine and unspotted cohabitation with [the] Bridegroom' (GNO VI, 189,16-190,3; tr. Norris 203). Later, however, they are identified with the soul and the Church, both of whom are incorporated into the identity of the Bride:

... all who have put on the divine armour surround the royal bed. They have become, as a whole group, the one Israel; and since, because there are twelve tribes that constitute this body of the brave in its fivefold form, the full total of the brave is completely summed up in the number sixty; they make up one formation and one army and one bed – that is, all shall become one church, one people, and one bride, fitted together into the communion of one body by one Commander, one Head of the church, one Bridegroom. (GNO VI, 197,13-198,2; tr. Norris 209)

While these male soldiers have an important role in guarding against temptation and eliciting the Bride's 'desire' (ἐπιθυμία) for the Bridegroom, they are – in the final analysis – subsumed into the role of the Bride. In this regard, Harrison makes a very pertinent remark (as long as we leave her Jungian importations aside):

... notice that ultimately the masculine activity of the soldier has an instrumental purpose. It defines the periphery, but the feminine activity is at the centre.[16]

This comment may seem surprising given Harrison's interpretation of the *Vit Moys*. For despite her awareness of the centrality of 'feminine activity' in this extract from the *Cant*, she does not feel compelled to re-evaluate her Jungian predilections. After all, the Jungian integration of 'masculine and feminine qualities' is at odds with the displacement of 'masculine activity' with 'feminine activity' described in the *Cant* above.

There is, then, a remarkable crowning view of 'femininity' at the heights of ascent that subsumes, and above all extends and enriches, all the positive 'male' traits that have proceeded it. The two forms of 'femininity' operative in Gregory's frame of reference – the passionate recalcitrant version and the passionate virginal (ascetic and epektastic) version – are not therefore *egal*, which gives

---

[16] V.E.F. Harrison, 'Gender, Generation and Virginity in Cappadocian Theology' (1996), 65-6.

us cause to consider whether one can speak unitarily of 'femininity', as Harrison does.

It is here at this point of gender reversal that Coakley finds the contemporary notion of gender 'fluidity' helpful as a point of comparison (and critique) with Butler's advocacy of subversive performativity. But the term 'fluidity' does not do sufficient justice to the maturational process Gregory describes. The 'gender switches and reversals' of spiritual growth are not amorphously 'fluid', but follow a set direction and diachronicity: transformation, in order words, must occur in a set order and at the right time. Attempting, therefore, to interpret Gregory's schema as the 'completion' of 'Butler's remorselessly sophisticated and tortured manoeuvres'[17] through an appeal to 'fluidity' means that Gregory's vision of spiritual growth is anachronistically framed by the postmodern concern to subvert 'gender binaries'.[18] In reality, it is *spiritual maturation* that is the real concern and motivation for Gregory's use of 'gendered' imagery.

4. Concluding Reflections

So to sum up the argument of this chapter: Harrison was right to observe a change between the *Vit Moys* and the *Cant* from normative masculinity to a supreme, spiritually normative femininity. The question is what you make of that change. It is not, I have argued here, an example contrasexual integration, a delicate balancing act between two complementary halves or parts of the soul – but a moment of triumphant displacement and disidentification, the Virgin Bride emerging supreme above all else.

Coakley was right to deny concretised settled 'gender' in Gregory's vision of ascent – but the term 'fludity', as I have shown, is misleading, implying endless anarchic gendered flux, which is normatively important for Butler, but not for Gregory. Nor, yet, is this transition to be confused with contemporary interests in *self*-identification, which characterises a great deal of post-modern gender theory. For Gregory, the collective – ecclesial – alignment of individuals to a set pattern of 'gendered' spiritual growth provides the context (and means) for individual sanctification.

We may consider, in closing, whether 'essentialism' – a much-disputed consideration in feminism and gender theory – remains in Gregory's vision of transformation. To respond in brief: what Gregory imagines here is not 'essentialism' in the world's modern terms as a fixed biology associated with inviolable cultural values. The supreme 'femininity' of the Virgin Bride is something that comes about through lengthy transformation *en route* to union with Christ. Subordination of this bride is not worldly subjugation (as evidenced by Macrina's

---

[17] S. Coakley, *Powers and Submissions* (2002), 166.
[18] *Ibid.* 164.

life), but a posture of loving obedience wrought through spiritual discipline and ascetic passion, and an acknowledgement of ontological differentiation between Creator and creature.

What I have sought to show in this chapter is the importance of interpreting Gregory's thought from the perspective of his diachronically theorised account of spiritual ascent. The maturations of the spiritual life are seldom considered in contemporary theological and secular reflections on 'gender'. So allow me, in closing, to suggest that a deeper appreciation of the soul's varied and shifting identifications with 'male' and 'female' characteristics at different chronological moments in spiritual ascent would not only revive an overlooked aspect of Christian spiritual reflection but also enrich contemporary discussions on that now widely contested issue of 'gender'.

CHAPTER 9

Creation, Fall and Redemption

Jonathan FARRUGIA

1. Introduction

The original context in which Gregory preached the homilies on the *Song of Songs* is debated,[1] however scholars agree on the point that the reason why they were delivered was to offer his audience a series of meditations on the biblical text, concentrating in particular on the ascetic journey the soul of the Christian is called to make in order to reach perfection.[2] In this long itinerary the Nyssen makes many references to the evil element that has soiled human nature after the fall. Therefore, one of the necessary pre-requisites for the soul to advance in the ascent towards perfection is to free itself of this evil stain.[3]

We shall therefore briefly illustrate how Gregory's interpretation of salvation history – generally associated with his treatises – is given in remarkable detail in this cycle of homilies.

2. Man: a divine creature tricked by evil

In about half of these fifteen homilies Gregory speaks of man's original condition in the garden and how this was lost because of his sin. The first reference to this is found in the second homily, where he states clearly with the words of the bride: 'In the beginning I was not created like this. [...] I was not black by nature, but this ugliness was brought on me from outside'.[4]

---

[1] Daniélou and many who followed him maintain that they were composed upon the request of the lady Olympiades and delivered for her and her friends in Constantinople towards the end of Gregory's life. Cahill has proposed that this was in fact a second stage in the development of these homilies which would have been first delivered at Nyssa as Lenten talks, then, eventually, were re-edited and sent to Olympiades for her and her friends to meditate upon: J.B. Cahill, 'The date and setting of Gregory of Nyssa's Commentary on the Song of Songs', *JThS* 32 (1981), 447-60.

[2] G. Maspero, 'In canticum canticorum', in L.F. Mateo-Seco and G. Maspero (eds), *The Brill dictionary of Gregory of Nyssa* (Leiden, 2010), 121.

[3] Many images are used to describe this stain, the first being the 'blackness' which makes the soul ugly: μέλαιναν οὖσαν ἐξ ἁμαρτίας *Cant* II (GNO VI, 46,11).

[4] *Cant* II (GNO VI, 50,10-6) Note: The English translations of the texts were made by the author.

Studia Patristica CI, 125-131.

Man, therefore, was not created a sinner by God. The original beauty of human nature is compared to childhood, because small children know no evil;[5] elsewhere it is compared to a golden stone[6] and a golden vase.[7] The soul, while it was still similar to God in all things, possessed the qualities of will, blessedness and incorruptibility.[8] Being thus endowed with all good things and being completely free from evil, all man had to do was to preserve these good gifts God entrusted to him, not being obliged to provide for himself.[9] As the bride says, it was something external that made man lose his brightness and turn black because of sin.

Along these homilies Gregory makes several references to free will, a quality which God gave to all rational creatures, not only to man. This made them capable of choosing freely and willingly what was pleasing to them.[10] At this point he introduces the devil as the one who used badly this freedom and became the inventor of evil. It was he who opened the path through which evil entered creation, becoming himself the enemy of all who seek to use their free will towards what is good.[11] He is described as a monster, an assassin with a sharp tongue, a dragon, a rebel, hell itself that opens its mouth.[12] In his hatred towards man, who still had a loving relationship with God, the devil tricked the first couple into believing that the prohibition of the fruit of the tree and the offer of an impassible life were wounds inflicted by God on them. He, instead, offered them his 'kiss' of all things that were pleasing and bright.[13] Human nature succumbed to his snare and was thus stripped of its original beauty, becoming black, because it got involved with vice.[14]

So human nature was created good, in the image of God, but before it grew its roots in the good and acquired unflinching stability there, it was tricked by the devil, disguised as the serpent, who brought him to neglect the goods he received from God and consequently was stripped of the goods it had been given.[15] Man's brightness was burnt, and his natural beauty shrivelled, just as a plant is burnt and dried by the onslaught of the sun. So, Gregory says in homily VII, the seed of sin was created by the curse of the serpent, and thus, along with the products of the good seed created by God, man found a further option: that of evil.[16]

---

[5] *Cant* II (GNO VI, 52,18-53,1).
[6] *Cant* IV (GNO VI, 100,16).
[7] *Cant* VII (GNO VI, 208,12).
[8] *Cant* XV (GNO VI, 448,5-9).
[9] *Cant* II (GNO VI, 54,5-7).
[10] *Cant* II (GNO VI, 55,4-7).
[11] *Cant* II (GNO VI, 55,7-16).
[12] *Cant* V (GNO VI, 165,7-14).
[13] *Cant* XIII (GNO VI, 378,6-9).
[14] τοῦ ἀρχετύπου κάλλους ἀποξενωθεῖσα τῇ πονηρᾷ γειτνιάσει τῆς κακίας πρὸς τὸ εἰδεχθὲς ἠλλοιώθης. *Cant* IV (GNO VI, 102,1-3).
[15] *Cant* II (GNO VI, 54,7-9).
[16] *Cant* VII (GNO VI, 241,12-3).

Speaking of free will in man, the bishop of Nyssa seeks to explain how this quality was involved in man's sin and how eventually it became the prime impulse for man's attraction to evil. First of all, in the second homily, when the bride is explaining how she lost her original beauty and became black, he says that this process of blackening was initiated by man's free will, not by God.[17] Later on, in the fourth homily, Gregory explains how human nature has been created in such a way as to be able to transform itself into the shape of that which it follows through its free will, just as the reflection in a mirror takes the form of what stands in front of it. Therefore when the soul gives in to an impulse towards a certain passion, it *becomes* the passion itself. Gregory does not fail to point out that this quality of the soul is not in itself negative, since it works both for virtues and vices.[18]

In man there is a movement which rises towards heaven (caused by the spiritual nature of the soul) and another that descends towards the ground (caused by the material nature of the body). Thus for one to go forth, the other must give way. Free will is found half way between these two and according to its choices it will give strength to one and relaxation to the other. So we understand that for Gregory free will is neutral. It is not pre-ordained towards evil or good; it will follow the greater impulse according to the strength of the person's reason and will in controlling his passions. The winning impulse will be the one with which free will sides.[19] But, since virtues and vices are opposites, these cannot abide simultaneously in the same person.[20] So when a person's free will tends towards evil, the good ceases to exist and vice versa.[21]

In short, therefore, man was created good and free. When confronted with a choice between good and evil, since he had no experience of evil and only a little experience of good, man's reason and will were not strong enough to control the impulse towards the sensual pleasure promised by the fruit, so he

---

[17] ἀσφαλίζεται τὴν τῶν μαθητευομένων διάνοιαν μὴ τῷ δημιουργῷ τὴν αἰτίαν τοῦ σκοτεινοῦ εἴδους ἀνατιθέναι ἀλλὰ τὴν ἑκάστου προαίρεσιν τοῦ τοιούτου εἴδους τὰς ἀρχὰς καταβάλλεσθαι. *Cant* II (GNO VI, 50,6-9).

[18] *Cant* IV (GNO VI, 102,4-103-5).

[19] Μέση δὲ ἀμφοῖν ἑστῶσα ἡ αὐτεξούσιος ἡμῶν δύναμίς τε καὶ προαίρεσις δι᾽ ἑαυτῆς ἐμποιεῖ καὶ τόνον τῷ κάμνοντι καὶ ἀτονίαν τῷ κατισχύοντι· ἐν ᾧ γὰρ ἂν γένηται μέρει, τούτῳ δίδωσι κατὰ τοῦ ἄλλου τὰ νικητήρια, *Cant* XII (GNO VI, 345,19-346,2).

[20] *Cant* IV (GNO VI, 103,5-7).

[21] *Cant* V (GNO VI, 157,21-158,7). Discussing this point in some further detail in Homily X, Gregory explains how human nature has two kinds of pleasure: that of the soul which is attained impassibly, and that of the body which is attained through passion. The one chosen by free will shall dominate the other. Those who choose the pleasure of the senses, therefore opting for evil, will not taste divine joy because their worse part will darken the better as we read in *Cant* X (GNO VI, 313,17-24). However, if man chooses to follow the impulses of his soul, his free will shall help him advance further along the way towards the good, changing from the degraded wooden or clay vase in which he was turned by sin back to the silver or golden vase of his original state, cf. *Cant* VII (GNO VI, 208,17-8).

freely[22] chose to disobey God's command not to eat from the tree, losing the special gifts God had bestowed on him.

3. The effects of evil on human nature

The act of disobedience committed by the first humans distorted not only their nature, but also that of all their descendants. Eating from the forbidden fruit man satisfied his gluttony for a moment, but then the fruit's sweetness turned bitter, filling man with corruption, and leading him to death. Tasting it, man became dead to the better life, exchanging his divine immortal life to an irrational and corruptible one. Hence the legacy the first parents passed on to their descendants was a dead life, because once death was united to human nature, all future generations were tainted with death; all future life was in truth death, being deprived of immortality.[23]

Apart from this, since the first choice made by man's free will was in the direction of evil, somehow free will, which had been created neutral, became warped. Even though man never lost his freedom, his natural impulses turned out to be more inclined towards what is not good rather than towards what is. Man became a slave of his own sin, being afraid to lose his contact with evil, especially the evil brought about by passions[24] which fight on the side of vice.[25] Choosing good did not become impossible, but it became decisively more difficult.

In these homilies Gregory does not make a clear reference to the 'double' creation of man[26] as he usually interprets *Gen* 1:27 in other works, but he does make a reference to the garments of skin with which God dressed man after eating the fruit. These garments of skin represent the passions which make man vulnerable to sin.[27]

---

[22] It is true that the devil tricked man into believing that the fruit was good for him, but this does not balance out the fact that man freely chose to obey the devil rather than God.

[23] *Cant* XII (GNO VI, 350,17-351,6).

[24] *Cant* II (GNO VI, 58,19-20).

[25] *Cant* II (GNO VI, 56,5-11); X (299,16-300,5).

[26] The biblical text states: 'So God created mankind in his own image, in the image of God he created them; male and female he created them' (*Gen* 1:27). In *Op hom* chapters 16 and 17 Gregory explains how first God created man in his own image, then he created them male and female. So at a first moment mankind had no gender distinction, just like God; eventually, since God foresaw that man would succumb to sin and would be subject to death, he divided mankind between males and females, in order to make it possible for them the procreate like other animals and thus the species would avoid extinction. At this point, however, human nature was still sinless, immortal and free from passions. These would eventually come after they were covered with the garments of skin (which are not to be identified with the body).

[27] τῆς γὰρ καθαρότητος ἐκπεσοῦσα τὸ ζοφῶδες εἶδος ἐνεδυσάμην (τοιοῦτος γὰρ τῷ εἴδει ὁ χιτὼν ὁ δερμάτινος) *Cant* II (GNO VI, 60,16-8).

Further discussion is offered regarding other effects of sin on human nature, which we cannot delve into in this study. The strongest among Gregory's comments is probably found in the fifth homily: human nature 'took upon itself the form of the serpent for all the ages it was lying on the ground looking at it'.[28] So from his fall till the time of redemption, man's glance was locked on the serpent, becoming ever more like it. Having stripped himself willingly of his divine image, man became a beast, taking on himself the irrational image through his animal behaviour.[29] Sin itself is a madness that ages the soul, leading it to death, to non-existence.[30]

4. Freedom from sin

Despite man's disobedience, God did not cease to be man's friend[31] and He still considered human nature as a good creation,[32] hence worthy of being saved. Apart from the indispensable role of the Incarnation and the sanctifying grace of the sacraments,[33] Gregory offers some other hints as to how man can strive towards his own salvation.

In the Prologue, Olympiades is praised for her purity of soul and thought, thus being untainted by any passion which dirties human nature;[34] this, then, is the path man has to follow in order to be worthy of enjoying God's salvation. To do this, man has to first shed off his old sinful self,[35] together with its desires and actions, as if it were a dirty garment.[36] Since man entered mortal life after dying to immortal life through sin, he will regain the original life if he dies to mortal life, dying, then, to sin.[37] In so doing, man takes upon himself the commitment to be always vigilant[38] and to strive towards perfection,[39] in order

---

[28] *Cant* V (GNO VI, 150,13-5).

[29] ἐπειδὴ γὰρ ἀποθέμενός ποτε τὸ θεῖον εἶδος ὁ ἄνθρωπος πρὸς τὴν ὁμοιότητα τῆς ἀλόγου φύσεως ἐθηριώθη. *Cant* VIII (GNO VI, 251,1-3).

[30] *Cant* I (GNO VI, 41,13-8).

[31] *Cant* XIII (GNO VI, 378,3-5).

[32] *Cant* XV (GNO VI, 449,12-3).

[33] In these homilies Gregory makes numerous references to the salvific value of Christ's birth, passion and resurrection, as he had already done in other sermons like the three Easter sermons, *Diem nat* and *Diem lum*. This is clearly a sign of his 'maturer' thought since in the *Homilies on the Beatitudes* – probably his oldest extant exegetical cycle of homilies – he makes no reference to this. Many times he also insists on the value of baptism, confession and the Eucharist in man's journey towards God.

[34] σου καθαρεύειν τὸν τῆς ψυχῆς ὀφθαλμὸν ἀπὸ πάσης ἐμπαθοῦς τε καὶ ῥυπώσης ἐννοίας, *Cant* Prol. (GNO VI, 4,4-5).

[35] *Cant* XI (GNO VI, 330,16-7).

[36] *Cant* I (GNO VI, 14,13-5); I (25,12-5).

[37] *Cant* XII (GNO VI, 351,9-13).

[38] *Cant* XI (GNO VI, 315,19-22).

[39] *Cant* III (GNO VI, 80,9-13); VI (188,3-4).

to put on the original immaculate garment woven by God[40] when He created human nature. It is important to note that God does not create a new nature for mankind; he will restore the soiled nature to the original state of incorruptibility.[41]

Gregory devises two particular ways how man can advance in this path of perfection. One is that of fear, the other that of love.

Loving God entails primarily drawing back to God[42] and looking at Christ as through a mirror, in order to assume His form in one's soul.[43] Contemplating Christ alone,[44] seeking his kiss,[45] leads to his imitation,[46] and this is the best way to attain perfection. Having a loving passion for God, greater than the other passions which tend towards sin, helps to reverse fallen human nature to its original state.[47] Desire, therefore, can be transformed into an aid to long for God, rather than for material things, and this chases away the evil one.[48] It is a return to the original state of innocence proper to children.[49] Those who follow this path are described as the children, or the queens who obey the Spouse out of love.[50]

Fearing God is the other way to attain perfection; it is good, but inferior to the former one. It is the fear of punishment, of being sent to hell,[51] where there is no memory of God and where there are no good things, that makes some people struggle to lead a good life. These are compared to the concubines of the Spouse, who obey him and are faithful to him out of submission and fear,[52] just like slaves.[53]

---

[40] *Cant* XI (GNO VI, 329,9-14).

[41] οὐ καινόν τι κάλλος ἐπ᾽αὐτῆς μηχανᾶται ὃ μὴ πρότερον ἦν, ἀλλ᾽ἐπὶ τὴν πρώτην ἐπανάγει χάριν, *Cant* IV (GNO VI, 101,1-3). This theme is found in many other of the Nyssen's sermons, particularly the *Diem lum* and the Easter homilies.

[42] *Cant* IV (GNO VI, 100,21-101,4).

[43] *Cant* II (GNO VI, 68,4-10). Earlier reference was made to man taking upon himself the form of the serpent after having looked at it for so long. Looking at Christ is the remedy to reject the serpent's form and regain the original divine image.

[44] *Cant* VI (GNO VI, 197,2-5); XIII (376,17-377,1).

[45] *Cant* I (GNO VI, 33,6).

[46] *Cant* III (GNO VI, 98,6-12).

[47] *Cant* I (GNO VI, 29,3-6).

[48] *Cant* IV (GNO VI, 118,18-119,11).

[49] *Cant* VI (GNO VI, 198,10-3); XIII (395,2-5).

[50] *Cant* XV (GNO VI, 461,7-11).

[51] *Cant* I (GNO VI, 15,18-16,1). It is interesting to point out that in these homilies – as in other works – Gregory seems undecided about what will be the final destiny of the wicked. In his treatises he says that all evil (hence including the evil-doers) will be crushed into non-existence, or that they will be saved nonetheless. Here and in other homilies, however, he makes clear references to the existence of hell (the place of crying and gnashing of teeth) as the place where the souls of the wicked will end up.

[52] *Cant* XV (GNO VI, 461,16-9).

[53] *Cant* I (GNO VI, 16,5-8).

In both cases the gift of memory[54] helps the progress in this path: remembering the sorry state in which man had brought himself will help him strive toward the better[55] in order to avoid falling back in that condition. Consequently, a soul which recognizes true beauty is no longer tricked by what in the world seems beautiful.[56]

In conclusion, Gregory states that at the fulfilment of time, love will erase all fear,[57] so eventually all those who in life seek to distance themselves from sin (be it out of fear or out of love) will have the same prize,[58] enjoying blessedness and incorruptibility for eternity in the presence of the Spouse.

5. Conclusion

As we have seen, then, in this exegetical cycle, addressed primarily to 'common' folk rather than to fellow theologians, Gregory succeeds in delivering his standard view of how human nature was created, lost its divine imprint and will eventually regain it, using clear and easily understandable language and imagery which fit very well with his mission as a bishop and as a preacher.

---

[54] *Cant* II (GNO VI, 47,1-5); VIII (252,5-6).
[55] *Cant* V (GNO VI, 160,13-5).
[56] *Cant* IV (GNO VI, 106,11-20).
[57] *Cant* XV (GNO VI, 466,5-9).
[58] *Cant* XV (GNO VI, 469,1-6).

CHAPTER 10

'I sleep but my heart is awake'
Gregory of Nyssa's Moral Reading of the *Song of Songs* 5:2

Joona SALMINEN

At the end of the tenth homily of *In Canticum*, St. Gregory of Nyssa comments on the verse 'I sleep but my heart is awake' (*Song* 5:2).[1] This article is focused on his moral reading of the passage. As spiritual progress is of paramount importance for Gregory,[2] in his homilies Gregory's aim is to instruct the 'fleshly folk for the sake of the spiritual and immaterial welfare of their souls.'[3] Being wakeful thus emerges as an important theme in his exegesis. According to Gregory:

Sleep is an image of death, for in death every perceptive activity of bodies is dissolved. There is no activity of seeing, or of hearing, or of smelling or tasting or of touching in the season of sleep. What is more, it relaxes the body's tension and brings about forgetfulness of the person's thoughts. It puts fear to sleep and tames aggression and relaxes the intensity of bitterness and effects an insensibility to all evils, as long as it prevails over the body. Hence from our text we learn this: that she who makes the boast that *I sleep but my heart lies awake* has risen higher than herself. For the truth is that insofar as only the intellect in itself is alive, without any distraction from the organs of sense perception, the bodily nature becomes inactive, as in slumber or profound sleep, and it is truly possible to say that through disuse the capacity to see all those shameful objects that regularly trouble childish eyes is put to sleep.[4]

Like the passage above, Gregory's *In Canticum* contains paradoxical language and expressions that are of great importance for Christian spirituality even today. In the quoted passage, Gregory shows dependence on Platonistic and Aristotelian strands. In relation to Christian mystical tradition in general and Gregory's thinking in particular, these philosophical undercurrents make his

---

[1] I use the English translation *Homilies on the Song of Songs* by R.A. Norris (Atlanta, 2012); and for the Greek text H. Langerbeck's edition in *Gregorii Nysseni opera* VI (Leiden, 1960). Before Gregory an influential commentary on *The Song* was that of Origen to whom Gregory also refers. See G. Maspero, 'Cant', in L.F. Mateo-Seco and G. Maspero (eds), *The Brill Dictionary of Gregory of Nyssa*, trans. S. Cherney (Leiden, 2010), 121-5.

[2] See J. Daniélou, *Platonisme et Théologie Mystique: essai sur la doctrine spirituelle de saint Grégoire de Nysse* (Paris, 1944), 22, 24, 192; see also H. Boersma, *Embodiment and Virtue in Gregory of Nyssa: An Anagogical Approach* (Oxford, 2013), 1.

[3] *Cant* prol., 4,7 (GNO VI, 3; Trans. Norris 3).

[4] *Cant* X (GNO VI, 312; Trans. Norris 327, 329).

Studia Patristica CI, 133-141.
© Peeters Publishers, 2021.

exegesis interesting. In what follows some of the paradoxical expressions of *Cant* X are analysed from the perspective of Gregory's moral teaching. It will be shown how the expression 'sleeping awake' is, in fact, a tropological interpretation of verse 5:2 of the *Song* and closely linked to both Gregory's Christology and his ascetical teaching.

Sleep, senses, and 'stranger sleep'

In early Christian asceticism, sleeping became a controversial topic because arousing dreams were considered as attachments to worldly pleasures.[5] Many ascetic authors considered sleep-related passions as signs that the dreamer was not making enough progress.[6] However, when it comes to Gregory, his idea might be slightly more positive because of his anthropology, teaching on trans-formation, and theory of restoration of the image of God.[7] Given that regarding sleep, Gregory's position differs from most early Christian ascetic authors, it needs to be asked what explains this different emphasis. Patricia Cox Miller has drawn attention to some events in Gregory's personal history in order to demonstrate his idea of dreaming.[8] In her view it was dreaming that gave Greg-ory the language he needed to describe both the border between the physical and spiritual world and ascetic identity.[9] Though I agree with this analysis, it needs to be highlighted that Gregory also develops a somewhat critical attitude toward sleeping and dreaming, for example, in the beginning of his 11th homily *In Canticum* as well as in his other works too.[10]

Since Daniélou, many scholars have pointed out that in Gregory's thinking in general, as in *In Canticum* too, the spiritual senses are supposed to take over the bodily ones.[11] When the person is sleeping her intellect (*nous*) can work

---

[5] P. Brown, *The Body and Society: Men, Women, and Sexual Renunciation in Early Christianity* (New York, 1988), 230; for background, analysis, and more references on sleeping in early Christian ascetic literature, see J. Salminen, *Asceticism and Early Christian Lifestyle* (diss., Helsinki, 2017), 48, 50-54.

[6] See S. Knuuttila, *Emotions in Ancient and Medieval Philosophy* (Oxford, 2004), 149, 173-4.

[7] J. Warren Smith has argued for the importance of transformation in Gregory's soteriology in *Passion and Paradise: Human and Divine Emotion in the Thought of Gregory of Nyssa* (New York, 2004). The theme of transformation is also important for Gregory's ascetical theory.

[8] P. Cox Miller, 'Dreaming the Body: An Aesthetics of Asceticism', in V.L. Wimbush and R. Valantasis (eds), *Asceticism* (Oxford, 1998), 281-300, 284, 289-90. See also P. Brown, *The Body and Society* (1988), 300.

[9] P. Cox Miller, 'Dreaming the Body' (1998), 296. See also the beginning of *Cant* XI about false dreaming.

[10] *Cant* XI (GNO VI, 315,15-317); in *De hominis opificio* and in *De mortuis non esse dolendum* Gregory also shows a critical attitude towards sleeping.

[11] See Sarah Coakley, 'Gregory of Nyssa', in P.L. Gavrilyuk & S. Coakley (eds), *The Spiritual Senses: Perceiving God in Western Christianity* (Cambridge, New York, 2012), 36-55; P. Brown, *The Body and Society* (1988), 300-1; H. Boersma, *Embodiment and Virtue in Gregory of Nyssa*

without being distracted by the senses; as Gregory puts it 'the capacity to see shameful objects' becomes inactive along with the body. This way the 'childish eyes' are no longer tempted and the person is almost like a corpse. Gregory uses the image of death to explain what sleeping is – the cessation of the senses. In his view, the one who sleeps is also immune to all evils because of the inactive body (this echoes 1*Tim* 5:6).

Gregory does not specify here what he means by 'shameful objects' but he mentions that usually people need sleep after drinking and also for digestion. However, the sleep mentioned in the passage is not of the ordinary sort but *xenos*, a stranger. He concludes that it is impossible for a sleeper to be awake and vice versa, so the passage must be talking about some other kind of sleep where the two opposites can take place at the same time.[12] In this he comes close to Aristotle who considered sleep (*hypnos*) and wakefulness (*egrēgorsis*) as opposites (*ta enantia epi tōn allōn*).[13] Gregory's description seems to imply a rather strict dualism between the body and the soul though wakefulness of the soul is gained through sleep. In the same context, he also mentions *ekstasis* as a result of drinking.[14] Something similar also happens during the 'stranger-sleep.'

In his theory of sleep as cessation of the senses, Gregory seems to follow Aristotle.[15] However, according to Aristotle it is only the intellectual part of the soul that sleeps while the imagination (*phantasma*) and senses (*aisthētikon*) are active to some extent.[16] For Gregory, in contrast, the cessation of the senses is related to contemplation and perceiving God. Sleep enables a person to have knowledge of God – not by bodily senses but while they are inactive. From the point of view of apophatic theology, this approach is remarkable because by *anaisthēsia*, lack of sensation, one is able to enter into a state in which he or she is no longer limited by sensory observations but is able to rise above oneself. Gregory maintains that in order to perceive the truth the intellectual part of the soul should not sleep but be active: at this point his approach turns towards Platonism.

(2013), 93. Boersma connects the spiritual senses to the Alexandrian tradition and especially to Origen and mysticism, whereas the focus of this article is to put more emphasis on the moralistic reading of Gregory's homilies; *cf.* J. Daniélou, *Platonisme et Théologie Mystique* (1944), 281. On the spiritual senses and Christian perfection, see S. Knuuttila, *Emotions in Ancient and Medieval Philosophy* (2004), 133-4.

[12] *Cant* X (GNO VI, 311,7-18).

[13] Aristotle, *De somno et vigilia* 453b25-30. In the same passage Aristotle considers sleep as deprivation (*sterēsis*) of wakefulness. See also *ibid.* 454b1-10.

[14] *Cant* X (GNO VI, 310,20).

[15] Aristotle, *De somno et vigilia* 454b25-30; 455a5-15.

[16] Aristotle, *De somno et vigilia* 455b1-5 (senses); about phantasms, see the references by M. Perälä, 'Sleep: Ancient Theories', in S. Knuuttila and J. Sihvola (eds), *Sourcebook for the History of the Philosophy of Mind. Philosophical Psychology from Plato to Kant* (Dordrecht, 2014), 173-86, 176: *De insomniis* 458b33-459a5, 459a21-2, 462a29-31.

Gregory seems to hold that sleeping is a natural function for humans, but, unlike Aristotle, he seems to give a positive evaluation of what happens during sleep.[17] In this matter, he comes close to Plato and his theory on dreams as media for divinations in *Timaeus* (71c-72a).[18] Richard Norris suggests that Gregory's account of sleeping should be understood in the light of *Phaed.* 64c-67b.[19] This is an accurate suggestion because 66d-e explains the dualism Gregory applies; however, it does not explain the metaphor of the 'stranger-sleep,' the figure of speech the explanation of *Song* 5:2 is all about. Gregory's intention seems to be to highlight that in order to get into a contemplative phase: the mind should be active, literally 'alive' (*monos nous bioteuei*), without senses causing it annoyance (*oudeni tōn aisthēriōn parenokhloumenos*).[20] This differs from how he defines death: a definition given by him holds that 'all bodily sensory activities are demolished' (*luetai pasa aisthētikē energeia tōn sōmatōn*). By contrast, the concept of stranger-sleep, then, seems to imply that it is composed of two opposites that normally would alternate but coincide in this particular case.[21] The image of death[22] is thus an example that illustrates the other half, the bodily one, of contemplation. It should be noted that in the same homily Gregory also links the theme of mortification of the flesh to the freedom of emotions and spiritual progress. Both forms of wakefulness are important to him. Being awake spiritually is a wonderful thing (a paradox in the Greek sense of the word) that enables one to progress in virtues, whereas the bodily awakening is a sign of discipline. Gregory's reading resembles what Plato writes in *Timaeus* (52b-c): because of our sleepy condition we are unable to understand the reality surrounding us and this also affects our moral evaluation.

At this point the early Alexandrian teachers Clement and Origen make an illuminating comparison.[23] For Clement, as for Gregory, sleeping is for digestion and resting from activities.[24] This connection was common in ancient thought; it is already apparent in Aristotle.[25] Though Clement thinks that sleeping is in accordance with human nature, he exhorts his students not to sleep

---

[17] *Cant* X (GNO VI, 311,11-4; 311,19-312,6).

[18] For further references and ancient discussion on divination through dreams, see M. Perälä, 'Sleep: Ancient Theories' (2014), 180-2.

[19] R.A. Norris, *Homilies* (2012), 329 n20.

[20] *Cant* X (GNO VI, 312,10-1).

[21] *Cant* X (GNO VI, 311,8-312,6). My translation. *Cf.* H. Boersma, *Embodiment and Virtue in Gregory of Nyssa* (2013), 97.

[22] Already Philo of Alexandria shared Plato's notion of equating dreaming with death and being awake to being alive; see *De somnis* I 150.

[23] Already Daniélou compared Clement, Origen and Gregory, *cf.* J. Daniélou, *Platonisme et Théologie Mystique* (1944), 274-5. This paragraph renders material from J. Salminen, *Asceticism and Early Christian Lifestyle* (2017), 50-2.

[24] Clement, *Paedagogus* II 9,78.

[25] Aristotle, *De somno et vigilia* 456b18-30; *cf.* 457b-32.

because he thinks they should be awake before God and demonstrate that by their actions.[26] Like Gregory, Clement links contemplation to being awake, not to sleeping.[27] From this perspective we can also understand Gregory's homily and how it emphasizes that the soul should be awake before God. The theme of waking is in many ways connected to reading the Scriptures and asceticism, but in this context I want to highlight particularly the moral dimension of it because, in addition to Clement, Origen, whose influence on Gregory is well known, also considers in his fifth homily on Genesis the sleeping Lot as an example of how vices attack a person who is incapable of 'knowing and sensing' (*nec sentire nec intelligere*).[28] For Origen, getting drunk leads to other vices and unvirtuous behaviour.[29] Origen's exegesis, then, suggests that the senses and the intellect are inactive while one is sleeping. What happens to Lot does not refer to having a rest. On the contrary, Origen's reading puts emphasis on being alert for vices of pride and vainglory. He explains that these vices are Lot's daughters because they come from the inside.[30] Origen's moral reading warns not to give in to carnal desires while the soul or intellect is sleeping.

Gregory's reading of *Song* 5:2 comes close to Origen's exegesis and Clement's exhortations, both of which carry a moralistic tune. The comparisons above also demonstrate that the originality of Gregory's thinking is not in his theory of sleep but in the language he uses to communicate his moral and ascetical teaching. His paradoxical expressions deserve more attention.

Paradoxes and pedagogy

It has been a custom in modern scholarship to pay attention to the paradoxical language Gregory applies in his commentary. Daniélou emphasizes that Gregory's commentary contains several paradoxes – such as 'bright darkness,' 'sober drunkenness' and, also, 'waking sleep,' the latter characterized as being 'among the most important of his expressions of the mystical life.'[31] This branch of research has produced a good amount of analysis on mystical language and called attention to the nuances of both apophatic and kataphatic theology.[32] However, as I argue, there are various kinds of paradoxes in the writings of

---

[26] Clement, *Paedagogus* II 9,79,3 and 81; my translation.
[27] Clement, *Paedagogus* II 9,80.
[28] Origen, *Gen. hom.* V 6.
[29] Origen, *Gen. hom.* V 3.
[30] Origen, *Gen. hom.* V 6.
[31] P. Cox Miller, 'Dreaming the Body' (1998), 290.
[32] See for example Andrew Louth, *The Origins of the Christian Mystical Tradition from Plato to Denys* (Oxford, 1981), 79, 85; S. Coakley (ed.), *Re-thinking Gregory of Nyssa* (Oxford, 2003); and F. Mateo-Seco, 'Mysticism', in L.F. Mateo-Seco and G. Maspero (eds), *The Brill Dictionary of Gregory of Nyssa* (2010), 519-30.

Gregory, but they have not always been recognized in the scholarship. Daniélou's account on bright darkness is a good example of a traditional analysis on paradoxical language. The distance between today's readers and Daniélou's treatise also illustrates many changes in the paradigm of patristic research.

In *Platonisme et Théologie Mystique* (1944) Daniélou noted that it is the doctrine of spiritual senses that lays the ground for Gregory's teaching on mystical life and knowledge of God. The mystical life is in practical terms the restoration of the *eikōn*, the image of God in man. This restoration is the same as achieving freedom from emotions: 'L'*apatheia* est cette restauration même.' According to Daniélou, the restoration of the image happens in the baptism that is the beginning of the purgative stage in one's life. There is an awareness of God and his presence in the human soul: *aisthēsis parousias* in Gregory's terms. Daniélou distinguishes between the mystical awareness and mystical union, the former, *connaissance mystique*, being a matter of the intellect and the latter, *union mystique*, a matter of the will. Daniélou describes the mystical life as a progress, constant movement towards God. He also refers to this process with the term bright darkness (*ténèbre lumineuse*) and emphasizes that Gregory is a part of the chain of the great tradition to which Philo, Clement of Alexandria, Plotinus, and Pseudo-Dionysius have also contributed.[33] Daniélou emphasizes that it is impossible to know God who shows himself as darkness.[34] He points out that in *In Canticum*, Gregory distinguishes three ways of salvation, darkness being the third way (*la troisième voie*) in addition to fear (*la crainte*) and hope (*l'espérance*). Though the darkness contains a negative element, it corresponds to positive things such as the soul's union with God through love. Daniélou's idea is that the mystical language implied here emphasizes the goal of the mystical life, union with God.[35]

As Daniélou emphasizes the repetitive use of paradoxical images in Gregory's writing, the concept of *sommeil vigilant* ('wakeful sleep') becomes important for his analysis as he connects ecstasy and wakeful sleep to each other and then shows how the idea of ecstasy was developed in Philo and in early Christian literature.[36] In Daniélou's view, Gregory constructs the new paradox (*une nouvelle oxymoron*) of sleeping awake (*sommeil-veille*) in order to say that if one wants to reach the *theōria physikē* he or she must wake up. Daniélou's analysis, however, is based on the beginning of the 11th homily of *In Canticum* and is not about the 'stranger-sleep.'[37] Elsewhere, when Daniélou analyses sleep in

---

[33] J. Daniélou, *Platonisme et Théologie Mystique* (1944), 187-9 see also 24-5.

[34] According to J. Daniélou, *Platonisme et Théologie Mystique* (1944), 208-10, 222, there are two kinds of darkness in Gregory: *ténèbre relative et transitoire*, darkness that is due to human capacities failing to perceive the inaccessible God, and *ténèbre absolue et permanente*, the absolute and permanent darkness that is God's very own nature.

[35] J. Daniélou, *Platonisme et Théologie Mystique* (1944), 211.

[36] *Ibid.*, 275, 277-8, 294, 300.

[37] *Ibid.*, 294-5.

the context of the 10th homily, he remarks that for Gregory this kind of sleep is *xenos*, a stranger, and that 'Gregory occasionally uses the word *paradoxos*.'[38] He begins the conclusion of his analysis by pointing out some similarities to other (later) mystics, but he nevertheless considers 'stranger-sleep' to be essential to what he calls the mystical life.[39]

Daniélou's analysis has been influential. It is in many ways due to his studies that Gregory has been seen as a mystic who uses paradoxical images when speaking about the ineffable God. However, recent scholarship has drawn attention to Gregory's asceticism as a framework for his doctrine.[40] Martin Laird in particular has related spiritual exercises to Gregory's exegesis of Solomonic Literature.[41] As a contribution to this discussion, I would like to point out that all the paradoxes applied by Gregory are not mystical in the same sense as the bright darkness described above. As this article demonstrates, Gregory uses paradoxical language also when it comes to moral teaching and the ascetic way of life. When discussing the issue of sleeping awake he uses the term *paradoxos* in a different way than on other, say, more mystical occasions. He distinguishes between certain opposites as 'things that are contrary to one another' and 'cannot naturally be together in the same place' using darkness and light as an example.[42] But when it comes to the paradoxical language in the context of the 'stranger-sleep,' the exact formulation is: *tis kainē kai paradoxos mixis tōn enantiōn kai sunodos peri autēn theōreitai*. So, rather, he is referring here to 'an astonishing mixture' of the two opposites that are active simultaneously.[43] Because the emphasis of the tenth homily is both on good deeds (*eupoiïa*) and contemplation of the Good (*theōria tou agathou*), the relationship between the 'mystical' and 'moral' reading of Scriptures in Gregory should be given a closer look.[44]

'Stranger sleep' and being awake

According to Gregory there is a 'double pleasure' (*diplē hēdonē*) in human nature. This is the key to understanding the meaning of sleep here: 'if one focuses attention on sense perception and seeks for oneself the pleasure it grafts into the body, one's life is spent without tasting the divine gladness.' For Gregory,

---

[38] *Ibid.*, 299. My translation.

[39] *Ibid.*, 300-1.

[40] See in particular S. Coakley's introduction in *Re-thinking Gregory of Nyssa* (2003), 5.

[41] M. Laird, 'Under Solomon's Tutelage: The Education of Desire in the *Homilies on the Song of Songs*', in S. Coakley (ed.), *Re-thinking Gregory of Nyssa* (2003), 77-96. For more on spiritual and physical exercises in early Christian asceticism, see Salminen, *Asceticism and Early Christian Lifestyle* (2017).

[42] *Cant* X (GNO VI, 297,19-298,5).

[43] *Cant* X (GNO VI, 311,16-8).

[44] *Cant* X (GNO VI, 307,16; 313,1-5).

then, though he considers *metriopatheia* to be sufficient for most people, it is the impassibility of the soul (*apatheia*) that helps one lead a good life and make right decisions (*proairesis*). The passions (*pathē*) distract one's attention. Only in contemplation (*theōria*) is one able to become immune to 'the pleasurable stirrings of the senses.' When one's desire (*epithymia*) is God-oriented, the person will see the world uncovered (*anepiskotēton*).[45] So, Gregory's definitions of death and stranger-sleep should be seen in the light of how he defines contemplation in the same homily. It means that the soul (1) has put to sleep everything that is bodily (*psykhe … pasan sōmatikēn katakoimēsasa kinēsin*) and (2) is 'wakened by the divine,' so that 'it embraces the revelation of God by pure and naked thought.'[46] Gregory concludes his homily with an exhortation that he and his listeners achieve the waking of the soul in the stranger-sleep.[47] By this he equates the heart (*kardia*) with the soul or mind (*nous*).

The point of Gregory's homily is not sleeping in the common sense of the word, but the stranger-sleep.[48] I suggest that what Gregory means by his commentary on *Song* 5:2 is that mental wakefulness and contemplation should always be active, and that even when one is awake his or her body is in a way sleeping because the mind is not distracted by the senses.[49] This is what he means by *anaisthēsia* and the soul being awake in Christ: impassibility results in decent moral behaviour. In fact, before his elaboration on the stranger-sleep he has discussed virtuous life, *i.e.*, being close to Christ in whom the soul is always awake. It was not unusual in Gregory's times to relate sleeping to moral suspension.[50] To take this analysis one step further, one could continue from what Daniélou called the soul's awareness of the presence of God within itself.[51] It would also be fruitful to apply this approach to Gregory's Trinitarian theology and see how ascetic life is related to God's transcendent nature and to his immanent presence in *energeia*.

In Christ 'I sleep but my heart is awake'

According to St. Gregory of Nyssa in his tenth homily *In Canticum*, it is in Christ that the two opposites, sleeping and being awake, can take place at the same time. By this he means that when bodily senses do not distract the intellect,

[45] *Cant* X (GNO VI, 313,17-24).

[46] *Cant* X (GNO VI, 314,3-7; Trans. Norris 330).

[47] *Cant* X (GNO VI, 314,8-10).

[48] See O. Clément, *The Roots of Christian Mysticism: Text and Commentary* (New York, 1995), 130: 'Ascesis then is an awakening from the sleep-walking of daily life.'

[49] J. Daniélou, *Platonisme et Théologie Mystique* (1944), 295 cites a lengthy passage on this from *Cant* XI.

[50] Perälä, 'Sleep' (2014), 173.

[51] *Cf.* J. Daniélou, *Platonisme et Théologie Mystique* (1944), 276.

one is able to make just decisions. Gregory's idea has its predecessors, for example, in the writings of Clement and Origen: comparison to them highlights the originality of Gregory's language. Thus 'sleeping awake' is not a paradox in the same way as for example 'bright darkness' that is central to Gregory's apophatic theology; rather 'sleeping awake' is a tropological interpretation of verse 5:2 of the *Song*, and serves as a moral instruction for those whom Gregory refers to as a 'fleshly folk.' When their desires stop distracting their intellect they are awake in Christ, in whom these opposites can coincide in this way. It would be problematic to strictly distinguish between the mystical and the moral reading of Scripture in this homily – rather, it should be noted that the *sensus mysticus* and the *tropologicus* are two sides of the same coin. Uninterrupted contemplation of the Good and good works go hand in hand with one another in Gregory's exegesis, as well as in his ascetical and moral teaching.

CHAPTER 11

Mystical Knowledge and Vision of God

Eirini ARTEMI

1. Introduction

This chapter seeks to provide an exposition on Gregory of Nyssa's work on how Moses could *know* and *see* God. Man and God stand on two very different planes of existence. Moses *knew* God, because he tried to leave with God's order. Every time that Moses made a movement that included a kind of his sacrifice, God appeared to him. God presented Himself to Moses through the burning bush. Moses had many *visions* of God, though God's revelation cannot be easily described. It is completely beyond human mind. Moses wanted to see God continuously. This erotic desire mirrors spiritual desire only in part; spiritual desire – and ultimately the divine nature – cannot be limited to erotic desire. Thus, Gregory highlights both God's imminence and transcendence. Moses wanted to see the same face of God. His desire was expressed to God. Man's Salvation is achieved through knowledge about God, but in Christian dimension. The knowledge for God is the result of belief in the revealed truth. For this high feat conquest has as assistant only the faith of man to God and the grace of God to man.

2. Man's *knowledge* and *agnoia* for God in Gregory's of Nyssa teaching

Gregory is regarded as an exponent of negative theology, and of the mystical tradition in Christianity. The supreme antinomy of the Triune God, unknowable and knowable, incommunicable and communicable, transcendent and immanent is the primary locus of his apophatism. He speaks about the unknowable and incommunicable of God in different ways. He demonstrates the presence of God in the world through examples, arguments and images. He explains how a man should try to become purified for realising the divine truth. In the *Life of Moses*, the *invisible*, *timeless*, *ineffable* of God cannot be understood. People make images of Him which reveal Him,[1] but the incomprehensibility and infinity

---

[1] *Eun* II (GNO I, 256).

Studia Patristica CI, 143-150.
© Peeters Publishers, 2021.

of God gives to human being a life of continual conversion in virtue, to an ever-lasting assimilation to God.[2]

He is unknowable in His *ousia*, eternal and beyond time. This eternality results in God's infinite expanse: 'But if the divine and unalterable nature is incapable of degeneracy ... we must regard it as absolutely unlimited in its goodness: and the unlimited is the same as the infinite'.[3] It is possible through His sanctifying grace to know His glory, holiness and magnificence, and yet his knowledge is beyond man's power. God promises that only those who are pure in heart can have a vision of God.[4] His essence is invisible, but He is visible in His *energeiai*, being perceived in the *idiomata* that surround Him. So, it is better for man to speak of the deeds of God, but remain silent concerning his divine nature.

God is not an *object* of knowledge but of admiration, 'how majestic is your name in all the earth!'.[5] The persons of the Godhead are infinite in goodness, power and life without distinction. The divine *ousia* has no *levels*, is singular, simple, without opposite. God cannot degrade overtime and change or lose His perfection.

God's essence cannot be approached. Man can feel the divine grace and glory, but as God's infinite nature cannot be fully conceived, so God does not seek to reveal Himself completely to those who seek Him. Rather, he reveals just enough to enlarge the desire of the soul for more so that the soul might ever press in closer and closer on its infinite path upwards.[6] Man's desire for the knowledge and the vision of God is constantly satisfied and yet never satisfied.[7]

The knowledge of God is sometimes synonym with the ignorance and vision of God in Gregory's writings. The divine darkness leads to enlightenment. It shows the encounter with God not as an act of comprehension but as a union beyond understanding.[8] He speaks for the vision of God, expressed in terms of darkness rather than the prevailing light imagery.[9] This relation between dark and light, knowledge and ignorance for God is important. Moses' vision began with light; afterwards God spoke to him in a cloud. But when Moses rose higher and became more perfect, he saw God in darkness. Gregory explains that where the divine is, understanding can not reach out to.[10] That knowledge

---

[2] *Vit Moys* II (GNO VII/1, 45).
[3] *Eun* I (GNO I, 77).
[4] V. Lossky, *The Mystical Theology of the Eastern Church* (New York, 1997), 81.
[5] *Ps* 8:9.
[6] *Hex* I (GNO IV/1, 15).
[7] *Vit Moys* II (GNO VII/1, 97).
[8] *Cant* VI (GNO VI, 179).
[9] M. Laird, *Gregory of Nyssa and the Grasp of Faith: Union, Knowledge, and Divine Presence* (Oxford, 2007), 111. D. Ang, *The Model of Paradox in Christian Theology: Perspectives from the Work of Henri de Lubac* (Sydney, 2011), 10.
[10] *Cant* VI (GNO VI, 167).

is cognitive, is perhaps the first assumption with which one must do away, if one is to properly understand Gregory's concept of the divine darkness. Yet cognitive knowledge is an assumption so basic to modern scientific thought that its influence is hardly given any consideration, it is taken entirely as a base fact in the general arena of learning. Yet it is this very idea which Gregory addresses: the entire way of knowing with which we approach the knowledge of God is an ability that goes beyond the confines and limitations of cognition with its inherent inability to comprehend the transcendent.[11] It is an awareness that plunges into the negative, into the darkness of that place *which understanding does not reach*, and there one finds the height of true knowledge. Gregory's concept of mystical apprehension is expressed in the image of divine darkness: a symbol that is perhaps one of his greatest gifts to the realm of Christian thought.[12] It is presented most clearly in his text, *The Life of Moses*, and it is primarily from that text that this brief examination shall be made.[13]

According to Gregory the knowledge about God is based on the human mind and cannot be the correct guide for the *vision* of God, but the ignorance for the divine nature is based on the human soul. Man searches for God, but only through his ignorance – the darkness of his mind with regards to God – he can discover the divine truth. Only then the finite human being can see the infinite God. The indwelling of the Trinity is within man. As the godhead dwells within the soul, so is the soul able to relate to the knowledge of it, in a manner of knowing that is no longer sensory. The soul acts as a mirror, which projects into one's knowledge the very nature of God. The contemplation of God is not effected by sight and hearing, nor is it comprehended by any of the customary perceptions of the mind.[14]

This is the beginning of the knowledge of God by the heart – by the intimate presence of God Himself. Yet it is only faint, and is still blurred, as one would expect within a cloud. The soul must still be purified, and must become ever more accustomed to this new way of knowing. It must, indeed, shed its reliance upon cognition, and embrace the seeming groundlessness of an *ineffable knowledge*.[15]

Generally, the ignorance of God can be equated to darkness. In contrast, God is light. Man's separation from God brought darkness to his mind and heart. If God is known as light, the loss of this knowledge is darkness; and, since eternal life consists in *knowing the Triune God*, absence of knowledge of God ends in the darkness of Hell. Light is the result for accompanying the union

[11] *Vit Moys* I (GNO VII/1, 26).
[12] A. Papanikolaou, *Being With God: Trinity, Apophaticism, and Divine–Human Communion* (Indiana, 2006), 18.
[13] *Vit Moys* II (GNO VII/1, 83).
[14] 1*Cor* 2:9. *Is* 6:4. *Vit Moys* II (GNO VII/1, 83).
[15] *Vit Moys* II (GNO VII/1, 83).

with God, whereas the dark reality can overrun human consciousness only when human consciousness dwells on the borders of eternal death and final separation from God.[16] Thus the obvious sense of darkness seems to be, above all, pejorative.[17] If a man accepts his ignorance of the eternal God, He can detect the real knowledge of Him. The human soul will capture God's vision only in its purification.[18]

Gregory teaches that only if darkness, 'and the ignorance for God on the Mount Sinai will be changed into the light of true knowledge of Mount Tabor, man will be able to have the vision of God, the glorious face of God incarnate and the eternal uncreated light of the Triune God'.[19] A soul that truly loves God, desires to be united with Him, tries to find this union through the vision and knowledge of God. Our true knowledge of God is that we do not and cannot know because that which we seek is beyond our cognition. By its very nature the Divinity is higher than knowledge and comprehension.[20]

3. Understanding mystical knowledge and the vision of God by Moses based on the *Song of Songs*

Gregory exposed the depth of God's contemplative and mystical nature in the *Life of Moses* and again in his *Commentary on the Song of Songs*. His homilies on the *Song of Songs* have long been considered, along with his *Life of Moses*, as a classic example of early Christian allegorical exegesis as well as the mature expression of Gregory's spiritual or mystical doctrine. This commentary on the *Song of Songs* is not for elite ascetics but for all serious Christians.[21] The context of this poem is not a record in the brain of what was perceived as a consequence of the sensorial experience of the soul's meeting with God, but only a translation of that mystical oneness with Him into a language of the outer senses.[22] Man can learn about God through the divine teaching of the songs of prophets who had God's illumination.[23]

The vision of God did appear in the Bible in two different and sometimes opposite types which are presented to be mutually exclusive. Some texts

---

[16] *Vit Moys* II (GNO VII/1, 86).

[17] *Vit Moys* II (GNO VII/1, 86).

[18] E. Artemi, 'The sixth oration of Gregory Nyssa into the beatitudes', *Koinonia* 45 (2002), 167-74.

[19] V. Lossky, *In the Image and Likeness of God* (New York, 1974), 31.

[20] E. Artemi, 'The sixth oration of Gregory Nyssa into the beatitudes' (2002), 173-4.

[21] M. DelCogliano, 'Review for Norris, Richard A., Jr., trans. Gregory of Nyssa: Homilies on the Song of Songs, Writings from the Greco-Roman World 13 (Atlanta, 2012)', *Review of Biblical Literature* (2013).

[22] W. Witalisz, 'I cluppe and I cusse as I wood wore': Erotic Imagery in Middle English Mystical Writings', *Text Matters* 3 (2006), 67.

[23] *Cant* I (GNO VI, 27).

characterize the vision of God as impossibility. In *Exodus*, God tells Moses: 'You cannot see My face; for no man can see My face and live',[24] while the psalmist notes that darkness is God's hiding place.[25] The Evangelist John writes: 'No one has ever seen God'[26] and Paul adds that God is He 'whom no one has ever seen or can see'.[27] There is a strange relation between the visibility and incomprehensibility of God. His visibility concerns His attributes and His incomprehensibility concerns His *ousia*.

So, God's existence is derived from His energies. They are in turn known both indirectly and directly. The indirect route relies on the order that is apparent in the cosmos. The fact that the universe is orderly made indicates that it is governed according to some rational plan, which implies the existence of a divine Planner.[28] For Gregory there is no doubt that when it is said that God is, this means that we can know his existence.

Such knowledge of God is brought out in his reflections on the life of Moses. His explanation is based on the sequence of three theophanies that marks Moses' life.[29] Moses is the image of every man who is thirsty for utter intimacy with God. These theophanies are stages on his journey to that intimacy.[30] It is an ascension of man that takes place in three stages. In the first, God presents Himself in light–fire, so He makes vanish any incorrect idea of Him. Then He appears in a cloud and then in darkness.

Each time that Moses made a movement that included some kind of sacrifice, God appeared. Moses left the palace of Pharaoh, because he wanted to participate in the suffering of his people and became their leader. Leaving Egypt, he went into the desert. There, God was present to him in the burning bush. Arriving at Mount Sinai, God revealed himself to Moses amidst thunder, voices, lightning and trumpets, and called Moses to go up to the mountain's top. Moses went up, indeed. The tubes did not frighten him nor the cloud that covered the mountain, nor thunder nor the darkness of the mountain where he met God. He met God and conversed with Him. God gave him the plates of Law. He carried the stone plates to the Jews, while his shining face was proof of God's appearance.[31]

The first theophany is the burning bush.[32] At this stage, Gregory takes light to be a symbol of knowledge. So the first stage of Moses' progress is the acquisition of purely intellectual knowledge of God.[33] This fact shows to Christians

---

[24] *Ex* 33:20.
[25] *Ps* 17 [18]:12.
[26] *Jn* 1:18. 1*Jn* 4:12.
[27] 1*Tim* 6:16.
[28] *Cant* I (GNO VI, 25); XI (GNO VI, 325); XII (GNO VI, 360). *Vit Moys* II (GNO VII/1, 84).
[29] *Cant* XII (GNO VI, 355).
[30] *Vit Moys* II (GNO VII/1, 115).
[31] *Cant* XII (GNO VI, 366).
[32] *Vit Moys* II (GNO VII/1, 93).
[33] *Vit Moys* II (GNO VII/1, 94).

what they should do to stand in the field of the true light. This is impossible
with feet in shackles, as these impede people to run toward the mountain
where the light of truth appears. Christians should get rid of any leather shoes
metaphorically, meaning they should get rid of their sins. Hence, they should
free themselves from being covered by dead skins in which their nature was
clad in the beginning, when Adam and Eve disobeyed God's will and went
away from Paradise.[34] When Moses stood before the burning bush and took
off his shoes, literally he got rid of the pleasures and any desires of this life.
This purgation the contemplative must experience to make progress toward
God.[35]

The second theophany occurred at the top of Mount Sinai.[36] The light was
replaced by darkness. Moses came closer to perfection. He saw God in a cloud
and, sheltered by a cloud, he participated in eternal life.[37] At this stage of man's
coming closer to God, the latter cannot be perceived with external senses. Some
sort of mystical awareness of God, however, is achievable internally. The senses
of sight and hearing are unable to *capture* the vision of God, but the more
intimate senses of smell, taste, and touch are used for the knowledge of God.[38]
A closer examination of the divine being who was hidden leads into a cloud,
which replaces visible things. As Moses ascended, the *inaccessible nature of
Divinity* was gradually revealed to him. He saw God in *his invisible and incomprehensible way*, in *a radiant cloud*.[39]

The third and final theophany revolved around Moses' vision of God's glory
from the cleft in a rock.[40] Moses had reached the summit. His physical journey
could go no further. One might be tempted, then, to assume that this is also where
his spiritual journey met its climax: the darkness has been reached, and perfection has been attained. Yet to Gregory's mind, perfection has here only been
attained in as much as the mountain's peak is but the beginning. Climbing up
the mountain of knowledge Moses has reached its summit, but it is now time
to begin a new spiritual journey.

Reading the *Song of the Songs* Gregory describes the three stages of man
obtaining knowledge of God.[41] Moses' vision began with light; afterwards
God spoke to him in a cloud. But when Moses rose higher and became more
perfect, he saw God in darkness.[42] Moses as the bride went into darkness. The

---

[34] *Gen* 2:4-3:24.
[35] *Vit Moys* I (GNO VII/1, 95); *Cant* I (GNO VI, 28). J. Beal, *Illuminating Moses: A History of
Reception from Exodus to the Renaissance* (Leiden, Boston, 2004), 349.
[36] *Vit Moys* II (GNO VII/1, 150-67).
[37] *Ibid.*
[38] *Cant* I (GNO VI, 40); III (GNO III, 77); IV (GNO VI, 115). *Vit Moys* II (GNO VII/1, 146).
[39] *Vit Moys* II (GNO VII/1, 168); *Cant* XI (GNO VI, 325).
[40] *Vit Moys* II (GNO VII/1, 170); *Cant* XI (GNO VI, 324).
[41] *Ex* 20:21; *Cant.* XI (GNO VI, 327).
[42] *Cant* XI (GNO VI, 332).

bride as Moses felt the divine presence, but they cannot realize Him.[43] Gregory comments on *Song* 3:1: 'On my bed at night I sought him whom my soul loved' and we find the bride, like Moses in the darkness where God was.[44] The bride's entry into this darkness marks an apophatic ascent in which the bride moves through the marketplace of various levels of knowledge in order to find her Beloved by means of faith. The bride like Moses was embraced by the divine night and seeks him hidden in darkness.[45] The bride and Moses realized that the one whom they seek are known in not knowing.[46]

The knowledge of God is a steep mountain and difficult to climb. Few people barely reach its base. If one were like Moses, one would ascend higher and hear the sound of trumpets which become louder as one advances. For the preaching of God is truly a trumpet blast, which strikes the hearing, already loud at the onset, but becomews louder at the end.[47] Moses did not feel enough of God's presence. He was avid in God's vision and insatiable. He was hungry to see God's face again and again. This desire was expressed to God as it was described in *Exodus*.[48] Gregory paralleled it as a dialogue between Moses and God.[49] The first asked the latter to see Him all the time. God let Moses see His back. This back of God symbolized God's manifestation to his creature in his divine energies.[50] As conclusion he wrote: 'Everyone who wants to see Him must have the will to follow Him unceasingly. The theoria of His person is a continuous and unstoppable march of man towards Him'.[51] At last three points are highlighted: Moses had theopties. They were not enough for him. He wanted to see more. He was insatiable. Viewing God further, is to follow incessantly the Word.[52]

The soul of man who wanted God's view must return to a state of paradise before his exile from it. In case, he was not ready to know and *see* God, he needs to try to *wash* the clothes of his heart from sins and clear his soul from earthly thoughts. He must get rid of any kind of marriage with the material things which tied him to the earth. As long as man has not reached this state of paradise again, the heaven, the vision and knowledge of God, remains obscured. Moses, however, tried to remove this hindrance of figurative thoughts.[53]

---

[43] *Cant* XI (GNO VI, 339).

[44] *Ex* 20:21; *Cant* VI (GNO VI, 193).

[45] *Cant* VI (GNO VI, 182); M. Laird, *Gregory of Nyssa and the Grasp of Faith Union, Knowledge, and Divine Presence* (New York, 2007), 87.

[46] *Cant* VI (GNO VI, 190-3).

[47] *Vit Moys* II (GNO VII/1, 21).

[48] *Ex* 33:12-23.

[49] *Cant* XII (GNO VI, 356).

[50] *Ex* 33:23. A.F. Kimel Jr., *Speaking the Christian God: The Holy Trinity and the Challenge of Feminism* (London, 1992), 152.

[51] *Cant* XII (GNO VI, 354).

[52] *Cant* XII (GNO VI, 356).

[53] *Cant* I (GNO VI, 27).

Christians are seeking to be united with God like the bride in the *Song of Songs* who tried hard to be united with her beloved. She wanted his kiss, to feel him as united with her. The bride like Moses desired to take part in God's theophany. The bridegroom kissing the bride was similar to the triune God speaking to Moses.[54]

4. Conclusions

The Divine darkness is not a synonym of blackness. It is not to compare with a room which has no lights. Divine darkness is a positive reality that helped Moses to discover God, hence it is rather luminous. Although this sounds like a contradiction in terms, luminous darkness expresses God's presence, which the soul can begin to perceive. Moses' knowledge of God was the result of His presence in him, the domain of the mystical life. In fact, the closer God comes to the soul, the more intense darkness becomes. And it is then, with all other things of this world cleared away, that the true vision God occurs: when the soul looks up to Him and never ceases to desire Him. The emphasis of this kind of spirituality is on *seeing* rather than *knowing*.[55] The soul, purified from sins has a reflection of God's light.[56] True knowledge and the vision of God consists 'in seeing that He is invisible, because He whom the soul seeks transcends all knowledge, separated from every part by his incomprehensibility as by darkness'.[57] The story of Moses and his vision of God is retold through the commentary of the *Song of the Songs*. Moses wanted to be united with God and to know Him as the bride tried to be united with her bridegroom. The ultimate goal of Moses, of the bride and of every Christian is to drive themselves to an infinite progress in the never-completed journey toward God. On this journey the love for God will be bigger and the wish to see God's attributes, not to know His essence, is what captures the soul of every believer in Christ.

---

[54] *Cant* I (GNO VI, 31).
[55] *Cant* I (GNO VI, 33).
[56] *Cant* III (GNO III, 77).
[57] *Vit Moys* II (GNO VII/1, 86).

CHAPTER 12

Johannine Eschatology of the *In Canticum*

Manabu AKIYAMA

1. Introduction

The *Song of Songs,* one of the 'five scrolls' (*ḥāmēš mᵉgillôt*), was read prob-ably from the 8th century A.D. on the feast of Judaic Easter,[1] since the election of the Judaic people as 'fiancée' of God has been celebrated on this holiday. However, we could suppose that beyond this ethnic restriction, the *Song of Songs* becomes a universal testimony to the way of the human beings toward the unity with God.

Gregory of Nyssa expresses the theory of 'apokatastasis' ('universal restora-tion') in a few passages of his works: for example, in *De anima et resurrec-tione*: 'Resurrection is the restoration of our nature to its original condition' (PG 46, 148,2; *cf.* also PG 46, 156,27)[2]. According to S. Lilla, 'the main feature of the resurrected body is that of the incorruptibility'.[3] We could say that in the exegetic works of Gregory, this theological point of view on the resurrection is applied especially to the interpretation of the Old Testament. In fact, when we interpret a biblical text from the viewpoint of the one who has already res-urrected, we could be recalled to the incorruptibility. It seems to me that in the *Homilies on the Song of Songs*, Gregory teaches us how we can participate in this incorruptibility from the reading of the *Song of Songs* on the basis of the spiritual path of the Bride.

We would like to make clear in this chapter how we can obtain this possibility of reading the *Song of Songs*, especially looking at a few problematic passages because of the difference of text commentated by Gregory.

2. 'Your name is perfumed ointment emptied out' (*Song* 1:3)

First of all, we would like to list two difficult passages which we meet at the beginning of the *Song of Songs*: 'Your name is perfumed ointment emptied

---

[1] H. Rózsa, *Az ószövetség keletkezése II: Bevezetés az ószövetség könyveinek irodalom- és hagyománytörténetébe* (Budapest, 2002), 393.
[2] Tr. by C.P. Roth, *On the Soul and the Resurrection: St. Gregory of Nyssa* (Crestwood, New York, 2002).
[3] S. Lilla (ed.), *Gregorio di Nissa: L'anima e la risurrezione* (Roma, 1992), 33.

out' (*Song* 1:3) and 'Young maidens have drawn you' (*Song* 1:4).[4] As for the first passage, the word 'ointment', *e.g.*, μύρον in Greek, corresponds to the Hebrew word in the original '*šemen*'. This Hebrew word appears in the *Song of Songs* three times: 1:3 (two times; 'The fragrance of your *perfumed ointments* is better than all spices, your name is *perfumed ointment* emptied out') and 4:10 ('The fragrance of your *perfumed ointments* is above all spices'). However, in the translation of the 4th chapter, the Septuagint does not use the word μύρον but ὀσμή, so a different text appears.

The Greek translation of the latter part of the first passage (*Song* 1:3) in the Septuagint is μύρον ἐκκενωθὲν ὄνομά σου.[5] The Hebrew text correspondent to this Greek translation should be '*šemen mûrāq šᵉmekā*'. In this case '*mûrāq*' is the form of the masculine passive participle (Hophal) of the verb '*rîq*'.[6] However, the current text in Hebrew is '*šemen tûraq šᵉmekā*'. So if this text is not corrupted, '*tûraq*' is the imperfect form of the second person masculine, or of the third person feminine, of Hophal of the verb '*rîq*'. If we interpret '*tûraq*' as the imperfect form of the third person feminine, we should explain the gender of the noun '*šemen*' as feminine, but this is an exceptional case.[7] Therefore, it seems that probably the subject of this sentence in Hebrew should be masculine 'you', while the masculine word '*šᵉmekā*' ('your name') should be put in apposition to this subject, 'you'. The translation would be, for instance, 'Your name, namely yourself, is poured forth as perfumed ointment'. Gregory, however, who reads here: 'Your name is perfumed ointment emptied out', interprets this text thus: 'the Nature that has no boundaries cannot be accurately comprehended by means of the connotations of words' (*Cant* I; GNO VI, 36,16-7). However, as we referred above, we would like to think that the phrase 'your name' is put in apposition to 'you' in this passage. In the following, we would like to interpret the original text better, in appreciation of the theology of Gregory.

3. 'Young maidens have drawn you' (*Song* 1:4)

As for *Song* 1:4, too, the text on which Gregory is based is different from the original Hebrew which reads: '*mošᵏēnî 'aḥᵃreykā*' ('Draw me after you'). The Greek translation of the Septuagint, however, reads εἵλκυσάν σε (sc. νεάνιδες),

---

[4] As for the English translation of Gregory's *Homilies on the Song of Song*, I use usually that of R.A. Norris Jr., *Gregory of Nyssa: Homilies on the Song of Songs*, Writings from the Greco-Roman World 13 (Atlanta, 2012). As for the translation from the Bible, I use that of the *New Jerusalem Bible*: *The New Jerusalem Bible*, Pocket Edition (London, 1990).

[5] Gregory uses a copy of a manuscript belonging to the Alexandrian family, which reads here not 'σου', but 'σοι'. A. Rahlfs (ed.), *Septuaginta*, vol. II (Stuttgart, 1935), 260.

[6] *Cf.* K. Elliger and W. Rudolph (eds), *Biblia Hebraica Stuttgartensia* (Stuttgart, 1904), 1325.

[7] *Cf.* F. Brown, S.R. Driver and Ch.A. Briggs (eds), *A Hebrew and English Lexicon of the Old Testament* (Oxford, 1906), 938 and 1032.

namely, 'they (sc. young maidens) have drawn you'. This translation corresponds to a text '*mᵉšāḵuḵā*'.[8] The original verb is in both cases '*māšaḵ*' ('attract'), but the subject, object and the mode of the verb are different respectively.

Incidentally, the words used in the *Song of Songs* are frequently common with those which we find in the *Gospel according to John*, for example: 'shepherd' (*Song* 1:8; *Jn* 10:11), 'spring' (*Song* 4:12; *Jn* 4:14), 'bread' (*Song* 5:1; *Jn* 6:51), 'one' (*Song* 6:9; *Jn* 17:22) etc. In addition to these words, we can find the verb 'draw' (ἕλκειν) which is used both in the *Song of Songs* and in the *Gospel according to John* in common (*Song* 1:4; *Jn* 6:44; 12:32); it is this word that appears here in *Song* 1:4. According to M. Simonetti[9] in fact, in the passage where Gregory describes the flight of the Bride's soul (*Cant* XV; GNO VI, 448 ss.), too, we can find the influence not only of the *Phaedrus* of Plato (246b-d), but also of the *Fourth Gospel* (*Jn* 6:44: 'No one can come to me unless drawn [ἑλκύσῃ] by the Father who sent me, and I will raise that person up on the last day'). In the *Fourth Gospel,* the same verb 'draw' is used in the eschatological words of Jesus who says: 'When I am lifted [ὑψωθῶ] from the earth, I shall draw [ἑλκύσω] all people to myself' (*Jn* 12:32). Therefore, we can suppose that Gregory would have interpreted the text in a different way, if the text of *Song* 1:4 had been: 'Draw me after you'.

In fact, Gregory often uses verbs which mean to 'draw' (*i.e.* ἕλκειν or ἐφέλκειν) in the second half of the *Homilies* to express the spiritual height of the Bride lifted up by the grace of God. Therefore, it seems to me that Gregory contemplates the spiritual progress of the Bride from the viewpoint of the crucified Jesus, *i.e.* Jesus lifted from the earth, on the basis of the description in the *Gospel according to John*.

4. Gregory and the *Gospel according to John*

It has often been noticed that the 'realized eschatology' is a feature of the *Fourth Gospel*. We could say that this eschatology is a mode of interpreting the action of Jesus during his lifetime from the point of view after his resurrection. This perspective of interpretation is noticeable from the outset of this *Gospel*. When we comprehend the Bible as a unity, we can, indeed, find in the figures or descriptions in the Old Testament the activity of the Holy Spirit who virtually descends after the death of Jesus on the cross (*Jn* 7:39). The author of this *Gospel* testifies to a sign that was given by the crucified Jesus: when 'one of the soldiers pierced his side with a lance, immediately there came out blood and water' (*Jn* 19:34). Before this moment, Jesus 'was already dead' (*Jn* 19:33). Therefore, this sign of 'blood and water' which poured forth from the crucified

[8] *Cf.* K. Elliger and W. Rudolph (eds), *Biblia Hebraica Stuttgartensia* (1904), 1326.
[9] M. Simonetti (ed.), *Gregorio di Nissa: La vita di Mosè* (Milano, 1984), 323.

Jesus has been explained in the byzantine tradition as an effusion of the Holy Spirit, that is, of the spirit of the resurrected. John Chrysostom, for example, explains this effusion of blood and water as the institution of the sacraments in the church.[10] Gregory, too, says: 'It was inevitable that not only the Son of man died, but also was crucified, in order that the cross became [theologian]' (*Trid*; GNO IX, 303,8-12).[11]

In a few passages of the *Homilies on the Song of Songs*, indeed, references to the *Fourth Gospel* often appear. In the last part of Homily 15, for example, Gregory expresses at length his eschatological hope of the unity of God and the humankind on the basis of chapter 17 of the *Fourth Gospel* (*Jn* 17:21). In this passage of the *Homily*, Gregory interprets the term 'glory' as 'bond' of this unity, and besides, says that the Holy Spirit is signified with this word of 'glory' (*Cant* XV; GNO VI, 467,3-16; cfr. *Jn* 17:22; 20:22).

Gregory refers not only to chapter 17, but also to chapter 7 of this *Fourth Gospel*, especially to the passage which contains the word of Jesus who says: 'Let anyone who is thirsty come to me! Let anyone who believes in me come and drink! As scripture says, "From his heart shall flow streams of living water"' (*Jn* 7:37-8). This passage, indeed, appears six times in his *Homilies on the Song of Songs*.[12] Gregory cites this passage once together with the explanation of the Evangelist: 'He said this concerning the Spirit, those who believe in him were going to receive' (*Jn* 7:39; *Cant* IX, GNO VI, 292,18-9). Immediately after this passage in the *Gospel*, however, the Evangelist adds: 'For there was no Spirit as yet, because Jesus had not yet been glorified [ἐδοξάσθη]'. In this way, at the end of this scriptural passage, the verb 'being glorified' [δοξάζεσθαι] appears. This verb is substantially a synonym of 'being crucified', since the cross means 'glory' in the theology of the Fourth Evangelist.

5. Myrrh, mortification and baptism

In the passage which we cited above from chapter 12 of the *Gospel according to John* (*Jn* 12:32: 'When I am lifted [ὑψωθῶ] from the earth, I shall draw [ἑλκύσω] all people to myself'), we can find the verb of 'being lifted' [ὑψοῦσθαι]. The verb 'lifting up' or 'being lifted up' is used also in chapter 3 of the same *Gospel* (*Jn* 3:14: 'As Moses lifted up [ὕψωσεν] the snake in the desert, so must the Son of man be lifted up [ὑψωθῆναι], so that everyone who believes may have eternal life in him').

According to the viewpoint of the *Fourth Gospel*, the figure of Jesus on the cross not only indicates his passion and death, but also implies his resurrection

---

[10] PG 59, 463B.

[11] *Cf.* G. Maspero, art. 'theologia', in L.F. Mateo-Seco and G. Maspero (eds), *The Brill Dictionary of Gregory of Nyssa* (Leiden, Boston, 2010), 727.

[12] GNO VI, 32,17; 248,7; 292,15-9; 303,14; 327.3; 414,11-2.

and ascension, since the crucified figure of Jesus, as we mentioned above, signifies the descent of the Holy Spirit (*Jn* 19:34), which happened, according to *Luke* (*Lk* 24:6; 24:51; *Acts* 1:9; 2:3), after Jesus' resurrection and ascension. In this sense, the cross transcends the temporality as well as represents eternity, *i.e.* the divinity existing in the beginning of the world; that is to say, the cross signifies the Holy Trinity. Gregory says indeed: 'The word 'piety' [τῆς εὐσεβείας] indicates the Holy Trinity as the only thing prior to the world' (*Antirrh*; GNO III/1, 222,14-15). It is necessary, however, that death precedes, and after death the resurrection happens. Gregory emphasizes this point in Homily 12 (GNO VI, 343-346). In this context, the keyword will be 'mortification' [νέκρωσις] (*2Cor* 4:10; cfr. GNO VI, 347,3-5).

According to Gregory, this mortification is represented symbolically with the word 'myrrh' (in Hebrew '*môr*'), used in the *Song of Songs*; this word appears, for example, in a phrase (*Song* 4:6): 'I shall go to the mountain of *myrrh* [σμύρνα]' (cfr. *Cant* VII; GNO VI, 242,19-243,1). In *Jn* 19:39, on the other hand, the word σμύρνα is used to embalm the corpse of Jesus. The symbolic interpretation of Gregory referred above is based on the significance of 'mortification' implied in this word 'myrrh'. Therefore, the word σμύρνα is put in relation with the sacrament of baptism (GNO VI, 249,13; 343,9; 405,15).

6. μύρον νάρδου and confirmation

The word μύρον, on the other hand, often appears in the *Gospel according to John* (*Jn* 11:2; 12:3 bis and 12:5). In *Jn* 12:3 the text of the *Gospel* reads: 'Mary brought in a pound of very costly *ointment, pure nard*, and with it anointed the feet of Jesus, wiping them with her hair; the house was filled with the scent of the *ointment*'. This act of Mary signifies the preparation of Jesus' burial (*Jn* 12:7). In the *Song of Songs*, on the other hand, the word of νάρδος (*nērd*ᵉ) appears in *Song* 1:12; 4:13; 4:14. Gregory says, juxtaposing *Song* 1:12 ('While the king rests in his own room, my *nard* yields its perfume') with *Jn* 12:3 (cited above): 'In the *Song of Songs*, the spikenard conveys to the Bride the scent of the Bridegroom, while in the *Gospel*, the sweetness that then filled the house becomes the ointment [χρῖσμα] of the whole body of the church in the whole cosmos, this suggests that the two have something in common to the point of seeming to be the same' (*Cant* III; GNO VI, 93,4-9).[13] Gregory, in this way, uses the word χρῖσμα for the purpose of explaining the behavior of Mary (GNO VI, 93,7). We could recognize here an allusion of Gregory to the ecclesiastic practice: in the Byzantine rite, indeed, the confirmation or χρῖσμα is administered together with baptism. According to the

---

[13] *Cf.* P. Meloni, *Il profumo dell'immortalità: L'interpretazione patristica di Cantico 1,3* (Roma, 1975), 197.

interpretation of the Byzantine church, 'on the occasion of the chrismation, the same thing happens that followed to the apostles in the day of Pentecost: the Holy Spirit descends'.[14] In this occasion, the unction is carried out with the *myron,* and each unction accompanies with the formula: 'The seal of the gift that is the Holy Spirit'.[15]

7. The glory, the King and the Trinity

Therefore, the chrismation or confirmation is a sacrament in which the baptized person receives the sign of a gift of the Holy Spirit through unction, so that he may become a living testimony to the resurrected Christ, more suitable for establishing the reign of God.[16] When we regard the figure of the crucified Jesus, from whom poured forth the Holy Spirit, we could say that the meaning of confirmation is an assimilating of the 'anointed' Christian to the body of Christ on the cross. Gregory, indeed, says in the book *Antirrheticus adversus Apolinarium*: 'Christ, who puts on himself the glory of the Holy Spirit before the ages (since the unction signifies this fact symbolically), and who decorates the person united with himself through the same unction, makes Christ without any difference' (*Antirrh*; GNO III/1, 222,5-9).

In the *Adversus Macedonianos*, too, Gregory, along with the Trinitarian contemplation, says: 'The ointment is not anything alien to the king by nature, nor the Spirit was arranged with the Holy Trinity as anything foreign and heterogeneous' (*Maced*; GNO III/1, 102,24-26). This sentence of Gregory corresponds with our observation that the crucified Jesus on the cross reveals the Holy Trinity. Moreover, according to Gregory, this King dominates the city of the restored and resurrected soul of humankind, that is, of heavenly Jerusalem (*Cant* XV, GNO VI, 442,15; cfr. GNO VI, 443,8: τὴν ψυχὴν ὑψωθῆναι). In Homily 12 on the *Song of Songs*, indeed, Gregory says, surprised at the height reached by the Bride: 'Do you see what a height [ὕψος] the Bride has reached?' (*Cant* XII; GNO VI, 367,16). In *Adversus Macedonianos*, on the other hand, Gregory says: 'The concept of unction hints at, by means of unspoken doctrines, that there cannot be found any distance [διάστημα] between the Son and the Holy Spirit' (GNO III/1, 102,32-103,4).[17] According to Gregory, although this concept of διάστημα is a feature of *epektasis* for humankind (*Cant* XV; GNO VI, 458-460), there is no separation among the Trinity, since the figure of Christ on the cross surpasses any temporality.

[14] I. Ivancsó, *Görög katolikus szertartástan* (Nyíregyháza, 2000), 185.

[15] *Catechism of the Catholic Church* (London, 1994), §1300.

[16] I. Ivancsó, *Görög katolikus szertartástan* (2000), 185.

[17] G. Maspero, art. 'chrism' in L.F. Mateo-Seco and G. Maspero (eds), *The Brill Dictionary of Gregory of Nyssa* (Leiden, Boston, 2010), 137-8.

Therefore, the sacrament of confirmation is administered by the King, and the anointed becomes a participant of the kingdom. In the *Song of Songs*, too, the 'king' appears (*Song* 1:4; 1:12). Though Gregory does not make any mention of the relationship between the text of the *Song of Songs* and the sacrament of confirmation, we could suppose on the basis of Gregory's theology that this 'king' represents Christ on the cross. Gregory, indeed, attributes the sacrament of chrismation to the glory which the Father gave to Jesus Christ, with the citation of a passage from chapter 17 of the *Fourth Gospel*: 'Jesus said: "Glorify me", as if he said, "Anoint me" (ὡσανεὶ χρῖσον), "with that glory I had with you before ever the world existed"' (*Jn* 17:5) (*Antirrh*; GNO III/1, 222,9-10). Gregory resumes: 'The glory observed before the world, before all of the creatures and all of the ages, with which the Only Son of God is glorified, is not anything other than the glory of the Spirit in our opinion' (*Antirrh*; GNO III/1, 222,11-4). In the following passage, Gregory recognizes that the Holy Trinity is the only thing prior to the world, as we have already cited above (*Antirrh*; GNO III/1, 222,14-5).

8. "He who is", the only Son of God and *Song* 1:3

Gregory cites from chapter 17 of the *Gospel according to John* in this way. However, immediately after this passage in *the Gospel*, Jesus says: 'I have revealed your name to those whom you took from the world to give me' (*Jn* 17:6). From the context of this passage, we can suppose that this 'name' indicates the title of God 'I AM', since Jesus often uses this title in this *Gospel*, for example: 'When you have lifted up the Son of man, then you will know that "I AM", and that I do nothing of my own accord. What I say is what the Father has taught me' (*Jn* 8:28); 'Before Abraham ever was, "I AM"' (*Jn* 8:58). In these passages we can notice an analogy with the name of God revealed in *Ex* 3:14 (ὁ ὤν).[18]

Gregory qualifies the cross to be 'theologian', as we observed above. When we place the crucified Jesus on the cross in the center of our theology, it becomes clear that Jesus is the only Son of God and that the name of God is truly 'I AM', since in the body of the crucified and dead Jesus, the life of resurrection is alive (*Jn* 19:34). In fact, Jesus says: 'Anyone who has seen me has seen the Father' and 'it is the Father, living in me, who is doing his works', 'I am in the Father and the Father is in me' (*Jn* 14:9-11). Gregory emphasizes the nature of the only Son of God on the basis of these passages of the *Gospel according to John*: 'The one, who is always in the Father and bears always the Father in himself and is united with Him, is and will be so, as he was before, and another Son except for him did not exist, neither was born nor will be ever' (*Theoph*; GNO III, 126,14-7).

---

[18] *Parola del Signore: la Bibbia; Traduzione interconfessionale in lingua corrente per la lettura, nuova versione NT* (Roma, 2000), 164.

As we have mentioned in the first part of this chapter, the text of *Song* 1:3 could be translated: 'Your name, namely yourself, is poured forth as perfumed ointment'. Although the importance of the 'perfume' seems to be emphasized mainly in the book by Mgr. Meloni,[19] the same importance could be given also to the 'name'. It is well known that in the *Book of Leviticus* the name of God is identified with God himself: 'Anyone who blasphemes the name of Yahweh will be put to death' (*Lv* 24:16). With regard to Jesus, first of all, his 'name' should be referred to the name of 'Christ' *i.e.* Χριστός, since the fourth Evangelist reveals his intention in the last part of the Gospel (*Jn* 20:31; cfr. *Jn* 1:12). Jesus indeed, the Only Son of God, after his death on the cross, became the true Χριστός by flushing out blood and water from his side, and put the glory of 'He who is'. At the same time, this sign testified to the divinity of the Holy Spirit. We could interpret a passage of the *Fourth Gospel* (*Jn* 8:28) in the Trinitarian context according to Gregory: when a person, who puts on the name of the 'Only Son of God', empties himself (*Phil* 2:7) by means of an experience of νέκρωσις, reveals 'He who is' who lets this person live (*Cant* XV, GNO VI, 444,2-3). It is this moment, indeed, that 'Christ' is born (*Jn* 19:30).

The Bride in the *Song of Songs* is invited by the Bridegroom, *i.e.* Christ, to experience this crucifixion. At the beginning of the *Song*, on the other hand, the Bride, who was full of the affection for the Bridegroom, can be regarded as already crucified (cfr. 1*Jn* 4:16): for her, the name of X in the second person singular is identified with the subject of this second person. The form of a second person is used generally in such a situation that the subject of the second person and that of the first person constitute a community. With regard to us, the situation, in which the subject of a second person coincides with the name of this subject, comes true when we are conscious in the name of X, of the *existence* of this subject in the second person (*Ex* 3:14). Then we get conscious of the fact that we constitute a community with this subject, and that we are a part of this community (*Jn* 1:14). It will be at this moment of our getting conscious that the resurrected Christ inhabits in ourselves. We could suppose that the Bride in the *Song of Songs* indicates this situation, when she says: 'Your name, namely yourself, is poured forth as perfumed ointment'. 'Your name' here is nothing other than 'Christ'.

9. Reconsideration on the text of *Song* 1:4

Gregory explains his theory of the *epektasis* with the citation from *Jn* 7:37 ('Let anyone who is thirsty come to me!') in the commentary on *Song* 4:8 (*Cant* VIII; GNO VI, 247-9), where an imperative invitation [δεῦρο] appears in the phrase of the Bridegroom ('Come [δεῦρο] from Lebanon, my promised

---

[19] P. Meloni, *Il profumo dell'immortalità* (1975), 184-206.

Bride, come from Lebanon, come on your way'): 'The wellspring of good things always draws the thirsty to itself' (ἐφέλκεται; GNO VI, 248,6), therefore 'the invitation to come to him that has been offered, and that ever and again draws us to better things (*cf.* ἐφελκομένη; GNO VI, 248,16) is never lacking to the person who is journeying upwards' (*cf.* ἑλκτικάς; GNO VI, 249,3).[20] Here Gregory often uses the verb ἕλκεσθαι (or ἐφέλκεσθαι), which has already appeared in *Song* 1:4 ('Young maidens have drawn you [εἵλκυσάν σε]'). The reading of the original Hebrew text (*Song* 1:4: 'Draw me after you'), therefore, does not disagree with the thought of Gregory at all.

We would like to develop our interpretation on this passage further. The Bride says: 'Let us rejoice [ἀγαλλιασώμεθα], and be glad in you' (*Song* 1:4). The verb 'rejoice' used here is the same one which appears in *Jn* 8:56 ('Your father Abraham *rejoiced* to think that he would see my Day; he saw it and was glad'). We could interpret 'Abraham', to which Jesus refers here in the *Gospel*, as a representative of 'us' in *Song* 1:4. This point of view, which we could regard as a kind of the conception of 'corporate personality', is developed clearly in the eschatological interpretation of Gregory on the figure of the Bride (*Song* 6:8-9; *Cant* XV, GNO VI, 456-469). On the basis of the eschatological viewpoint of Gregory, we can extend this 'we' to the universal level. In this way, with the interpretation of Gregory, the *Song of Songs* could acquire an universal and eschatological nature.

10. Conclusion: Place of eschatological encounter of divinity and humankind

It seems to me that not only the Evangelist John, but also Jesus himself found in the text of the *Song of Songs* the source of his thought. The image of the crucified Christ on the cross surpasses any temporality, since it includes new life as well as death in itself. It is true, indeed, that not only the image of Christ is anointed by the 'glory' there, but also his name itself means the 'anointed'. According to Gregory, the *Song of Songs* invites us to participate in this Christ through the stages of spiritual path of the Bride; however, in the beginning of this path, the name of the aim of this *epektasis* is already specified: it is 'Christ', the Only Son of God, the center of the Trinity. When we apply and develop the interpretation of Gregory on the *Song of Songs*, we will be able to make clear the divine property of the human soul in an universal sense: our soul can experience death and resurrection, by means of nourishing in itself the figure of Christ on the cross, or more succinctly, the name of 'Christ'.

[20] R.A. Norris Jr., *Gregory of Nyssa* (2012), 261.

PART III
APOKATASTASIS

CHAPTER 13

Origen and Gregory of Nyssa

Vito LIMONE

1. Premise

In past years *Song* 1:5: 'I am black and beautiful, o daughters of Jerusalem, like the tents of Qedar, like the curtains of Solomon' has given rise to a huge debate among the scholars attentive to the problem of racism because of the negative connotation ascribed to the adjective 'black'.[1] Anyway, we have evidence that the association of blackness with negative meanings was typical of the Greco-Roman world,[2] later incorporated into the early Christian culture.[3] Indeed, in their readings of *Song* 1:5 the Church Fathers make no secret of their derogatory attitudes toward blackness,[4] even if it plays a significant role in their allegorical exegesis of this verse.

Without addressing the controversial issue about the early Christians' views of blackness, the chief aim of this chapter is to explore the interpretations of *Song* 1:5 of Origen of Alexandria and Gregory of Nyssa and compare them. The preconditions of this cross-check are that, firstly, we owe Origen the earliest extensive analysis of *Song* 1:5, which also Gregory is influenced by, as

---

* Earlier drafts of this article were presented at the XIII International Colloquium on Gregory of Nyssa, held in Rome, on Sept. 17-20, 2014, at the Pontifical University of the Holy Cross, and at the 'Seminario de Posgrado y Doctorado en Letras y en Filosofía: Trinidad y lenguajes de la forma estética: figuras y senderos', held in Buenos Aires, on Sept. 10-13, 2018, at the Universidad Católica Argentina, Facultad de Filosofía y Letras.

[1] For a recent evaluation of this issue see Mark S.M. Scott, 'Shades of Grace: Origen and Gregory of Nyssa's Soteriological Exegesis of the "Black and Beautiful" Bride in Song of Songs 1:5', *HThR* 99 (2006), 65-6, 77-81.

[2] Helpful and comprehensive contributions to this topic are Frank M. Snowden, *Before Color Prejudice. The Ancient View of Blacks* (Cambridge, MA., London, 1983), and Robert E. Hood, *Begrimed and Black. Christian Traditions on Black and Blackness* (Minneapolis, 1994).

[3] In particular, the early Christians consider the Ethiopians as instantiations of blackness, which stand for the evil or the demons that tempt them – on this: Jean Marie Courtès, 'The Theme of "Ethiopia" and "Ethiopians" in Patristic Literature', in Jean Devisse (ed.), *The Image of the Black in Western Art. II/1: From the Early Christian Era to the 'Age of Discovery': From the Demonic Threat to the Incarnation of Sainthood* (New York, 1979), 9-32. See also F.M. Snowden, *Before Color* (1983), 99-108, and R.H. Hood, *Begrimed* (1994), 73-90.

[4] An overview of the patristic readings of *Song* 1:5 is: Giancarlo Gaeta, 'Nera e bella. L'esegesi antica di Cantico 1, 5-6', *ASE* 2 (1985), 115-23.

Studia Patristica CI, 163-176.
© Peeters Publishers, 2021.

he expressly claims,[5] and secondly, they both draw the attention to the eschatological core of the verse.[6] In this regard, the present study consists of two main sections: one is devoted to Origen's use of *Song* 1:5 (2.), with focus on its occurrences in his *Commentary* (henceforth *CCt*; 2.1.) and in the I of his homilies on the *Song* (henceforth *HCt*; 2.2.); the other investigates how Gregory employs *Song* 1:5 in the II of his homilies on the *Song* (henceforth *In Ct*; 3.), in light of Origen's heritage.

Before turning to Origen, we must at least mention the circulation of *Song* 1:5 in the Jewish-Christian debate in the II-III centuries. As far as the Jewish tradition is concerned, the bride, who calls herself black and beautiful, is Israel; the bridegroom is Jhwh; the daughters of Jerusalem are the Church, that presumes to have displaced Israel as Jhwh's beloved: in rabbinic literature the blackness of the bride is Israel's sin of idolatry, in particular the worship of the golden calf, whereas the beauty is the everlasting intimacy with Jhwh, restored by its repentance, namely, the construction of the Tabernacle of Testimony.[7]

A similar interpretation of *Song* 1:5 is provided by Hippolytus, who wrote the earliest extant Christian commentary on the *Song* (likely in years 211-218),[8]

---

[5] Greg. Nys., *In Ct.* I (GNO VI, 13.3-4) – on his acquaintance with Origen's commentary. Two erudite studies on Origen's reading of *Song* 1:5 are Ernst Benz, '"Ich bin schwarz und schön" (*Hohes Lied* 1,5). Ein Beitrag des Origenes zur Theologie der *negritudo*', in Hans-Jürgen Greschat and Hermann Jungraithmayr (eds), *Wort und Religion: Kalima na Dini. Studien zur Afrikanistik, Missionswissenschaft, Religionswissenschaft. E. Damman zum 65. Geburtstag* (Stuttgart, 1969), 225-42, and Lenka Karfíková, 'Fusca sum et formosa. Die Heiligkeit der Kirche und die Heiligkeit der Seele nach den Hohelied-Auslegungen des Origenes', in Theresia Hainthaler, Franz Mali and Gregor Emmenegger (eds), *Heiligkeit und Apostolizität der Kirche. Forscher aus dem Osten und Westen Europas an den Quellen des gemeinsamen Glaubens* (Innsbruck, Wien, 2010), 311-34. See also the study of M.S.M. Scott, 'Shades of Grace: Origen and Gregory of Nyssa's Soteriological Exegesis of the "Black and Beautiful" Bride in Song of Songs 1:5' (2006).

[6] Unlike the majority of the Church Fathers, who agree about the allegorical sense of the *Song*, Theodore of Mopsuestia believes that the book was composed by the king Solomon in order to defend himself from the accusation of having married a black (= not Jewish) woman; Theod. Mops., *In Ct.* (PG 66, 699-700). On Theodore: G. Gaeta, 'Nera a bella' (1985), 117 n. 9; about Solomon's shame: Louis Ginzberg, *The Legends of the Jews. IV: From Joshua to Esther* (Baltimore, London, 1998), 128-9.

[7] The *Song of Songs Rabbah* (on *Song* 1:5-6) passes down to us the account of Rabbi Isaac, that a black maidservant is persuaded that her master is going to divorce his wife and marry her, because he saw her hands stained, but a companion of hers warns her that the master will never divorce his wife and prefer the maidservant, who is black from birth. The meaning of this parable is that Jhwh does not disavows Israel, despite its sin of idolatry, and the Church can not replace Israel. Most of the agadic passages transmitted by Rabbi Isaac are from Rabbi Yohanan, who operated in Caesarea around the same time Origen delivered public sermons there. On this see Reuven Kimelman, 'Rabbi Yohanan and Origen on the Song of Songs: A Third Century Jewish-Christian Disputation', *HThR* 73 (1980), 567-95.

[8] A sum of the various scholars' views and this proposal of datation are in Yancy W. Smith, *Hippolytus' Commentary on the 'Song of Songs' in Social and Critical Context*, Dissertation Presented at the Faculty of the Brite Divinity School (Fort Worth, 2009), 8-14. The Slav fragments of it are published in German translation in *Hippolytus. Exegetische und Homiletische Schriften,*

which shares many similarities with the later Origen's *CCt*.[9] According to Hippolytus, the bride is allegory of the Synagoge, which is 'black' due to the sin and 'beautiful' due to the faith, while the bridegroom is Christ.[10] On the one side, Hippolytus restates the identification of the bride with the Jews, in line with the rabbinic exegesis,[11] on the other side he renews the reading of the bridegroom as Christ.

In sum, the Judeo-Christian literary production before Origen documents such a use of *Song* 1:5 that the bride stands for Israel, which benefits from its neverending belonging to Jhwh, though it once betrayed him, and the bridegroom is Jhwh, or – as in the case of Hippolytus – Christ.

2. Origen of Alexandria

As aforesaid, Origen is the earliest Christian author who formulates an extensive analysis of *Song* 1:5. It is worth noting that the *Song* is at the heart of Origen's interest, since he devotes to it a continuous commentary[12] and two

---

GCS I = Hipp. I (Leipzig, 1897), 343-74; the Georgian fragments were later edited by G. Garitte in 1965 in CSCO 263 (= CSCO 264, for the Latin translation).

[9] Nicephorus, patriarch of Costantinople, argues that Origen's father, Leonidas, died during the time that Hippolytus was very popular; see Carl De Boor (ed.), *Nicephori Archiepiscopi Costantinopolitani Opuscula Historica* (Leipzig, 1880), 94. In addition, J. Daniélou conjectures that Origen met Hippolytus during his vist to Rome and Hippolytus encouraged the Alexandrine to comment on the Scripture; see Jean Daniélou, *Origène* (Paris, 1948), 20; on Origen's trip to Rome: Eus., *HE*. VI 19, 10 (SC 41, 108).

[10] Hipp., *In Ct. 1,5* (CSCO 264, 26.31).

[11] As it was extensively pointed out by Gertrud Chappuzeau, 'Die Auslegung des Hohenliedes durch Hippolyt von Rom', *JbAC* 19 (1976), 45-81.

[12] That is, a 'lemmatic' commentary; on the analogies between the late antique philosophical commentaries and Origen's *CCt* see: Ilsetraut Hadot, 'Les introductions aux commentaires exégétiques chez les auteurs néoplatoniciens et les auteurs chrétiens', in Michel Tardieu (ed.), *Les règles de l'interprétation* (Paris, 1987), 99-122, esp. 111-9. We must not forget that Origen also authored a juvenile commentary on the *Song*, which is witnessed by: Hier., *Ep.* 33,4 (CSEL 54, 256.16-7), and: *FrCt* 1 (*app.*) (ed. M.A. Barbàra, 288 = SC 302, 327) – on *FrCt* see below, n. 14. The scholars disagree about the literary genre of this juvenile commentary: the majority of them sees it as a commentary in the proper sense, see: Henri Crouzel, 'Introduction', in Luc Brésard, Henri Crouzel and Marcel Borret (eds), *Origène. Commentaire sur le Cantique des Cantiques. I*, SC 375 (Paris, 1991), 10; Manlio Simonetti, 'Introduzione', in *id.* (ed.), *Origene. Il Cantico dei Cantici* (Milan, 1998), xv; *id.*, 'Cantico dei Cantici', in Adele Monaci Castagno (ed.), *Origene. Dizionario* (Rome, 2000), 60; some argue that it consists of occasional remarks on the *Song*, the so called 'scholia', see Olivier Rousseau, 'Introduction', in *id.* (ed.), *Origène. Homélies sur le Cantique des Cantiques*, SC 37 (Paris, 1953), 8; Martin N. Esper, *Allegorie und Analogie bei Gregor von Nyssa*, Habelts Dissertationsdrucke: Reihe klassische Philologie 30 (Bonn, 1979), 155 n. 5; finally, Éric Junod is persuaded that it is a discontinuous commentary, the so called 'sēmeiōseis', see 'Que savons-nous des «scholies» (σχόλια – σημειώσεις) d'Origène?', in Gilles Dorival and Alain Le Boulluec (eds), *Origeniana Sexta. Actes du Colloquium Origenianum Sextum, Chantilly, 30 août-3 sept. 1993*, BETL 118 (Leuven, 1995), 133-49, esp. 139-40.

homilies. With respect to the former, originally in ten books, written in years 240-245, between Athens and Caesarea, it has been passed down to us in the partial Latin translation by Rufinus (only the prologue and the first four books);[13] nevertheless, a huge corpus of Greek fragments of the *CCt*., coming from the epitome of Procopius of Gaza (centuries V-VI), was recently edited by Maria Antonietta Barbàra.[14] Concerning the two homilies, delivered at Caesarea after 245,[15] they have been transmitted only in the Latin version of Jerome.[16] The Alexandrine's exegesis of *Song* 1:5 occurs at the beginning of the book II of his *CCt*, to which the sub-section 2.1. will be devoted, and in the I of his *HCt*, which will be examined in 2.2.

2.1. *The Exegesis of* Song *1:5 in the* Commentary on the Song

Origen supplies two interpretations of *Song* 1:5: the literal and the allegorical. With regard to the former, he ascribes the statement: 'I am black and beautiful' to the bride, who responds to the daughters of Jerusalem, who accuse her of being black, namely ugly: although she is black, and ugly, as far as her complexion goes, she is beautiful with respect to her inward parts,

---

[13] On this Eus., *HE*. V 32, 2 (SC 41, 134), and Hier., *Ep*. 33,4 (CSEL 54, 288.10-3). For a detailed scrutiny of the various views on the *CCt* and a proposal of datation: Vito Limone, 'Origen on the *Song of Songs*. A Reassessment and Proposal of Dating of his Writings on the *Song*', *SP* 94 (2017), 195-204. Rufinus' translation of the *CCt* is dated to 410-411, see Caroline P. Hammond, 'The last ten years of Rufinus' life and date of his move south from Aquileia', *JTS* n.s. 28 (1977), 372-427, 393-4, 429; Giorgio Fedalto, *Rufino di Concordia tra Oriente e Occidente* (Rome, 1990), 149.

[14] Maria Antonietta Barbàra (ed.), *Origene. Commentario al Cantico dei Cantici. Testi in lingua greca*, Biblioteca Patristica 42 (Bologna, 2005). When quoted, these fragments are shortened *FrCt* (as above, n. 12).

[15] Pierre Nautin speculated that Origen may have delivered a three year cycle of homilies on the Old Testament in Caesarea under the reign of Gordian III (238-244); see Pierre Nautin, 'Introduction', in *id*. (ed.), *Origène. Homélies sur Jérémie*, SC 232 (Paris, 1976), 15-21; *id*., *Origène. Sa vie et son œuvre*, Christianisme antique 1 (Paris, 1997), 403, 411, 434; *id*., 'Introduction', in Pierre Nautin and Marie-Thérèse Nautin (eds), *Origène. Homélies sur Samuel*, SC 328 (Paris, 1986), 57-60. Nevertheless, this conjecture was rejected some years ago by various scholars, *e.g.* Adele Monaci Castagno, *Origene predicatore e il suo pubblico* (Milan, 1987), 59-64; Vittorio Peri, *Omelie origeniane sui Salmi. Contributo all'identificazione del testo latino*, Studi e testi 289 (Vatican, 1980), 129 n. 68; Antonio Grappone, 'Annotazioni sulla cronologia delle omelie di Origene', *Augustinianum* 41 (2001), 27-58; *id*., 'Annotazioni sul contesto liturgico delle omelie di Origene', *Augustinianum* 41 (2001), 329-62. The later dating of Origen's homilies has been recently confirmed by the discovery of the Greek homilies on the *Psalms*, *e.g. H36Ps*. I 2 (GCS n.F. 19/ Orig. XIII 35ʳ) = *H36Ps*. I, 1 (SC 411, 62), and *H77Ps*. VIII 1 (GCS n.F. 19/ Orig. XIII 299ᵛ-300ʳ); on the contribution of the recently found homilies on the *Psalms* to the dating of Origen's homiletical corpus see Adele Monaci Castagno, 'Contesto liturgico e cronologia della predicazione origeniana alla luce delle nuove *Omelie sui Salmi*', *Adamantius* 20 (2014), 238-55.

[16] Dated to 383, as it results from Jerome's dedicatory letter to Damasus (382-384); see Hier., *HCt. praef.* (SC 37, 58). On this: M. Simonetti, 'Introduzione', in *Origene. Il Cantico dei Cantici* (1998), xv.

and compares her own beauty with that of the tents of Qedar and the curtains of Solomon.[17]

Concerning the allegorical meaning of *Song* 1:5, Origen offers two main interpretations. According to the first interpretation, the bride is the Church gathered from among the Gentiles, *i.e.* those who have come from paganism to faith in Christ; the daughters of Jerusalem stand for the Jews. In light of these definitions, Origen argues that the accusation of blackness by the daughters of Jerusalem against the bride signifies that the Jews blame the Gentiles for their state of being unenlightened by the wisdom of the patriarchs and particularly by the Mosaic law.[18] At this stage, the Alexandrine distinguishes two kinds of enlightenment, or beauty: the external and the internal. Although the Gentile Church is deprived of the external enlightenment, that is, of Jewish education and Mosaic law, it nevertheless boasts of an internal enlightenment, that is, its primordial participation in God, of which the beauty of the bride consists. Indeed, Origen comments that the beauty of the bride, or of the Gentile Church, means that God created all humans in the image of himself through the Word of God and, therefore, also the Gentile Church was created in the image of God and benefits from the divine enlightenment from birth.[19] This might be called the 'protological' meaning of the bride's beauty, supported by *Gen* 1:27.[20]

---

[17] Orig., *CCt* II 1, 1 (SC 375, 260). 'Qedar', a Hebrew name which stands for 'blackness', was the second-born of Ishmael (*Gen.* 25:13) and means that the 'blackness' did not affect the glory of the Ishmaelites, who had extended to the boundaries of the Medes and the Persians. The 'curtains of Solomon' remind us of the Tabernacle of Witness which, according to *Ex.* 26:7, was made of goatskins; on this see Orig., *CCt* II 1, 51-54 (SC 375, 290-2).

[18] Orig., *CCt* II 1, 3 (SC 375, 262).

[19] Orig., *CCt* II 1, 4: 'Namque et in me est illud primum, quod *ad imaginem Dei* (*Gen* 1:27) in me factum est; et nunc accedens ad Verbum Dei recepi speciem meam' (SC 375, 262).

[20] This 'protological' meaning reminds us of the controversial 'doctrine of the pre-existence of the souls', which includes the original creation of the soul in the image of God (*Gen* 1:26-7) and the subsequent fall (*Gen* 2:6-7). Several are the bibliographical references to this topic; we just mention some comprehensive studies on it: Giulia Sfameni Gasparro, 'Doppia creazione e peccato di Adamo nel *Peri Archon* di Origene: fondamenti biblici e presupposti platonici dell'esegesi origeniana', in Ugo Bianchi (ed.), *La «doppia creazione» dell'uomo negli alessandrini, nei cappadoci e nella gnosi*, Nuovi Saggi 70 (Rome, 1978), 43-82; *ead.*, 'Restaurazione dell'immagine del celeste e abbandono dell'immagine del terrestre nella prospettiva origeniana della doppia creazione', in U. Bianchi (ed.), *Arché e Telos. L'antropologia di Origene e di Gregorio di Nissa: Analisi storico-religiosa. Atti del Colloquio, Milano, 17-19 maggio 1979*, SPM 12 (Milan, 1981), 231-66; *ead.*, 'La doppia creazione di Adamo e il tema paolino dei due uomini nell'esegesi di Origene', *SP* 13 (1982), 897-902 (now reprinted in: *ead.*, *Origene. Studi di antropologia e di storia della tradizione*, Nuovi Saggi 90 [Rome, 1984], 139-55); Manlio Simonetti, 'Alcune osservazioni sull'interpretazione origeniana di *Genesi* 2,7 e 3,21', *Aevum* 36 (1962), 370-81 (now reprinted in: *id.*, *Origene esegeta e la sua tradizione*, LCA n.s. 2 [Brescia, 2004], 111-22); Peter W. Martens, 'Origen's Doctrine of Pre-Existence and the Opening Chapters of Genesis', *ZAC* 16 (2013), 516-49; Ilaria Ramelli, 'Preexistence of Souls? The ἀρχή and τέλος of Rational Creatures in Origen and Some Origenians', *SP* 56 (2013), 167-226. There is no agreement among the scholars about the significance of this theory in Origen's thought: *e.g.* some think

Additionally, this 'protological' meaning of the beauty is documented by a Greek fragment related to *Song* 1:5, corresponding to the Latin translation by Rufinus.[21] In this fragment Origen takes the bride as the Gentile Church, the daughters of Jerusalem as the Jews, the blackness as the fact that the Gentile Church does not boast of a Jewish education, and the beauty as the participation in the Word which it receives at its birth. In sum, both the Latin version of Rufinus, which passes down to us Origen's reading of *Song* 1:5, and the corresponding Greek fragment attest to the 'protological' meaning of beauty: the bride is the Gentile Church; the daughters of Jerusalem are the Jews; blackness is the lack of the Jewish education which affects the Gentiles; beauty is the communion with God through the Word that the Gentile Church receives at the creation.

In addition to the above interpretation of the bride as the Gentile Church, Origen identifies her with the soul.[22] Given the 'protological' meaning of beauty, he claims that, although the soul is 'black' because of sin, it has the opportunity to get back to the primordial communion with God thanks to repentance and faith in Christ.[23] As we shall see in due course, Origen shows preference for the former interpretation, whereas Gregory for the latter.[24]

For Origen some forerunners of the allegorical content of *Song* 1:5 are to be found in five texts in the Old Testament. The rest of his exegesis of the verse is entirely devoted to the investigation of these texts.[25]

The first text is *Num* 12:1-2: since Moses takes an Ethiopian wife, Mary and Aaron speak ill of him and say with indignation: 'Has the Lord spoken to Moses only? Has he not also spoken to us?' To Origen this narrative lacks coherence, in other words, it is a case of 'defectus litterae': Mary and Aaron's statement is not consistent with Moses' marriage with the Ethiopian woman.[26]

---

of it as a core doctrine of the Alexandrine's theology, see Henri Crouzel, *Théologie de l'image de Dieu chez Origène* (Paris, 1956), 147; some see its roots in the Judeo-Hellenistic doctrine of the divine foreknowledge, see Marguerite Harl, 'Recherches sur l'origénisme d'Origène: la "satiété" (κόρον) de la contemplation comme motif de la chute des âmes', *SP* 8 (1966), 374-405; *ead.*, 'La préexistence des âmes dans l'œuvre d'Origène', in Lothar Lies (ed.), *Origeniana quarta*, Innsbrucker theologische Studien 19 (Innsbruck, Wien, 1987), 247-68.

[21] Orig., *FrCt* 7: Λέγει δὲ ἡ ἐξ ἐθνῶν ἐκκλησία ταῦτα πρὸς τὰς ἐξ Ἰσραὴλ ψυχάς, ἤτοι τὴν Ἰερουσαλήμ, ὁμολογοῦσα τὸ μέλαν, διὰ τὸ μὴ ἐκ λαμπρῶν μηδὲ πεφωτισμένων εἶναι πατέρων, διὸ καὶ σκοτασμῷ παραβάλλεσθαι – καλὴ δὲ διὰ τὸν λόγον ὃν παρεδέξατο – καὶ δέρρεσιν ἐοικέναιτοῦ Σαλομών, ἃς εἶχεν, μεθ᾽ὧν ἄλλων ἐκέκτητο ἐν τῇ δόξῃ αὐτοῦ (*Mt* 6:29) (ed. Barbàra, 158). See *CCt* II 1, 51-53; 55 (SC 375, 290-2).

[22] See Orig., *CCt* II 1, 6-7 (SC 375, 264).

[23] This interpretation is supported by the reference to *Jn* 1:14; *Col* 1:15, and *Heb* 1:3.

[24] A overall study about the differences between Origen and Gregory is Franz Dünzl, 'Die Canticum-Exegese des Gregor von Nyssa und des Origenes im Vergleich', *JbAC* 36 (1993), 94-109.

[25] In *CCt* II 1, 8-19 (SC 375, 264-70) Origen offers an overview of these five texts.

[26] For a thorough discussion of this principle: Manlio Simonetti, *Lettera e/o allegoria. Un contributo alla storia dell'esegesi patristica*, SEA 23 (Rome, 1985), 85-6, 102, 115. This principle was not introduced by Origen, but it originated from the philosophical *milieu* and was implemented by the early Christians; on this Jean Pépin, *La tradition de l'allégorie. De Philon d'Alexandrie à Dante. Études historiques*, EEA 120 (Turnhout, 1987), 167-86; see also Ilaria Ramelli, 'The

This incoherence leads Origen to search for the mystical meaning of the text: Moses, who stands for Christ, gets married with the Ethiopian woman, the Gentile Church, and is criticised by Mary and Aaron, respectively the Synagoge and the priesthood.[27] What Mary and Aaron say of Moses is thus allegory of the jealousy of the Jews who disapprove of the Lord's revelation to the Gentiles.

Origen dedicates an in-depth attention to the episode of 1*Kings* 10:1-10, in which the Queen of Sheba goes to Jerusalem and visits Solomon to have some proof of his wisdom.[28] The Queen of Sheba who combines the characteristics of both the bride of *Song* 1:5 and the Ethiopian woman of *Num* 12:1-2, is an allegory of the Gentile Church; Solomon is an allegory of Christ; finally, the Queen of Sheba's desire to meet Solomon means that the Gentile Church, dissatisfied with the philosophers' responses to her doubts about God, the creation of the world, and the immortality of the soul, expects from Christ the dissolution of her doubts.[29]

The third text is the *Ps* 67/68:31-3, in particular 32b: 'Ethiopia will strech out her hands to God'.[30] In a similar way to what is said of the Ethiopian woman in *Num* 12:1-2, once again Origen understands Ethiopia as the Gentile Church, and the fact that she strechtes out her hand to God signifies that the Gentiles get the gift of salvation from God through Christ. In addition, the Alexandrine exposes the thesis that salvation came to the Gentiles through Israel's offence and that, at the end of time, the salvation of Israel will follow the salvation of the Gentiles, as Origen underlines afterwards.

With respect to the above texts Origen employs the allegorical interpretation of the female character, that is, the Ethiopian woman in *Num* 12:1-2, the Queen of Sheba in 1*Kings* 10:1-10, and Ethiopia in *Ps* 67/68:32b, as the Gentile Church. In case of the fourth text, *Sophon* 3:8-11, especially 3:8a: 'From beyond the rivers of Ethiopia will I receive the dispersed ones', he restates the notion of the individual soul.[31] For Origen this verse has a double meaning. Firstly, it denotes that salvation comes to both the Gentile Church, allegorized by those

---

Philosophical Stance of Allegory in Stoicism and Its Reception in Platonism, Pagan and Christian: Origen in Dialogue with the Stoics and Plato', *IJCT* 18 (2011), 335-71.

[27] Orig., *CCt* II 1, 21-5 (SC 375, 272-4). Origen understands Moses as the law elsewhere: *HEx* II 4 (SC 321, 84); *HLev* VI 2 (SC 286, 272); XIV 3 (SC 287, 240); *HIos* I 3 (SC 71, 100); or as the law of God, or the spiritual law, that is, Christ: *HEx* III 3 (SC 321, 102); IV 6 (SC 321, 130); V 4 (SC 321, 160); V 5 (SC 321, 166); XIII 2 (SC 321, 378). A parallel of *CCt* II 1, 21-25 is *HNum* VI 4, 1-2 (SC 415, 156-60). As Marcel Borret has already pointed out (*Origène. Commentaire sur le Cantique I* [1991], 272 n. 1), the roots of this conception of Moses as the spiritual law are to be found in Philo of Alexandria; see Phil. Alex., *Vit. Mos.* I 162; II 4 (102; 194 Arnaldez *et alii* = Phil. XXII).

[28] Orig., *CCt* II 1, 26-41 (SC 375, 274-84). Origen supports the historical content of this episode with the reference to Flavius Josephus; see: *CCt* II 1, 15 (SC 375, 268), and: Ios. Flav., *Ant. Iud.* II 249-50 (IV, 272 Thackeray).

[29] Orig., *CCt* II 1, 27 (SC 375, 276).

[30] Orig., *CCt* II 1, 42 (SC 375, 284-6).

[31] Orig., *CCt* II 1, 43-45 (SC 375, 286-8). See above, n. 22.

who are surrounded by the rivers of Ethiopia, and to the Jews, represented by those who are beyond the rivers of Ethiopia. Secondly, it signifies that, though all the souls are 'blackened' by sins, they are destined to salvation thanks to repentance and faith in Christ. As in his comment on *Ps* 67/68:32b, Origen recalls the above argument that Israel will be saved after the fullness of the Gentiles is saved, on the basis of *Rm* 11:25.[32]

The last text is *Jer* 38:6-18, in which Ebed-Melech, Ethiopian and eunuch, draws up the prophet Jeremias from the pit. One more time Origen takes Ebed-Melech who is of Ethiopian descent as the Gentile Church that is, on the one side, 'blackened' by sins and, on the other side, made 'beautiful' by her faith in Christ.[33]

In addition to the above 'protological' meaning, in his comments on the last three texts – *Ps* 67/68:32b, *Sophon* 3:8-11, and *Jer* 38:6-18 – Origen introduces another meaning of the beauty of the bride, which might be called 'eschatological': the beauty of the bride signifies that all the Gentiles are destined to be saved before the Jews at the end of time.

On the basis of the data collected until now, we can formulate at least three main conclusions about Origen's exegesis of *Song* 1:5 in his *CCt*.

First, the Alexandrine understands the bride as either the Gentile Church or the soul, her blackness as the lack of Jewish education or sins, and her beauty as the participation in the Godhead through Christ the Word.

Secondly, Origen singles out two core meanings of the beauty of the bride: the 'protological' and the 'eschatological' – the former is that the Gentiles partake of the Godhead at the creation, the latter is that at the end of time all the Gentiles will be saved before the Jews; by the way, we must highlight that, although the former occurs at the beginning of the exegesis of *Song* 1:5, the latter is prevailing in the course of the exegesis.

---

[32] See Orig., *CCt* II 1, 45 (SC 375, 286); see also above, n. 30.

[33] Orig., *CCt* II 1, 46-9 (SC 375, 288-90). Origen notes that the Hebrew name 'Ebed-Melech' stands for 'servant of kings'. The hypothesis that Origen had at hands one or more dictionaries from Hebrew to Greek is confirmed by some passages, *e.g. HEx* V 2 (SC 321, 152); *HIer* XIII 2 (SC 238, 56); *CIo* II 33, 197 (SC 120, 340); *HNum* XX 3 (SC 461, 38); XXVII 12 (SC 461, 322-42). On the ethymological sources of Origen for the Hebrew onomastics see Franz Wutz, *Onomastica Sacra: Untersuchungen zum 'Liber Interpretationis Nominum Hebraicorum' des hl. Hieronymus,* TU 11/1-2 (Leipzig, 1914-1915); Ronald E. Heine, 'Interpretations of Hebrew Names in Origen', *VC* 10 (1956), 103-23; *id.,* 'The Interpretation of Names in the *Genesis* and *Exodus Homilies*', in Ronald E. Heine (ed.), *Origen. Homilies on Genesis and Exodus*, Fathers of the Church 17 (Washington D.C., 1981), 389-97. Additionally, the definition of Ebed-Melech as eunuchus leads Origen to quote *Mt* 19:12 and explain it in a mystical sense, that is, he has in himself no seed of wickedness (see *CCt* II 1, 48 [SC 375, 288]). An acute study about the association between a literal reading of *Mt* 19:12 and the practice of castration, with respect to Origen (see Eus., *HE* VI 8, 1-3 [SC 41, 95-6]), is Christoph Markschies, 'Kastration und Magenprobleme? Einige neue Blicke auf das asketische Leben des Origenes', in *id., Origenes und sein Erbe. Gesammelte Studien*, TU 160 (Berlin, New York, 2007), 15-34.

Finally, he supports his interpretation of *Song* 1:5 with reference to some texts in the Old Testament, in particular the episode of Moses and the Ethiopian woman in *Num* 12:1-2, the Queen of Sheba in 1*Kings* 10:1-10, *Ps* 67/68:32b, *Sophon* 3:8-11, and finally the story of Ebed-Melech and the prophet Jeremiah in *Jer* 38:6-18.

2.2. *The Exegesis of* Song *1:5 in the* Homilies on the Song

As aforementioned, Origen focuses on *Song* 1:5 also in the first homily of his *HCt*.[34]

The starting point of the Alexandrine's interpretation of this verse is here its paradoxical content, as far as the literal level is concerned: in fact, the bride calls herself, on the one hand, 'black', that is, ugly, and on the other hand, 'beautiful'. For Origen, if we move from the literal to the mystical level, the content of *Song* 1:5 is no more contradictory. This assumption leads him to put forward two allegorical readings of *Song* 1:5, which are the same as in the *CCt*: the bride means either the individual soul or the Gentile Church.

First of all, Origen considers the bride as the soul which is 'black' because of sins, but can become 'beautiful' thanks to repentance. In particular, he stresses that beauty is not a property which the soul has at its birth, but it is a property which it can get progressively, namely, in the course of its process of purification, and that it can receive at the end of this process.[35] In contrast with the *CCt*, this interpretation of 'beauty' rules out the 'protological' meaning, that beauty denotes the primordial communion of the soul with the divine Word, and relaunches the 'eschatological' meaning, that beauty signifies the perfection which the soul is destined to receive at the end of its spiritual progression. Additionally, this reading is supported by the quotation of *Song* 8:5, in which the bride who was black at the beginning of the *Song* is described as white at the end of the *Song*.

Before drawing attention to the other allegorical interpretation, namely, that of the bride as the Gentile Church, Origen states that the mystical content of *Song* 1:5 is to be found in some texts in the Old Testament, in particular the episode of Moses and the Ethiopian wife in *Num* 12:1-2, *Ps* 67/68:31-3, *Sophon* 3:8-11 – these texts are the same as in *CCt* – and the episode of the woman subject to bleeding in *Mt* 9:18-26.[36]

---

[34] Orig., *HCt* I 6 (SC 37, 71-4).

[35] Orig., *HCt* I 6: 'Paenitentiam egit a peccatis, speciem ei est largita conversio et ideo *speciosa* cantatur. Quia vero necdum omni peccatorum sorde purgata, necdum lota est in salutem, *nigra* dicitur, sed in atro colore non permanet; fit et candida. Itaque quando ad maiora consurgit et ab humilibus incipit ad alta conscendere, dicitur de ea: *quae est ista, quae adscendit dealbata* (*Song* 8:5)' (SC 37, 71).

[36] This episode was employed by the Gnostics in order to explain the difference between the pleromatic Sophía and the extra-pleromatic Sophía, or Sophía Achamoth, that is, Sophía after her

Concerning the second allegorical interpretation of *Song* 1:5, Origen takes the bride as the Gentile Church, which is 'black', since it lacks the Jewish education, but is 'beautiful', since it is nevertheless saved by Christ.[37] Once again, he supports this reading with reference to the episode of the Queen of Sheba and Solomon. There is a difference between the quotation of this episode in the *CCt* and here: in fact, in the *CCt* Origen derives the episode from 1*Kings* 10:1-10, whereas in the *HCt* he refers to *Mt* 12:42. This difference is confirmed by the fact that in the *HCt* the 'men of this generation', whom *Mt* 12:42 speaks of, is an allegory of Israel, whereas in the *CCt* we have no mention of it, since this expression does not occurr in 1*Kings* 10:1-10. By the way, Origen restates the 'eschatological' meaning of beauty: though the Gentiles are deprived of the Jewish education, they are destined to be saved at the end of time, before the Jews.

In short, we can now underscore the similarities between Origen's exegesis in the *CCt* and in the *HCt*. Firstly, the Alexandrine employs both the allegorical readings: the bride is either the Gentile Church or the individual soul. Secondly, the same texts in the Old Testament are recalled in support of his interpretetation both in the *CCt* and in the *HCt*: *Num* 12:1-2; *Ps* 67/68:31-33, *Sophon* 3:8-11, the episode of the Queen of Sheba (the episode of Ebed-Melech does not occur in the *HCt*). Finally, the 'eschatological' meaning of beauty, that the Gentile Church will be saved before the Jewish people at the end of time, is common to the *CCt* and *HCt*, while the 'protological' meaning, that it partakes of the Word at the creation, is mentioned in the *CCt* and is not registered in the *HCt* at all.

3. Gregory of Nyssa

Although Gregory's exegesis of *Song* 1:5 is considerably shorter than Origen's, he expressly recovers some key elements of the Alexandrine's interpretation, on the one hand, and he also includes some details which are new to

---

fault and her fall out of the divine Pleroma; on this see: Iren., *AH* I 3, 3 (SC 264, 54). This reading of this episode was known to Origen, as it results from: Orig., *C. Cels.* VI 35 (SC 147, 264). Origen's quotation of *Mt* 9:18-26 might be in contrast with the Gnostics: in fact, the Alexandrine understands the woman subject to bleeding as the soul which converts from the sins to the faith in Christ, whereas the Gnostics consider her as allegory of the double facet of Sophía. On this see Vito Limone, 'La Sposa e l'Agnello. La mistica di Origene nel *Commento al Cantico dei Cantici*', in *id.* (ed.), *Origene. Commento al Cantico dei Cantici*, Theánthropos 1 (Panzano in Chianti, Florence, 2014), 76-9. A comprehensive study about the difference between Origen and the Gnostics with respect to the use of the nuptial metaphor and the *Song* is Gaetano Lettieri, 'Origene intrreprete del *Cantico dei Cantici*. La risoluzione mistica della metafisica valentiniana', in Luigi F. Pizzolato and Marco Rizzi (eds), *Origene maestro di vita spirituale / Origen Master of Spiritual Life*, SPM 22 (Milan, 2001), 141-86.

[37] Orig., *HCt* I 6 (SC 37, 73-4).

his predecessor, on the other hand.[38] As aforementioned, Gregory explores *Song* 1:5 at the opening passages of the second homily of his *In Ct*. Before examining in detail what Gregory says of this verse, it is worth noting some literary features of his homiletical corpus on the *Song*.

In contrast to Origen's writings on the *Song* (*CCt* and *HCt*), which have been passed down to us in the Latin translations by Rufinus and Jerome – except for the *FrCt* –, we have the chance to access Gregory's corpus of the 15 homilies on the *Song* in the original Greek. They were likely delivered over the last years of Gregory's life, probably right before 394, as it results from the analogies between the *In Ct* and the *De vita Moysis* which is dated to his old age as well.[39] In regard to the place in which they were delivered, scholars tend to agree about Nyssa, in Cappadocia.[40]

With respect to Gregory's reading of *Song* 1:5, his starting point is the contrast between the 'beauty' of the bride and her 'blackness'.[41] First of all, he reformulates the contrast between the 'beauty' of the bride and her 'blackness', or her uglyness, as the contrast between what is internal and what is external – this is to be found also in Origen's *CCt*.[42] On the basis of this correspondence between the contrast 'beauty'/'blackness' and the contrast 'internal'/'external',

---

[38] Several are the studies about the differences between Origen and Gregory concerning their interpretations of the *Song*; see *e.g.*, Anneliese Meis, 'Orígenes y Gregorio de Nisa, "*In Canticum*"', in G. Dorival and A. Le Boulluec (eds), *Origeniana Sexta* (1995), 599-616; *ead.*, 'Das Paradox des Menschen im *Canticum-Kommentar* Gregors von Nyssa und bei Origenes', in Wolfgang A. Bienert and Uwe Kühneweg (eds), *Origeniana Septima. Origenes in den Auseinandersetzungen des 4. Jahrhunderts*, BETL 137 (Leuven, 1999), 469-96.

[39] According to Franz Dünzl, the *De vita Moysis* was earlier than the *In Ct*; see Franz Dünzl, 'Gregor von Nyssa's *Homilien zum Canticum* auf dem Hintergrund seiner *Vita Moysis*', VC 44 (1990), 371-81. This hypothesis is shared by Claudio Moreschini, 'Le omelie sul *Cantico dei Cantici* di Gregorio di Nissa', in Vito Limone and Claudio Moreschini (eds), *Origene, Gregorio di Nissa. Sul Cantico dei Cantici* (Milan, 2016), 90 n. 4. In light of this hypothesis, F. Dünzl argues that the *In Ct* were delivered by Gregory after 394; see *Braut und Bräutigam: Die Auslegung des Canticum durch Gregor von Nyssa*, Beiträge zur Geschichte der biblischen Exegese 32 (Tübingen, 1993), 32.

[40] For Jean Daniélou the *In Ct* were delivered at Constantinople; on this see Jean Daniélou, 'La chronologie des œuvres de Grégoire de Nysse', *SP* 7 (1966), 159-69, 168. Nevertheless, this thesis has been rejected by the scholars who agree about Nyssa, in Cappadocia: Joseph B. Cahill, 'The Date and Setting of Gregory of Nyssa's Commentary on the *Song of Songs*', *JTS* n.s. 32 (1981), 450-3; Ronald E. Heine, 'Gregory of Nyssa's Apology for Allegory', *VC* 38 (1984), 360-70; F. Dünzl, *Braut und Bräutigam* (1993), 26 (see also Franz Dünzl [ed.], *Gregor von Nyssa. In Canticum Canticorum Homiliae / Homilien zum Hohenlied*, Fontes Christiani 16/1 [Freiburg i. Br., 1994], 25); Pierre Maraval, 'Biografia', in L.F. Mateo-Seco and G. Maspero (eds), *Gregorio di Nissa. Dizionario* (Rome, 2007), 117-29; C. Moreschini, 'Le omelie sul *Cantico dei Cantici*' (2016), 90-2.

[41] Greg. Nys., *In Ct* II (GNO VI, 43,8-9). On this M.S.M. Scott, 'Shades of Grace' (2006), 72.

[42] See Orig., *CCt* II 1, 1: '*Fusca quidem sum* – vel *nigra* –, quantum ad colorem spectat, o *filiae Hierusalem, formosa* vero, si quis interna membrorum liniamenta perspiciat' (SC 375, 261).

Gregory compares the bride with the tents of Solomon and devotes a detailed section to the description of the Tabernacle of Testimony. He claims that we can not see how much the Tabernacle is 'beautiful' inside if we see it from outside: in fact, inside the Tabernacle is provided with gold, silver, precious stones, and bright colours, whereas outside it is made of dark goatskins and linen.[43]

Additionally, Gregory applies the above scheme 'internal'/'external' also to the *Song* itself. He conceives of it as a writing which, according to its 'external' facet, that is, to the literal interpretation, speaks of the relationship between a bride and a bridegroom, whereas, according to its 'internal' facet, that is, to the mystical and allegorical interpretation, it is about the interplay of the individual soul with Christ the Word. Concerning *Song* 1:5, Gregory proves to opt for the understanding of the bride as the individual soul – the interpretation of it as the Gentile Church does not occur here, in contrast with the above mentioned exegesis of Origen.[44]

Given these premises – the contrast 'internal'/'external' and the interpretation of the bride as the individual soul –, Gregory exposes the allegorical meaning of *Song* 1:5. To Gregory the bride is an allegory of the soul, her blackness stands for sins, her beauty is the spiritual perfection, that is, the participation in God through the Word, and the daughters of Jerusalem are the souls which are still at a lower stage of their spiritual progression and are encouraged to tend to God by the example of the bride.[45] Two core doctrines of Gregory, strictly related to each other, contribute to the understanding of his conception of beauty,[46] in so far as it is offered in the circumstance of the exegesis of *Song* 1:5: the assumption of the ontological difference between the soul and God and the well-known theory of 'epéktasis'. The former implies the absolute ontological difference (διάστημα) between God and creation, namely, the infinity and the finitude,[47] whereas the latter explicates

---

[43] Greg. Nys., *In Ct* II (GNO VI, 43,9-44,7). A parallel text is *Vit. Moys.* II 170 (GNO VII/1, 95,10-96,13).

[44] Greg. Nys., *In Ct* II (GNO VI, 44,7-45,15).

[45] Gregory's allegorical reading of *Song* 1:5 is expressed in Greg. Nys., *In Ct* II (GNO VI, 45,16-47,1).

[46] We can find an extensive analysis of Gregory's conception of the beauty in Anthony Meredith, 'The Good and the Beautiful in Gregory of Nyssa', in Herbert Eisenberger (ed.), *Hermeneumata. Festschrift für H. Hörner zum sechzigsten Geburtstag* (Heidelberg, 1990), 137-40. Furthermore, the topic of the beauty is to be found also in Gregory's *On Virginity*; on this see Morwenna Lodlow, 'Useful and Beautiful: A Reading of Gregory of Nyssa's *On Virginity* and Proposal for Understanding Early Christian Literature', *Irish Theological Quarterly* 79 (2014), 219-40.

[47] On this see Ekkehardt Mühlenberg, *Die Unendlichkeit Gottes bei Gregor von Nyssa. Kritik am Gottesbegriff der klassischen Metaphysik*, Forschungen zur Kirchen- und Dogmengeschichte 16 (Göttingen, 1996), and Thomas Böhm, *Theoria, Unendlichkeit, Aufstieg. Philosophische Implikationen zu »De Vita Moysis« von Gregor von Nyssa*, VC.Suppl. 35 (Leiden, New York and Köln, 1996). In a sense, an anticipation of this doctrine is to be found in Philo of Alexandria, as

that, despite this inextinguishable difference, the created soul has the natural desire for the infinite God, and this desire is endless, since its difference from the Creator can not be removed.[48] Both these core implications of Gregory's thought shed light on the above use of the notion of beauty: it is neither a property which the soul receives at its creation, as in the aforementioned 'protological' meaning of Origen, nor only a gift which the soul has from the divine Word, but it is the spiritual perfection, or the participation in God through the Word, to which the individual soul tends and which it can never completely possess. Once again we have to do with an 'eschatological' meaning of the beauty of *Song* 1:5. Nevertheless, Origen and Gregory offer two different formulations of this 'eschatological' meaning of the beauty of the bride: both in the *CCt* and in the *HCt* Origen intends beauty to be the salvation which the Gentile Church is destined to get at the end of time, before the Jews, although in the *HCt* he also speaks of beauty as the spiritual perfection of the soul; Gregory thinks of beauty as the final step of the infinite spiritual progression of the soul.

Anyway, at the heart of Gregory's reading of *Song* 1:5 we can see the idea that beauty is the 'eschatological' destination which attracts all the souls. Gregory does not employ any of the Old Testament texts which Origen mentions: he supports his view of *Song* 1:5 with reference to *Rm* 1:13-5, in which Paul, who was once persecutor of the Christians, now preaches the Gospel, and to *Ps* 86/87:3-4, in which David sees Babylon, Ethiopia, and Tyre among the inhabitans of the Heavenly Jerusalem.[49]

4. Conclusions

On the basis of the data collected until now, we can register the similarities and differences between Origen' and Gregory's readings of *Song* 1:5.

Both Origen and Gregory assume the literal and the allegorical interpretations of the verse: in particular, the former considers the bride as the Church Gentile, or the individual soul, whereas the latter intends her solely as the individual soul.

With respect to the bride's beauty, Origen outlines two core meanings, the 'protological' – beauty signifies the unity of the Gentile Church and Christ

pointed out by Albert-Kees Geljon, 'Divine Infinity in Gregory of Nyssa and Philo of Alexandria', *VC* 59 (2005), 152-77. See also Clem. Alex., *Strom.* II 2, 5-6 (SC 38, 35-37); VI 17, 150-1; 154 (SC 446, 360-4; 368-70).

[48] A comprehensive study on this theory in Gregory's *In Ct* is Maria Laura di Paolo, 'Desiderio del bello e inestinguibilità della relazione nell'*In Canticum* di Gregorio di Nissa', *Acta Philosophica* 27 (2018), 119-33. See also Ilaria Vigorelli, 'Desiderio e beatitudine: *schesis* nell'*In Canticum Canticorum* di Gregorio di Nissa', *Annales Theologici* 28 (2014), 277-300.

[49] Greg. Nys., *In Ct* II (GNO VI, 48,14-50,4).

from the primordial creation (documented only by the *CCt* and the *FrCt* 7) – and the 'eschatological' – beauty is an allegory of the salvation of the Gentile Church at the end of time (in *CCt* and *HCt*), or of the spiritial perfection at the end of the soul's progression to Christ (only in the *HCt*).

In regard to Gregory, though he makes no reference to the 'protological' meaning, he employs the 'eschatological' meaning, but in a sense different from Origen's: for Gregory the beauty of the bride stands for the final step of the infinite progression of the soul towards God.

CHAPTER 14

Gregory and Evagrius

Ilaria L.E. RAMELLI

Gregory's mystical eschatology, as his mystical theology and many other aspects of his thought, seem to have exerted a remarkable influence on Evagrius Ponticus. Nyssen in turn was the most perceptive follower of Origen (hence, among much else, his adhesion to Origen's eschatological doctrine of universal restoration[1]). Origen and Nyssen, together with Nazianzen, seem to have been Evagrius' most prominent inspirers. I have argued elsewhere[2] that, in addition to Gregory Nazianzen, Gregory of Nyssa too – and Origen, both through Gregory, who was a faithful Origenian, and probably also independently – greatly impacted Evagrius' thought, in practically all fields of philosophical theology, from Trinitarian theology and Christology to anthropology, psychology, and eschatology, as well as in ideas about social justice and poverty.[3]

A large bundle of notions that Evagrius inherited from Nyssen – and, through Nyssen, from Origen – is related to mystical eschatology, which in both of them included the doctrine of apokatastasis, the eschatological restoration of all rational creatures.[4] Nyssen defended it as an 'orthodox' Christian doctrine, and to this effect he related it to his Christological anti-subordinationism – just

---

[1] Morwenna Ludlow, *Universal Salvation: Eschatology in the Thought of Gregory of Nyssa and Karl Rahner* (Oxford, 2000); Ilaria Ramelli, *The Christian Doctrine of Apokatastasis: A Critical Assessment from the New Testament to Eriugena* (Leiden, 2013), 372-440; Rowan Greer, *One Path for All: Gregory of Nyssa on the Christian Life and Human Destiny* (Eugene, OR, 2015).

[2] In *Evagrius' Kephalaia Gnostika* (Leiden, Atlanta, 2015), and more systematically in 'Gregory Nyssen's and Evagrius' Biographical and Theological Relations: Origen's Heritage and Neoplatonism', in Ilaria Ramelli, Kevin Corrigan, Giulio Maspero and Monica Tobon (eds), *Evagrius between Origen, the Cappadocians, and Neoplatonism*, SP 84 (Leuven, 2017), 165-231.

[3] For this point see Ilaria Ramelli, *Social Justice and the Legitimacy of Slavery: The Role of Philosophical Asceticism from Ancient Judaism to Late Antiquity* (Oxford, 2016), 172-210 on Gregory, and esp. 204-8 on Evagrius.

[4] Analysis of this doctrine in I. Ramelli, *Apokatastasis* (2013), with the reviews by Anthony Meredith, *International Journal of the Platonic Tradition* 8 (2014), 255-7; Mark Edwards, *Journal of Theological Studies* 65 (2014), 718-24; Johannes van Oort, *VC* 64 (2014), 352-3; Chris De Wet, *Journal of Early Christian History* 5 (2015), 184-6; Steven Nemes, *Journal of Analytic Theology* 3 (2015), 226-33; George Karamanolis, *International Journal of the Platonic Tradition* 10 (2016), 142-6; Robin Parry, *International Journal of Systematic Theology* 18 (2016), 335-8.

Studia Patristica CI, 177-206.
© Peeters Publishers, 2021.

as Origen had done, as I hope to have thoroughly demonstrated.[5] Evagrius and
Nyssen may also have closer biographical relations than is generally assumed,[6]
and allusions to Gregory of Nyssa may lie behind several of Evagrius' references to his own teachers. Both Gregory and Evagrius require a holistic approach
to their thought, which does not divide their theological/speculative and their
spiritual/ascetic works.

I shall thus investigate some important points of Gregory's mystical eschatology and will briefly outline their influence on Evagrius.

Gregory interpreted the heart as a mystical faculty, that through which a
human creature comes into communion with God – the way in which Origen
interpreted 'heart', implying not only *nous* but a pure *nous*, what unites a human
to God (a concept further developed by Evagrius), and the seat of love (which
was so central to Origen's own eschatology[7]). This is clear from Gregory's
exegesis of the beatitude 'Blessed are the pure in heart, for they shall see God'
– meaning participating in God through purity of life, which reflects God's pure
beauty – in *Beat.* 6 and *In Cant.*[8] The fact that Origen's notion of the heart as
mystical faculty emerges in later works of Gregory and not in the earlier *De
hominis opificio* is one of the many proofs that it is not the case that – as is
sometimes repeated – Gregory followed Origen's ideas initially and then abandoned them.[9] Gregory indeed posited the expression of the heart, namely love,
ἀγάπη and ἔρως (as a strong form of ἀγάπη) as a factor in the mystical ascent
to God. It might sound as a contradiction that he also indicated virginity as a factor in the mystical ascent to God: virginity 'deifies / divinises [θεοποιοῦσαν]
those who share in her pure mysteries' (*Virg.* 1). But there is no contradiction,
since the love he is speaking of is spiritual, and virginity is a characteristic of

---

[5] Arguments in my 'Gregory of Nyssa's Trinitarian Theology in *In Illud: Tunc et ipse Filius*:
His Polemic against "Arian" Subordinationism and Apokatastasis', in Volker Drecoll and Margitta
Berghaus (eds), *Gregory of Nyssa: The Minor Treatises on Trinitarian Theology and Apollinarism*
(Leiden, 2011), 445-78; 'Origen's Anti-Subordinationism and Its Heritage in the Nicene and
Cappadocian Line', *VC* 65 (2011), 21-49. On Evagrius' dependence on Origen and Nyssen
regarding the doctrine of apokatastasis, see my commentary in *Evagrius' Kephalaia Gnostika*
(2015) and 'Gregory Nyssen's and Evagrius' Relations' (2017).

[6] 'Evagrius and Gregory: Nazianzen or Nyssen? A Remarkable Issue that Bears on the Cappadocian (and Origenian) Influence on Evagrius', *Greek, Roman, and Byzantine Studies* 53 (2013), 117-37.

[7] See my 'Eros and Ascent in Gregory of Nyssa between Origen and Ps.Dionysius', lectures
at the SBL Annual Meetings, San Antonio, 19-22 November 2016 and Boston, 18-21 November
2017, forthcoming in Kevin Corrigan (ed.), *Eros and Ascent in Platonism*.

[8] On which see Alexander Abecina, 'Gregory of Nyssa's Change of Mind about the Heart',
JThS 68 (2017), 121-40; on God's beauty in Gregory see my 'Good / Beauty', in Lucas F. Mateo-
Seco and Giulio Maspero (eds), *Brill Dictionary of Gregory of Nyssa* (Leiden, 2010), 356-63; trans.
Athanasios Ziakas, 'Τὸ ὅμορφο καὶ τὸ ἀγαθό στον Γρηγόριο Νύσσης', *Φιλοσοφεῖν* (Thessalonika)
13 (January 2016), 381-92; David Konstan, *Beauty. The Fortunes of an Ancient Greek Idea* (Oxford,
2014), 217-18, 249; Nadine Schibille, *Hagia Sophia and the Byzantine Aesthetic Experience*
(Oxford, 2016), 178.

[9] A full study on this point is in preparation.

God, meaning essentially purity and the abstention from any evil, so that by imitating it one ascends mystically towards God.

The heart as mystical faculty is related to a pure *nous*. Nyssen arguably inspired Evagrius with the concept of the unified soul as *nous*, which is the channel of the mystical knowledge of God: 'When the soul becomes simple [ἁπλῆ], unitary [μονοειδής], and perfectly similar to God [θεοείκελος], *it will find the truly simple and immaterial Good*'.[10] Indeed, the concept of the unified *nous*, as subsuming body and soul – a key theory in Evagrius – was already in Nyssen, as is confirmed also by *Beat.* GNO VII/2, 160,11-20: body and nous 'must become one'. This is exactly Evagrius' view as well, and within this concept of the unified *nous* it is necessary to read Gregory's and Evagrius' notion of the subsumption of body into soul into *nous*. Gregory's idea that the superior component assimilates the inferior to itself (so does intellect with soul and soul with body) was already embraced by Origen:[11] within the human being, the inferior nature must assimilate itself to the superior, which is in the image of God. This point will return prominently in Evagrius and later in Eriugena, in connection with the eschatological restoration. For Nyssen, too, the assimilation of human nature to the divine will take place at the eschatological restoration: 'The two must become one, and the conjunction will consist in a *transformation into the better nature* [τὸ κρεῖττον]'.[12]

Gregory's mystical eschatology culminated – as was the case with Origen – in restoration (apokatastasis) and deification (θέωσις). Unlike Nazianzen, however, Nyssen uses θέωσις terminology very rarely, only twice θεοποιέω and twice συναποθεόω – a neologism – in the whole of his work.[13] Sometimes he also speaks of deification without this terminology, for instance when he mentions, like Clement, a pre-eschatological deification during the present life (Clement's gnostic becomes 'god, although getting around in flesh', *Strom.* 7.101.4). Likewise for Gregory, a human, if free from any evil, 'becomes a god [θεὸς γίνεται] through this habit', since, according to Jesus, 'those who approach God should themselves become gods' (θεοὺς γίνεσθαι, *Or. Dom.* 5). Gregory uses συναποθεόω to express the indispensable contribution given by Christ to human deification – hence the notion of συν-, expressing the union of Divinity and humanity through Christ: like Athanasius, Gregory remarks that Christ 'mingled himself with our mortal nature so that, by communion with his Divinity, humanity might also be deified' (συναποθεώθη, *Or. cat.* 37). Indeed, again like Athanasius, Gregory insists that the Logos became incarnate that, 'by becoming what we are, it might make us as the Logos is'.[14]

---

[10] *An. et res.* 93C = GNO III/3, 69,16-8.

[11] *Dial. Her.* 12 and *passim*.

[12] *Beat.* 7.

[13] On Gregory's deification theory see Norman Russell, *The Doctrine of Deification in the Greek Patristic Tradition* (Oxford, 2005), 225-32.

[14] *Antirrh.* 11, GNO III/1, 146.

As is the case with Origen, the eschatological doctrine of restoration in Gregory is present throughout his production, from the beginning to the end. This is the core of Gregory's mystical eschatology and must be understood against the backdrop of Gregory's intellectualistic ethics. In this framework, as in Origen's, freedom is not freedom to sin, which is enslavement to sin, but freedom from passions and evil, to adhere to the Good without obstacles, actualising one's human, rational nature in God's image and therefore free.[15] According to ethical intellectualists – going back to Socrates, Plato, and the Stoic – freedom is knowledge; will depends on intellect. Evil is chosen when mistaken for a good, out of insufficient knowledge and/or obnubilation. So, Origen Socratically traced the origin of sin to ignorance and wrong belief: 'Scripture rightly called sin "ignorance"';[16] 'whoever sins entertains wrong beliefs'.[17]

The choice of evil is the fruit of a deceived, mistaken intellect that must be instructed and cured. This is the task of Christ-Logos. If one's intellect is illuminated and achieves the knowledge of the Good, one will adhere to it. Such illumination makes the object of *Princ.* 2.11. Restoration is here said to rest on enlightenment and direct vision of truth. Origen, inspiring Gregory's mystical eschatological theory of infinite *epektasis*,[18] depicts the process of instruction and nourishment in knowledge as without end: the intellect '*continues to feed on suitable foods in the right measure ... this food is for all the contemplation and knowledge of God*'.[19] In his *Commentary on the Song of Songs*, Gregory's model for *Cant.*, Origen spoke of a continual renewal in rational creatures, in an infinite tension toward God's image: the face of the soul 'is renewed every day after the image of its Creator';[20] 'always will they forget what is behind and tend toward what is ahead';[21] 'those souls are made new every day into the image of the One who created them ... they restore the image of God's Son by becoming new themselves'.[22]

Based on the same notion of continually 'becoming new', Gregory supported apokatastasis within his mystical eschatology and as linked to *epektasis*,[23] until

---

[15] 'If, thanks to our solicitude in this life or purification by fire in the next, our soul will be able to liberate itself from irrational emotions, nothing will be left to prevent it from contemplating the Good ... it will be found joined to what is proper and familiar to itself [οἰκεῖον]' (*An et res.* GNO III/3, 66,11-8).

[16] 'Recte autem hic peccatum insipientiam nominavit' (*H*.1 *Ps* 37:4).

[17] 'Male credit quicumque peccat' (*H.Ez.* 9.1).

[18] Models of which are Paul, Moses in *Vit.Mos.*, and Abraham in *CE* GNO I, 252,16-253,22.

[19] *Princ.* 2.11.7.

[20] *C.Cant.* 4.2.17; *cf.* 2*Cor* 4:6; *Col* 3:10.

[21] *C.Cant.* 3.13.36; *cf. Phil* 3:13.

[22] 'Illae animae cotidie innovantur ad imaginem eius qui creavit eas ... per innovationem sui imaginem in se reparant Filii Dei' (*C.Cant.* 3.8.10; *cf. Col* 3:10).

[23] The link between Gregory's apokatastasis and epektasis is argued by Ilaria Ramelli, 'Apokatastasis and Epektasis in *In Cant.*: The Relation between Two Core Doctrines in Gregory and Roots in Origen', in Giulio Maspero, Miguel Brugarolas and Ilaria Vigorelli (eds), *Proceedings of the*

the end of life, in his *Homilies on the Song of Song*. For example, in *In Cant.* 4 he claims that the τέλος is 'that love may always increase and develop, until the One who "wants all to be saved and reach the knowledge of Truth"[24] *has fulfilled his will ...* until the Bridegroom's good will is *accomplished*. This will is that all humans be saved and reach the knowledge of Truth'. Gregory claims that God's universally saving will shall be fulfilled, and this will happen through an infinite, epektatic movement of increment of mystical love.

Much earlier, Gregory had led the foundations of his mystical eschatology culminating in apokatastasis and epektatic mystical union in *De anima et resurrectione*, a remake of Plato's *Phaedo* in light of Origen's Christianised Platonism,[25] and *In illud: Tunc et Ipse Filius*. Gregory's argument for apokatastasis entirely occupies the latter.[26] Here Gregory was closely inspired by Origen, not only in his main argument, but also in his tiniest details, including Biblical exegetical details (such as the recourse to *Ps* 61:2) and literal borrowings. During Christ's eschatological reign (*1Cor* 15:25-6), which Eusebius after Origen called διορθωτικὴ καὶ θεραπευτική, all enemies will submit voluntarily to Christ and God, and will thereby be liberated from evil, while the last enemy, death, will be destroyed. Their conversion to the Good will begin with those who are closest to the Good and end with those who are the farthest. The Good, in its ordered conquest, will reach even 'the extreme limit of evil', having evil disappear completely. In this way, 'nothing will remain opposed to the Good', who is God. After the abolition of evil, 'the whole lump of human nature, joined to its first fruits ... will receive exclusively the dominion of the Good'.

Gregory explains that 'all will have God' means that all will be one with God; mystical unity, Henosis (ἕνωσις) with God will obtain when all will constitute the 'body of Christ' after purification and illumination. Indeed, not even one being in all creation will be lost: μηδὲν ἔξω τῶν σωζομένων, 'No being will remain outside the number of the saved' (*Tunc et Ipse* 21 Downing); 'No being created by God will fall outside of the Kingdom of God' (*ibid.* 14 Downing).

Like Origen, Gregory relates the final situation (after evil) with that obtaining at the beginning (before evil), although both also agreed that the end will be not only similar to, but also better than, the beginning: 'Every being that had its origin from God will return such as it was from the beginning [ἐξ ἀρχῆς], when it had not yet received evil'.[27] Following Origen very closely,

---

XIII International Colloquium on Gregory of Nyssa, Rome, 17-20 September 2014 (Leiden, 2018), 312-39.

[24] *1Tim* 2:4.

[25] See my 'Gregory of Nyssa on the Soul (and the Restoration): From Plato to Origen', in Neil McLynn (ed.), *Gregory of Nyssa: Historical and Philosophical Perspectives* (Oxford, 2018), 110-41.

[26] Argument in Ilaria Ramelli, '*In Illud: Tunc et Ipse Filius...* (1Cor 15:27-28): Gregory of Nyssa's Exegesis, Its Derivations from Origen, and Early Patristic Interpretations Related to Origen's', *SP* 44 (2010), 259-74.

[27] *Tunc et Ipse* 14 Downing.

from 1*Cor* 15:28 Gregory deduces that, if God must eventually be 'all in all,' then evil will no longer exist in any being, because God, the supreme Good, could never be found in evil. Gregory repeats Origen's argument almost word for word, especially from *Princ.* 3.6.2-3: 'When God becomes 'all in all', we cannot admit of evil, lest God be found in evil ... And not only in few or in many, but in all God will be all, when there will be no longer death, nor death's sting,[28] nor evil, absolutely. Only then will God really be "all in all"'. Gregory expands on Origen's argument:

'God will be all in all': in the last sentence Paul with his discourse clearly demonstrates the ontological non-subsistence of evil, by saying that God will be in all, and that for each one God will be all. For it is clear that it will be the case that God is 'in all' only when in the beings it will be impossible to detect any trace of evil. For it is utterly unlikely that God may ever be found in evil. Therefore, either God will not be in all, in case any trace of evil should remain in beings, or else, if it is really necessary to believe that God will be 'in all', along with this conviction the non-existence of evil is also demonstrated. For it is impossible for God to be found in evil.[29]

The eschatological submission of all creatures will not be slavish subjection, but a voluntary choice, resulting in 'sovereignty, incorruptibility, and beatitude'. The final subjection of Christ to God is the subjection of all humans – Christ's body – to God, a subjection that will mean their salvation: 'The subjection of humans to God is salvation for those who submit in this way, according to the prophet's saying that his soul is subject to God because from God comes salvation through submission'.[30] The recourse to *Ps* 61:2, here and in *Tunc et Ipse*, as a Biblical proof that the eventual submission will be aimed at salvation, is the same as Origen's in support of the same thesis.

The doctrine of apokatastasis repeatedly emerges in *De anima et resurrectione*, a dialogue in which Macrina plays the same role as Socrates and Diotima do in Plato's dialogues. The first part is devoted to the immateriality and immortality of the soul (the Platonic doctrine, thoroughly assimilated in Christian Platonism), and the second part to the resurrection (the Jewish-Christian doctrine). Gregory, like Origen, entertains a holistic concept of resurrection, involving not only the body, but also the soul and the intellect – a threefold, integral resurrection, which Evagrius will develop – and coinciding with the eventual restoration.[31] The strong link between anastasis and apokatastasis, resurrection and restoration, is illustrated by Macrina (145C-149B). It is grounded in the definition of the resurrection itself as the restoration or reconstitution (ἀποκατάστασις) of human nature to its original condition. This definition is

---

[28] 1*Cor* 15:55-6.
[29] *Tunc et Ipse* 17 Downing.
[30] *Ref. conf. Eun.* GNO II, 396-7.
[31] On anastasis as apokatastasis in Gregory: *Apokatastasis* (2013), 401-5; for the unity between the Platonic and the Jewish-Christian doctrine: 'Gregory on the Soul (and the Restoration)'.

frequent in Gregory, occurring also, for instance, at *Eccl.* GNO V, 296,16-8: 'Resurrection is nothing other than the complete restoration to the original condition [ἡ εἰς τὸ ἀρχαῖον ἀποκατάστασις]', and often elsewhere.[32]

Gregory by this equation, far from intending to reduce apokatastasis to the resurrection of the body, rather expanded the notion of resurrection into that of body, soul, and intellect – which will be developed systematically by Evagrius.[33] Indeed, anastasis coincides with apokatastasis if it is understood holistically: like Origen and like Evagrius later, Gregory entertains a holistic notion of resurrection, which involves not only the restoration of the body to its original, prelapsarian state, but also the restoration of the soul and intellect of each human being to its integrity before sin. This is a whole process that starts with the resurrection of the body and continues with purification and illumination of the soul and intellect if need be, and culminates in an endless epektatic process in which the notions of mystical eschatological Henosis and Theosis take up a strongly dynamic drift in Gregory. In *De anima et resurrectione*, the resurrection of the body is the beginning of the restoration; for some, who are already pure, it is also the end, since their restoration will be completed at once (although their epektatic motion will never end); for others, there will be a long process before the completion of their restoration. The resurrection of soul and intellect may actually be achieved in some cases after a long purification, but it will be achieved for all.

In his definition of the resurrection as a restoration Gregory follows in the footsteps of Origen, who already entertained a holistic notion of resurrection-restoration and used ἀποκατάστασις in reference to the resurrection, for example of Christ, or of Lazarus.[34] By Origen Methodius was inspired when he called the resurrection of all Christians 'an ἀποκατάστασις' (*Res.* 3,2). Origen explicitly defined apokatastasis as the perfection of the resurrection: τὸ τέλειον τῆς ἀναστάσεως.[35]

Resurrection is thus the restoration of human nature to its original condition, prior to the emergence of evil, as Macrina explains. But the original condition of humanity, as was planned and created by God from the beginning, was free from evil, suffering, and bodily decay and death; 'human nature was something divine, before the human being acquired the impulse towards evil'.[36] And in the τέλος it will return to being so, in conformity with the principle of similarity – but not identity – between the ἀρχή and the τέλος that was a pillar of Origen's (and Plotinus') thought and was embraced by Gregory, and later by Evagrius. The body will remain, but it will be made glorious and freed from

---

[32] *Mort.* GNO IX, 51,16-20; *Hom. op.* 17.2; *Or. dom.* PG 44, 1148C; *Pulch.* GNO IX, 472.
[33] Full argument in 'Gregory's and Evagrius' Relations'.
[34] *Comm. Io.* 20.11; 28.6.
[35] *Comm. Io.* 10,37.
[36] *An. et res.* 148A.

secondary aspects such as the division into genders, which is accessory and not ontologically intrinsic to the human being.[37] It was provided only because of the fall, but it cannot exist in the image of God. This tenet, also expressed in *De hominis opificio*, will remain unchanged in Gregory up to his last work (*In Cant.* 7). Macrina, interpreting 1*Cor* 15:35-8, remarks that the omnipotent God not only gives back to each human being its body, which had been dissolved, but bestows on human nature 'a more magnificent constitution',[38] the 'spiritual body' of 1*Cor* 15:44. That incorruptible and glorious body (1*Cor* 15:52), free from πάθη, will no longer facilitate sin; thus, it will no longer prevent the soul from remaining in the Good.

Macrina makes clear that the aim that God intends to pursue with the resurrection is apokatastasis, the restoration of all humans – and indeed all rational beings and all creatures of God – to a state of original perfection with a view to their infinite spiritual development (*epektasis*). Those who have pursued virtue in this life will rise immediately in a perfect state; those who have not will still need purification after their resurrection. God will eliminate from them all that which is spurious and alien to their nature, that is, sin and evil: 'after the purification and vanishing of these passions thanks to (God's) solicit and much needed care, with the therapy of fire, instead of those defects there will appear their positive counterparts: incorruptibility, life, force, grace, glory, and every other similar prerogative that we conjecture can be contemplated in the Godhead itself and in its image, human nature'.[39]

Macrina, like Origen, regards *Phil* 2:9-10 as a prediction of the submission/ salvation of all rational creatures, angels, humans, and demons, after their purification, 'when finally, after long cycles of aeons, evilness has disappeared, only the Good will remain, and even those creatures [the demons] will concordantly and unanimously admit the sovereignty of Christ' (72B). In line with Origen's position, Gregory deems otherworldly sufferings purifying rather than retributive: the aim of the whole cathartic process is the annihilation of sin and evil (100-105A). The same as Origen declared in *Cels.* 8.72: Christ-Logos, 'more powerful than any evil or illness of the soul', applies the necessary therapy to everyone, according to God's will, and 'the end and perfection of all will be the elimination of evil';[40] likewise in *Hom. in Ier.* 1.15: 'evil must subsist absolutely nowhere, in no respect' (δεῖ μηδαμῶς συνεστάναι).

In the same way, Gregory envisages the radical eschatological annihilation of evil: 'Evil must necessarily be eliminated, absolutely and in every respect, once and for all, from all ... God who is "all" will also be "in all". And in this

---

[37] See, *e.g.*, my 'Patristic Anthropology and the Issue of Gender', in Roberta Franchi and Anelyia Barnes (eds), *More than Female Disciples* (Turnhout, 2020).

[38] *An. et res.* 153C.

[39] *An. et res.* 157C-160C.

[40] Τὸ τέλος τῶν πραγμάτων ἀναιρεθῆναί ἐστι τὴν κακίαν.

it seems to me that Scripture teaches the complete disappearance of evil. For, if in all beings there will be God, clearly in them there will be no evil'.[41] In the last sentence Gregory, as also in *Tunc et Ipse* (pointed out above), is taking over Origen's argument that God's eschatological, mystical presence 'all in all' radically excludes the eschatological subsistence of evil.

Unity with God and with other rational creatures (ἔνωσις with θέωσις) is the culmination of Gregory's mystical eschatology. In *An. et res.* 132C-136A Macrina, remembering Origen's allegorisation of the eschatological heavenly feasts in which all *logika* will participate, interprets the Feast of Tabernacles[42] as an expression of the eventual apokatastasis: all rational creatures will enjoy harmony – in the homogeneous orientation of their wills towards the Good – and unity after the disappearance of evil. The access to the Temple is allegorised as all *logika*'s access to the eventual restoration, which comes from knowledge and voluntary adhesion to God (133D). The angels are the 'horns of the altar' around which all *logika* will celebrate the eschatological feast of unity.[43] *Phil* 2:10 here supports again the doctrine of apokatastasis (136A): Macrina explains that St. Paul in this passage prophesied the eventual 'universal harmony with the Good', *i.e.* with God: Henosis and Theosis as the consummation of Gregory's mystical eschatology.

Gregory's mystical eschatology, culminating in universal restoration and Henosis, is proclaimed in many works of his, from the earliest to the latest, and in disparate literary genres: from the dialogue (*An. et res.*) to the exegetical treatise/homily (*Tunc et Ipse* and *In Cant.*), from consolatory literature (*De infantibus praemature abreptis*) to the 'catechetical handbook' *Oratio catechetica*, and other works. In his *Oratio catechetica*, Gregory includes it among the basic Christian doctrines, which catechists should impart to all. Chapter 26, 64-7 Mühlenberg, even includes the devil in the mystical restoration of all creation to God – mystical here qua based on the Mystery of God's Inhumanation.

Gregory argues that God's salvific plan keeps divine justice and goodness together – the same theodicy as Origen supported against Marcionites and 'Gnostics,' developing his doctrine of apokatastasis. Gregory's mystical eschatology, as emerges from this passage too, joins God's 'judgement according to justice' and God's 'goodness of the purpose inspired by love for humanity'. Christ, 'by rendering what one has deserved, through which the deceiver [the devil] is deceived in turn, shows God's justice', since the devil 'receives in

---

[41] *An. et res.* 101-4.

[42] *Ps* 117:27.

[43] See Ilaria Ramelli, 'Harmony between *arkhē* and *telos* in Patristic Platonism and the Imagery of Astronomical Harmony Applied to the Apokatastasis Theory', *International Journal of the Platonic Tradition* 7 (2013), 1-49; Ilaria Vigorelli, 'Soul's Dance in Plotinus and Gregory of Nyssa', in *Evagrius between Origen, the Cappadocians, and Neoplatonism* (2017), 59-75.

exchange those things whose seeds he has sown by means of his own free choice. For he is deceived in turn by [Christ's] human appearance, he who first deceived the human being with the seduction of pleasure'. But the purpose of this operation also shows God's goodness and love:

The devil plotted his deception aiming at the destruction of human nature, while Christ, who is *just, good, and wise at the same time*,[44] used the intention of deception *aiming at the salvation of the destroyed*. Thus, he benefited not only the one who had perished [the human being], but *also the one who had perpetrated that ruin against us* [the devil]. For, when death is approached by life, darkness by light, and corruption by incorruptibility, there occurs the disappearance of the worse element and its passage into nonbeing. This is *beneficial to the one who is purified* from those worse elements ... the approach of the divine power, like fire, to death, corruption, darkness, and whatever product of evilness[45] had *grown upon the inventor of evil* [the devil], produced the disappearance of what is against nature and therefore *benefited the nature itself* [the devil as created substance] by purification, although that separation is painful.

Indeed, not even the adversary himself would doubt that what has happened is *both just and salvific* [δίκαιόν τε καὶ σωτήριον], in consideration of the benefit produced. Let me now explain this benefit with another simile. Those who are amputated and cauterised for therapeutic reasons ... if health returns thanks to these treatments, and the suffering caused by cauterisation disappears, will be grateful to those who have applied that therapy ... When there will be *the restoration of those who now lie in evilness into their original state* [ἡ εἰς τὸ ἀρχαῖον ἀποκατάστασις τῶν νῦν ἐν κακίᾳ κειμένων], a unanimous thanksgiving will be elevated by all creation, *both those who have been punished in purification and those who needed not even a beginning of purification*.

These and such things are made possible by *the great Mystery of the Inhumanation of God* [τὸ μέγα μυστήριον τῆς θείας ἐνανθρωπήσεως]. For, thanks to all the respects in which Christ has mixed with humanity, having passed through all that is proper to human nature, birth, nourishment, growth, and having even gone as far as the trial of death, he has accomplished all the tasks I have mentioned, both *liberating the human being from evilness* [τόν τε ἄνθρωπον τῆς κακίας ἐλεύθερον] *and healing even the inventor of evilness* [καὶ αὐτὸν τὸν τῆς κακίας εὑρετὴν ἰώμενος, the devil]. For the purification from illness, as painful as it may be, is the definitive healing of the sickness.

Mystical eschatology is delineated here, because the mystery of salvation was made possible by the mystery of the inhumanation of God, as Gregory explains. Christ heals – as a physician and purifying fire, themes dear to Origen – and removes all evil both from humanity, thanks to his Inhumanation (as is also explained in *Tunc et Ipse*, in which the body of Christ is all humanity) and from the devil himself, whose purification is 'both just and salvific'. This appears a more outspoken position than that of Origen himself, who posited

---

[44] Gregory is using the principle of the *akolouthia* of all virtues that was developed by Origen on the basis of a Stoic tenet (see my *Origen of Alexandria Philosopher and Theologian* [in preparation]).

[45] I emend the reading ἔγκονον, kept by Mühlenberg in the GNO edition, into ἐγκόνου.

with some circumspection the salvation of the devil – not as enemy and evil, but as a creature that, once healed, voluntarily converts to God.[46] If the devil is saved, it is difficult to attach to Gregory the eternal damnation of any human. Some people, indeed, having been purified on earth, will need no purification in the other world; others will be purified in the next world.

To the power of Christ's Inhumanation Gregory returns shortly afterwards, in *Or. Cat.* 32, in which he echoes Origen (especially *Cels.* 3.28): Christ has assumed human nature in its totality; therefore, all of it participates in the liberation from evil and the union with the divinity that Christ has realised with his incarnation, death, and resurrection and which will be full in the *telos*. The power of Christ's risen body transmits the resurrection to all humanity, which Christ has assumed in his Inhumanation.[47]

The motif of the deception of the devil,[48] used by Gregory in *Or. cat.* 26, is central to his understanding of the original sin: in his Socratic-Platonic ethical intellectualism, sin is the result of a wrong choice which depends on a wrong judgement; it is ultimately due to ignorance.[49] Adam and Eve sinned, which was evil, because it looked good, and it looked good because they were deceived by the devil. In *Hom. op.* 20, the very name of the forbidden tree, 'of the knowledge of good and evil', is said to express the double nature of the fruit: 'it looks good [καλὸν εἶναι δοκεῖ], but, in that it causes the ruin of those who taste it, it turns out to be the culmination of all evil', κακοῦ παντὸς ἔσχατον. Sin comes from an obfuscation of the intellect: 'The adversary, having mingled evilness [κακία] to the human faculty of choice [προαίρεσις], produced an obfuscation and darkening of the capacity for reasoning well [εὐλογία]'.[50] Indeed, for Gregory the demons' main work of temptation consists precisely in deception, in giving to evil an appearance of good, in deceiving humans through oracles, divination, and the like,[51] and in having humans judge in a superficial way, without a proper exercise of free will.[52]

Since the eschatological, universal restoration is made possible by Christ's inhumanation, sacrifice, and resurrection, and dovetails with a holistic vision of the resurrection, Gregory's concept of apokatastasis – like that of Origen – is thoroughly Christian. The ontological non-subsistence of evil and its final

[46] *Princ.* 3.6.5. On Origen's position and reticence see *Origen of Alexandria*, Ch. 2.

[47] *In S. Pascha* GNO IX, 245-53; *Or. cat.* 37, GNO III/4, 93-5.

[48] On which see Nicholas Constas, 'Divine Deception in Greek Patristic Interpretations of the Passion Narrative', *HTR* 97 (2004), 139-63; I. Ramelli, *Apokatastasis* (2013), 385-90.

[49] Analysed in reference to sin in my 'Was Patristic Sin Different from Ancient Error? The Role of Ethical Intellectualism and the Invention of "Original Sin"', invited lecture, in *The Invention of Sin*, international conference, Institute of Advanced Studies of the University of Paris, 13-14 April 2017 (forthcoming).

[50] *Or. cat.* GNO III/4, 26,3-5.

[51] *C. fatum* GNO III/2, 59,6-12;15-6.

[52] *V. Greg. Thaum.* PG 46, 937.30.

vanishing was a metaphysical tenet of Platonism, but Gregory, like Origen, also
found it in the Bible, especially in 1*Cor* 15:23-8, and indeed they grounded it
in the authority of Scripture, and not in that of Plato or Plotinus. At the same
time, they were indebted to Hellenistic Jewish apologetics from Aristobulus
onwards and Christian apologetics from Justin, Tatian and Clement onwards
and found that Plato agreed with the Bible, in that he was inspired by either the
Bible or Jewish thought, or by the very author and matter of the Bible, God's
Logos.[53] This is a fundamental presupposition of Christian Platonism.

Gregory, like Origen and Evagrius after him, often hammers home that evil
must eschatologically disappear in the most radical way, in accord with its
ontological non-subsistence, in *De anima et resurrectione*, *In illud: Tunc et
Ipse Filius*, *Oratio catechetica*, as seen, but also *In Inscriptiones Psalmorum*,
for instance at GNO V, 100,25 and 101,3. Here Gregory claims that evil is
not 'from eternity', ἐξ ἀϊδίου – since only God is, according to him and to
Origen – and therefore it will not subsist eternally (an argument that Evagrius
will take over in *KG* 1.49-50). Gregory, indeed, points to 'a great philosophical truth' in the dogma 'that evil is not from eternity [ἐξ ἀϊδίου]' and
therefore 'will not subsist forever [εἰς ἀεί]. For what does not exist always
[ἀεί] will not exist forever [εἰς ἀεί] either'. This is an application of the
Platonist perishability axiom, which was well known to Origen and the Cappadocians.[54] This also makes clear that in Gregory's mystical eschatology there
is no room in the least for evil, from neither the ontological nor the ethical point
of view.

Shortly after, in fact, Gregory asserts the eschatological 'complete elimination of evil' (ἀναίρεσις τοῦ κακοῦ) on the basis of both evil's ontological
negativity and of Christ's action – likewise, in *Tunc et Ipse* it is the Inhumanation of Christ that liberates rational creatures from evil. Since evil has no
ontological subsistence, as opposed to God – absolute Good and Being – to be
found in evil is tantamount to non being: 'Being in evil properly means *non-
being*, since evil itself has no ontological subsistence of its own; what originates
evil, indeed, is rather a lack of Good'.[55] *De tridui spatio* also announces the
eschatological vanishing of evil, which is made dependent on the action of
Christ, as in *Tunc et Ipse* and *Or. cat.* 26. In *Trid.* GNO IX, 285,7-286,12 Gregory
meditates on the days between Christ's death and resurrection. They are

[53] See, *e.g.*, my 'Philo as Origen's Declared Model. Allegorical and Historical Exegesis of
Scripture', *Studies in Christian-Jewish Relations* 7 (2012), 1-17.
[54] On this axiom and its importance in Gregory see my 'Gregory of Nyssa', in Sophie Cartwright
and Anna Marmodoro (eds), *A History of Mind and Body in Late Antiquity* (Cambridge, 2018),
283-305.
[55] *Inscr. Ps.* GNO III/2, 62-3. See also *V. Mos.* 2.175: 'Out of love for us, who had been corrupted in our being due to foolishness, Christ has accepted to be created just as we are, to bring
back to being what had ended up out of being [τὸ ἔξω τοῦ ὄντος γενόμενος]' that is, out of the
Good, far from God.

connected with Christ's threefold victory over evil, respectively in the man, the woman, and the serpent, representing the devil – this intimates again the purification of the devil from evil, as in *Or. cat.* 26. Each day 'was devoted to the healing of a kind of those who were infected with evil' and during the third day death 'was completely eliminated'.[56] Evagrius will probably echo Gregory's interpretation, when stating that Christ worked miracles on Friday and Saturday and on the third day, Sunday, he reached his aim: 'If today is that which is called Friday, in which our Saviour was crucified, indeed, all those who are dead are the parable/image of his sepulchre; those in which the justice of God is dead, which will revive on the third day and will rise, when it will take on a spiritual body, if it is true that "today and tomorrow he works miracles, and on the third day is done"' (*KG* 1.90).

Inscr. Ps. GNO III/2, 101,18-21 also predicts the mystery of the eschatological annihilation of evil: 'When evil is no more, neither will there be anyone who is conformed to it. Therefore, once evilness has perished and its form has vanished into nonbeing, all will take up the form of Christ, and one and the same form will shine in all, the form that had been applied to human nature from the beginning'. The annihilation of evil will coincide with the restoration of the 'form of Christ' – the opposite of the form of evil because Christ, qua God, is Good – the ideal form of humanity projected by God and realised by Christ's Inhumanation.

Gregory insists on the restoration as the eschatological annihilation of evil in the same work, at GNO III/2, 155: the nature of evil, which is no creature of God (and therefore was not created in order to exist, as Origen would claim), 'is unstable [ἄστατος] and passes away [παροδική], being opposed to the creatures of God and to the nature of God, stable in being qua Being itself – as Bardaisan of Edessa, known to Gregory, declared, when asserting that being in evil cannot be with stability.[57] This is why evil will disappear, Gregory argues: 'It did not come into existence in the beginning with the creation' and 'will not continue to exist eternally along with the beings that have ontological consistence. For the beings that derive their existence from the One who is the Being continue to exist eternally'. This is why evil, which 'is out of the One who is', will disappear 'at the universal restoration of all into the Good [ἐν τῇ τοῦ παντὸς πρὸς τὸ ἀγαθὸν ἀποκαταστάσει]'. Evil will pass away, since it is nonbeing, unstable, and finite, as opposed to God who is infinite. This is why an eternal permanence in evil is impossible. In *Hom. op.* 21 Gregory opposes the immutability of divine will, which is always in the Good, to the mutability of creatures' will, which can be in evil but cannot remain there stably: 'It is absolutely certain that divine will is characterised by immutability, whereas the

---

[56] Καταργεῖται, *ibid.* GNO IX, 285,21-3.

[57] See my *Bardaiṣan of Edessa: A Reassessment of the Evidence and a New Interpretation* (Piscataway, 2009), 138-42.

mutability of our nature does not remain stable, not even in evil'. Since evil is finite and unstable, an infinite progression in evil is impossible: 'As a consequence, after the extreme limit of evil [τὸ πέρας τῆς κακίας], there comes again the Good [ἡ τοῦ ἀγαθοῦ διαδοχή] ... I believe that in reference to us, too, it must be considered that, even if we should have crossed the boundary of evilness [διεξελθόντες τὸν τῆς κακίας ὅρον] and reached the culmination of the shadow of sin [ἐν τῷ ἄκρῳ γενώμεθα τῆς κατὰ τὴν ἁμαρτίαν σκιᾶς], we shall return to live again in the Light'. Only an epektatic movement towards the Good can happen, because the Good, God, is infinite, whereas there can be no *epektasis* towards evil.

Gregory posits God as ἄπειρον and evil as limited qua God's opposite (see above *Hom. op.* 21). While Plotinus described absolute evil as ἄπειρον,[58] Gregory, who described the Good (*i.e.* God) as ἄπειρον, intended to describe evil as finite and limited, in order to ascribe to it opposite characteristics. As a consequence, only evil qua limited, and not the Good, which is infinite and is God, can cause satiety (κόρος): 'Our appetite, purified from all this, will orient its energy toward one single object of will, desire, and love. It will not entirely abolish our natural impulses toward the old things, but it will reorient them toward the participation in the immaterial goods. For in that state there will be a ceaseless love for the true Beauty, a praiseworthy eagerness for the treasures of wisdom, the beautiful and noble love for glory that is reached in the communion of the Kingdom of God, a sublime passion, which will never be sated and will never be deluded in its good desire by the satiety [κόρος] of these objects'.[59]

De Vita Mosis deals with the soul's ascent towards God, a theme that is close to that of the Homilies on the Song of Songs – entirely devoted to the soul's mystical ascent to God. According to Martin Laird, mystical union is present in the latter work, but more difficult to find in the former.[60] Andrew Louth and J. Warren Smith, instead, tend to read *De Vita Mosis* as intimating the progression from purification to illumination to union[61] – which will become central to Evagrius' spiritual life and thought. This contradiction may be solved looking at the epektatic nature of the mystical union itself in Gregory's view: this is not an experienced, finite, and concluded moment, but always calls for more. Within this framework, indeed, it is significant that Gregory insists on apophatic theology, which in his thought is grounded in the infinity of God, who can never be grasped. This is why God meets Moses 'in darkness [γνόφος], which indicates the unknown and unseen [τὸ ἄγνωστόν τε καὶ

---

[58] *Enn.* 1.8.9.
[59] *Mort.* 19 Lozza.
[60] Martin Laird, *Gregory of Nyssa and the Grasp of Faith: Union, Knowledge, and Divine Presence* (Oxford, 2004), 50-1.
[61] A. Louth, *The Origins* (1981), 81-6; J. Warren Smith, *Passion and Paradise: Human and Divine Emotion in the Thought of Gregory of Nyssa* (New York, 2004), 150-82.

ἀθεώρητον]'.[62] In *V. Mos.* GNO VII/1, 57,8-58,3, Gregory focuses on the eventual apokatastasis as restoration and notes that Moses' outstretched hands prefigure the cross of Christ and its salvific effects: Moses, stretching out his arms during the plagues of Egypt, saved not only the Israelites, but the Egyptians as well, who symbolise sinners; likewise Jesus with his Cross saves sinners too. The plague of darkness (*Ex* 10:21) suggests to Gregory that Christ's Cross can dissipate even the 'outer darkness' of hell: Moses removed the darkness from Egypt, and Christ with his Cross removes even the outer darkness that, with Gehenna, in the Gospel is a designation of hell (*Mt* 8:12):

> Perhaps someone, based on the fact that after three days of suffering in darkness even the Egyptians participated in the light, could be induced to understand in this passage the announcement of the restoration [τὴν ἀποκατάστασιν] that we expect will come to pass in the end, in the Kingdom of Heavens: the restoration of those who had been condemned to Gehenna … both this and the outer darkness are dispelled when Moses outstretched his arms for the salvation of those who lay in darkness.[63]

Something similar is maintained in *Or. cat.* 32: Christ, by outstretching his arms on the Cross, is said to have embraced and unified all, and attracted all to himself, according to *Jn* 12:32. This is why his Cross can be seen as a recapitulation, an ἀνακεφαλαίωσις,[64] which in Gregory dovetails with apokatastasis. Their connection is clear especially from *Ascens.* 327, where Gregory explicitly joins universal recapitulation and universal restoration in Christ, who 'has recapitulated all in himself, who ranks first among all, he who has restored all [ἀποκαταστήσας τὰ πάντα] to the first creation'.

In Cant. 15, a later work, refers to mystical eschatology often, and clarifies that this is a result of mystical love. Mystical love will produce the eschatological Henosis. The exegetical context, on the *Song of Songs*, is particularly appropriate to this treatment. The conclusion of the homily at stake is entirely devoted to the description of restoration, after the complete vanishing of evilness from all and the attainment of mystical communion with God-the Good. First Gregory makes it clear, in accord with Paul and Origen, that 'God receives everyone in his order, giving to each one in proportion to his deserts', which is also the classical definition of justice. God's justice, however, does not contradict God's love, as seen in *Or. cat.* 26, analysed above. Thus, Gregory quotes *Rm* 8:35,38-9 concerning God's unfailing love: 'Nobody will ever be able to separate us from God's love, in Christ Jesus: neither life nor death, neither present nor future, nor anything else of what exists'. Gregory points to Paul's, and Origen's,

---

[62] *V. Mos.* GNO VII/1, 89,11-2.

[63] Notably, interpolations and glosses to this passage, as often in *De anima et resurrectione*, aimed at denying that Gregory supported the theory of apokatastasis. Some even attempted to delete from this passage the term ἀποκατάστασις.

[64] *Trid. sp.* GNO IX/1, 298-303; *C. Eun.* 3, GNO II, 121-2.

differentiation between doing good out of love and avoiding evil out of fear, and remarks:

But if, as it is written,[65] love will utterly dispel fear, and fear, by transforming itself, will become love, then it will be found that what is saved constitutes a unity [μονὰς τὸ σωζόμενον], since all will be unified with one another [πάντων ἀλλήλοις ἑνωθέντων], in connaturality with the only Good [ἐν τῇ πρὸς τὸ μόνον ἀγαθὸν συμφυΐᾳ], thanks to perfection.[66]

The description of the initial and final Monad will be taken over by Evagrius. This final ἕνωσις is one of the most important characterisations of mystical eschatology in both Origen and Gregory (and later Evagrius), and will involve all rational creatures, as is explained immediately afterwards: 'The run for this beatitude is common to all the souls of every order ... until all look at *the same object of their desire and become one and the same thing* and no evilness [κακία] will any longer remain in anyone. Then God will really be "all in all"'.[67] For all, thanks to the union with one another, and their union of wills directed to the same object of love (God), will be 'joined in communion with the Good', *i.e.* God. This is the peak of Gregory's mystical eschatology.

In *An. et res.* 129BC and 152A, Gregory explains the meaning of Henosis with God, *i.e.* the consummation of mystical eschatology and God's aim for his rational creatures. This is coming to be in God and participating in God's goods:

God's goal [σκοπός] is one and only one: after the realisation, through each single human being, of the full totality – when some will be found to have been already purified from evil during the present life, while others will have been healed by means of fire for the given periods, and yet others will have not even tasted, in this life, either good or evil to the same extent – *to bestow on all the participation in the goods that are in the God-head*, of which Scripture says that no eye has ever seen and no ear has heard them, nor are they graspable through reasoning. Now, this, I think, is nothing but *coming to be in the Godhead itself.*

God's aim is restoration, Henosis, and Theosis: the return of all human (and rational) beings to God and their – for Gregory, progressive – participation in the goods of God, who is the Good itself and the source and sum of all goods. This is 'being in God'.[68] The possibility of Henosis and Theosis is grounded Christologically. By means of his Inhumanation and Resurrection, Christ has united again in a perpetual communion the two natures, intelligible and sense-perceptible, which in humanity had become separate. This unification included

[65] 1*Jn* 4:18.
[66] GNO VI, 466-7.
[67] 1*Cor* 15:28.
[68] This notion has similarities with Theosis in Hilary of Poitiers as read by Janet Sidaway, *The Human Factor: 'Deification' as Transformation in the Theology of Hilary of Poitiers* (Leuven, 2016), a sound reconstruction apart from the evaluation of Origen's influence on Hilary's exegesis of 1*Cor* 15:24-8; see my review in *Latomus* 77 (2018), 884-7.

the whole human race (γενικωτέρῳ τινὶ λόγῳ, *Or. Cat.* 16). The aim of Christ's resurrection was 'to recall back the original grace [πρώτη χάρις] that which belongs to human nature, and thus allow us to return to the absolutely eternal life' (τὴν ἀΐδιον ζωήν *ibid.*). Here and elsewhere, Gregory refers ἀΐδιος to the eternal life, thus indicating that it will be absolutely eternal, whereas he never refers ἀΐδιος to death, punishment or fire in the world to come: to these he only applies the Biblical αἰώνιος, which never means 'eternal' unless it refers to God.[69]

The unity of human nature is the foundation of the universality of the resurrection and apokatastasis: 'Because the totality of the whole human nature forms, so to say, one living being [ἑνός τινος ὄντος ζῴου], the resurrection of one part of it [sc. Christ] extends to the whole, and, in conformity with the continuity and *unity of the (human) nature* [κατὰ τὸ συνεχές τε καὶ ἐνωμένον τῆς φύσεως], passes on from the part to the whole' (*Or. cat.* 32). This is why, just as the principle of death, becoming operative in the case of one human being, from this one passed on to the whole human nature, likewise the principle of the resurrection, from one human being, and through it, extends to all humankind (*Or. cat.* 16).[70]

Human nature, united by the bond of Henosis, will be eschatologically invested by the glory of the Spirit, which brings it to perfection:

'That all may be one; just as you, Father, are in me and I am in you, so may also they be one in us'.[71] And the bond of this unity is the glory. Now, no sensible person could deny that it is the Holy Spirit who is called 'Glory', if one takes into consideration the words of the Lord; for he says: 'The glory that you have given me I have given them'.[72] Having taken up human nature, he received the glory he possessed from eternity, from before the world existed. And because this human nature was glorified by the Spirit [in Christ], the communication of the glory of the Spirit has taken place on all that which belongs to the same nature [πᾶν τὸ συγγενές], beginning from the disciples.[73]

Through the συγγένεια between Christ and all human beings – which is an aspect of his Christian elaboration of the doctrine of οἰκείωσις, anticipated

---

[69] See Ilaria Ramelli and David Konstan, *Terms for Eternity. Αἰώνιος and ἀΐδιος in Classical and Christian Authors* (Piscataway, 2007; new edition 2013), reviewed by Carl O'Brien, *CR* 60 (2010), 390-1.

[70] By the unity of the whole human nature in Christ, by whom the 'mass' of humanity is joined to the Father: 'By assuming in body and soul the first fruits of the common nature, [the Son] has sanctified it, preserving it in himself pure from every evil and uncontaminated, to consecrate it in incorruptibility to the Father of incorruptibility, and to attract to himself, through it, all that belongs to the same species by nature [πᾶν τὸ συγγενὲς κατὰ τὴν φύσιν] and is of the same family [ὁμόφυλον], to readmit those disinherited to the inheritance of filial adoption, God's enemies to the participation in his divinity' (*Perf.* GNO VIII/1, 197;206).

[71] *Jn* 17:21.

[72] *Jn* 17:22.

[73] *In Cant.* GNO VI, 467,2-17.

by Origen[74] – Gregory can motivate 'the common salvation of human nature':
'the only-begotten Son of God himself resurrects the human being united to himself, by separating the soul from the body and then joining them again. In this
way, the common salvation of human nature is achieved. This is why he is also
called the Initiator of Life. Indeed, the Only-Begotten God, by dying for us and
rising again, has reconciled the universe to himself, ransoming by means of his
flesh and blood, as war prisoners, all of us who participate in him through a bond
of blood [διὰ τοῦ συγγενοῦς ἡμῶν αἵματος]'.[75] Christ's συγγένεια with humanity is of body and soul together, since Christ took up both; therefore, when Christ
'resurrects the human being united to himself', he performs the resurrection of all
human beings, and not only their bodily resurrection, but also their spiritual resurrection, by which humanity is restored to the Good, i.e. God. This is how Gregory's
idea of συγγένεια between Christ and humanity relates to his holistic concept of
resurrection – inherited from Origen and taken over and systematised by Evagrius.

The Henosis that is the peak of Gregory's mystical eschatology parallels the
unity that the intellectual soul must achieve in its spiritual progress – what
Evagrius will develop in his notion of the unified nous: 'When the soul becomes
simple [ἁπλῆ], unitary [μονοειδής], and perfectly similar to God [θεοείκελος],
it will find the truly simple and immaterial Good'.[76] This unification is made
possible, again, by Christ, in that in Christ human nature finds its unity and is
united to the divinity: 'By participating in the purest being, human weakness
is transformed into what is better and stronger ... human smallness is united to
divine greatness'.[77] The divine nature in this union is unaffected by the defects
of human nature, but rather human nature receives divine perfection. This
notion that the superior component assimilates the inferior to itself was already
supported by Origen:[78] within the human being, the inferior nature must assimilate itself to the superior, which is in the image of God. This idea will return
prominently both in Evagrius' concept of unified nous – the result of the subsumption of body into soul and soul into nous – and in Eriugena, in the description of the process of reditus.[79] The assimilation of human nature to God will
take place in the eschatological apokatastasis according to Gregory: 'The two
must become one, and the conjunction will consist in a transformation into
the better nature [τὸ κρεῖττον]'.[80] As mentioned, indeed, Gregory's mystical

[74] See arguments on Gregory in my 'Οἰκείωσις in Gregory's Theology: Reconstructing His
Creative Reception of Stoicism', in Johan Leemans and Matthieu Cassin (eds), Gregory of Nyssa:
Contra Eunomium III (Leiden, 2014), 643-59; on Origen in eadem, 'The Stoic Doctrine of Oikeio-
sis and its Transformation in Christian Platonism', Apeiron 47 (2014), 116-40.
[75] Contr. c. Apoll. GNO III/1, 154.
[76] An. et res. 93C.
[77] C.Eun. 3.4.
[78] Dial. Heracl. 12 and passim.
[79] See my Apokatastasis (2013), 773-815.
[80] Beat. 7.

eschatology culminates in Henosis and Theosis. Origen already put θέωσις as the zenith of his mystical eschatology, for instance in *Or.* 27.13 (θεοποιηθῶμεν), *Comm. in Matt.* 17.32 (θεοποιηθῆναι), and *Martyr.* 35, where the Logos deifies humans (ἀπὸ τοῦ Λόγου θεοποιηθεῖσι). Origen speaks in terms of 'communion with the divine'[81] and possibly of becoming God.[82]

Mario Baghos[83] insists on the importance of virtue as having strong eschatological consequences for Nyssen, and on the importance for him of beginning the process of restoration *hic et nunc* in the life of the Church. All this is correct and I have underscored myself the pivotal importance of virtue in Gregory's thought elsewhere, showing how it relates to his theology of freedom and eschatology.[84] Baghos also recognises that for Gregory even those who are outside the Church will be given an opportunity in the future life, because God wants all humans to be saved.[85] This is because virtue is voluntary – both Origen and Gregory went back again and again to Plato's definition of virtue as 'something that has no master' (ἀδέσποτον) in the myth of Er[86] – and this is framed within their ethical intellectualism: the choice of virtue is the true exercise of freedom; the choice of evil is never free. Because of their ethical intellectualism,[87] Gregory, like Origen, could consider free will to be compatible with divine providence, which will enable the goal itself of mystical eschatology: universal restoration, Henosis and Theosis.

Indeed, Origen already insisted that individual free will acted in a synergy with salvific providence: 'God providentially takes care of everyone, respecting all *logika*'s free will'.[88] Rational creatures will eschatologically submit to God for the sake of their own salvation and will adhere to God *voluntarily*: 'All the

---

[81] Ἡ πρὸς τὸ θεῖον κοινωνία, *Cels.* 3.80.

[82] Γίγνεσθαι θεόν, *Sel. Ps.* 2369.

[83] Mario Baghos, 'Reconsidering Apokatastasis in St. Gregory of Nyssa's *On the Soul and Resurrection* and the *Catechetical Oration*', *Phronema* 27 (2012), 125-62, republished with revisions in Doru Costache and Philip Kariatlis (eds), *Cappadocian Legacy: A Critical Appraisal* (Sydney, 2012), 387-415.

[84] 'Baptism in Gregory of Nyssa's Theology and its Orientation to Eschatology', in David Hellholm, Tor Vegge, Oyvind Norderval and Christer David Hellholm (eds), *Ablution, Initiation, and Baptism. Late Antiquity, Early Judaism, and Early Christianity* (Berlin, 2011), 1205-32; 'The Eucharist in Gregory of Nyssa as Participation in Christ's Body and Preparation of the Restoration and *Theōsis*', in David Hellholm and Dieter Sänger (eds), *The Eucharist: Its Origins and Contexts. Sacred Meal, Communal Meal, Table Fellowship, in Late Antiquity, Early Judaism, and Early Christianity* (Tübingen, 2017), 1165-84; I. Ramelli, *Social Justice and the Legitimacy of Slavery* (2016), 182-5.

[85] M. Baghos, 'Reconsidering Apokatastasis in St. Gregory of Nyssa's *On the Soul and Resurrection* and the *Catechetical Oration*' (2012), 161-2.

[86] For Gregory's use of this key Platonic concept see I. Ramelli, *Social Justice and the Legitimacy of Slavery* (2016), Chs 4-6.

[87] On which see my 'Apokatastasis and Epektasis' (2018) and especially 'Was Patristic Sin Different from Ancient Error?' (forthcoming).

[88] *Princ.* 3.5.8. Cf. *Princ.* 2.1.2; 3.5.5; I 8,3 etc., until the later *C.Matt.* 10.3.

world will submit to the Father, not by violence or necessity that compels to
subjection, but by means of word, reason, teaching, imitation of the best, good
norms, and even threats, when appropriate'.[89] Origen elaborated his doctrine of
apokatastasis on the basis of his defence of free will against 'Gnostic' deter-
minism, as is clear from Book 3 of *De principiis*, which begins with this
defence of free will, within a concern for theodicy, and concludes with the
theory of universal restoration.[90] The process of instruction is not interrupted
by death, because the intellectual soul – God's image – does not cease to live
after its separation from the mortal body, and at resurrection it will receive the
same body, but incorruptible, which will be no hindrance to intellectual activity
and mystical love of God. This activity and mystical love of God will grow
forever in *epektasis*. This aspect was anticipated by Origen and developed especially by Gregory of Nyssa.

Origen already maintained that rational creatures will never lose their free
will: for instance, he asserted that 'Free will [*liberum arbitrium*] will always
[*semper*] remain available to rational creatures',[91] and it will become the instrument of their restoration, salvation, and deification (although free will is necessary but not sufficient to this end, which depends primarily on 'Christ's Cross
and his death'[92]): 'That *free mastery over ourselves* [ἐξουσία] *could remain* in
our nature, but *evil might be removed* from it, divine Wisdom excogitated this
plan: allow the human being to do whatever it wanted and taste all the evils it
wished, and thus learn from experience what it preferred to the Good, and then
come back, with desire, to its original beatitude, voluntarily [ἑκουσίως], ban-
ishing from its own nature all that which is subject to passions and irrational,
by purifying itself in this life by meditation and philosophy, or by plunging after
death into the purifying fire'. The taste of evil will produce desire for the Good,
who is God;[93] therefore, turning towards the Good will be a *voluntary* action,
dictated by each one's free will.

In various passages in *De anima et resurrectione* and *De infantibus*, Gregory
uses αἰών and αἰώνιος in reference to purifying punishment – *never* using
ἀΐδιος or ἀϊδιότης in this case – and this while he explicitly denies that it is
eternal. Absolute eternity (ἀϊδιότης), according to Gregory as well as to Origen,

---

[89] *Princ.* 3.5.8.

[90] Full demonstration in my 'La coerenza della soteriologia origeniana: dalla polemica contro
il determinismo gnostico all'universale restaurazione escatologica', in *Pagani e cristiani alla ricerca
della salvezza. Atti del XXXIV Incontro di Studiosi dell'Antichità Cristiana, Roma, Istituto Patris-
tico Augustinianum, 5-7 maggio 2005* (Rome, 2006), 661-88.

[91] *C.Rom.* 5.10.

[92] *Ibid.* See also *C.Rom.* 4.11.73-5 on 'the blood of Christ' (*sanguis Christi*) as the main factor
of salvation, much stronger than 'our faith' and our 'works of justice' – which nevertheless are
necessary to salvation.

[93] On desire and *eros* as the engine of the return towards God in Gregory, see the aforementioned
'Eros and Ascent' (forthcoming).

belongs only to God and to the eternal life of those united to God.[94] As seen above, indeed, Gregory is adamant that evil is neither infinite nor eternal; it did not exist from the beginning and will not exist forever – only God does. Gregory does mention an αἰωνία suffering for those who are punished, or purified, in the other world,[95] but, like Origen, Didymus and others, he is aware that αἰώνιος in the Bible does not mean 'eternal' unless it refers to God and what relates to God. In Scripture, in Origen, in Gregory, and in other patristic authors, αἰώνιος, when it does not refer to God – mostly it does in Biblical quotations – refers to the aeon/world (αἰών) to come. The αἰώνιος death, the αἰώνιος punishment, or the αἰώνιον fire mentioned in the Bible are understood by Gregory as pertaining to the world to come; he never calls them 'eternal' (ἀΐδια).

Later on, Germanus of Constantinople in the eight century mistakenly thought that Gregory with αἰώνιος meant 'eternal'. But since he also found the doctrine of apokatastasis supported throughout Gregory's works, and he was unable to explain away this apparent contradiction, he was forced to maintain that Gregory's manuscripts had been interpolated by Origenists.[96] In this way he could account for the doctrine of universal restoration that he did find unmistakably expressed in Gregory's works. That Gregory, like Origen and other Fathers, did not understand αἰώνιος punishment or perdition, or αἰώνιον fire, as 'eternal', but as lasting for an indefinite period – depending on each single case – in the world to come was understood well by Severus of Antioch, who easily recognised the presence of the doctrine of eschatological restoration in Gregory's works, and personally rejected it: Severus 'does not approve what was said by Saint Gregory, the bishop of Nyssa, concerning apokatastasis'.[97] Nevertheless, he did find this doctrine expressed in Gregory's oeuvre. Barsanuphius of Gaza, who – like Germanus and Severus – rejected the doctrine of universal restoration, also acknowledged that Gregory clearly taught this doctrine: 'Gregory of Nyssa speaks clearly of apokatastasis'.[98]

Likewise, 'perdition' in Gregory does not include a connotation of eternity. In the Gospel of Luke, in the parables of the lost sheep, the lost drachma, and the prodigal son, these things or people are all 'lost' (ἀπώλολε), but they are found again. Gregory too, when he uses the lexicon of perdition (ἀπώλεια) and being lost (ἀπόλλυμι), does not mean an eternal perdition. Significantly, he uses the term ἀποκατάστασις, precisely when he comments on the parable of

[94] See I. Ramelli and D. Konstan, *Terms for Eternity* (2007; 2013), 172-84; my 'Αἰώνιος and αἰών in Origen and Gregory of Nyssa', *SP* 48 (2010), 57-62.

[95] *E.g.* in *C. usur.* PG 46, 436.

[96] *Ap.* Photius *Bibl.* Cod. 233.

[97] Τῷ ἐν ἁγίοις Γρηγορίῳ, τῷ ἐπισκόπῳ Νύσσης, τὰ εἰρημένα περὶ ἀποκαταστάσεως οὐκ ἀποδέχεται (Photius *Bibl.* cod. 232).

[98] Περὶ ἀποκαταστάσεως σαφῶς λέγει ὁ αὐτὸς Γρηγόριος ὁ Νύσσης (*C. opin. Orig.* PG 86, 891-902).

the *lost* sheep[99] – since that sheep was lost but then restored, as was already highlighted by Origen and the *Dialogue of Adamantius*.[100] Origen envisaged the eschatological 'reintegration of the lost',[101] whose perdition, therefore, cannot be considered eternal; likewise, Gregory speaks, to be sure, of the 'perdition of those condemned',[102] but, by stating at the same time that it will extend for an indefinite period and that its goal is purification, he clearly excludes its eternity: 'because of the profundity of inveterate evil, the punishment *provided for the purpose of purification* will tend to an indefinite duration'.[103] Tending towards does not mean to reach, and 'indefinite' is not synonymous of 'eternal'; if its end is purification and not retribution, as Gregory expressly states, this punishment cannot endure eternally.

Αἰώνιος refers to purification in *Infant*. GNO III/2, 91,23-92,2, where it is explicitly stated again that this purification (κάθαρσις), far from being eternal – in which case it would not be a purification – will come to an end, after long, when God will restore the purified person 'to the totality of those who are saved' (τῷ τῶν σῳζομένων πληρώματι). Similarly, Gregory speaks of a διαιωνίζουσα suffering in fire,[104] meaning that it will extend indefinitely through the αἰών to come, but is not eternal (ἀΐδιος): it will not endure in the final apokatastasis, as is especially clear from *An. et res.*, *Tunc et Ipse*, and *Or. cat.* 26. It is precisely by αἰώνιον fire (*An. et res.* 100A) that souls will be purified for the purpose of salvation: it will destroy evil (*ibid.* 157A) and cease when such purification is achieved. Even Epiphanius, who disagreed with Origen and Nyssen, had to add ἀϊδίως ('eternally') to διαιωνίζειν to mean 'endure eternally',[105] since διαιωνίζειν per se did not imply eternity.

Otherworldly punishment may only endure for an indefinite duration – depending for each one on the measure of one's own sins – through the future aeon(s) (διαιωνίζειν), but is not eternal as only God is, and as life in God is. In *An. et res.* 101.17-43, Gregory is clear that purifying punishment (κόλασις) 'is measured out over an entire aeon', συνδιαμετρεῖται πρὸς ὅλον αἰῶνα, as a parallel to the expression εἰς αἰώνιόν τι διάστημα, 'for a given interval in the future aeon'. Here διάστημα manifestly refers to a limited interval, within Gregory's concern for the opposition of 'diastematic' vs 'adiastematic'.[106] The very verb συνδιαμετρεῖται confirms the limited nature of this punishment,

---

[99] *In Eccl.* GNO V, 305.
[100] See my 'The *Dialogue of Adamantius*: A Document of Origen's Thought?' *SP* 52 (2012), 71-98; 56 (2013), 227-73.
[101] *Princ.* 3.5.7.
[102] Τὴν τῶν κατακρίτων ἀπώλειαν, *Infant*. GNO III/2, 96,3-5.
[103] Εἰς ἄπειρον παρατείνεται ἡ διὰ τῆς καθάρσεως κόλασις (*ibid.* 87,10-2).
[104] *Benef.* GNO IX, 100,5.
[105] *AH* 2.160.16.
[106] See my *Tempo ed eternità in età antica e patristica: filosofia greca, ebraismo e cristianesimo* (Assisi, 2015), Ch. 3.

since infinite is beyond measure, and eternity is adiastematic, being beyond extensions and limited intervals (διαστήματα); it transcends the dimension (διάστημα) of time. This is why in the same passage Gregory observes that we shall pay our debts 'up to the last coin' and shall come to an end of this payment – conceived as a limited interval – sooner or later, finally attaining complete purification and liberation from sin.

The ἄληκτον ὀδυρμόν in *Cast. aegre fer.* GNO X/2, 328,16 is an incessant lamentation, since those who are suffering are continually lamenting, but it is not described as eternal. Indeed, if for Gregory the devil will be saved, as is clear from *Or. cat.* 26, analysed above, a fortiori all humans will, through the necessary purification. Consistently, Gregory deems the eschatological αἰώνιον fire a purifying fire, which aims at the elimination of evil:

The nature of evil, at last, will be reduced to non-being, completely disappearing from being, and God's purest goodness will embrace in itself every rational creature, and none of the beings that have come to existence thanks to God will fall out of the King-dom of God, when every evilness that has mixed with beings, as a kind of spurious matter, will have been consumed by the fusion of the purifying fire, and thus every being that has come to existence thanks to God will return to being such as it was at the beginning, when it had not yet received evil.[107]

Gregory interprets the fire of hell or Gehenna as purifying fire in many other passages as well.[108] This provides the purification necessary for the final Heno-sis and Theosis, the culmination of Gregory's mystical eschatology.

That for Gregory mystical ascent is always grounded in the principle of doing justice is underscored, in different ways, by both Andrew Louth and myself.[109] This will also become a prominent feature in Evagrius.[110] In a num-ber of passages, Gregory hammers home this principle, and even in Homily 4 on the Lord's Prayer, he identifies the bread to be asked for as the 'bread of justice'. This is a bread that comes from justice, not injustice. It must be a bread coming from one's own sweat and labour (*Gen* 3:19), not from the oppression of other people (*Or. Dom.* 55.20). Refraining from oppressing other people is a principle of what Gregory calls 'spiritual asceticism', on the basis of which each one will determine one's own eschatological scenario.

This is one of the large cluster of notions related to mystical eschatology that Evagrius inherited from Gregory. One of the main aspects of Nyssen's mystical theology, the infinity of God, in which Gregory grounded his doctrine of *epek-tasis*, was emphasised by Evagrius in turn as the basis of *epektasis*, which in

---

[107] *Tunc et Ipse*, 13-4 Downing.

[108] *E.g. Mort.* 15, p. 64 Lozza; 16, p. 66 Lozza. *Or. cat.* 26, which I have already examined, is relevant to purification by fire and consequent eschatological restoration.

[109] Andrew Louth, *The Origins of the Christian Mystical Tradition* (2nd ed., Oxford, 2007), 90-3; I. Ramelli, *Social Justice and the Legitimacy of Slavery* (2016), Chs. 5-6.

[110] As investigated in 'Gregory Nyssen's and Evagrius' Relations' (2017).

Evagrius takes the form of God's impossibility to satiate. Like Gregory, Evagrius maintains that God never ceases to satiate intellects, which points to
God's infinity. Evagrius is depicting the final unity, which 'will be an indescribable peace. There will be only bare intellects who continually satiate themselves from God's impossibility to satiate' (*KG* 1.65). This passage is clearly
influenced by Nyssen's notion of infinite *epektasis*. The intellects will continually strive towards God, who is infinite, achieving a unity among them and with
God that is not static, but always dynamic. The theme of satiation is Origenian
and was taken over by both Gregory and Evagrius: God, being infinite, will
never fill the intelligences with satiety (κόρος) in the end.[111] This is essential,
because κόρος was the cause of the fall of the *noes* at the beginning, but in the
end there will be no new fall, and this thanks to love, as argued by Origen[112]
– who was followed by both Nyssen and Evagrius. Like Origen and Nyssen,
Evagrius also sees the eschatological restoration as mystical unity (a union not
of substances but of wills) and peace (since the wills of all rational creatures
shall be oriented toward the Good), as is clear from *KG* 1.65 as well as from
the *Letter to Melania*.

Evagrius' *Letter to Melania*, *Kephalaia Gnostika*, and other works, teach the
eschatological restoration, as Origen and Gregory had done – displaying both
the terminology and the concept of apokatastasis itself.[113] In the extant Greek
works, too, Evagrius employs the terminology of apokatastasis (ἀποκαθίστημι,
ἐπιστρέφω). In *KG* 3.60, the original reference to apokatastasis is transparent
and the Greek lexicon of apokatastasis underlies the Syriac version.[114]

Evagrius' mystical eschatology is central to the whole of his thought, since
his concept of the *telos*, like those of Origen and Nyssen, is closely related to
the rest of his philosophical theology. This is, indeed, entirely oriented toward
the *telos*, *i.e.* the realisation of God's plan for all rational creatures. In *Sentence* 58 Evagrius, reminiscent of Origen and Nyssen, identifies the true identity of each rational creature with what it was at the beginning, in God's plan,
before its fall. What rational creatures were in the ἀρχή, before their fall, will
be restored in the end, at apokatastasis, when their soul has achieved impassibility, *apatheia*[115] – which at the same time does not exclude love, which is
an important factor of deification.[116]

---

[111] The meaning here is 'impossibility to satiate', not 'insatiability', which is the translation
by François Guillaumont (p. 49: *insatiabilité*), followed by Luke Dysinger, who ascribes this
'insatiability' to the intellects ('their insatiability'), although the possessive suffix in Syriac is
singular, -*h*, which refers back to the unity and state of peace mentioned by Evagrius soon before.

[112] *Apokatastasis* (2013), 169-72.

[113] As explored in *ibid.* 461-514.

[114] *Evagrius Ponticus' Kephalaia Gnostika* (2015), 175-6 and *passim*.

[115] On this ideal in Evagrius see now Monica Tobon, *Apatheia and Anthropology in Evagrius
of Pontus* (London, 2020).

[116] See my *Evagrius Ponticus' Kephalaia Gnostika* (2015), lxxvii-lxxxi.

Rational creatures' bodies will be subsumed into soul, and their souls will be subsumed into intellects, and intellects will become fully pure and be immersed in divine life and knowledge, in a truly mystical eschatology and eschatological Henosis:

And there will be a time when the body, the soul, and the intellect will cease to be separate from one another, with their names and their plurality, since the body and the soul will be elevated to the rank of intellects. This conclusion can be drawn from the words, 'That they may be one in us, just as You and I are One'. Thus there will be a time when the Father, Son, and Spirit, and their rational creation, which constitutes their body, will cease to be separate, with their names and their plurality. And this conclusion can be drawn from the words, 'God will be all in all'.[117]

Both scriptural quotations here were among the favourite of Origen and Nyssen in reference to the mystical eschatological Henosis: *Jn* 17:22 and 1*Cor* 15:28.

Evagrius in *KG* 4.34 uses the same biblical passage (*Mt* 18:23-5; *Lk* 7:41) as Nyssen[118] to establish that otherworldly punishments will stop after 'the full payment of one's debt'. Evagrius also relied on 1*Tim* 2:4-6, cited in *Gnostikos* 22: one must want all humans to be saved and to attain the knowledge of truth, which is what God wants. Evagrius maintains here that the awareness of what Scripture reveals concerning the *telos* brings joy – a mystical joy in view of the eschatological universal restoration. Based on his radical eschatological optimism, the same as Nyssen's, Evagrius exhorts his disciples to hope, joy, and confidence, also in *Praktikos* 12.[119] Evagrius' eschatological optimism was based on metaphysico-theological optimism: the absolute priority of Good over evil, Good being God. This is a tenet inherited from Origen and Nyssen. Evil, which did not exist at the beginning, does not properly exist, and will completely vanish in the end. This notion, which Evagrius expresses in the last sentence of *KG* 1.9 and elsewhere, perfectly corresponds to Origen's and Nyssen's idea of apokatastasis as the final destruction of evil, which befits its ontological non-existence.[120] In *KG* 1.40 Evagrius avers: 'There was a time when evil did not exist, and there will be a time when, likewise, it will no more exist, whereas there was no time when virtue did not exist, and there will be no time when it will not exist. For the germs of virtue are impossible to destroy'. Origen's argument that evil did not exist in the beginning and therefore will not exist in the end had already been taken up by Nyssen. As pointed out above,

---

[117] *Letter to Melania*, 22.

[118] *An. et res.* 101-4 = GNO III 3,74-7.

[119] *Praktikos* 20, 25-6, 27-8, 46-7. Therefore, Evagrius warns against wrath, hatred, affliction, memory of suffered injuries, sadness, and lack of confidence, and urges to hope in God; lacking hope in God's Providence is a serious sin, a yielding to the devil.

[120] See my 'Christian Soteriology and Christian Platonism. Origen, Gregory of Nyssa, and the Biblical and Philosophical Basis of the Doctrine of Apokatastasis', *VC* 61 (2007), 313-56.

Nyssen identified a 'great philosophical point' in the theory that 'evil is not from eternity'.[121] Thus, it cannot subsist eternally:[122] 'Therefore, it has been demonstrated that evil is not from eternity, nor will it remain forever. For that which has not been forever will not continue to exist forever either'.[123]

Evagrius' mystical eschatology depends on his protology. The germs of virtue are indestructible – Evagrius claims in above-mentioned *KG* 1.40 – because they were planted by God in souls, whereas God never planted germs of vice, which do not belong to our nature: they were not part of God's original plan, and therefore they will not endure in Evagrius' mystical eschatology. This argument derives from Origen.[124] Evagrius' equation between God, Good, and Being – as opposite to evil which has no ontological existence – so that being outside of the Good (*i.e.*, in evil) is being outside of Being (*i.e.*, nonexistence), was already clear in Origen and is emphasised by Nyssen, *e.g.* in *Mos.* 2.175: Christ became a human 'in order to draw back into Being that which had ended up outside of Being'. The pole of the Good is the ontologically positive one; evil's nonexistence also implies its non-eternity. Evagrius also knew from Gregory that God-Good alone is infinite, while evil is finite.

According to Evagrius, as to Origen and Nyssen, the *telos* is the removal of evil and ignorance, the restoration of intellectual creatures, and deification, that is, entering the life of God. This is the culmination of mystical eschatology: Henosis with God. This is the true life of the intellectual soul or *nous*: this is the life that God meant from the beginning. In *KG* 1.41, Evagrius draws on Philo, the New Testament, Clement, Origen, and Nyssen, when arguing that the illness and death of the soul[125] are secondary to its life and health; again, the positive pole is primary; the negative one, not subsisting from the beginning, cannot endure forever. Origen even corrected Plato (who maintained that some people have committed such grave injustices as to become 'incurable', ἀνίατοι), or better his 'Gnostic' contemporary interpreters: 'nothing is impossible for the Omnipotent; no being is incurable [*insanabile*, ἀνίατον] for the One who created it'.[126] For 'in souls, there is no illness caused by evilness that is impossible to cure for God-Logos, who is superior to all'.[127] As seen above, Nyssen was so sure of this as to maintain in *Or.Cat.* 26 that Christ will heal even the devil, thanks to the mystery of his Inhumanation.

---

[121] *Inscr. Ps.* GNO V, 100,21-5.
[122] See my 'Christian Soteriology' (2007).
[123] *Ibid.* 101.3.
[124] *C.Rom.* 6.5.78-102.
[125] See my 'ΚΟΙΜΩΜΕΝΟΥΣ ΑΠΟ ΤΗΣ ΛΥΠΗΣ (Luke 22,45): A Deliberate Change', *ZNW* 102 (2011), 59-76; 'Philo's Doctrine of Apokatastasis: Philosophical Sources, Exegetical Strategies, and Patristic Aftermath', *StPhilo* 26 (2014), 29-55.
[126] *Princ.* 3.6.5; my *Apokatastasis* (2013), 388-90.
[127] *Cels.* 8.72.

Evagrius tackles the foregoing motif of the death of the intellectual soul, a Philonic, Origenian, and Nyssian theme, not only in *KG* 1.40-1, which is all about the priority of life over death and good/virtue over evil(ness)/vice, but also in *KG* 1.64: 'The true life of rational creatures is their natural activity, whereas their death is their activity against nature. Now, if the one who is naturally made to cast away the true life is mortal of this kind of death, which of the beings is immortal? This is because every rational nature is liable to opposition'. The life of a rational creature is its adhesion to the Good; the opposite, adhesion to evil, is its death. The soul is mortal of the real death, which comes from the soul's adhesion to sin: Origen already argued in this sense in the *Dialogue with Heraclides* and elsewhere, and Nyssen had too. Rational creatures should be immortal, and were meant to be so, but they fell into death because of sin. Sin is against the nature of rational creatures, which is good, being created by God and for virtue. Death is contrary to their nature. This is the opposition which Evagrius mentions, which is also related to rational creatures' being constitutively suspended between the choice of Good and evil. Only God, indeed, is Good itself, like Plato's Idea of Good;[128] creatures are good insofar as they are created by God and participate in this absolute Good. If rational creatures choose not to participate in Good, they fall into its opposite, evil, which is against their nature.

Evagrius' mystical eschatology is hinted at in several other passages. In *KG* 3.68 Evagrius states: 'Just as the first rest of God indicates the removal of evil and the vanishing of thick bodies, likewise the second, too, indicates the vanishing of bodies, secondary beings, and the diminution of ignorance'. Heavy bodies at the resurrection will disappear by being transformed into fine, immortal bodies, as they were before the fall. The ultimate reality in Evagrius' mystical eschatology is not the destruction of bodies, but their subsumption into souls, and souls into *noes* – and *noes* in Henosis with God.[129] The diminution of evil is the premise of apokatastasis, for Origen and Nyssen as well as for Evagrius.[130] Origen, followed by Nyssen especially in *Tunc et Ipse*, as pointed out above, argued from 1*Cor* 15:28 that, since God 'will be all in all', in the *telos* 'we cannot admit of evil, lest God be found in evil'.[131] The final eviction of evil is also a consequence of its aforementioned ontological negativity, a tenet of Origen's and Nyssen's thought. This is the notion that Evagrius posits in *KG* 1.1 and everywhere: the absolute ontological priority of Good/God over evil, which is nonbeing. At the second rest of God and the final ἕνωσις and

---

[128] *KG* 1.1.

[129] See my 'Evagrius Ponticus, the Origenian Ascetic (and not the Origenistic "Heretic")', in John McGuckin (ed.), *Orthodox Monasticism, Past and Present* (New York, 2014 = Piscataway, NJ, 2015), 147-205.

[130] See my 'Christian Soteriology' (2007).

[131] *Princ.* 3.6.2-3; see my *Apokatastasis* (2013), 143-4.

θέωσις, rational creatures will be freed from ignorance, which is the counterpart of evil, and from bodies, which are not evil but will be subsumed into souls
and thence into intellects. Intellects, as mentioned, will be unified inside – by
the subsumption of body and soul – and united with God.

Evilness (κακία) is not proper to the body, but to the rational faculty,[132]
which can choose between virtue and vice. The latter is assimilated by Evagius
to the 'dirtiness' of the rational nature (*KG* 3.75). Likewise in *KG* 4.36: 'The
intelligible fat is the thickness that, due to evilness, sticks to the intellect'.
A similar image was used by Nyssen: the evil committed by each one is a thick,
dirty glue or mud that sticks to the soul. This will be difficult and painful to
remove for the sinner to return clean in the end, which is the goal that God
wants to achieve with this painful purification.[133]

According to Evagrius as well, the eventual submission of all to Christ will
be mystical and will coincide with their eschatological salvation. In *KG* 3.79,
Evagrius uses the same sense of 'underworld', related to demons, as is found
in Origen's and Nyssen's interpretation of *Phil* 2:10-1 on the bending of all
knees before Christ, in heaven, on earth and in the underworld, denoting the
voluntary submission of all rational creatures to Christ, angels (in heaven),
humans (on earth[134]), and demons (underneath). I think especially of Nyssen,
Tunc et Ipse 20 Downing, and Origen, *Princ.* 1.2.10 and 1.6.2, where everyone's submission to Christ in heaven, on earth, and in the underworld (angels,
humans and demons) is understood as the salvation of all, since it is voluntary
and entails conversion and volitional adhesion. Evagrius wholly agrees that
'submission is the assent of the rational nature's will toward the knowledge of
God'.[135] The equation between submission to Christ and God and salvation
was drawn by Origen and Nyssen,[136] and followed closely by Evagrius. For
this equation to stand, one must posit that submission will be voluntary. This is
what Origen and Nyssen postulated, and what Evagrius too makes clear in the
quotation from *KG* 6.68, speaking of the assent of rational creatures' will.
That salvation coincides with the knowledge of God not only was upheld by
Origen and Nyssen, but was suggested by *1Tim* 2:4 – to which most supporters
of apokatastasis, including Nyssen and Evagrius, appealed.

Evagrius takes over again Origen's and Nyssen's identification of the eschatological submission of all to Christ as universal salvation in *KG* 6.15: 'Christ's
feet are practical virtue and contemplation. Now, if he "puts all his enemies under
his feet", all of them will know practical virtue and contemplation'. *1Cor* 15:25,

---

[132] *KG* 3.75-6; 3.53.

[133] *An. et res.* 100A = GNO III/3, 73; commentary in my *Gregorio di Nissa sull'Anima* (2015).

[134] I read '*brw* in Syriac, after a suggestion by Sebastian Brock. See my commentary in *Evagrius Kephalaia Gnostika* (2015), 189-90.

[135] *KG* 6.68.

[136] See my 'Christian Soteriology' (2007) and '*In Illud: Tunc et Ipse Filius…* (1Cor 15.27-28):
Gregory of Nyssa's Exegesis' (2010), 259-74.

remarkably, is part of the eschatological revelation of 1*Cor* 15:24-8 that Origen and Nyssen used as a major Biblical pillar for apokatastasis.[137] Evagrius here focuses on v. 25 and interprets the submission of all under Christ's feet as their acquisition of practical virtue (the goal of *praktikē* or ascetic life) and contemplation (*theōria*). This will lead to their perfection. Also in *KG* 6.27, Evagrius, like Origen and Nyssen, interprets the eschatological universal submission to Christ and God as universal salvation, in that this submission will be voluntary: 'If it is the case that "all peoples will come and worship before the Lord", it is evident that the peoples who want war will also come. Now, if this is true, the whole nature of rational creatures will adore the Name of the Lord, him who reveals the Father who is in him. For this is the Name that is "above all names"'. Here the universal adoration before the Lord is described in the words of *Ps* 85:9, and it is understood as universal salvation, including the enemies who are said to be subjected in the end (1*Cor* 15:24-6), given that it will be the adoration of the Name that reveals the Father, which for this reason is said to be superior to all names in *Phil* 2:9. Consequently, even the enemies will know the Father – and this knowledge, according to Evagrius' ethical intellectualism, which he shared with Origen and Nyssen (see briefly above), entails a fully volitional adhesion.

Like Nyssen and Origen, Evagrius teaches that the submission of all to Christ, who will submit to God (1*Cor* 15:28), will take place at the end of all aeons, in the *telos*, when all will be brought to unity: 'When Christ will no longer be imprinted on the various aeons and in names of every sort, then he too "will submit to God the Father", and he alone will rejoice in the knowledge of God, a knowledge which is not distributed over the aeons and the progresses of rational creatures'.[138] Evagrius' conception of several aeons before the final apokatastasis is close to Origen's and Nyssen's. During the aeons, rational creatures increase their virtue and knowledge, and get purified; after this has been accomplished, all aeons will cease and the fullness of divine ἀϊδιότης will remain. Evagrius adheres to Origen and Nyssen in claiming that the succession of aeons is not infinite, but it had a beginning and will thus have an end.[139] Aeons are necessary to rational creatures' spiritual and intellectual development.

Evagrius in *KG* 6.27 and elsewhere interprets 1*Cor* 15:28 exactly in the same way as Nyssen in *Tunc et Ipse*.[140] The eventual subjection of the Son to the Father, mentioned and interpreted by Evagrius, is announced in 1*Cor* 15:28, the same passage Gregory comments on in *Tunc et Ipse* to support apokatastasis.

---

[137] See my 'Christian Soteriology' (2007); *Apokatastasis* (2013), 137-215, 372-440.

[138] *KG* 6.33.

[139] *KG* 5.89. On the aeons in Origen and Nyssen see my 'Αἰώνιος and αἰών' (2010) and *Apokatastasis* (2013) the sections on Origen and Nyssen.

[140] See I. Ramelli, 'Gregory of Nyssa's Trinitarian Theology' (2011), 445-78.

Developing Origen's argument, Nyssen interpreted the final subjection of the Son to the Father not as a sign of subordination, but as the subjection of humanity or even all *logika*, *i.e.* the creatural component assumed by Christ-Logos (his 'body'), not the divine one. Nyssen thereby joined anti-subordinationism and the apokatastasis doctrine, as Evagrius also did, who followed both theories. Like Origen, they both posited restoration as an important aspect of their mystical eschatology, which culminated in Henosis and Theosis.

CHAPTER 15

Gregory of Nyssa and ἀποκατάστασις τῶν πάντων

Magdalena MARUNOVÁ

1. The Issue

In this short Chapter we pose two questions: does the restoration of all (ἀποκατάστασις τῶν πάντων) apply to the irrational nature, or does it include the rational nature only? And why does Gregory only speak of the rational nature?

Let us first concentrate on Gregory's concept of apokatastasis with regard to the rational nature. Gregory recalls that according to Jesus Christ's words people who will take part 'in the resurrection from the dead will neither marry nor be given in marriage'... and 'are like the angels'.[1] For Gregory this resurrection means a restoration (ἀποκατάστασις) to the primal state in paradise, *i.e.* a return to the isangelic life (to which the first creation belongs).[2] In the resurrection the primal dignity shall be restored to both mankind as a whole and every individual. In this way the image of God will be complete again.[3]

Gregory of Nyssa was influenced by Origen,[4] whose ideas he partly accepted and partly rejected.[5] Gregory believes, like Origen, in the idea of a universal restoration (*apokatastasis*) and of an educational character in Divine punishment, meaning that the purifying fire after one's death cannot be eternal.[6] In

---

[1] See *Lk* 20:35-6.

[2] See *Op hom* 17 (PG 44, 188CD).

[3] See *An et res* (PG 46, 156C); *Op hom* 16 (PG 44, 185CD); *Op hom* 17 (PG 44, 188CD); *Op hom* 17 (PG 44, 189B); *Op hom* 18 (PG 44, 192-6); *Op hom* 21 (PG 44, 204A).

[4] See M. Ludlow, *Universal Salvation: Eschatology in the Thought of Gregory of Nyssa and Karl Rahner* (Oxford, 2000); 37; I.L.E. Ramelli, *The Christian Doctrine of Apokatastasis (A Critical Assessment from the New Testament to Eriugena)* (Leiden, Boston, 2013), 1-221.

[5] Gregory refused Origen's concept of the finitude and comprehensibility of God's nature, the pre-existence of souls and their fall into the body (see *e.g. Op hom* 28). See M. Ludlow, *Universal Salvation* (2000), 37.

[6] See *An et res* (PG 46, 89B; 152AB); *Inscr* I,7 (GNO V, 50,4-18). See A. Andreopoulos, 'Eschatology and Final Restoration (Apokatastasis) in Origen, Gregory of Nyssa and Maximos the Confessor', in *Theandros, An Online Journal of Orthodox Christian Theology and Philosophy* [online] 1, 2004: <http://www.theandros.com/restoration.html>, 2; J.P. Burns, 'The Economy of Salvation: Two Patristic Traditions', *TS* 37 (1976), 598-619, 604; D.A. Salomon, 'The Concept of Apokatastasis or the Restoration of All Things in Jesus Christ According to Gregory of Nyssa',

---

Studia Patristica CI, 207-213.

Gregory's writings the term *apokatastasis* usually signifies the restoration of all things, in which all creation, including soul and body, or the whole rational nature will reach the kingdom of heaven.[7] Everything will be restored to the primal state before sin, and evil will be destroyed. All mankind is the image of God, therefore salvation must apply to every individual person who has been created.[8] In human nature there is something homogeneous with God, so that human beings could enjoy God. Due to this homogeneity, God attracts human nature to himself. [9] The restoration to the primal state before sin and regaining similarity to God is the goal of human life.[10]

Referring to *Phil* 2:10 and *1Cor* 15:25-8 Gregory relates the universal restoration to all, including the fallen angels.[11] Every rational being will be in harmony with each other and everyone will be freed from evil – there will be unity with God and harmony of all rational beings, human beings, angels and demons (because demons will admit Christ's lordship).[12]

The return to the primal state before sin can be reached through the purifying fire.[13]

Gregory (like Origen) regards evil as a distortion or deficiency of good or as a lapse into the opposite direction from good: evil does not have its own real existence. Contrary to good, evil is not unlimited, it is finite.[14] Thus Gregory says about the ever-moving human nature:

When it has finished the course of wickedness and reached the extreme limit of evil, then that which is ever moving, finding no halting point for its impulse natural to itself when it has run through the lengths that can be run in wickedness, of necessity turns

<www.romancatholicism.org/nyssa-apokatastasis.html> (without pagination); I. Ramelli, *The Christian Doctrine of Apokatastasis* (2013), 377-9.

[7] See *Or dom* 4 (GNO VII/2, 49,1-15): ὡς ἂν γένοιτό ... μετουσία ... τοῦ τε νοεροῦ τῆς ψυχῆς ... τῆς τε γεηρᾶς ταύτης σαρκὸς ἐν τῇ ἀποκαταστάσει τῶν πάντων εἰς τὸν οὐράνιον χῶρον τῇ ψυχῇ συμμετοικιζομένης ... πᾶσα ἡ λογικὴ ... φύσις ... τὴν οὐράνιον λαχοῦσα μακαριότητα. *Inscr* II, 14 (GNO V, 155,11): ἐν τῇ τοῦ παντὸς πρὸς τὸ ἀγαθὸν ἀποκαταστάσει. See M. Ludlow, *Universal Salvation* (2000), 38.

[8] See *Op hom* 16 (PG 44, 185CD); 17; 22; *cf.* J.P. Burns, 'The Economy of Salvation' (1976), 602-3.

[9] See *Or cat* (GNO III/4, 17,11-18,4); see also *Op hom* 2 (PG 44, 133B).

[10] *Mort* (GNO IX/1, 51,16-8): ὁ δὲ σκοπὸς καὶ τὸ πέρας τῆς διὰ τούτων πορείας ἡ πρὸς τὸ ἀρχαῖον ἀποκατάστασις, ὅπερ οὐδὲν ἕτερον ἢ ἡ πρὸς τὸ θεῖόν ἐστιν ὁμοίωσις; *Op hom* 16 (PG 44, 185CD); *Op hom* 17 (PG 44, 188CD); *Op hom* 17 (PG 44, 189B); see also *Op hom* 18 (PG 44, 192-6); *Op hom* 21 (PG 44, 204A).

[11] See *Trid spat* (GNO IX/1, 285,7-286,12): ... ἐν τρισὶν ἡμέραις τῶν ὄντων τὸ κακὸν ἐξοικίζεται, ἐξ ἀνδρῶν ἐκ γυναικῶν καὶ ἐκ τοῦ γένους τῶν ὄφεων, ἐν οἷς πρώτοις ἡ τῆς κακίας φύσις ἔσχε τὴν γένεσιν.

[12] See *An et res* 72b; I. Ramelli, 'Harmony between Arkhe and Telos in Patristic Platonism and the Imagery of Astronomical Harmony Applied to Apokatastasis', *The International Journal of the Platonic Tradition* 7 (2013), 1-49, 19.

[13] See also *Or cat* 26 (GNO III/4, 67,7-13); *Or cat* 35 (GNO III/4, 91,14-92,4).

[14] See *Op hom* 21 (PG 44, 201C); *Inscr* II,8 (GNO V, 101,2-4): τὸ μὴ ἐξ ἀϊδίου τὴν κακίαν εἶναι μηδὲ εἰς ἀεὶ παραμένειν αὐτὴν ἐνεδείξατο. ὃ γὰρ μὴ ἀεὶ ἦν, οὐδὲ εἰς ἀεὶ ἔσται.

its motion towards good: for as evil does not extend to infinity, but is comprehended by necessary limits, it would appear that good once more follows in succession upon the limit of evil; and thus, as we have said, the ever-moving character of our nature comes to run its course at the last once more back towards good.[15]

The restoration cannot signify a return to a state that is absolutely identical to the original, because human mutability has approached the angelic state that existed before sin.[16] In *In inscriptiones Psalmorum* Gregory says that human beings should use their mutability so that they may turn to good and return to the place from which they have fallen.[17]

The return to the original state can be seen as sinlessness, not using the sexual differentiation, and as immortality.

2. Who are the 'All' Who Shall be Restored?

In some texts Gregory speaks about the restoration of 'all', in other texts he deals with the 'rational nature' or 'human beings'. When enumerating 'all' who shall be restored, he seems to restrict himself to the rational nature. But does the restoration relate to other, lower levels of creation?

There are many texts in which Gregory speaks about the restoration of human beings, *i.e.* in *Oratio catechetica*,[18] *De oratione dominica*,[19] *De mortuis non esse dolendum*,[20] *De hominis opificio*,[21] *In Ecclesiasten*,[22] *Contra Eunomium III*,[23] *De virginitate*,[24] *Oratio consolatoria in Pulcheriam*,[25] *De beatitudinibus*,[26] *De anima et resurrectione*,[27] *Epistula canonica ad Letoium*.[28]

In many of these texts he speaks about the restoration to the original state and about the restoration of the image of God in human beings.

---

[15] *Op hom* 21 (PG 44, 201BC; translated by H.A. Wilson).

[16] See *Op hom* 16 (PG 44, 184A); *Op hom* 16 (PG 44, 184CD): Αὐτὴ γὰρ ἡ ἐκ τοῦ μὴ ὄντος εἰς τὸ εἶναι πάροδος, κίνησίς τίς ἐστι καὶ ἀλλοίωσις, τοῦ μὴ ὄντος εἰς τὸ εἶναι κατὰ τὸ θεῖον βούλημα μεθισταμένου. See also *Or cat* 6 (GNO III/4, 24,1ff.); *Or cat* 8 (GNO III/4, 35,18f.); *Or cat* 21 (GNO III/4, 55,11ff.).

[17] See *Inscr* I,7 (GNO V, 46,24-47,8).

[18] *Or cat* 26 (GNO III/4, 67,7-20); *Or cat* 35 (GNO III/4, 88,12-8); *Or cat* 35 (GNO III/4, 91,1-12).

[19] *Or dom* 2 (GNO VII/2, 30,22).

[20] *Mort* (GNO IX/1, 51,16-8).

[21] *Op hom* 17 (PG 44, 188CD), *Op hom* 26 (PG 44, 224C).

[22] *Eccl* 1 (GNO V, 296,12-8).

[23] *Eun* III (GNO II, 51,8).

[24] *Virg* (SC 119, 12,4,2).

[25] *Pulcher* (GNO IX/1, 472,8-10).

[26] *Beat* (PG 44, 1292,25-9).

[27] *An et res* (PG 46, 108,8; 137,27; 148A; 156C).

[28] *Epist* (PG 45, 232C).

There are many texts in which Gregory speaks about the restoration of the rational nature, about angels and human beings, too: *De tridui inter mortem et resurrectionem domini nostri Iesu Christi spatio*,[29] *De vita Moysis* II,[30] *In Illud: Tunc et ipse filius*,[31] *De beatitudinibus*;[32] in *In ascensionem Christi* Gregory says that Christ was not only a man among men but that he also has united his nature with the angelic nature.[33]

In some texts he speaks about the restoration of all: In *De oratione dominica* Gregory first mentions the rational creation which is divided into incorporeal nature (which are the angels who live in the upper region) and corporeal nature, *i.e.* human beings living on the earth to which they are akin because of the body.[34] Perhaps this is the Divine intention that the whole creation would be brought

into relationship with itself, so that neither the lower portion should be without part in the heavenly heights, nor heaven wholly without a share in the things pertaining to earth. Thus the creation of man would effect in each of the elements a participation in the things belonging to the other; for the spiritual nature of the soul, which seems to be decidedly akin to the heavenly powers, dwells in earthly bodies, and in the restoration of all, this earthly flesh will be translated into the heavenly places together with the soul (ἐν τῇ ἀποκαταστάσει τῶν πάντων).[35]

Man seems to be a connection and mediator between the intelligible nature and the corporeal nature that is on the earth. It could be presumed that man represents both of these parts of creation and thus both will be restored. Something of this kind could be indicated in *De hominis opificio* 16, where a human being is a mean between the divine incorporeal nature and the irrational nature of animals.[36]

In *In Ecclesiasten* Gregory speaks of a higher philosophy about beings which shows that the universe contains everything and the harmony of beings does not admit any dissolution.[37] In *In inscriptiones Psalmorum* Gregory says that all evil will be removed in the restoration of the universe to the good,[38] and in *In ascensionem Christi* Christ restores everything to the state that was in the first creation.[39]

---

[29] *Trid spat* (GNO IX/1, 285,7-286,12).
[30] *Vit Moys* II (GNO VII/1, 57,10).
[31] *Tunc et ipse* (GNO III/2, 13,22-14,13).
[32] *Beat* (PG 44, 1300,42-52).
[33] See *Ascens* (GNO IX/1, 326,4-6).
[34] *Or dom* 4 (GNO VII/2, 48,18-27).
[35] *Or dom* 4 (GNO VII/2, 48,28-49,8; translated by Hilda C. Graef).
[36] *Op hom* 16 (PG 44, 181BC).
[37] *Eccl* 7 (GNO V, 406,1-7).
[38] *Inscr* II,14 (GNO V, 155,11-4).
[39] *Ascens* (GNO IX/1, 327,3): ὁ εἰς τὴν πρώτην κτίσιν ἀποκαταστήσας τὰ πάντα.

As Ilaria Ramelli stresses, Gregory speaks about harmony of the whole creation, not only of the rational nature.[40] In *In Illud: Tunc et ipse filius* Gregory says that the entire creation will be in harmony with itself.[41]

It could be useful to recall Gregory's division of universe or beings. Having examined many of Gregory's texts, David L. Balás provides a clearly hierarchical division of beings.[42] Beings are divided into uncreated and created ones (it is a basic and the most important classification);[43] created beings are divided into intelligible and sensible ones; intelligible are divided into celestial (angels) and terrestrial ones (human beings – with their intelligible part); sensible are divided into living ones and those that are devoid of life; the living ones are divided into sentient and non-sentient ones; the sentient ones are divided into rational (which are human beings – who are also intelligible terrestrial), and irrational ones.

For example in *De hominis opificio* Gregory describes in compliance with the biblical narration the hierarchy of creation and starts with inanimate things, continues with plants and animals up to human beings. Gregory says that food for animals is created first, animals come next so that they could minister man who comes last, after everything has been made. According to Gregory, there is a philosophical doctrine concerning the soul in Moses' narration, a doctrine which has also been discovered by a 'pagan philosophy', though not clearly comprehended.[44] Gregory sees a hierarchy within living creatures and in accordance with Aristotle[45] he divides the power of life or soul into three levels: the power of growth and nutrition, which is called the vegetative soul (φυσική; it can be seen in plants); another form of life that includes the previous form, is the power of sense perception (αἰσθητική), which belongs to the irrational animals; and the rational soul (λογική), in which perfect bodily life can be seen: the human nature is nourished and perceives, it partakes of reason and is ordered by mind (λόγου μετέχουσα, καὶ νῷ διοικουμένη).[46] The perfect and true soul, the soul proper (κυρίως ψυχή), is, according to Gregory, only the intellectual and immaterial soul,[47] everything that is not so is soul in the figurative sense (ὁμωνύμως);[48] actually it is not soul, but a certain vital energy

[40] See I. Ramelli, 'Harmony between Arkhe and Telos' (2013), 20.

[41] See *Tunc et ipse* (GNO III/2, 20,11-2).

[42] See D.L. Balás, Μετουσία θεοῦ. *Man's Participation in God's Perfections according to Saint Gregory of Nyssa* (Roma, 1966), 23-53; especially the synthesis on p. 50.

[43] See D.L. Balás, 'Christian Transformation of Greek Philosophy Illustrated by Gregory of Nyssa' s Use of the Notion of Participation', *Proceedings of the American Catholic Philosophical Association* 40 (1966), 152-7; especially p. 154.

[44] See *Op hom* 8 (PG 44, 144CD). Here Gregory speaks about Plato's and Aristotle's division of the parts of the soul.

[45] See Aristotle, *De anima* II 3,414a29-33.

[46] See *Op hom* 8 (PG 44, 144D-145A).

[47] *Op hom* 14 (PG 44, 176B).

[48] See Aristotle, *Cat.* 1a1ff., where Aristotle speaks about homonyms.

associated with the appellation of the 'soul'.[49] For this reason the animal nature besides plants has been given to man for being eaten, because, as Gregory says, it is not so distant from the vegetative life.[50] The animal nature is due to a sense perception slightly better than that which is nourished and grows without this power.[51] Yet, in another place when speaking about the food in paradise, Gregory says that something absolutely different to normal material food and drinking must be understood, *i.e.* the word of God.[52] This would indicate that no creature fed on another,[53] nor even on plants.

As there is a hierarchy within the whole creation, from inanimate things to human, in the same way the human being has been hierarchically arranged and the image of God is expressed in the whole human compound (τὸ ἀνθρώπινον σύγκριμα): the highest part, *i.e.* the mind (νοῦς), is the image and mirror of God; the body, if it is functioning normally, is the image of image (εἰκὼν εἰκόνος), *i.e.* of the mind; the mind is a mirror reflecting the appearance of what is received by it, and the nature being controlled by mind is then the mirror of the mirror (κατόπτρου κάτοπτρον).[54]

According to the aforementioned view, if there is a basic difference between the uncreated and created beings, it is not possible to designate a radical difference between human beings and the lower levels of creation (*i.e.* animals and plants, if concentrating on the living nature only), because both these levels and human beings are distant from the uncreated nature in the same manner.

In *Oratio catechetica* Gregory says that in terms of dignity everything is inferior to and unworthy of God in the same measure. God is absolutely unapproachable and inaccessible by anything, by the whole universe, and transcends all that exists, both in earth and heaven, by his sublimity.[55]

Furthermore, as Gregory says, everything has been created by the Divine will[56] and 'God is in His own nature all that which our mind can conceive of good; rather, transcending all good that we can conceive or comprehend.'[57]

In the 25th chapter of *De hominis opificio* Gregory says that (according to *Psalm* 104/103) sinners will perish from the earth.[58] 'For how shall any one be called by the name of sin, when sin itself exists no longer?'[59]

According to Gregory every evil will be removed in the apokatastasis and sinners will be purified of sin. This suggests that the other levels of creatures

---

[49] See also *Op hom* 14 (PG 44, 176B); *Op hom* 30 (PG 44, 256BC).
[50] See *Gen* 9:3.
[51] See *Op hom* 15 (PG 44, 176D-177A).
[52] See *Op hom* 19 (PG 44, 196CD).
[53] See *Gen* 1:29-30.
[54] See *Op hom* 12 (PG 44, 161CD; 164A).
[55] See *Or cat* 27 (GNO III/4, 69,12-70,2).
[56] See *Op hom* 1 (PG 44, 132AB).
[57] See *Op hom* 16 (PG 44, 184A; translated by H.A. Wilson); and *Eccl* 7 (GNO V, 406,7-15).
[58] See *Ps* 104(103):31.35.
[59] See *Op hom* 25 (PG 44, 224B; translated by H.A. Wilson).

(animals and plants) should be freed from death as well because death is a consequence of sin which, moreover, has been introduced into the whole creation by the rational nature. This assertion could indicate that everything, from the rational nature to the lowest level of creation, will be restored.

But Gregory in his definition of the soul claims that the soul proper (κυρίως ψυχή) is the human soul, while the others are only souls in the figurative sense. When Gregory speaks of the human mind as a mirror of God and of the body as a mirror of a mirror, we could ask why he does not consider such a reflection also in the entirety of created nature. Why does this reflection not proceed to the lower parts of the soul (to the souls of animals and plants), if these parts are also in human beings?

3. Conclusion

Gregory speaks about the restoration of 'all' and about harmony in the whole creation; nevertheless he does not mention the restoration of the irrational nature. He concentrates on the rational nature, on human beings and angels. Perhaps it is the strong influence of Plato and Aristotle on Gregory that results in a lack of interest in the lower than rational levels of nature. There is also the fact mentioned above, namely that souls other than the rational ones are souls only in a figurative sense. In addition, according to Gregory, God did not give the mind (νοῦς) to human beings, but he shares it with them. The human mind is unknowable and thus it is similar to the Divine nature which is incomprehensible for men. This is perhaps the basic difference between the rational and the other created nature in Gregory's view. These could be the main reasons why Gregory speaks only of the rational nature in connection with the *apokatastasis*.

And there are the main points on the basis of which I think he should have included (but actually has not) the irrational nature into the number of those restored: First, the main ontological difference in Gregory's view is that between the uncreated and created nature (not between rational and irrational); and second, both death and evil will be removed in the *apokatastasis* – death is a consequence of evil which has been introduced into the whole creation by the rational nature.

Though Gregory could silently presuppose the restoration of the lower levels of creation, he does not mention it explicitly. As it stands, his doctrine of *apokatastasis* concerning the restoration of all, as it regards the lower levels of creation, has not been worked out.

This study was funded by the Czech Science Foundation (GAČR 19-180465: 'The relationship between the uncreated God and created beings according to Gregory of Nyssa as a follow-up to the Alexandrian biblical exegesis') and the Charles University Research Centre Programme (No. 204053).

CHAPTER 16

Apokatastatis and Eternal Hell

Marta PRZYSZYCHOWSKA

1. Introduction

The problem with Gregory of Nyssa is that at first glance his thought takes two incongruous ways: one way is his teaching about human nature as an ontic unity; about its creation as a unity yet before individual human beings were created; about its fall as a unity, about its deification thanks to the fact that God's Son took on the entire human nature understood as a unity; finally, about its restoration as a unity at the moment of resurrection, that is about apokatastasis, a return to the beginning. This part of Gregory's teaching is coherent and logical, but unfortunately seems hardly reconcilable with the other, no less essential current in his thought: Gregory speaks equally clearly about man's freedom, his free will, his right to make free choices, and about consequences of such choices, which may as well be eternal damnation. I think there is a missing piece of the puzzle that allows Gregory to think about those two parts simultaneously. The piece missed by us, not him, of course, is the relationship between human nature and individual man.

2. Apokatastasis as a part of a system

According to Gregory 'the ultimate goal of the journey is a return to the beginning (ἡ πρὸς τὸ ἀρχαῖον ἀποκατάστασις), that is becoming similar to God'.[1] Apokatastasis is a return to the original state. That is why we need to know, first of all, what was at the beginning.

Gregory thinks that God created man in two stages/acts. In the first one, He created one, undividable human nature without gender.

In saying that *God created man* the text indicates, by the indefinite character of the term, all mankind; for was not Adam here named together with the creation, as the history tells us in what follows; yet the name given to the man created is not the particular, but the general name: thus we are led by the employment of the general name of

---

[1] *Mort* (GNO IX, 51,168).

Studia Patristica CI, 215-222.
© Peeters Publishers, 2021.

our nature to some such view as this – that in the Divine foreknowledge and power all humanity is included in the first creation.[2]

Only in the second act of creation God produced an individual man with specific gender. Gregory innovatively resolves an apparently unsolvable aporia: what was the origin of gender since a man was created in the image of God and there is no gender in God. Gregory says that in the second act of creation God created man with gender *foreseeing* the fall that was to come.[3] It seems that the second act of creation was necessary precisely in order to allow human nature to achieve its plenitude (πλήρωμα). If man did not commit the first sin, the foreseen number of human beings would come into being in the angelic way (very mysterious).[4]

As a result of the second act of creation the first individual man – Adam came into being. But apart from determination of sex Adam did not yet experience any other consequences of the sin (foreseen by God). All other results of the sin became apparent only after the sin had been committed. All attributes that we associate with the present human condition, including corporeality susceptible to transition, death and passions, Gregory calls an animal aspect of life. When he talks about the consequences of the sin he refers to the image of clothes made of animal skin (*Gen* 3:21) and interprets them in an allegorical way. Human nature, rational and close to God, put on itself a strange element and we will get rid of it only upon resurrection.[5]

We should examine in details the reality that was produced in the first act of creation – human nature. As far as I know, Gregory of Nyssa was the first Father of the Church who came up with a precise definition of nature. Although the definition was elaborated during his polemics with Eunomius regarding the unity of God's nature, there is no doubt it applies to human nature as well, because Gregory compares God's nature to the human one and he considers the comparison clear to the audience. Here is the definition of nature presented in his small work *To Ablabius*:

Nature (ἡ φύσις) is one, at union in itself (αὐτὴ πρὸς ἑαυτὴν ἡνωμένη), and an absolutely indivisible unit (μονάς), not capable of increase by addition or of diminution by subtraction, but remains the same (ὅπερ ἐστίν), in its essence being and continually remaining one, inseparable even though it appears in plurality, continuous, complete, and not divided with the individuals who participate in it.[6]

In his other works Gregory also talks about 'one body of our nature'[7] and names nature 'one vivid being'.[8] Gregory considers human nature to be one

---

[2] *Op hom* 16 (PG 44, 185, tr. Moore-Wilson, NPNF II 5, 406).
[3] *Cf. Op hom* 16 (PG 44, 185).
[4] *Cf. Op hom* 17 (PG 44, 189-92).
[5] *Cf. An et res* (PG 46, 148).
[6] *Abl* (GNO III/1, 41,2-7, tr. Moore-Wilson, NPNF II 5, 332).
[7] *Tunc et ipse* (GNO III/2, 16,17-8).
[8] *Or cat* 32 (GNO III/4, 78,14).

οὐσία. In the homily *To the words: in the image and resemblance*, he compares the way in which the first three human beings were created according to the relation between three divine persons, and he calls these first three people three heads of the entire human nature (τῆς ἀνθρωπότητος). Then he calls them consubstantial (ὁμοούσιοι) as they follow the example of the Trinity in whose image they were created.[9] Similarly, in the treatise *Concerning the difference between essence and hypostasis*, he calls men consubstantial (ὁμοούσιοι).[10] As in reference to divine nature we talk about one essence (οὐσία) and three hypostases, similarly in reference to human nature we deal with one essence (οὐσία) and many hypostases.[11]

Does Gregory really treat divine οὐσία and human οὐσία equally? Divine persons are not separated from each other by time and place and human persons, whose number is as well specified as the number of divine persons, do not appear simultaneously and at the same place.[12] But there is another very important difference: human persons are separated by will – that is the reason why we talk about many men instead of one as we should do.[13]

The concept of the unity of human nature provides a basis for the most important parts of Gregory's teaching, especially anthropology, if not for his entire theology. The entire human nature suffered the consequences of Adam's sin; similarly, the entire one as a unity gained deification and renovation through the very fact of Incarnation, in which it was assumed by God's Son. Gregory rarely uses the formulas of the Nicene Council when he speaks about Incarnation. He usually describes that mystery with an expression that *the Word assumed human nature*[14] as in the following passage:

The Word, who was with God at the beginning, became a flesh out of love to men and through the communion with our weak nature mixed with man (τῷ ἀνθρώπῳ ἀνακραθείς) and took our entire nature (πᾶσαν ἐν ἑαυτῷ τὴν ἡμετέραν φύσιν δεξάμενος) in order to deify humanity (τὸ ἀνθρώπινον) by mixing it with God and sanctifying through that germ (διὰ τῆς ἀπαρχῆς ἐκείνης) the whole 'dough' of our nature.[15]

In *Contra Eunomium* we find yet a different image. Gregory refers to the parable of the lost sheep (*Mt* 18:12) in order to explain the mystery of Redemption.

---

[9] *De eo, quid sit, ad imagiem Dei et ad similitudinem* (PG 44, 1329).

[10] *Diff ess hyp* (PG 32, 325).

[11] *Cf. Graec* (GNO III/1, 29,9-11).

[12] Although human persons live in different times, human nature remains immutable despite the flow of time, cf. *Eun* I 173-5 (GNO I, 78,11-27).

[13] *Cf. Graec* (GNO III/1, 25,8-17).

[14] The terms that are characteristic of Gregory include: ἡ μίξις/mixing, ἡ ἀνάκρασις/mixing with others, ἡ ἕνωσις/union, ἡ συνάφεια/junction – and the related verbs. However, Gregory never used them in the meaning of mixing God's and human nature into one. An in-depth analysis of the use of all those terms by Gregory was performed by J.R. Bouchet, 'Le vocabulaire de l'union et du rapport des natures chez saint Grégoire de Nysse', *Revue thomiste* 68 (1968), 533-82.

[15] *Antirrh* (GNO III/1, 151,14-20).

That comparison evocatively shows the unity of human nature, which is so real that we can talk about human nature as if it were one organism:

We too went to make up the sacred hundred sheep, the rational beings. But when the one sheep – our nature (ἡμετέρα φύσις) – was led astray from the heavenly way by evil, and was dragged down to this parched salty place, the flock which had not strayed did not add up to the same number as before, but are said to be ninety-nine.[16]

The entire human nature fell, and similarly the entire one as a unity was healed through the fact that the Word assumed it, namely through the Incarnation. This way of thinking inevitably leads Gregory to the conviction that entire human nature will be restored – and this is the idea of apokatastasis. It arises from his conviction that human nature forms a unity and thanks to that unity it suffered the consequences of the first sin and was redeemed in Incarnation. Upon the resurrection it will return to its original state, which means that unavoidably the *entire* human nature must be restored.

3. Damnation as a consequence of man's free choice

On the other hand, the conviction that man has free will provides a basis for Gregory's entire moral teaching. A human being is capable of obedience but he is not forced to it by any external obligation or by natural necessity (ἀνάγκη φύσεως).[17] Thanks to free will a human person is able to lead a virtuous life and to receive a reward for such a life. If a virtue was an effect of any necessity, it could not be followed by a merit.[18] A free choice of man may also direct itself to evil and the consequence of such a choice (if not regretted) would be eternal punishment.

We must not forget the places where Gregory clearly talks about the existence of eternal hell and damnation.

Everyone gains a proper reward: the one, who led virtuous life, gets a joyful stay in the kingdom of heaven; men who were inhuman and evil get the fire punishment that remains forever (διαιωνίζουσα).[19]

It is worth to examine the verb used here by Gregory: διαιωνίζω. At first glance it seems to have something in common with αἰών – the term that means 'time'. But in other places where Gregory uses the verb it never means anything temporal, just the opposite: it means eternal duration.[20]

---

[16] *Eccl* 2 (GNO V, 305,2-7; tr. Hall-Moriarty 52).
[17] *Cf. Ref Eun* 139 (GNO II, 372,15-6).
[18] *Cf. Or cat* 5 (GNO III/4, 19,15-20,2).
[19] *Benef* (GNO IX, 100,2-5).
[20] *Cf. Inscr* II 16 (GNO V, 146,1); *Pulcher* (GNO IX, 472,6); *Eccl* 5 (GNO V, 365,20); *Cant* 2 (GNO VI, 66,18).

Gregory believes that a misdeed may always be forgiven, but a man who rejects God's grace himself renounces his salvation.[21] He also says that after the resurrection men will gain a different fate: it may be the fate of a good or of a bad servant.[22] The indispensable condition that makes someone able to stay with the just after death is to fight evil,[23] which is impossible after death.[24]

Gregory points to Judas as an example of a man who suffers eternal punishment:

For, as to the latter (Judas), on account of the depth of the ingrained evil, the chastisement in the way of purgation will be extended into infinity (εἰς ἄπειρον).[25]

The term ἄπειρον is one of the most important words in Greek philosophy. In various philosophical schools it acquired somewhat different shades of meaning, but it always meant something infinite, endless, boundless, indefinable and indeterminable.

4. It may happen that a man does not partake in human nature

In order to understand that Gregory's teaching about apokatastasis does not stand in contradiction to his conviction about free will and possible damnation we have to remember his teaching about grace that actually is a consequence of his concept of double creation. He thinks that human nature is not so much oriented to God as that it *contains* grace in itself. A man was created in such a way that grace constitutes a part of his nature. Gregory uses specific terms to describe this reality. He says:

The operation of looking upon God is nothing less than the life-nourishment appropriate, as like to like, to an intellectual nature.[26]

He does not hesitate to say that divine beauty is *really our* beauty thanks to the fact that we have God's image in ourselves.[27] In his small work *About the early diseased children* that issue provides a basis for Gregory's deliberation on the fate of dead children. He arrives at a conclusion that salvation may not be called a reward in a strict sense because it is something natural for man as perceiving objects is something natural for the one who has healthy eyes.[28] Whatever man makes out of his *nature*, it is a work of *grace*.

---

[21] *Cf. Bapt* (GNO X/2, 363,14-20).
[22] *Cf. Bapt* (GNO X/2, 368,15-9).
[23] *Cf. Bapt* (GNO X/2, 370,2-7).
[24] *Inscr* II 11 (GNO V, 121,10-1).
[25] *Infant* (GNO III/2, 87,10-2; tr. Moore-Wilson, NPNF II 5, 378).
[26] *Infant* (GNO III/2, 79,2-3, tr. Moore-Wilson, NPNF II 5, 375).
[27] *Mort* (GNO IX, 42,18-21).
[28] *Cf. Infant* (GNO III/2, 81,7-15).

We can clearly see that it is impossible to interpret Gregory's thought in the categories recognized and used in the West to describe the relationship between nature and grace. Jean Daniélou proposed a thesis that in Western theology *nature* means corporal and intellectual life while supernatural life is something added; for Gregory and the entire East, on the other hand, *human nature* contains intellectual and supernatural life, while the sensual aspect is something added.[29]

Does it mean that a man who sins renounces his own nature? Yes, it does – Gregory is straightforward about it. Already the first sin took human nature down to the level of existence which is alien to it, because it is a level of irrational animals. Summing up the introduction of sex determination to human nature Gregory openly says:

For he truly was made the beast, who received in his nature the present mode of transient generation, on account of his inclination to material things.[30]

So even the state that we recognize as *natural* and obvious is actually an effect of sin. That is the reason why a child coming to the world does not possess human nature perfectly because he/she is born with the consequences of the original sin. José Vives noticed that according to Gregory a man is a human being inasmuch as he is able to partake in that nature – it means in mind and freedom. So a man only becomes a human being in the course of his life: an embryo possesses a human nature in an embryonic way; a child in a childish way, and an adult in a mature way.[31] Gregory compares an embryo to a grain from which slowly a man grows up.[32]

In a word: a man can partake in human nature more or less, so he may be more or less a human being. The reason could be age or a stage of development – we may call it a natural cause (though these are really the effects of the original sin), or own decisions and choices of everyone. A man may cease to be a human being as a consequence of his own free choices:

When he says earthborn and sons of men he distinguishes those who are fleshly and earthly and irrational from those who are being saved and who have an impress of human nature in themselves. Now likeness to the divine is the distinguishing impress of humanity (ἴδιος δὲ χαρακτὴρ ἀνθρώπου ἡ πρὸς τὸ θεῖον ὁμοίωσις).[33]

Misbehaviour may – according to Gregory's own words – really change a man into an animal, for instance into a dog[34] or a lion.[35]

---

[29] *Cf. Platonisme et Théologie mystique* (Paris, 1954), 54.

[30] *Op hom* 17 (PG 44, 189-92, tr. Moore-Wilson, NPNF II 5, 407).

[31] *Cf.* J. Vives, 'El pecado original en San Gregorio di Nisa', in *Pecado original; XXIX Semana Española de Teología* (Madrid, 1970), 188f.

[32] *Cf. Mort* (GNO IX, 50,23-52,4), *Op hom* 29 (PG 44, 236).

[33] *Inscr* II 12 (GNO V, 130,1-5; tr. Heine 175).

[34] *Cf. Inscr* II 16 (GNO V, 173,26-174,5).

[35] *Cf. Inscr* II 14 (GNO V, 156,20-7).

5. Apokatastasis and damnation

Summing up, human nature, produced at the first creation, burdened with animal properties after the fall, was divinized in Incarnation and will without doubt return to its original state. Does it mean that all people will be saved? Yes, it does; it must happen to allow human nature save its unity. We would want it to mean that everyone will be saved and will come back to the unity with God. But Gregory clearly states that sinners will be condemned for eternity. So the entire human nature will be unified with God, but not everyone considered to be a human being is really a man and participates in human nature. There are people who reject God out of their own fault, which means that they reject their own nature, as living with God is an essence of humanity.[36]

When Gregory speaks about apokatastasis he always refers to human nature understood as an ontic unity. In his work *In illud: tunc ipse Filius* he stresses that 'nothing that was created by God will be excluded from the saved',[37] but we have to see the context: Gregory refers to the salvation of the *body* of Christ which is 'human nature with which He was united'.[38] Even when he writes about the purifying fire after death, which is a fate of those who were not baptized, he says that the aim of that purification is so that after long ages pure nature will be preserved for God.[39] It seems that Gregory claims that it is possible to purify and spiritually develop after death for those who did not practice virtue during their lives. Often the following text has been quoted as a proof that Gregory believed in the salvation of all people:

The rest (those who did not practice virtue in the present life) will be liberated from material passion thanks to the purifying fire and thanks to the desire for the good they will return to grace that was meant [for human nature] from the beginning.[40]

But we need to take a look at the following phrase:

The desire for something opposite does not last in the nature (τῇ φύσει) forever.[41]

This way of thinking is clearly shown in his disquisition from *On the inscriptions of the Psalms*; first, Gregory speaks about the end of evil and if we took that part out of the context it would be a proof of his belief in the salvation of all people.

---

[36] Giulio Maspero actually came to the same conclusion when he stated: 'But if man will have chosen to live as a beast, he will be in eternity that what he has chosen, since he cannot be man if he has rejected he who is the model of man, he who reveals man to man himself' (*Trinity and Man* [Leiden, Boston, 2007], 90).

[37] *Tunc et ipse* (GNO III/2, 21,2-3).

[38] *Tunc et ipse* (GNO III/2, 21,10-1).

[39] Cf. *Or cat* 35 (GNO III/4, 92,1-3).

[40] *Mort* (GNO IX, 56,21-57,2).

[41] *Mort* (GNO IX, 57,2-3).

There will be no destruction of humanity, in order that the divine work not be rendered useless, being obliterated by non-existence. But in its stead sin will be destroyed and will be reduced to non-being.[42]

But in the next sentence Gregory says:

Then he again repeats the same word about those who return at evening, and who are hungry as a dog, and who go around the city in a circle showing, I think, through the repetition of the word, that men, insofar as they are now in either wickedness or in that which is better, will also be in the same afterwards. For the person who now goes about in a circle in disregard for God, and does not live in the city, nor guard the human imprint on his own life, but is changed into a beast by his choice and has become a dog, will also be punished at that time by being cast out of the city above in a famine of good things.[43]

So, human nature will be restored, but there are people who will not take part in that restoration because out of the original sin in which they were born or out of their own evil choices they do not partake in human nature.

---

[42] *Inscr* II 16 (GNO V, 174,23-175,2; tr. Heine 212).
[43] *Inscr* II 16 (GNO V, 175,9-19; tr. Heine 212f.).

PRINTED ON PERMANENT PAPER • IMPRIME SUR PAPIER PERMANENT • GEDRUKT OP DUURZAAM PAPIER - ISO 9706

N.V. PEETERS S.A., WAROTSTRAAT 50, B-3020 HERENT